"....the re[al]
will never get
in the books"

# "...the real war will never get in the books"

## Selections from Writers During the Civil War

Edited by

### LOUIS P. MASUR

OXFORD UNIVERSITY PRESS

New York          Oxford

## Oxford University Press

Oxford    New York

Athens   Auckland   Bangkok   Bombay
Calcutta   Cape Town   Dar es Salaam   Delhi
Florence   Hong Kong   Istanbul   Karachi
Kuala Lumpur   Madras   Madrid   Melbourne
Mexico City   Nairobi   Paris   Singapore
Taipei   Tokyo   Toronto

and associated companies in
Berlin   Ibadan

First published in 1993 by Oxford University Press, Inc.,
200 Madison Avenue, New York, New York 10016

First issued as an Oxford University Press paperback, 1995

Oxford is a registered trademark of Oxford University Press

Library of Congress Cataloging-in-Publication Data

". . . the real war will never get in the books"
Selections from Writers During the Civil War
edited by Louis P. Masur.
p.   cm.
Includes bibliographical references and index.
ISBN 0-19-506868-8
ISBN 0-19-509837-4 (PBK.)
1. Authors, American—19th century—Correspondence.
2. United States—History—Civil War, 1861–1865—Literary collections.
3. United States—History—Civil War, 1861–1865—Personal narratives.
4. Authors, American—19th century—Diaries.
5. American literature—19th century.
I. Masur, Louis P.
PS128.H39   1993
810.8'0358'09034—dc20   92-24446

*The following page is regarded as an extension of the copyright page.*

2 4 6 8 10 9 7 5 3 1

Printed in the United States of America

The author gratefully acknowledges considerations granted by the following sources:

Henry Adams's letters reprinted, by permission of Harvard University Press, from *The Letters of Henry Adams, Vol. 1: 1858–1868*, edited by J. C. Levenson et al. Copyright © 1982 by Harvard University Press.

Louisa May Alcott's journal reprinted by permission of Houghton Library, Harvard University.

Lydia Maria Child's letters reprinted courtesy of the Department of Rare Books, Cornell University Library; the William L. Clements Library, the University of Michigan; and Houghton Library, Harvard University.

Ralph Waldo Emerson's journals reprinted, by permission of Harvard University Press, from *The Journals and Miscellaneous Notebooks of Ralph Waldo Emerson, Vol. 15: 1860–1866*, edited by Linda Allardt and David Hill. Copyright © 1982 by Harvard University Press.

Charlotte Forten's journals reprinted, by permission of Oxford University Press, from *The Journals of Charlotte Forten Grimké*, edited by Brenda Stevenson. Copyright © 1988 by Oxford University Press.

Nathaniel Hawthorne's letters reprinted, by permission of the Ohio State University Press, from the Centenary Edition of the Works of Nathaniel Hawthorne, Vol. XVIII, *The Letters, 1857–1864*. Copyright © 1987 by the Ohio State University Press.

William Gilmore Simms's letters, reprinted by permission of the University of South Carolina Press, from *The Letters of William Gilmore Simms. Vol. 4 and Vol. 6*, edited by Mary Simms Oliphant. Copyright © 1955, 1982 by University of South Carolina Press.

Harriet Beecher Stowe's letters reprinted courtesy of the Stowe-Day Foundation.

Walt Whitman's letters reprinted, by permission of New York University Press, from *The Correspondence of Walt Whitman, Vol. 1: 1842–1867*, edited by Edwin Haviland Miller. Copyright © 1961 by New York University.

For Benjamin and Sophie
and Jonathan, Molly, Sam, Max, Gracie,
Jackson, Moses, and Zoë


"the luckiest
Thing is having been born"

MARK STRAND

# Preface

The Civil War was a written war. It was written by soldiers who kept diaries. It was written by family members who corresponded with soldiers at the front. It was written by journalists who reported from the battlefields and by editors who reshaped their newspapers and magazines to accommodate the desire for news of the war. And it was written by the nation's writers. These writers—the novelists, essayists, and poets—struggled to capture the texture of the extraordinary and the everyday. One writer who contemplated more deeply than most the meaning of this written war was Walt Whitman: "I have become accustomed to think of the whole of the Secession War in its emotional, artistic and literary relations."[1]

The literary dimensions of the Civil War have eluded us. From the start, critics have searched for timeless works of literature inspired by the war. In seeking some American version of *The Iliad,* they have focused on what was written about the war following the war and have neglected what was penned at the time. As early as 1862, John Weiss, a Unitarian minister, expressed his hope that the conclusion of the war would make a great literature possible: "the pen is becoming tempered in the fires of a great national controversy." Five years later, the impatient William Dean Howells, editor of the *Atlantic Monthly,* was ready to pass judgment. He set the terms for future critical discussion when he lamented that the war "has laid upon our literature a charge under which it has hitherto staggered very lamely."[2]

The two most important studies of the literature of the Civil War—Edmund Wilson's *Patriotic Gore: Studies in the Literature of the American Civil War* (1962) and Daniel Aaron's *The Unwritten War: American Writers and the Civil War* (1973)—brilliantly probed the "literary reverberations" of the Civil War. Both authors worked within the framework suggested by Howells, seeking to assess the literature, defined mostly as fiction, that came out of the war. Wilson observed that the war produced "a remarkable literature which consists mostly of speeches and pamphlets, private letters and diaries, personal memoirs and journalistic reports," but he lamented that it was not a period in which "belles lettres flourished." Aaron covered even more ground than Wilson and gave greater attention to what was written during the war, but as a literary critic he felt compelled to point out the "literary dearth" of the Civil War, the "paucity of 'epics' and 'masterpieces,'" hence the title of his book.[3]

To a certain extent, Wilson and Aaron, in evaluating the literature of the war, took their lead from the writers themselves, who felt cut off from their creative wellsprings. In different ways, the best-selling writers of the day lamented how difficult it was to write while the war raged on about them. Harriet Beecher Stowe asked "who could write fiction when fact was so imperious and terrible?" William Gilmore Simms announced: "I am literally doing nothing in letters." Lydia Maria Child proclaimed: "I can never write unless my mind is *free*." And Nathaniel Hawthorne declared himself "mentally and physically languid." By looking only for sustained works of fiction, and by taking these authors at their word, we have forsaken the moving and remarkable literature of the Civil War—the letters, diaries, speeches, and essays of the nation's leading writers. Despite their concerns, Stowe and Hawthorne published probing pieces in the *Atlantic Monthly;* Simms and Child sent stirring letters to a variety of correspondents. It is one of the paradoxes of writing and the war that whenever these authors lamented their inability to compose they did so in some of their finest prose.

This volume gathers portions of those writings. The personal letters, diary entries, and journal articles of the most distinguished writers at the time constitute a striking literary and intellectual landscape. These wartime writings expose the connections between the political, the personal, and the creative. They illustrate how art grows out of experience and how experience is understood through literary art. The fourteen individuals included in this volume labored to find the words by which they could comprehend, and with which they hoped to influence, the war that fixed their attention. Their words ring with immediacy and authority not only because of their talents as writers but also because they addressed the central issues of the day. These writers examined secession, military life, emancipation, and the transition from slavery to freedom. They provided biographical sketches of those well-known and those almost unknown—Abraham Lincoln, P.G.T. Beauregard, Stonewall Jackson, and Robert Gould Shaw as well as soldiers dying in hospitals and African-Americans struggling for freedom. In whatever they wrote they told stories, stories about womanhood and manhood, stories that were by turns comic and tragic, romantic and realistic. In some of their stories, these writers also revealed the paternalistic racism characteristic of their class. Events compelled them to think hard about the individual and society, truth and falsehood, nature and death. In doing so, they charted the contours of American culture at the time. Both as literary and historical sources, the work produced by the nation's preeminent writers during the war provides an original perspective on the conflict.

Nearly all of the writers included in this volume were nationally prominent at the time of the Civil War, though reputations have fluctuated since. Some of these writers—Nathaniel Hawthorne, Harriet Beecher Stowe, Ralph Waldo Emerson, Frederick Douglass, Herman Melville, and Walt Whitman—were widely known and read then and are widely read today. Others—Lydia Maria Child, William Gilmore Simms, Thomas Wentworth Higginson, and John De Forest—were best-selling authors in the nineteenth century but, except by scholars, are largely forgotten and unknown today. Still others—Henry Adams, Louisa May Alcott, and John Esten Cooke—had the bulk of their writings and reputations ahead of them, whereas at least one talented young writer—Charlotte Forten—abandoned the pen.[4]

The selection of writers in this volume is not intended to be comprehensive. The very notion of who is prominent, of who is worth reading and accordingly whose work is preserved, is embedded to a certain extent in the outcomes of the Civil War.[5] This volume is unable to redress that imbalance. For example, there are too many Northerners and too few Southerners and Westerners. In large part, there is more available material by Northern writers than Southern or Western ones. The most prominent Southern writer associated with the Civil War, Mary Chesnut, is not included here because much of her diary was composed long after the war and her unrevised Civil War diary is readily available in print. Two additional Southern writers deserving of attention are Augusta Evans and Charles Henry Smith. But Evans's wartime novel resists editing and the original dialect in Smith's letters, published under the pseudonym Bill Arp, makes for difficult reading. Fortunately, Evans's *Macaria; or, Altars of Sacrifice* (1863), and Smith's *Bill Arp, So Called* (1866), as with numerous additional Civil War titles, have been recently reissued.

Many professional writers experienced the Civil War and left creative work from those years (the poets Henry Timrod and John Greenleaf Whittier, for example). Other writers and critics were either too young at the time of the war or failed to write extensively about the conflict in extant novels, stories, essays, letters, or diaries composed during the war. Among these are Ambrose Bierce, William Wells Brown, George Washington Cable, Emily Dickinson, Bret Harte, William Dean Howells, Henry James, Sidney Lanier, James Russell Lowell, John Trowbridge, and Mark Twain. To be sure, the war had an impact on each of these writers, but this volume is limited to writings about the Civil War penned during the war.

The fourteen writers are arranged alphabetically. This order has resulted in some happy coincidences. The book begins with Henry Adams, the most aristocratic of the group, and concludes with Walt Whitman, the most democratic. Louisa May Alcott felt liberated by the war; Lydia Maria Child, who follows, felt constrained. Another fortuitous pairing is John Esten Cooke and John De Forest, the two writers who saw the most military action during the war. The intellectual ruminations of Ralph Waldo Emerson's journals are succeeded by the personal confessions of Charlotte Forten's diary; Nathaniel Hawthorne, who had his doubts about the conflict, is followed by Thomas Wentworth Higginson, who had none. Wherever possible, the selections that follow preserve the original capitalization, spelling, and punctuation schemes of the authors. It does not matter in what order these writers are read. Each selection stands alone as a testament to the struggle for understanding and each is enriched by comparison with another.

A recurring issue for these writers was how to construct literature from real life, how to make words out of war. This was not a new issue for everyone. Nearly a decade before the Civil War, Melville anticipated what every writer would soon attempt when he advised Hawthorne to take "a skeleton of actual reality [and] to build about [it] with fulness & veins & beauty."[6] For each writer, there was no escaping the skeletons of the Civil War. Cooke, De Forest, and Higginson, found them in battle; Alcott, Emerson, Forten, Hawthorne, and Melville, found them on temporary journeys to the front; Adams, Child, Douglass, Stowe, and Simms, found them in their homes.

Whitman too lived with the skeletons of reality. No one was more determined than he to put flesh on experience, to convey in words the meaning of the war. His poems, letters, articles, and recollections speak simultaneously to the deepest truths of the war and the impossibility of ever knowing those truths. As he tended to the wounded and dying in various army hospitals, he jotted down facts and thoughts in little notebooks. Years later, he declared that simply by looking at these pages "the actual army sights and hot emotions of the time [come] rushing like a river in full tide through me." These leaves of war, whether Whitman's "tiny, . . . blood-stain[ed] leaves," Emerson's "iron" leaves, or Cooke's "stray" leaves, are collected in this volume. Taken together, they introduce the literary Civil War. They illuminate "the real war" that Whitman, better than anyone, knew "will never get in the books."

# Acknowledgments

A Mellon Fellowship in the Humanities at Harvard University, followed by an appointment to History and Literature, provided the time and resources to complete this book. My thanks go to Robert Allison, Randall Burkett, Marcia Dambry, James Engell, Pat Hoy II, Steven Jaffe, Richard Hunt, Susan Hunt, Margo McCarty, Peter Mancall, Jan Thaddeus, Louise Townsend, and Thomas Underwood. I owe a special debt of gratitude to Aaron Sachs for showing me that teaching and friendship are inseparable. At Mather House, I got a second chance at undergraduate life thanks to the invitation of Jeffrey and Nancy Williamson. Words cannot express my appreciation to Jason Abrevaya, Scot Landry, Roger Landry, Tai Wong and the rest of the team that allowed me to share in the 1991–92 B-League Intramural Basketball Championship: Brett Allen, John DiGeorge, Phil Mahowald, Tae Song, Bryan Tawney, and Joe Vavpetic.

The idea for this volume grew out of discussion with Rachel Toor. This is my second project with Sheldon Meyer who continues to provide invaluable advice and encouragement. I am also grateful to Joellyn Ausanka, Leona Capeless, Karen Wolny, and the many other people at Oxford who have helped shape this book.

I have kept James Goodman, Douglas Greenberg, David Masur, John Phillips, Mark Richman, Bruce Rossky, and Thomas Slaughter largely clear of this work but in other ways I have asked a great deal of them. I am lucky to have such giving, long-lasting friendships. I am even luckier for the love of Jani, Benjamin, and Sophie Masur. Every day they teach me that "Outside/ outside myself/ there is a world." Every day they help me realize my dreams and visions.

*Cambridge, Mass.*                                                                      L.P.M.
*August 1992*

# Contents

"...the real war
will never get
in the books"

Henry Adams, 1860 *(Courtesy of the Massachusetts Historical Society)*

# Henry Brooks Adams
## (1838–1918)

Henry Adams always knew for whom he wrote. It was not for himself, or his friends, or his family, but for the ages. He was twenty-two when he informed his brother Charles that he "would like to think that a century or two hence when everything else about us is forgotten, my letters might still be read and quoted as a memorial of manners and habits at the time of the great secession of 1860."[1]

He could afford such grandiosity and, as it turned out, would live up to it as well. The great-grandson and grandson of Presidents, Adams expected himself to assume a position of intellectual and social influence. As he put it in the *Education* more than half a century later, no child "held better cards than me."[2] His genealogy (back to the Massachusetts Bay Colony), his training (Harvard and Europe), and his finances (legacies from John Quincy Adams and Peter Chardon Brooks) meant independence and confidence. But it brought a burden as well.

Descended from glory, Adams needed to make his own place in family history. He knew the Civil War was the defining event for his generation. Weary of serving in England as amanuensis to his father, he desired a more heroic and dramatic mode of participation. Time and again he decided to come home to the battlefield, and then he would hesitate. His letters to his brother, who seemed nearly monthly to be climbing into the higher ranks of military command, undulate with confused and forbidden desires. His place was on the field of action, yet England was where he could do the most good. He would seek a commission presently, but having survived scarlet fever as a child, his physical and emotional constitution forbade his going to war.

In the end, he remained in England. But if, in one sense, Adams missed the war, the war did not miss him. Late in 1863 he confided: "I don't want to talk about the war, yet what else is there to mention."[3] In talking about it, Adams introduced ideas and feelings that persisted for decades. Intellectually, he searched for the equations that would unlock history and society, contemplated the nature of democratic institutions and the power of scientific laws, and flirted with mysticism. Emotionally, he alternated between hope and despair, he craved something more yet sensed he must settle for something less. The letters grab us because they are immediate and honest, unvarnished. Here was a privileged youth, "somewhat left out of the American swim" in John Jay Chapman's words, struggling to find his place among a generation marked forever by "Cyclopean battles," by mythic acts and tales of struggle and survival, death and renewal.[4]

The stories told in the correspondence differ from the stories told in the *Education*. The first-person Henry of the letters drafted history by experience; the third-person Henry of the *Education* composed history by memory. The one Henry separated himself from those who fought in the war and at times lamented his life of inaction; the other Henry described himself as one of several hundred thousand men who were "rolled . . . into the surf of a wild ocean . . . to be beaten about for four years by the waves of war." The one Henry thought glory and goodness possible in the world; the other believed only "in the sheer chaos of human nature." The one Henry imagined a future and thought about his place in it; the other longed for the pre-Civil War past. And finally, the one Henry, on a July day, after receiving news of the Federal victory at Gettysburg, exclaimed that "our generation has been stirred up from its lowest layers and there is that in its history which will stamp every member of it until we are all in our graves. We cannot be commonplace"; the other Henry agreed that the war forever changed his world, but it was precisely how common his generation turned out to be that made it all seem so tragic.[5]

1. HA to Charles Francis Adams, Jr. [London, 4 July 1861][6]

. . . As to your going to the war, I will tell you plainly how the case seems to me to stand. The Chief[7] is unwilling to do anything about it. His idea is that the war will be short and that you will only destroy all your habits of business without gaining anything. If you will take my advice you will say no more about it; only make arrangements so as not to be taken by surprise, and when the time comes, just write and notify him. He will consent to that as a "fait accompli" which he cannot take the responsibility of encouraging himself. As for mamma she drives us all crazy by worrying to let you go. When you are gone she will give us no rest worrying till you're killed. This is my advice, for I see that it is your only way. . . .

## 2. HA to CFA, Jr., London, 26 July 1861

. . . You say that you wanted to go off with Gordon's Regiment. I tell you, sir, I would give my cocked hat and knee breeches to be with them at this moment. Egad I don't understand being sorry for them. I have no doubt that barring a few lives and legs and arms lost, they'll all like it and be the better for it. And as for the lives and legs, if they estimate theirs as low as I do mine, the loss won't amount to much. Pain is the only thing I should fear, but after all, one's health is just as likely to be benefitted as to be hurt by a campaign, bullets and all, so that this doesn't count. My own task however lies elsewhere and I should be after all hardly the material for a soldier; so that I do my own work and resign the hope of becoming a hero. . . .

## 3. HA to CFA, Jr., London, 5 August 1861

P.S. 6 August. . . . After studying over the accounts of the battle and reading Russell's letter to the *Times*, I hardly know whether to laugh or cry.[8] Of all the ridiculous battles there ever were fought, this seems to me the most so. To a foreigner or to any one not interested in it, the account must be laughable in the extreme. But the disgrace is frightful. The exposé of the condition of our army is not calculated to do us anything but the most unmixed harm here, though it might have the good effect at home of causing these evils to be corrected. If this happens again, farewell to our country for many a day. Bull's Run will be a by-word of ridicule for all time. Our honor will be utterly gone. But yesterday we might have stood against the world. Now none so base to do us reverence. Let us stop our bragging now and hence-forward. Throw Bulls Run in the teeth of any man who dares to talk large. In spite of my mortification, I could not help howling with laughter over a part of Russell's letter. Such a battle of heels. Such a bloodless, ridiculous race for disgrace, history does not record. Unpursued, untouched, without once having even crossed bayonets with the enemy, we have run and saved our precious carcasses from a danger that does not exist. Our flag, what has become of it? Who will respect it? What can we ever say for it after this.

My determination to come home is only increased by this disgrace. I cannot stay here now to stand the taunts of everyone without being able to say a word in defence. Unless I hear from you at once, I shall write myself to Gov. Andrew and to Mr. Dana and to everyone else I can think of, and raise Heaven and earth to get a commission. If we must be beaten, and it looks now as though that must ultimately be the case, I want to do all I can not to be included among those who ran away. . . .

### 4. HA to CFA, Jr., London, 28 December 1861

. . . You are going into the army. I do not think it my duty to express any regrets at the act, or at the necessity for it. They are understood, and I do not mean to make the thing any harder for either you or myself, by mourning or maundering about it. About my own fortunes I am becoming more and more callous and indifferent; but about yours, I feel differently, and if it were not for the strange madness of the times, which has left no longer any chance of settled lives and Christian careers, I should be vehement against your throwing yourself away like this. As it is, I can only tell you to do what you think best, and I shall be always ready to stand by you with what aid I can give. . . .

### 5. HA to CFA, Jr., London, 15 March 1862

. . . Meanwhile it worries me all the time to be leading this thoroughly useless life abroad while you are acting such grand parts at home. You would be astonished at the change in opinion which has taken place here already. . . . The truth is, as our swarm of armies strike deeper and deeper into the South, the contest is beginning to take to European proportions of grandeur and perfection like nothing of which they ever heard or read. They call us insane to attempt what, when achieved, they are almost afraid to appreciate. A few brilliant victories, a short campaign of ten days or a fortnight, rivalling in its vigor and results those of Napoleon, has positively startled this country into utter confusion. . . . The English on hearing of Fort Donelson and the Fall of Nashville, seem to think our dozen armies are already over the Saint Lawrence and at the gates of Quebec. They don't conceal their apprehensions and if we go on in this way, they will be as humiliated as the South itself. The talk of intervention, only two months ago so loud as to take a semi-official tone, is now out of the minds of everyone. . . . Mr. Mason . . . maintains now that the South always expected to lose the border States and that now that they are retiring to the cotton region the war has just begun.[9] He cooly talks this stuff to the English people as if they hadn't always asserted that the border-states were a vital point with them. We on the other hand, no longer descend to argue such stories, or to answer the new class of lies; but smile blandly and compassionately on those who swallow them and remark that so far as advised, the nation whom we have the honor to represent, is satisfied with the progress thus far made, and sees no reason to doubt that the Union will be maintained in its fullest and most comprehensive meaning. . . .

Here I am, more dry-nurse than ever, dabbling a little, a very little in society;

reading a little; copying a great deal; writing nothing, and not advancing an inch.
I envy you who at least has an enemy before you. My enemy is only myself.

### 6. HA to CFA, Jr., London, 11 April 1862

... I have no doubt that, if I were to stay here another year, I should become
extremely fond of the place and the life. There is, too, a certain grim satisfaction in the idea that this people who have worn and irritated and exasperated
us for months, and among whom we have lived nearly a year of what was, till
lately, a slow torture, should now be innocently dancing and smiling on the
volcano, utterly unconscious of the extent of hatred and the greediness for
revenge that they've raised. When the storm does finally burst on them, they
will have one of their panics and be as astonished as if they'd never heard of
anything but brotherly affection between the two nations. Of course it would
be out of the question for me to hint at the state of things to them. I have only
to smile and tell gross lies, for which God forgive me, about my feelings toward
this country, and the kindness I have received here, which, between ourselves,
so far as the pure English go, has been brilliantly conspicuous for its almost total
absence. . . .

You may think all this nonsense, but I tell you these are great times. Man has
mounted science, and is now run away with. I firmly believe that before many
centuries more, science will be the master of man. The engines he will have
invented will be beyond his strength to control. Some day science may have the
existence of mankind in its power, and the human race commit suicide, by
blowing up the world. Not only shall we be able to cruize in space, but I'll be
hanged if I see any reason why some future generation shouldn't walk off like
a beetle with the world on its back, or give it another rotary motion so that
every zone should receive in turn its due portion of heat and light. . . .

I despise a mail that does not tell of a victory, and indeed for some time past
we have been pampered. But every time that the telegram comes and its yellow
envelope is torn open, I feel much like taking a little brandy to strengthen me
up to it. There is a nervous tremor about it that is hard to master. The 24th did
well at Newbern. I wish to God I had been with it, or were with the Richmond
army now. I feel ashamed and humiliated at leading this miserable life here, and
since having been blown up by my own petard in my first effort to do good, I
haven't even the hope of being of more use here than I should be in the
army. . . .

### 7. HA to CFA, Jr., London, 8 May 1862

One always begins to doubt at the wrong time, and to hesitate when one should
strike hardest. Knowing this my infirmity, I have made it my habit here abroad

to frown it down with energy, and to persuade myself, when seeing most cause for anxiety, that the moment of suspense was nearest to its end. It needs to be here, among a people who read everything backwards that regards us, and surround us with a chaos of croaking worse than their own rookeries, to understand how hard it is always to retain one's confidence and faith. The late indecisive military events in America, are looked upon here as the sign of ultimate Southern success. I preach a very different doctrine and firmly believe that the war in its old phase is near its end. I do not see how anything but great awkwardness on our part can prevent the main southern army from being dispersed or captured in Virginia. But there is no doubt that the idea here is as strong as ever that we must ultimately fail, and unless a very few weeks show some great military result, we shall have our hands full again in this quarter. There is no fear of armed intervention, or even, I think, of immediate recognition; but a moral intervention is not impossible; or rather it is inevitable without our triumph before July. By moral intervention I mean some combined representation on the part of the European powers, in friendly language, urging our two parties to come to an understanding. If this catches us still in Virginia, it will play mischief. The worst of it is that the Government here are forced to it. The suffering among the people in Lancashire and in France is already very great and is increasing enormously every day without any prospect of relief for months to come. This drives them into action, and has at least the one good side that if we do gain decisive advantages so as to make the Southern chances indefinitely small, we shall have Europe at our control and can dictate terms.

On the other hand, if it is right to suppose that we shall soon end the war, I am afraid we have got to face a political struggle that will be the very deuce and all. The emancipation question has got to be settled somehow, and our accounts say that at Washington the contest is getting very bitter. The men who lead the extreme Abolitionists are a rancorous set. They have done their worst this winter to over-ride the Administration rough-shod, and it has needed all Seward's skill to head them off. If we are completely victorious in the field, we shall see the slave-question come up again worse than ever, and Sumner and Chandler and Trumbull and the rest are just the men to force a new explosion.[10] Gradual measures don't suit them, and yet without their support it will be hard to carry gradual measures. I have immense confidence in Seward however, and there is said to be the most perfect confidence between him and the President, so that we shall go into the struggle with a good chance of carrying it through.

As for this country, the simple fact is that it is unanimously against us and becomes more firmly set every day. From hesitation and neutrality, people here are now fairly decided. It is acknowledged that our army is magnificent and that we have been successful and may be still more so, but the feeling is universal against us. If we succeed, it will still be the same. It is a sort of dogged, English prejudice, and there is no dealing with it. . . .

## 8. HA to CFA, Jr., London, 16 May 1862

... One thing is certain, labor in America is dear and will remain so; American cotton will always command a premium over any other yet known; and can be most easily produced. Emancipation cannot be instantaneous. We must rather found free colonies in the South such as you are now engaged in building up at Port Royal; the nucleus of which must be military and naval stations garrisoned by *corps d'armée*, and grouped around them must be the *emeriti*, the old soldiers with their grants of land, their families, their schools, churches and Northern energy, forming common cause with the negroes in gradually sapping the strength of the slave-holders, and thus year after year carrying new industry and free institutions until their borders meet from the Atlantic, the Gulf, the Mississippi and the Tennessee in a common centre, and the old crime shall be expiated and the whole social system of the South reconstructed. Such was the system of the old Romans with their conquered countries and it was always successful. It is the only means by which we can insure our hold on the South, and plant colonies that are certain of success. It must be a military system of colonies, governed by the Executive and without any dependence upon or relation to the States in which they happen to be placed. With such a system I would allow fifty years for the South to become ten times as great and powerful and loyal as she ever was, besides being free. ...

## 9. HA to CFA, Jr., London, 22 May 1862

... I dread the continuance of this war and its demoralizing effects, more than anything else, and happy would be the day when we could see the first sign of returning peace. It's likely to be hard enough work to keep our people educated and honest anyway, and the accounts that reach us of the whole-sale demoralization in the army of the West, from camp-life, and of their dirt, and whiskey and general repulsiveness, are not encouraging to one who wants to see them taught to give up that blackguard habit of drinking liquor in bar-rooms, to brush their teeth and hands and wear clean clothes and to believe that they have a duty in life besides that of getting ahead, and a responsibility for other people's acts as well as their own. The little weaknesses I speak of are faults of youth; but what will they become if America in its youth takes a permanent course towards every kind of idleness, vice and ignorance.

As for our position here, it is all that could be wished. Everyone congratulates us on the successes of our arms and there is no longer any hint at even a remonstrance, though there are questions between the Governments which in our bitter state of feeling may bring difficulty. I am very anxious to avoid anything of this sort. We must have peace for many years if we are to heal our wounds and put the country on the right track. We must bring back or create a respect for law and order and the Constitution and the civil and judicial authorities. The nation has been dragged by this infernal cotton that had better have been burning in Hell, far away from its true course, and its worst passions and tastes have been developed by a forced and bloated growth. It will depend on the generation to which you and I belong, whether the country is to be brought back to its true course and the New England element is to carry the victory, or whether we are to be carried on from war to war and debt to debt and one military leader to another, till we lose all our landmarks and go ahead like France with a mere blind necessity to get on, without a reason or a principle. No more war's. Let's have peace for the love of God. . . .

## 10.  HA to CFA, Jr., London, 5 September 1862

. . . As to your speculations about the end of the war and a peace, I won't say that I wouldn't consent to argue about it some day, but you know perfectly well that until we've driven the South into their cotton fields we have no chance even to offer those terms. Perhaps on the broad national question I look at the matter differently from you. Apart from other causes, I am here in Europe and of course am influenced by European opinion. Firmly convinced as I am that there can be no peace on our continent so long as the southern people exist, I don't much care whether they are destroyed by emancipation, or in other words a vigorous system of guerilla war carried on by negroes on our side, or by the slower and more doubtful measures of choaking them with their own cotton. Perhaps before long we shall have to use both weapons as vigorously as we now are using the last. But one thing is clear to my mind, which is that we must not let them as an independent state get the monopoly of cotton again, unless we want to find a powerful and a bitterly hostile nation on our border, supported by all the moral and social influence of Great Britain in peace; certain in war to drag us into all the European complications; sure to be in perpetual anarchy within, but always ready to disturb anything and everything without; to compel us to support a standing army no less large than if we conquer them and hold them so, and with infinite means of wounding and scattering dissension among us. We must ruin them before we let them go or it will all have to be done over again. And we must exterminate them in the end, be it long or be it short, for it is a battle between us and slavery.

I see that your regiment is ordered to Virginia which shows a gleam of reason in the war-department. . . . For my own part I confess that I value human life at a pretty low price, and God knows I set no higher value on my own than on others. I always was a good deal of a sceptic and speculator in theories and think precious small potatoes of man in general and myself in particular. But I confess to feeling very badly when the news comes of our disasters and losses. Poor Stephen Perkins! Poor Hamilton Kuhn![11] What on earth was Union or the national future to Hamilton Kuhn! One would have booked him for a single care in life as he grew older; that of his own comfort. With Stephen it was different. I have a kind of an idea that Stephen thought much as I do about life. He always seemed to me to take rather a contemptuous view of the world in general, and I rather like to imagine him, after the shock and the pain was over, congratulating himself that at last he was through with all the miseres of an existence that had bored him and that offered him little that he cared for; and now he could turn his mind to the exploring of a new life, with new duties and a new career, after having done all that man can do to discharge his debt to God and his fellow-men in the old. . . .

## 11. HA to CFA, Jr., London, 21 November 1862

. . . The truth is, the experience of four years has done little towards giving me confidence in myself. The more I see, the more I am convinced that a man whose mind is balanced like mine, in such a way that what is evil never seems unmixed with good, and what is good always streaked with evil; an object never seems important enough to call out strong energies till they are exhausted, nor necessary enough not to allow of its failure being possible to retrieve; in short, a mind which is not strongly positive and absolute, cannot be steadily successful in action, which requires quickness and perseverance. I have steadily lost faith in myself ever since I left college, and my aim is now so indefinite that all my time may prove to have been wasted, and then nothing left but a truncated life.

I should care the less for all this if I could see your path any clearer, but while my time *may* prove to have been wasted, I don't see but what yours *must* prove so. At least God forbid that you should remain an officer longer than is necessary. And what then? The West is possible; indeed, I have thought of that myself. But what we want, my dear boy, is a *school*. We want a national set of young men like ourselves or better, to start new influences not only in politics, but in literature, in law, in society, and throughout the whole social organism of the country. A national school of our own generation. And that is what America has no power to create. In England the Universities centralize ability and London gives a field. So in France, Paris encourages and combines these influences. But with us, we should need at least six perfect geniuses placed, or rather, spotted over the country and all working together; whereas our generation as yet has not produced one nor the promise of one. It's all random, insulated work, for special and temporary and personal purposes, and we have no means, power or hope of combined action for any unselfish end. . . .

I have given up the war and only pray for its end. The South has vindicated its position and we cannot help it, so, as we can find no one to hold us together, I don't see the use of shedding more blood. Still, my boy, all this makes able men a necessity for the future, and if you're an able man, there's your career. I have projects enough and not unpromising ones for some day, but like most of my combinations, I suppose they'll all end in dust and ashes. . . .

## 12.  HA to CFA, Jr., London, 23 January 1863

. . . The Emancipation Proclamation has done more for us here than all our former victories and all our diplomacy. It is creating an almost convulsive reaction in our favor all over this country. The London *Times* is furious and scolds like a drunken drab. Certain it is, however, that public opinion is very deeply stirred here and finds expression in meetings; addresses to Pres. Lincoln; deputations to us; standing committees to agitate the subject and to affect opinion; and all the other symptons of a great popular movement peculiarly unpleasant to the upper classes here because it rests altogether on the spontaneous action of the laboring classes and has a pestilent squint at sympathy with republicanism. But the *Times* is on its last legs and has lost its temper. They say it always does lose its temper when it finds such a feeling too strong for it, and its next step will be to come round and try to guide it. We are much encouraged and in high spirits. If only you at home don't have disasters, we will give such a checkmate to the foreign hopes of the rebels as they never yet have had. . . .

## 13.  HA to CFA, Jr., London, 27 March 1863

. . . [B]etween our Government at home and our active and energetic allies here, we seem to have made progress. I went last night to a meeting of which I shall send you a report; a democratic and socialist meeting, my boy; most threatening and dangerous to the established state of things; and assuming a tone and proportions that are quite novel and alarming in this capital. And they met to notify Government that "they would not tolerate" interference against us. I can assure you this sort of movement is as alarming here as a slave-insurrection would be in the South, and we have our hands on the springs that can raise or pacify such agitators; at least as regards our own affairs, they making common cause with us. I never quite appreciated the "moral influence" of American democracy, nor the cause that the privileged classes in Europe have to fear us, until I saw how directly it works. At this moment the American question is organising a vast mass of the lower orders in direct contact with the wealthy. They go our whole platform and are full of the "rights of man." The old revolutionary leaven is working steadily here in England. You can find millions of people who look up to our institutions as their model and who talk with utter contempt of their own system of Government. . . .

## 14. HA to CFA, Jr., London, 16 April 1863

. . . Here I find myself again in the old atmosphere of smoke and fog, atmospheric, moral and political. The other side means mischief and we know it. But they will not open against us until we do something which will rouse national anger. Then you will see us struggle *in vasto*. Oh, ye Gods! why not make a man of tanned leather as to his heart! The more I strive to be callous, the more I become only silent! Rage boils up in my throat. My only consolation is the thought that as yet we have weathered the storm in spite of all the convictions of our foreign friends, and some day—God forgive me for the folly of wishing for what could do no good and must do harm to everyone—but some day I hope to see the time when America alone will take France and England both together on her hands, and be strong enough to knock their two skulls against each other till they crack. Fifty more years of peace would do it. A hundred years of union and peace would place Europe so low in the ranks as no longer to create jealousy. . . .

## 15. HA to CFA, Jr., London, 1 May 1863

. . . And so two years have passed over and gone, and still I am abroad and still you are a Captain of Cavalry. You meanwhile are near twenty-eight years old. I shall never on this earth see my twenty-fifth birthday again. Does not this fact suggest certain ideas to you? Can a man at your time of life be a Cavalry Captain and remain a briefless solicitor? Can a man of my general appearance pass five years in Europe and remain a candidate for the bar? In short, have we both wholly lost our reckoning and are we driven at random by fate, or have we still a course that we are steering though it is not quite the same as our old one? By the Apostle Paul I know not. Only one fact I feel sure of. We are both no longer able to protect ourselves with the convenient fiction of the law. Let us quit that now useless shelter, and steer if possible for whatever it may have been that once lay beyond it. Neither you nor I can ever do anything at the bar. . . .

You don't catch me entering the army now. Donner-r-r-wetter! it would be like entering college Freshman when all one's friends were Seniors. . . . No, my warlike brother! My hand could at best use a rapier. It is not made for a sabre. I should be like a bewildered rabbit in action, being only trained to counsel. My place is where I am, and I never was so necessary to it as now. All thoughts of escape even for a day, have vanished. We are covered with work, and our battles are fierce and obstinate. . . .

## 16. HA to CFA, Jr., [London,] 17 July 1863

We are in receipt of all your sanguinary letters, as well as of news down to the 4th, telling of Cyclopean battles, like the struggles of Saturn and Terra and Hyperion for their empire, lasting through sunrise after sunrise, in an agony such as herald the extinction of systems.[12] It's a pity that we're civilized. What a grand thing Homer would have made of it; while in our day, men only conceive of a battle as of two lines of men shooting at each other till one or the other gives way. At this distance, though, even now it's very grand and inspiring. There's a magnificence about the pertinacity of the struggle, lasting so many days, and closing, so far as we know on the eve of our single national anniversary, with the whole nation bending over it, that makes even these English cubs silent. Dreadful I suppose it is, and God knows I feel anxious and miserable enough at times, but I doubt whether any of us will ever be able to live contented again in times of peace and laziness. Our generation has been stirred up from the lowest layers and there is that in its history which will stamp every member of it until we are all in our graves. We cannot be commonplace. The great burden that has fallen on us must inevitably stamp its character on us. I have hopes for us all, as we go on with the work.

And I, though I grumble at my position here and want to go home, feel at times that I don't know what I say, in making my complaints. I want to go into the army! to become a second lieutenant in an infantry regiment somewhere in the deserts of the South! I who for two years have lived a life of intellectual excitement, in the midst of the most concentrated society of the world, and who have become so accustomed to it that I should wither into nothing without it! Why, the thing's absurd! Even to retire to a provincial life in Boston would be an experiment that I dread to look forward to! But for me to go into the army is ridiculous! . . .

## 17. HA to CFA, Jr., London, 2 October 1863

. . . I imagine that this mischance [Rosecrans's defeat at Chickamauga] ensures us another year of war, unless the army of the Potomac shows more energy than usual and more success than ever yet. The truth is, everything in this universe has its regular waves and tides. Electricity, sound, the wind, and I believe every part of organic nature will be brought some day within this law. But my philosophy teaches me, and I firmly believe it, that the laws which govern animated beings will be ultimately found to be at the bottom the same with those which rule inanimate nature, and, as I entertain a profound conviction of the littleness of our kind, and of the curious enormity of creation, I am quite ready to receive with pleasure any basis for a systematic conception of it all. Thus (to explain this rather alarming digression) as a sort of experimentalist, I look for regular tides in the affairs of man, and of course, in our own affairs. In every progression, somehow or other, the nations move by the same process which has never been explained but is evident in the ocean and the air. On this theory I should expect at about this time, a turn which would carry us backward. The devil of it is, supposing there comes a time when the rebs suddenly cave in, how am I to explain that!

This little example of my unpractical, experimento-philosophico-historico-progressiveness, will be enough. It suffices to say that I am seeking to console my trouble by chewing the dry husks of that philosophy, which, whether it calls itself submission to the will of God, or to the laws of nature, rests in bottom simply and solely upon an acknowledgment of our own impotence and ignorance. In this amusement, I find, if not consolation at least some sort of mental titillation. Besides, I am becoming superstitious. I believe Nick Anderson's killed, though I've not yet seen his ghost. Write me that he's not yet gone under, and I will say defiance to the vague breath of similar chimeras. . . .

## 18. HA to CFA, Jr., London, 30 October 1863

If it weren't for our anxiety about you, I think we should get on swimmingly in these times. The war has taken a chronic shape, and it seems pretty clear that it must burn itself out, or perhaps I should say, burn the rebels out. After having passed through all the intermediate phases of belief, I have come out a full-blown fatalist, and what has greatly aided the result has been the observation of the steady movement of affairs at home. The world grows, my friend, just like a cabbage; or if the simile is vulgar, we'll say, like an oak. The result will come when the time is ripe, and the only thing that disgusts me much is the consciousness that we are unable to govern it, and the conviction that a man of sense can only prove his possession of a soul, by remaining in mind a serene and indifferent spectator of the very events to which all his acts most eagerly contribute. This has been in one form or another the result of every philosophical system since men became conscious of the inexplicable contradiction of their existence, and though it may seem damned nonsense to you with bullets flying round, it does very well for a theory of existence so long as it has no occasion to regulate the relation between one man and another. But there I confess, it rubs, and naturally enough. So I can contemplate with some philosophy the battles and the defeats, which are indeed only of the same sort of interest as the story of Marathon or Naseby, a degree intensified, but not so with your hasards.[13] The race will go on all right or wrong; either way it's the result of causes existing but not within our reach; but unfortunately if you were to get into trouble, you might not go on at all, which from my point of view would be disagreeable to us all, yourself inclusive, and would not admit of the application of your old though fallacious maxim that life is a system of compensations, a maxim probably just, if we speak of the race as a unit.

Such are, or have been, my reflections during the past week on hearing of Lee's advance and of the severe skirmishing that has been going on. . . .

## 19. HA to CFA, Jr., London, 1 July 1864

We have had nothing but excitement this week. Naturally we were delighted to hear that you had succeeded in crossing the James undisturbed, and it relieved our minds of great anxiety. But it came to us coupled with the story that Petersburg was captured, and that of course raised our hopes extremely. This morning they are very much cooled down by the announcement of the battles of the 17th and 18th, so that the reaction may give my epistle today a shade of blueness not warranted perhaps by the facts. It is a remarkable proof of human folly, and a strong encouragement of the philosopher, to see how really weak our minds naturally are, and how little the severest training can keep them from making damned idiots of themselves by trusting their hopes and wishes. As the balance shifts slowly between the Federal and Confederate, and the anxiety of the wise man is merely to learn which scale falls, we wretched creatures on each side are always looking for some sudden change that will reverse the whole order of creation. The ups and downs are rough on such poor things as nerves, but the strain is wearing rather from its long continuance than from its immediate pressure. Through them all, some party is continually getting ahead slowly, and some day or other I suppose the infinite region of barren lies will be passed, as you have left the Wilderness behind you, and we shall come out upon some firm and evident truth. . . .

## 20. HA to CFA, Jr., London, 8 July 1864

. . . [W]hat is practicable seems to be a summary ejection of us gentlemen from our places next November, and the arrival of the Democratic party in power, pledged to peace at any price. This is my interpretation of the news which now lies before me.[14]

Shall you be sorry? not for the failure of course, for our feelings on that subject are well enough known to us. But for the loss of our power. For my own part, I don't know. I am not sure. It is becoming clear that we must have peace. All the talk of our orators of the impossibility of disunion is damned nonsense, between you and me. If we fail to get Richmond, as I imagine we have failed, there will be a popular majority for disunion in the North, and the question of terms ought not to stand long against the pressure for peace North and South. But this work is not for us to do, and I don't envy the men that are to do it.

Therefore I am not sure that we shall not be lucky to escape the task of accomplishing the humiliation of the country.

But the struggle to die is painful. The next nine months will be slow to pass, and I wish either that one could put one's nerves into one's pocket, bottled stoutly up; or that one could run away from the future. I would like much to go to bed, and sleep peacefully till next March. I want to escape the alternation of hope and dread; the hectic phenomena of our decline; and bid farewell to my strangely disastrous experience as a politician. . . .

## 21. HA to CFA, Jr., London, 25 November 1864

. . . The election is over then, and after all that excitement, worry and danger, behold all goes on as before! It was one of those cases in which life and death seemed to hang on the issue, and the result is so decisive as to answer all our wishes and hopes. It is a curious commentary upon theoretical reasoning as to forms of Government, that this election which ought by all rights to be a defect in the system, and which is universally considered by the admirers of "strong Governments" to be a proof of the advantage of their own model, should yet turn out in practice a great and positive gain and a fruitful source of national strength. After all, systems of Government are secondary matters, if you've only got your people behind them. I never yet have felt so proud as now of the great qualities of our race, or so confident of the capacity of men to develop their faculties in the mass. I believe that a new era of the movement of the world will date from that day, which will drag nations up still another step, and carry us out of a quantity of old fogs. Europe has a long way to go yet to catch us up. . . .

## 22. HA to CFA, Jr., Florence, 10 May 1865

I can't help a feeling of amusement at looking back on my letters and thinking how curiously inapt they have been to the state of things about you. Victories and assassinations, joys, triumphs, sorrows and gloom; all at fever point, with you; while I prate about art and draw out letters from the suniest and most placid of subjects. I have already buried Mr. Lincoln under the ruins of the Capitol, along with Caesar, and this I don't mean merely as a phrase. We must have our wars, it appears, and our crimes, as well as other countries. I think Abraham Lincoln is rather to be envied in his death, as in his life somewhat; and if he wasn't as great as Caesar, he shares the same sort of tomb. History repeats itself, and if we are to imitate the atrocities of Rome, I find a certain amusement in conducting my private funeral service over the victims, on the ground that it is most suitable for such associations, of any in the world. . . .

Louisa May Alcott *(Courtesy of the University of Virginia Library)*

# Louisa May Alcott
## (1832–1888)

Thirty years old, Alcott longed "to fly at some body and free my mind on several points."[1] Precisely what those points were she never specified, but it is clear she sought escape from the numbing rules established by her pedagogical father, Bronson Alcott, and from the restraining conventions imposed on women by American society. She craved action. As much as she loved solitude (how could she not, growing up neighbors to Emerson and Thoreau?), she wanted to experience the physical as well as the mental, wanted to test herself against flesh as well as scripture. "I long to be a man," she confessed. That line can be read in many ways; one of its meanings is that Alcott longed to leave her father's parlor and find the independence and vitality that eluded her in Concord.

The Civil War gave her a chance, and she took it. In the Fall of 1862 she applied to serve as a nurse in Washington. On December 11, she received orders to report to the Union Hotel Hospital, a converted tavern. And there she set to work. What she knew about nursing came from caring for her dying sister a few years earlier and reading Florence Nightingale's recently published *Notes on Nursing* (1860). But experience did not matter as much as fortitude. For three weeks, she bathed and fed and comforted men being rushed in from the battle at Fredericksburg. For three weeks, Alcott endured fetid odors and piercing screams. For three weeks, she worked twelve-hour shifts and shuddered at the death all around her.

And then she took ill, shot down by typhoid fever. High fevers caused her delirious dreams, and the treatment, huge doses of calomel, caused mercury poisoning that resulted in life-long physical ailments. On January 16, 1863, Bronson Alcott came to retrieve his stricken daughter; they returned to Concord a week later. For two months Louisa recuperated.

"To go very near to death teaches one to value life," she wrote in her journal.[2]

From Washington, Alcott had written letters home and signed some of them Nurse Tribulation Periwinkle, one of many personas that she employed throughout her writing career. Recovered from her illness, she revised some of these letters and published them in four installments in *The Commonwealth*, an antislavery weekly. The response was favorable, and when James Redpath offered to reprint these letters as a book, Alcott accepted. She was not pleased at receiving only five cents per copy sold, but Redpath promised to contribute to war orphans out of his profits and it was, after all, her first book.

It has been said that all the themes of a writer's lifetime can be found in her first book. *Hospital Sketches* contains light and darkness, comedy and tragedy, salvation and sin. There are scenes that focus on the domestic, the familial, and the moral. Such scenes, extended into books, would make Alcott the best-selling author of *Little Women* (1868), *Little Men* (1871), and *Jo's Boys* (1886). And there are scenes shaped by passion, anger, and satire. These would characterize other novels and stories including *Work* (1873) and *A Modern Mephistopheles* (1877). Until recently, Alcott's reputation has stood mainly on the former and not the latter. Despite its popularity at the time, *Hospital Sketches* was omitted from the first collections of Alcott's complete work. Seen as too realistic, it was cast aside by those who wanted all her writing to resemble *Little Women*.

Readers at the time, however, praised *Hospital Sketches* for its "fluent" narrative, "quiet" humor, and "graphic" focus.[3] The book brought what Whitman would later call the "real war" into the homes of Northerners removed from the battlefields. Readers could not get enough of it and Alcott was pleasantly overwhelmed by her sudden literary reputation. "To this day," she exclaimed, "I cannot see why people like a few extracts from topsy turvey letters written on inverted tin kettles, in my pantry, while waiting for gruel to warm or poultices to cool, for boys to wake and be tormented, on stairs, in window seats & other sequestered spots favorable to literary inspiration. People are very kind & very easily pleased & I'm much obliged, but I dont understand it at all & probably never shall."[4]

After *Hospital Sketches*, Alcott continued to have "warlike matters simmering in my head."[5] She applied to go to Port Royal to teach the freed slaves. While waiting for permission that was never granted, she wrote a story called "My Contraband," which first appeared in the *Atlantic Monthly* as "Brothers." The tale is an abolitionist tract that depicts the horrors endured by slaves and salutes the bravery of the black soldiers who attacked Fort Wagner. At another level, "Brothers" is about hidden desires and suppressed hatreds. The narrator, Nurse Dane, who had survived typhoid fever, is asked to care for a Confederate captain and is assigned a mulatto servant, Bob, to help her. She is drawn to the contraband and learns that the captain and servant are half-brothers; even worse, the captain had raped Bob's wife, Lucy, and sold him to traders in the deep South. Bob unsuccessfully tries to kill the captain. Learning that Lucy had committed suicide after he was sold, Bob enlists with the Massachusetts 54th. He returns from battle fatally wounded and is treated by the narrator, who discovers that Bob has taken a surname for himself—Dane.

In 1869, *Hospital Sketches* combined with other writings was published in a new edition; "My Contraband; or, the Brothers" was included in this collection of *Camp and Fireside Stories*. By then the war was behind her, though what she said about her nursing days in November 1863 most likely held for the rest of her life: "it was a most interesting experience & I never tire of thinking and talking about 'my boys'."

## 1. Journal of Louisa May Alcott[6]

*April.* [1861]—War declared with the South, and our Concord company went to Washington. A busy time getting them ready, and a sad day seeing them off, for in a little town like this we all seem like one family in times like these. At the station the scene was very dramatic, as the brave boys went away perhaps never to come back again.

I've often longed to see a war, and now I have my wish. I long to be a man, but as I can't fight, I will content myself with working for those who can. . . .

*September, October.* [1862]— . . . War news bad. Anxious faces, beating hearts, and busy minds.

I like the stir in the air, and long for battle like a warhorse when he smells powder. The blood of the Mays is up! . . .

*November.*—Thirty years old. Decided to go to Washington as a nurse if I could find a place. Help needed, and I love nursing, and *must* let out my pent-up energy in some new way. Winter is always a hard and a dull time, and if I am away there is one less to feed and warm and worry over.

I want new experiences, and am sure to get 'em if I go. So I've sent in my name, and bide my time writing tales, to leave all snug behind me, and mending up my old clothes,—for nurses don't need nice things, thank Heaven!

*December.*—On the 11th I received a note from Miss H. M. Stevenson telling me to start for Georgetown next day to fill a place in the Union Hotel Hospital. Mrs. Ropes of Boston was matron, and Miss Kendall of Plymouth was a nurse there, and though a hard place, help was needed. I was ready, and when my commander said "March!" I marched. Packed my trunk, and reported in B.[oston] that same evening.

We had all been full of courage till the last moment came, then we all broke down. I realized that I had taken my life in my hand, and might never see them all again. I said, "Shall I stay, Mother?" as I hugged her close. "No, go! and the Lord be with you!" answered the Spartan woman, and till I turned the corner she bravely smiled and waved her wet handkerchief on the doorstep. Shall I ever see that dear old face again?

So I set forth in the December twilight, with May and Julian Hawthorne as escort, feeling as if I was the son of the house going to war.

Friday, the 12th, was a very memorable day, spent in running all over Boston to get my pass, etc., calling for parcels, getting a tooth filled, and buying a veil,—my only purchase. A. C. gave me some old clothes, the dear Sewalls money for myself and boys, lots of love and help, and at 5 P.M., saying "goodby" to a group of tearful faces at the station, I started on my long journey, full of hope and sorrow, courage and plans.

A most interesting journey into a new world full of stirring sights and sounds, new adventures, and an evergrowing sense of the great task I had undertaken.

I said my prayers as I went rushing through the country white with tents, all alive with patriotism, and already red with blood.

A solemn time, but I'm glad to live in it, and am sure it will do me good whether I come out alive or dead.

All went well, and I got to Georgetown one evening very tired. Was kindly welcomed, slept in my narrow bed with two other room-mates, and on the morrow began my new life by seeing a poor man die at dawn, and sitting all day between a boy with pneumonia and a man shot through the lungs. A strange day, but I did my best, and when I put mother's little black shawl round the boy while he sat up panting for breath, he smiled and said, "You are real motherly, ma'am." I felt as if I was getting on. The man only lay and stared with his big black eyes, and made me very nervous. But all were well behaved, and I sat looking at the twenty strong faces as they looked back at me,—hoping that I looked "motherly" to them, for my thirty years made me feel old, and the suffering round me made me long to comfort every one. . . .

*January.* [1863]—I never began the year in a stranger place than this, five hundred miles from home, alone among strangers, doing painful duties all day long, & leading a life of constant excitement in this greathouse surrounded by 3 or 4 hundred men in all stages of suffering, disease & death. Though often home sick, heart sick & worn out, I like it—find real pleasure in comforting tending & cheering these poor souls who seem to love me, to feel my sympathy though unspoken, & acknowledge my hearty good will in spite of the ignorance, awkwardness, & bashfulness which I cannot help showing in so new & trying a situation. The men are docile, respectful, & affectionate, with but few exceptions, truly lovable & manly many of them. John Suhre a Virginia blacksmith is the prince of patients, & though what we call a common man, in education & condition, to me is all that I could expect or ask from the first gentleman in the land. Under his plain speech & unpolished manner I seem to see a noble character, a heart as warm & tender as a woman's, a nature fresh & frank as any child's. He is about thirty, I think, tall & handsome, mortally wounded & dying royally, without reproach, repining, or remorse. Mrs Ropes & myself love him & feel indignant that such a man should be so early lost, for though he might never distinguish himself before the world, his influence & example cannot be without effect, for real goodness is never wasted.

Mon 4th—I shall record the events of a day as a sample of the days I spend—

Up at six, dress by gas light, run through my ward & fling up the windows though the men grumble & shiver; but the air is bad enough to breed a pestilence & as no notice is taken of our frequent appeals for better ventilation I must do what I can. Poke up the fire, add blankets, joke, coax, & command, but continue to open doors & windows as if life depended on it; mine does, & doubtless many another, for a more perfect pestilence-box than this house I never saw—cold, damp, dirty, full of vile odors from wounds, kitchens, wash rooms, & stables. No competent head, male or female, to right matters, & a jumble of good, bad, & indifferent nurses, surgeons & attendants to complicate the Chaos still more.

After this unwelcome progress through my stifling ward I go to breakfast with what appetite I may; find the inevitable fried beef, salt butter, husky bread & washy coffee; listen to the clack of eight women & a dozen men; the first silly, stupid or possessed of but one idea, the last absorbed in their breakfast & themselves to a degree that is both ludicrous and provoking, for all the dishes are ordered down the table *full* & returned *empty*, the conversation is entirely among themselves & each announces his opinion with an air of importance that frequently causes me to choke in my cup or bolt my meals with undignified speed lest a laugh betray to these pompous beings that a "child's among them takin notes." Till noon I trot, trot, giving out rations, cutting up food for helpless "boys," washing faces, teaching my attendants how beds are made or floors swept, dressing wounds, taking Dr. FitzPatrick's orders, (privately wishing all the time that he would be more gentle with my big babies,) dusting tables, sewing bandages, keeping my tray tidy, rushing up & down after pillows, bed linen, sponges, book & directions, till it seems as if I would joyfully pay down all I possess for fifteen minutes rest.

At twelve the big bell rings & up comes dinner for the boys who are always ready for it & never entirely satisfied. Soup, meat, potatoes, & bread is the bill of fare. Charley Thayer the attendant travels up & down the room serving out the rations, saving little for himself yet always thoughtful of his mates & patient as a woman with their helplessness. When dinner is over some sleep, many read, & others want letters written. This I like to do for they put in such odd things & express their ideas so comically I have great fun interiorally while as grave as possible exteriorally. A few of the men word their paragraphs well & make excellent letters. John's was the best of all I wrote. The answering of letters from friends after some one has died is the saddest & hardest duty a nurse has to do.

Supper at five sets every one to running that can run & when that flurry is over all settle down for the evening amusements which consist of newspapers, gossip, Drs last round, & for such as need them the final doses for the night. At nine the bell rings, gas is turned down & day nurses go to bed.

Night nurses go on duty, & sleep & death have the house to themselves. . . .

My work is changed to night watching or half night & half day, from twelve to twelve. I like it as it leaves me time for a morning run which is what I need to keep well, for bad air, food, water, work & watching are getting to be too much for me. I trot up & down the streets in all directions, some times to the Heights, then half way to Washington, again to the hill over which the long trains of army wagons are constantly vanishing & ambulances appearing. That way the fighting lies, & I long to follow. . . .

## 2. *Hospital Sketches* (Boston, 1863)

### CHAPTER III: A DAY

"THEY'VE come! they've come! hurry up, ladies—you're wanted."

"Who have come? the rebels?"

This sudden summons in the gray dawn was somewhat startling to a three days' nurse like myself, and, as the thundering knock came at our door, I sprang up in my bed, prepared

"To gird my woman's form,
And on the ramparts die,"

if necessary, but my room-mate took it more coolly, and, as she began a rapid toilet, answered my bewildered question,—

"Bless you, no child; it's the wounded from Fredericksburg; forty ambulances are at the door, and we shall have our hands full in fifteen minutes."

"What shall we have to do?"

"Wash, dress, feed, warm and nurse them for the next three months, I dare say. Eighty beds are ready, and we are getting impatient for the men to come.

Now you will begin to see hospital life in earnest, for you won't probably find time to sit down all day, and may think yourself fortunate if you get to bed by midnight. Come to me in the ball-room when you are ready; the worst cases are always carried there, and I shall need your help."

So saying, the energetic little woman twirled her hair into a button at the back of her head, in a "cleared for action" sort of style, and vanished, wrestling her way into a feminine kind of pea-jacket as she went.

I am free to confess that I had a realizing sense of the fact that my hospital bed was not a bed of roses just then, or the prospect before me one of unmingled rapture. My three days' experiences had begun with a death, and, owing to the defalcation of another nurse, a somewhat abrupt plunge into the superintendence of a ward containing forty beds, where I spent my shining hours washing faces, serving rations, giving medicine, and sitting in a very hard chair, with pneumonia on one side, diptheria on the other, five typhoids on the opposite, and a dozen dilapidated patriots, hopping, lying, and lounging about, all staring more or less at the new "nuss," who suffered untold agonies, but concealed them under as matronly an aspect as a spinster could assume, and blundered through her trying labors with a Spartan firmness, which I hope they appreciated, but am afraid they didn't. Having a taste for "ghastliness," I had rather longed for the wounded to arrive, for rheumatism wasn't heroic, neither was liver complaint, or measles; even fever had lost its charms since "bathing burning brows" had been used up in romances, real and ideal; but when I peeped into the dusky street lined with what I at first had innocently called market carts, now unloading their sad freight at our door, I recalled sundry reminiscences I had heard from nurses of longer standing, my ardor experienced a certain chill, and I indulged in a most unpatriotic wish that I was safe at home again, with a quiet day before me, and no necessity for being hustled up, as if I were a hen and had only to hop off my roost, give my plumage a peck, and be ready for action. A second bag at the door sent this recreant desire to the right about, as a little woolly head popped in, and Joey, (a six years' old contraband), announced—

"Miss Blan is jes' wild fer ye, and says fly round right away. They's comin' in, I tell yer, heaps on 'em—one was took out dead, and I see him,—ky! warn't he a goner!"

With which cheerful intelligence the imp scuttled away, singing like a blackbird, and I followed, feeling that Richard was *not* himself again, and wouldn't be for a long time to come.

The first thing I met was a regiment of the vilest odors that ever assaulted the human nose, and took it by storm. Cologne, with its seven and seventy evil savors, was a posy-bed to it; and the worst of this affliction was, every one had assured me that it was a chronic weakness of all hospitals, and I must bear it. I

did, armed with lavender water, with which I so besprinkled myself and premises, that, like my friend, Sairy, I was soon known among my patients as "the
nurse with the bottle." Having been run over by three excited surgeons,
bumped against by migratory coal-hods, water-pails, and small boys; nearly
scalded by an avalanche of newly-filled tea-pots, and hopelessly entangled in a
knot of colored sisters coming to wash, I progressed by slow stages up stairs
and down, till the main hall was reached, and I paused to take breath and a sur-
vey. There they were! "our brave boys," as the papers justly call them, for cow-
ards could hardly have been so riddled with shot and shell, so torn and shattered, nor have borne suffering for which we have no name, with an
uncomplaining fortitude, which made one glad to cherish each as a brother. In
they came, some on stretchers, some in men's arms, some feebly staggering
along propped on rude crutches, and one lay stark and still with covered face,
as a comrade gave his name to be recorded before they carried him away to the
dead house. All was hurry and confusion; the hall was full of these wrecks of
humanity, for the most exhausted could not reach a bed till duly ticketed and
registered; the walls were lined with rows of such as could sit, the floor covered
with the more disabled, the steps and doorways filled with helpers and lookers
on; the sound of many feet and voices made that usually quiet hour as noisy as
noon; and, in the midst of it all, the matron's motherly face brought more comfort to many a poor soul, than the cordial draughts she administered, or the
cheery words that welcomed all, making of the hospital a home.

The sight of several stretchers, each with its legless, armless, or desperately
wounded occupant, entering my ward, admonished me that I was there to
work, not to wonder or weep; so I corked up my feelings, and returned to the
path of duty, which was rather "a hard road to travel" just then. The house had
been a hotel before hospitals were needed, and many of the doors still bore their
old names; some not so inappropriate as might be imagined, for my ward was
in truth a *ball-room,* if gun-shot wounds could christen it. Forty beds were prepared, many already tenanted by tired men who fell down anywhere, and
drowsed till the smell of food roused them. Round the great stove was gathered
the dreariest group I ever saw—ragged, gaunt and pale, mud to the knees, with
bloody bandages untouched since put on days before; many bundled up in blankets, coats being lost or useless; and all wearing that disheartened look which
proclaimed defeat, more plainly than any telegram of the Burnside blunder.[7] I
pitied them so much, I dared not speak to them, though, remembering all they
had been through since the rout at Fredericksburg, I yearned to serve the dreariest of them all. Presently, Miss Blank tore me from my refuge behind the piles
of one-sleeved shirts, odd socks, bandages and lint; put basin, sponge, towels,
and a block of brown soap into my hands, with these appalling directions:

"Come, my dear, begin to wash as fast as you can. Tell them to take off socks, coats and shirts, scrub them well, put on clean shirts, and the attendants will finish them off, and lay them in bed."

If she had requested me to shave them all, or dance a horn-pipe on the stove funnel, I should have been less staggered; but to scrub some dozen lords of creation at a moment's notice, was really—really—. However, there was no time for nonsense, and, having resolved when I came to do everything I was bid, I drowned my scruples in my washbowl, clutched my soap manfully, and, assuming a businesslike air, made a dab at the first dirty specimen I saw, bent on performing my task *vi et armis*[8] if necessary. I chanced to light on a withered old Irishman, wounded in the head, which caused that portion of his frame to be tastefully laid out like a garden, the bandages being the walks, his hair the shrubbery. He was so overpowered by the honor of having a lady wash him, as he expressed it, that he did nothing but roll up his eyes, and bless me, in an irresistible style which was too much for my sense of the ludicrous; so we laughed together, and when I knelt down to take off his shoes, he "flopped" also and wouldn't hear of my touching "them dirty craters. May your bed above be aisy darlin', for the day's work ye are doon!—Woosh! there ye are, an bedad, it's hard tellin' which is the ditiest, the fut or the shoe." It was; and if he hadn't been to the fore, I should have gone on pulling, under the impression that the "fut" was a boot, for trousers, socks, shoes and legs were a mass of mud. This comical tableau produced a general grin, at which propitious beginning I took heart and scrubbed away like any tidy parent on a Saturday night. Some of them took the performance like sleepy children, leaning their tired heads against me as I worked, others looked grimly scandalized, and several of the roughest colored like bashful girls. One wore a soiled little bag about his neck, and, as I moved it, to bath his wounded breast, I said,

"Your talisman didn't save you, did it?"

"Well, I reckon it did, marm, for that shot would a gone a couple of inches deeper but for my old mammy's camphor bag," answered the cheerful philosopher.

Another, with a gun-shot wound through the cheek, asked for a looking-glass, and when I brought one, regarded his swollen face with a dolorous expression, as he muttered—

"I vow to gosh, that's too bad! I warn't a bad looking chap before, and now I'm done for; won't there be a thunderin' scar? and what on earth will Josephine Skinner say?"

He looked up at me with his one eye so appealingly, that I controlled my risibles, and assured him that if Josephine was a girl of sense, she would admire the honorable scar, as a lasting proof that he had faced the enemy, for all women thought a wound the best decoration a brave soldier could wear. I hope Miss Skinner verified the good opinion I so rashly expressed of her, but I shall never know.

The next scrubbee was a nice looking lad, with a curly brown mane, and a budding trace of gingerbread over the lip, which he called his beard, and defended stoutly, when the barber jocosely suggested its immolation. He lay on a bed, with one leg gone, and the right arm so shattered that it must evidently follow; yet the little Sergeant was as merry as if his afflictions were not worth lamenting over, and when a drop or two of salt water mingled with my suds at the sight of this strong young body, so marred and maimed, the boy looked up, with a brave smile, though there was a little quiver of the lips, as he said,

"Now don't you fret yourself about me, miss; I'm first rate here, for it's nuts to lie still on this bed, after knocking about in those confounded ambulances, that shake what there is left of a fellow to jelly. I never was in one of these places before, and think this cleaning up a jolly thing for us, though I'm afraid it isn't for you ladies."

"Is this your first battle, Sergeant?"

"No, miss; I've been in six scrimmages, and never got a scratch till this last one; but it's done the business pretty thoroughly for me, I should say. Lord! what a scramble there'll be for arms and legs, when we old boys come out of our graves, on the Judgment Day: wonder if we shall get our own again? If we do, my leg will have to tramp from Fredericksburg, my arm from here, I suppose, and meet my body, wherever it may be."

The fancy seemed to tickle him mightily, for he laughed blithely, and so did I; which, no doubt, caused the new nurse to be regarded as a light-minded sinner by the Chaplain, who roamed vaguely about, informing the men that they were all worms, corrupt at heart, with perishable bodies, and souls only to be saved by a diligent perusal of certain tracts, and other equally cheering bits of spiritual consolation, when spiritous ditto would have been preferred.

"I say, Mrs.!" called a voice behind me; and, turning, I saw a rough Michigander, with an arm blown off at the shoulder, and two or three bullets still in him—as he afterwards mentioned, as carelessly as if gentlemen were in the habit of carrying such trifles about with him. I went to him, and, while administering a dose of soap and water, he whispered, irefully:

"That red-headed devil, over yonder, is a reb, damn him! You'll agree to that, I'll bet? He's got shet of a foot, or he'd a cut like the rest of the lot. Don't you wash him, nor feed him, but just let him holler till he's tired. It's a blasted shame to fetch them fellers in here, along side of us; and so I'll tell the chap that bosses this concern; cuss me if I don't."

I regret to say that I did not deliver a moral sermon upon the duty of forgiving our enemies, and the sin of profanity, then and there; but, being a red-hot Abolitionist, stared fixedly at the tall rebel, who was a copperhead, in every sense of the word, and privately resolved to put soap in his eyes, rub his nose the wrong way, and excoriate his cuticle generally, if I had the washing of him.

My amiable intentions, however, were frustrated; for, when I approached, with as Christian expression as my principles would allow, and asked the question—"Shall I try to make you more comfortable, sir?" all I got for my pains was a gruff—

"No; I'll do it myself."

"Here's your Southern chivalry, with a witness," thought I, dumping the basin down before him, thereby quenching a strong desire to give him a summary baptism, in return for his ungraciousness; for my angry passions rose, at this rebuff, in a way that would have scandalized good Dr. Watts. He was a disappointment in all respects, (the rebel, not the blessed Doctor,) for he was neither fiendish, romantic, pathetic, or anything interesting; but a long, fat man, with a head like a burning bush, and a perfectly expressionless face: so I could hate him without the slightest drawback, and ignored his existence from that day forth. One redeeming trait he certainly did possess, as the floor speedily testified; for his ablutions were so vigorously performed, that his bed soon stood like an isolated island, in a sea of soap-suds, and he resembled a dripping merman, suffering from the loss of a fin. If cleanliness is a near neighbor to godliness, then was the big rebel the godliest man in my ward that day.

Having done up our human wash, and laid it out to dry, the second syllable of our version of the word war-fare was enacted with much success. Great trays of bread, meat, soup and coffee appeared; and both nurses and attendants turned waiters, serving bountiful rations to all who could eat. I can call my pinafore to testify to my good will in the work, for in ten minutes it was reduced to a perambulating bill of fare, presenting samples of all the refreshments going or gone. It was a lively scene; the long room lined with rows of beds, each filled by an occupant, whom water, shears, and clean raiment, had transformed from a dismal ragamuffin into a recumbent hero, with a cropped head. To and fro rushed matrons, maids, and convalescent "boys," skirmishing with knives and forks; retreating with empty plates; marching and counter-marching, with unvaried success, while the clash of busy spoons made most inspiring music for the charge of our Light Brigade:

> "Beds to the front of them,
> Beds to the right of them,
> Beds to the left of them,
>   Nobody blundered.
> Beamed at by hungry souls,
> Screamed at with brimming bowls,
> Steamed at by army rolls,

> Buttered and sundered.
> With coffee not cannon plied,
> Each must be satisfied,
> Whether they lived or died;
> All the men wondered."

Very welcome seemed the generous meal, after a week of suffering, expo- sure, and short commons; soon the brown faces began to smile, as food, warmth, and rest, did their pleasant work; and the grateful "Thankee's" were followed by more graphic accounts of the battle and retreat, than any paid reporter could have given us. Curious contrasts of the tragic and comic met one everywhere; and some touching as well as ludicrous episodes, might have been recorded that day. A six foot New Hampshire man, with a leg broken and per- forated by a piece of shell, so large that, had I not seen the wound, I should have regarded the story as a Munchausenism,[9] beckoned me to come and help him, as he could not sit up, and both his bed and beard were getting plentifully anointed with soup. As I fed my big nestling with corresponding mouthfuls, I asked him how he felt during the battle.

"Well, 'twas my fust, you see, so I ain't ashamed to say I was a trifle flustered in the beginnin', there was such an all-fired racket; for ef there's anything I do spleen agin, it's noise. But when my mate, Eph Sylvester, caved, with a bullet through his head, I got mad, and pitched in, licketty cut. Our part of the fight didn't last long; so a lot of us larked round Fredericksburg, and give some of them houses a pretty consid'able of a rummage, till we was ordered out of the mess. Some of our fellows cut like time; but I warn't a-goin to run for nobody; and, fust thing I knew, a shell bust, right in front of us, and I keeled over, feel- ing' as if I was blowed higher'n a kite. I sung out, and the boys come back for me, double quick; but the way they chucked me over them fences was a caution, I tell you. Next day I was most as black as that darkey yonder, lickin' plates on the sly. This is bully coffee, ain't it? Give us another pull at it, and I'll be obleeged to you."

I did; and, as the last gulp subsided, he said, with a rub of his old handkerchief over eyes as well as mouth:

"Look a here; I've got a pair of earbobs and a handkercher pin I'm goin' to give you, if you'll have them; for you're the very moral o'Lizy Sylvester, poor Eph's wife: that's why I signalled you to come over here. They ain't much, I guess, but they'll do to memorize the rebs by."

Burrowing under his pillow, he produced a little bundle of what he called "truck," and gallantly presented me with a pair of earrings, each representing a cluster of corpulent grapes, and the pin a basket of astonishing fruit, the whole large and coppery enough for a small warming-pan. Feeling delicate about depriving him of such valuable relics, I accepted the earrings alone, and was obliged to depart, somewhat abruptly, when my friend stuck the warming-pan in the bosom of his night-gown, viewing it with much complacency, and perhaps, some tender memory, in that rough heart of his, for the comrade he had lost.

Observing that the man next him had left his meal untouched, I offered the same service I had performed for his neighbor, but he shook his head.

"Thank you, ma'am; I don't think I'll ever eat again, for I'm shot in the stomach. But I'd like a drink of water, if you aint too busy."

I rushed away, but the water-pails were gone to be refilled, and it was some time before they reappeared. I did not forget my patient patient, meanwhile, and, with the first mugful, hurried back to him. He seemed asleep; but something in the tired white face caused me to listen at his lips for a breath. None came. I touched his forehead; it was cold: and then I knew that, while he waited, a better nurse than I had given him a cooler draught, and healed him with a touch. I laid the sheet over the quiet sleeper, whom no noise could now disturb; and, half an hour later, the bed was empty. It seemed a poor requital for all he had sacrificed and suffered,—that hospital bed, lonely even in a crowd; for there was no famliar face for him to look his last upon; no friendly voice to say, Good bye; no hand to lead him gently down into the Valley of the Shadows; and he vanished, like a drop in that red sea upon whose shores so many women stand lamenting. For a moment I felt bitterly indignant at this seeming carelessness of the value of life, the sanctity of death; then consoled myself with the thought that, when the great muster roll was called, these nameless men might be promoted above many whose tall monuments record the barren honors they have won.

All having eaten, drank, and rested, the surgeons began their rounds; and I took my first lesson in the art of dressing wounds. It wasn't a festive scene, by any means; for Dr. P., whose Aid I constituted myself, fell to work with a vigor which soon convinced me that I was a weaker vessel, though nothing would have induced me to confess it then. He had served in the Crimea, and seemed to regard a dilapidated body very much as I should have regarded a damaged garment; and, turning up his cuffs, whipped out a very unpleasant looking housewife, cutting, sawing, patching and piecing, with the enthusiasm of an accomplished surgical seamstress; explaining the process, in scientific terms, to the patient, meantime; which, of course, was immensely cheering and comfortable. There was an uncanny sort of fascination in watching him, as he peered and probed into the mechanism of those wonderful bodies, whose mysteries he understood so well. The more intricate the wound, the better he liked it. A poor private, with both legs off, and shot through the lungs, possessed more attractions for him than a dozen generals, slightly scratched in some "masterly retreat"; and had any one appeared in small pieces, requesting to be put together again, he would have considered it a special dispensation.

The amputations were reserved till the morrow, and the merciful magic of ether was not thought necessary that day, so the poor souls had to bear their pains as best they might. It is all very well to talk of the patience of woman; and far be it from me to pluck that feather from her cap, for, heaven knows, she isn't allowed to wear many; but the patient endurance of these men, under trials of the flesh, was truly wonderful; their fortitude seemed contagious, and scarcely a cry escaped them, though I often longed to groan for them, when pride kept their white lips shut, while great drops stood upon their foreheads, and the bed shook with irrepressible tremor of their tortured bodies. One or two Irishmen anathematized the doctors with the frankness of their nation, and ordered the Virgin to stand by them, as if she had been the wedded Biddy to whom they could administer the poker, if she didn't; but, as a general thing, the work went on in silence, broken only by some quiet request for roller, instruments, or plaster, a sigh from the patient, or a sympathizing murmur from the nurse.

It was long past noon before these repairs were even partially made; and, having got the bodies of my boys into something like order, the next task was to minister to their minds, by writing letters to the anxious souls at home; answering questions, reading papers, taking possession of money and valuables; for the eighth commandment was reduced to a very fragmentary condition, both by the blacks and whites, who ornamented our hospital with their presence. Pocket books, purses, miniatures, and watches, were sealed up, labelled, and handed over to the matrons, till such times as the owners thereof were ready to depart homeward or campward again. The letters dictated to me, and revised by me, that afternoon, would have made an excellent chapter for some future history of the war; for, like that which Thackeray's "Ensign Spooney" wrote his mother just before Waterloo, they were "full of affection, pluck, and bad spelling"; nearly all giving lively accounts of the battle, and ending with a somewhat sudden plunge from patriotism to provender, desiring "Marm," "Mary Ann," or "Aunt Peters," to send along some pies, pickles, sweet stuff, and apples, "to yourn in haste," Joe, Sam, or Ned, as the case might be.

My little Sergeant insisted on trying to scribble something with his left hand, and patiently accomplished some half dozen lines of hieroglyphics, which he gave me to fold and direct, with a boyish blush, that rendered a glimpse of "My Dearest Jane," unnecessary, to assure me that the heroic lad had been more successful in the service of Commander-in-Chief Cupid than that of Gen. Mars; and a charming little romance blossomed instanter in Nurse Periwinkle's romantic fancy, though no further confidences were made that day, for Sergeant fell asleep, and, judging from his tranquil face, visited his absent sweetheart in the pleasant land of dreams.

At five o'clock a great bell rang, and the attendants flew, not to arms but to their trays, to bring up supper, when a second uproar announced that it was ready. The new comers woke at the sound; and I presently discovered that it took a very bad wound to incapacitate the defenders of the faith for the consumption of their rations; the amount that some of them sequestered was amazing; but when I suggested the probability of a famine hereafter, to the matron, that motherly lady cried out: "Bless their hearts, why shouldn't they eat? It's their only amusement; so fill every one, and, if there's not enough ready tonight, I'll lend my share to the Lord by giving it to the boys." And, whipping up her coffee-pot and plate of toast, she gladdened the eyes and stomachs of two or three dissatisfied heroes, by serving them with a liberal hand; and I haven't the slightest doubt that, having cast her bread upon the waters, it came back buttered, as another large-hearted old lady was wont to say.

Then came the doctor's evening visit; the administration of medicines; washing feverish faces; smoothing tumbled beds; wetting wounds, singing lullabies; and preparations for the night. By eleven, the last labor of love was done; the last "good night" spoken; and, if any needed a reward for that day's work, they surely received it, in the silent eloquence of those long lines of faces, showing pale and peaceful glances that lighted us to bed, where rest, the sweetest, made our pillows soft, while Night and Nature took our places, filling that great house of pain with the healing miracles of Sleep, and his diviner brother, Death.

#### CHAPTER IV: A NIGHT

... The night whose events I have a fancy to record, opened with a little comedy, and closed with a great tragedy; for a virtuous and useful life untimely ended is always tragical to those who see not as God sees. My headquarters were beside the bed of a New Jersey boy, crazed by the horrors of that dreadful Saturday. A slight wound in the knee brought him there; but his mind had suffered more than his body; some string of that delicate machine was over strained, and, for days, he had been reliving, in imagination, the scenes he could not forget, till his distress broke out in incoherent ravings, pitiful to hear. As I sat by him, endeavoring to soothe his poor distracted brain by the constant touch of wet hands over his hot forehead, he lay cheering his comrades on, hurrying them back, then counting them as they fell around him, often clutching my arm, to drag me from the vicinity of a bursting shell, or covering up his head to screen himself from a shower of shot; his face brilliant with fever; his eyes restless; his head never still; every muscle strained and rigid; while an incessant stream of defiant shouts, whispered warnings, and broken laments, poured from his lips with that forceful bewilderment which makes such wanderings so hard to overhear.

It was past eleven, and my patient was slowly wearying himself into fitful intervals of quietude, when, in one of these pauses, a curious sound arrested my attention. Looking over my shoulder, I saw a one-legged phantom hopping nimbly down the room; and, going to meet it, recognized a certain Pennsylvania gentleman, whose wound-fever had taken a turn for the worse, and, depriving him of the few wits a drunken campaign had left him, set him literally tripping on the light, fantastic toe "toward home," as he blandly informed me, touching the military cap which formed a striking contrast to the severe simplicity of the rest of his decidedly *undress* uniform. When sane, the least movement produced a road of pain or a volley of oaths; but the departure of reason seemed to have wrought an agreeable change, both in the man and his manners; for, balancing himself on one leg, like a meditative stork, he plunged into an animated discussion of the war, the President, lager beer, and Enfield rifles, regardless of any suggestions of mine as to the propriety of returning to bed, lest he be court-martialed for desertion.

Anything more supremely ridiculous can hardly be imagined than this figure, scantily draped in white, its one foot covered with a big blue sock, a dingy cap set rakingly askew on its shaven head, and placid satisfaction beaming in its broad red face, as it flourished a mug in one hand, an old boot in the other, calling them canteen and knapsack, while it skipped and fluttered in the most unearthly fashion. What to do with the creature I didn't know; Dan was absent, and if I went to find him, the perambulator might festoon himself out of the window, set his toga on fire, or do some of his neighbors a mischief. The attendant of the room was sleeping like a near relative of the celebrated Seven and nothing short of pins would rouse him; for he had been out that day, and whiskey asserted its supremacy in balmy whiffs. Still declaiming, in a fine flow of eloquence, the demented gentleman hopped on, blind and deaf to my graspings and entreaties; and I was about to slam the door in his face, and run for help, when a saner and second phantom, "all in white," came to the rescue, in the likeness of a big Prussian, who spoke no English, but divined the crisis, and put an end to it, by bundling the lively monoped into his bed, like a baby, with an authoritative command to "stay put," which received added weight from being delivered in an odd conglomeration of French and German, accompanied by warning wags of a head decorated with a yellow cotton night cap, rendered most imposing by a tassel like a bell-pull. Rather exhausted by his excursion, the member from Pennsylvania subsided; and, after an irrepressible laugh together, my Prussian ally and myself were returning to our places. . . .

"This is my first battle; do they think it's going to be my last?"

"I'm afraid they do, John."

It was the hardest question I had ever been called upon to answer, doubly hard with those clear eyes fixed on mine, forcing a truthful answer by their own truth. He seemed a little startled at first, pondered over the fateful fact a moment then shook his head, with a glance at the broad chest and muscular limbs stretched out before him:

"I'm not afraid, but it's difficult to believe all at once. I'm so strong it don't seem possible for such a little wound to kill me."

Merry Mercutio's dying words glanced through my memory as he spoke: "'Tis not so deep as a well, nor so wide as a church door, but 'tis enough."[10] And John would have said the same could he have seen the ominous black holes between his shoulders, he never had; and, seeing the ghastly sights about him, could not believe his own wound more fatal than these, for all the suffering it caused him.

"Shall I write to your mother, now?" I asked, thinking that these sudden tidings might change all plans and purposes; but they did not; for the man received the order of the Divine Commander to march with the same unquestioning obedience with which the soldier had received that of the human one, doubtless remembering that the first led him to life, and the last to death.

"No, ma'am; to Laurie just the same; he'll break it to her best, and I'll add a line to her myself when you get done."

So I wrote the letter which he dictated, finding it better than any I had sent; for, though here and there a little ungrammatical or inelegant, each sentence came to me briefly worded, but most expressive; full of excellent counsel to the boy, tenderly bequeathing "mother and Lizzie" to his care, and bidding him good bye in words the sadder for their simplicity. He added a few lines, with steady hand, and, as I sealed it, said, with a patient sort of sigh, "I hope the answer will come in time for me to see it"; then, turning away his face, laid the flowers against his lips, as if to hide some quiver of emotion at the thought of such a sudden sundering of all dear home ties.

These things had happened two days before; now John was dying, and the letter had not come. I had been summoned to many death beds in my life, but to none that made my heart ache as it did then, since my mother called me to watch the departure of a spirit akin to this in its gentleness and patient strength. As I went in, John stretched out both hands:

"I knew you'd come! I guess I'm moving on, ma'am."

He was; and so rapidly that, even while he spoke, over his face I saw the grey veil falling that no human hand can lift. I sat down by him, wiped the drops from his forehead, stirred the air about him with the slow wave of a fan, and waited to help him die. He stood in sore need of help—and I could do so little; for, as the doctor had foretold, the strong body rebelled against death, and fought every inch of the way, forcing him to draw each breath with a spasm, and clench his hands with an imploring look, as if he asked, "How long must I endure this, and be still!" For hours he suffered dumbly, without a moment's respite, or a moment's murmuring; his limbs grew cold, his face damp, his lips

white, and, again and again, he tore the covering off his breast, as if the lightest
weight added to his agony; yet through it all, his eyes never lost their perfect
serenity, and the man's soul seemed to sit therein, undaunted by the ills that
vexed his flesh.

One by one, the men woke, and round the room appeared a circle of pale
faces and watchful eyes, full of awe and pity; for, though a stranger, John was
beloved by all. Each man there had wondered at his patience, respected his
piety, admired his fortitude, and now lamented his hard death; for the influence
of an upright nature had made itself deeply felt, even in one little week. Presently, the Jonathan who so loved this comely David, came creeping from his
bed for a last look and word. The kind soul was full of trouble, as the choke in
his voice, the grasp of his hand, betrayed; but there were no tears, and the farewell of the friends was the more touching for its brevity.

"Old boy, how are you?" faltered the one.

"Most through, thank heaven!" whispered the other.

"Can I say or do anything for you anywheres?"

"Take my things home, and tell them that I did my best."

"I will! I will!"

"Good bye, Ned."

"Good bye, John, good bye!"

They kissed each other, tenderly as women, and so parted, for poor Ned
could not stay to see his comrade die. For a little while, there was no sound in
the room but the drip of water, from a stump or two, and John's distressful
gasps, as he slowly breathed his life away. I thought him nearly gone, and had
just laid down the fan, believing its help to be no longer needed, when suddenly
he rose up in his bed, and cried out with a bitter cry that broke the silence,
sharply startling every one with its agonized appeal:

"For God's sake, give me air!"

It was the only cry pain or death had wrung from him, the only boon he had
asked; and none of us could grant it, for all the airs that blew were useless now.
Dan flung up the window. The first red streak of dawn was warming the grey
east, a herald of the coming sun; John saw it, and with the love of light which
lingers in us to the end, seemed to read in it a sign of hope of help, for, over his
whole face there broke that mysterious expression, brighter than any smile,
which often comes to eyes that look their last. He laid himself gently down;
and, stretching out his strong right arm, as if to grasp and bring the blessed air
to his lips in a fuller flow, lapsed into a merciful unconsciousness, which
assured us that for him suffering was forever past. He died then; for, though
the heavy breaths still tore their way up for a little longer, they were but the
waves of an ebbing tide that beat unfelt against the wreck, which an immortal
voyager had deserted with a smile. He never spoke again, but to the end held

my hand close, so close that when he was asleep at last, I could not draw it away. Dan helped me, warning me as he did so that it was unsafe for dead and living flesh to lie so long together; but though my hand was strangely cold and stiff, and four white marks remained across its back, even when warmth and color had returned elsewhere, I could not but be glad that, through its touch, the presence of human sympathy, perhaps, had lightened that hard hour.

When they had made him ready for the grave, John lay in state for half an hour, a thing which seldom happened in that busy place; but a universal sentiment of reverence and affection seemed to fill the hearts of all who had known or heard of him; and when the rumor of his death went through the house, always astir, many came to see him, and I felt a tender sort of pride in my lost patient; for he looked a most heroic figure, lying there stately and still as the statue of some young knight asleep upon his tomb. The lovely expression which so often beautifies dead faces, soon replaced the marks of pain, and I longed for those who loved him best to see him when half an hour's acquaintance with Death had made them friends. As we stood looking at him, the ward master handed me a letter, saying it had been forgotten the night before. It was John's letter, come just an hour too late to gladden the eyes that had longed and looked for it so eagerly: yet he had it; for, after I had cut some brown locks for his mother, and taken off the ring to send her, telling how well the talisman had done its work, I kissed this good son for her sake, and laid the letter in his hand, still folded as when I drew my own away, feeling that its place was there, and making myself happy with the thought, that, even in his solitary place in the "Government Lot," he would not be without some token of love which makes life beautiful and outlives death. Then I left him, glad to have known so genuine a man, and carrying with me an enduring memory of the brave Virginia blacksmith, as he lay serenely waiting for the dawn of that long day which knows no night.

Lydia Maria Child, circa 1865 *(Courtesy of the Boston Public Library)*

# Lydia Maria Child
## (1802–1880)

"I never can write unless my mind is *free*," lamented Lydia Maria Child in 1863.[1] At no time was her mind as pinioned as during the Civil War. For four decades Child had published novels, advice books, anthologies, letters, children's stories, and reform tracts. With works such as *Hobomok* (1824), *The Frugal Housewife* (1829), and *Letters from New York* (1843–45), she became a widely known and best-selling author. But from early on her romantic and literary sensibilities clashed with her moral and political concerns. She refused to look away from those less fortunate than herself. Like so many New England intellectuals of the period, she came to identify with the ordeal of black men and women in America and committed herself to the struggle against slavery.

There is no doubt that *An Appeal in Favor of That Class of Americans Called Africans* (1833) damaged her standing within the literary circles of the time. The Boston Athenaeum in effect banned her; outraged readers stopped buying her books. Child's response was to thrust herself even more deeply into the abolitionist crusade. She continued to write Romances such as *Philothea* (1836), and stories and essays for literary magazines such as the *Columbian Lady's and Gentleman's Magazine*, and she wrote antislavery tracts as well. For a time in the 1840s, she edited the *National Anti-Slavery Standard*. And on the eve of the Civil War, her exchange of letters on the subject of John Brown with the wife of Virginia's Senator James Mason, the author of the Fugitive Slave Act, appeared in a pamphlet. It is likely that as many as 300,000 copies were printed.

Obsessed with the fate of the slave during the Civil War, Child could not write novels because as long as others were not free to create their own lives, she did not feel free to create fictional ones. Her sense of enslavement did not, however, silence her. Even more than usual, correspondence became an outlet for her creative energies. Her letters are filled with telling stories and mythic analogies, as well as personal, political meditations.

She involved herself in the literary aspects of the Civil War in other ways as well. A volume called *Incidents in the Life of a Slave Girl* appeared in 1861, with Child listed as editor on the title page. The author, Harriet Jacobs, was a former fugitive slave living in New York. The volume is now recognized as a rare and important slave narrative by a black woman. Child advised Jacobs what to omit (a chapter on John Brown) and what to recall (Nat Turner's rebellion). She helped market the book, and she wrote an introduction that offered the work "for the sake of my sisters in bondage, who are suffering wrongs so foul, that our ears are too delicate to listen to them."[2]

Toward the close of the War, Child wanted to do more for emancipated slaves than simply root for them. She told the abolitionist Gerrit Smith that "the Freed men and women are fast learning to read, and are much taken up with the new acquisition. There seem to be very few books *suitable* to their condition."[3] So Child compiled one. Published in 1865, *The Freedmen's Book* contained biographical sketches of prominent black figures in history, selections from political speeches by Republicans, stories, hymns, prayers, poems and practical advice. The contributors included Harriet Beecher Stowe, Charlotte Forten, Harriet Jacobs, John Greenleaf Whittier, Frederick Douglass, and William Lloyd Garrison.

Child wrote more than one-third of the selections. She offered biographical portraits of Ignatius Sancho, Benjamin Banneker, Toussaint L'ouverture, Phillis Wheatley, James Forten, Frederick Douglass, and others. She hoped that the book would be read aloud and that black men and women "would derive fresh strength and courage from this true record of what colored men have accomplished, under great disadvantage."[4]

It was meant to be a book that inspired, a book that provided blacks with what we today would call role models. Only a handful of writers at the time appreciated the myriad problems of emancipation, and Child sought through literary means to work through those problems and give the freedmen hope. But it is impossible not to squirm as we read her "Advice from an Old Friend." The Christian, middle-class pieties that characterized the community of reformers permeate the piece. Slavery is merely a "disadvantage" to be overcome; sobriety, industry, cleanliness, and honesty are the keys to rising in the world on one's own accord;

Republicans and abolitionists would always provide protection. This was a potent formula. In later years, Booker T. Washington would achieve great prominence by upholding similar values. Reading the essay, we wish Child better understood racism, better understood the economic and social roots of inequality, better understood that a cry from the heart was as necessary to the black cause as advice from the head. Still, Child was no hypocrite, and *The Freedmen's Book* contributed to the slow and continuing process of unearthing and creating African-American history.

The end of the war gave Child back her freedom and her writing. She published *A Romance of the Republic* (1867), a novel about race and racism, but it was not well received, and she allowed the criticism to shackle her fiction. She continued her activities on behalf of blacks, and Indians as well, and she thought much about matters beyond the grave. Twenty years before her death, she told Wendell Phillips that she wanted to be buried in ground "belonging to the *colored people*," and that on her stone should be inscribed: "Buried in this place, at her own request, among her brethren and sisters of dark complexion, as the last testimony it is in her power to bear against the wicked, cruel, and absurd prejudice, which so grievously oppresses them in a country that boasts loudly of its free institutions." While her body lies near those of two former slaves, her words have yet to be carved into stone.[5]

## 1. LMC to John Greenleaf Whittier,[6] Medford, April 4, 1861[7]

... With regard to the present crisis of affairs, I think the *wisest* can hardly foresee what turn events will take; but *whatever* way they may develop, I have faith that the present agitation will shorten the existence of slavery; and we ought to be willing to suffer *anything* to bring about *that* result. The ancient proverb declares that "whom the gods would destroy, they first make mad"; and surely the South are mad enough to secure destruction. My *own* soul utters but *one* prayer; and that is, that we may be effectually separated from *all* the Slave-States. My reasons are, first, that we can in no *other* way present to the world a fair experiment of a free Republic; second, that if the Border-States remain with us, we shall be just as much bound to deliver up fugitives as we now are; third, those Border-States will form a line of armed sentinels between us and the New Confederacy of "Slave-own-ia," (as *Punch* wittily calls it) preventing the escape of slaves from the far South, just as they now do; lastly, we shall continue to be demoralized, politically and socially, by a *few* slave-states, as much as we should by all of them; they will always be demanding concessions of principle, and our politicians will always be finding reasons for compromise. There is no *health* for us, unless we can get *rid* of the accursed thing. My prayer is, "Deliver us, O Lord, from this body of Death!"

This does not arise from any sectional or partisan feeling; but simply because my reason, my heart, and my conscience, *all* pronounce this Union to be *wicked*. The original compact is *wrong;* and the attempt to obey the laws of *man,* when they are in open conflict with the laws of *God,* must *inevitably* demoralize a nation, and ultimately undermine all true prosperity, even in a material point of view. . . .

## 2. LMC to Lucy Osgood,[8] Wayland, April 26, 1861

. . . The excitement reaches us here only in very faint echoes. Now and then, a cart-horse goes by with a small U.S. flag at his ears. I am surprised at the unanimity of all parties in supporting the government; and I thank God that I live to see the day when it is risky to talk in praise of the South. Nevertheless, I do not think there is much of either right principle, or good feeling, at the foundation of this unanimous Union sentiment. Our merchants are alarmed about dangers to commerce; our national vanity is piqued by insults to the U.S. flag, likely to render it contemptible in the eyes of the world; great numbers of the people think there is an imperious necessity of defending the government *now,* lest there should soon *be* no government to protect us from utter anarchy; and still greater numbers are ready to rush into whatever is the fashion. Two-thirds would be as ready as ever to throw *away* sop to Cerberus,[9] if he would only be content to spare the passengers in *our* boat, and eat everybody else. But thank God, Cerberus is ferocious to eat up *every*thing. May he continue so, till the work of complete separation is accomplished!

Rumor says that 30 Florida slaves, who escaped to Fort Pickens and offered their services in defence of the U.S., were sent back to their masters, in chains; and that our Mass'ts General Butler proposes to employ the soldiers under his command in putting down a projected insurrection of slaves in Maryland.[10] God knows I want to love and honor the flag of my country; but how *can* I, when it is used for *such* purposes? When men strive to enslave others, the spirit of justice within me cries out, "May God do unto them, and more also!" . . .

## 3. LMC to Lucy Searle,[11] Wayland, June 5, 1861

. . . I am glad to see some amendment with regard to sending back fugitive slaves. Those at Fort Monroe are to be protected so long as Virginia continues in rebellion. God grant that all the slave-holders may rebel, and remain in rebellion, till the emancipation of their slaves is accomplished! Success to Jeff. Davis, till he goads the free states into doing, from policy and revenge, what they have not manhood to do from justice and humanity! It is a dreadful thing, a most demoralizing thing, to have the laws of one's country at such variance with the laws of God. I never realized it so fully as when I heard your good, conscientious, intelligent friend say that he would send back a fugitive slave because the Constitution required it. When our fathers joined hands with slave-holders to form the Constitution, with their feet on the prostrate and helpless slaves, they did sad work for their descendants. If my father had made a compact with a rich neighbor that I would help him rob a poor one, I should break the compact. Law is not law, if it violates principles of eternal justice. If drunken foreigners are hired to vote for a member of Congress, and the vote of that member causes the enactment of the Fugitive Slave Law, probably because he wishes to obtain some still higher office, am I bound to sell my soul to perdition because the iniquity has been found into law? The dictionary does not contain words enough to express my detestation of all laws framed for the support of tyranny. To keep that unrighteous compact with fellow-citizens was bad enough, but to keep it with rebels, who have over and over again violated all their part of the compact, is adding imbecility and absurdity to wickedness.

## 4. LMC to Lucy Searle, Wayland, June 9, 1861

... The fact is I identify myself so completely with the slaves, that I am kept in alternating states of anxiety and wrath, concerning their rendition by officers of the U.S. If I wake up in the middle of the night, it is the first thing I think of. I long to get at the poor creatures, to tell them to run away to Canada or Hayti, and not trust to the promises of the U.S. always perfidious and cruel to the colored man.

I am waiting with great anxiety to see what will be the results of this war; for if things are patched up on the old foundation, I will quit the country, and lay my bones on a foreign soil; *any* soil not cursed by a Fugitive Slave Law. Under that law I will not live.

It is a beautiful peaceful Sabbath. Cloud-shadows are flitting over the broad green meadows, in front of my window; and all is so still that one might "hear the grass grow," if the ear were fine enough. It seems difficult to realize the fierce passions that are raging a few hundred miles from us. You will think it strange and perhaps wrong, that I do not wish them to be less fierce, at present. I want the "irrepressible conflict" to intensify to a focus that will kindle a fire powerful enough to sweep over and effectually destroy the *cause* of the conflict. This does not arise from partisan feelings on my part, from any hatred to slave-holders, or any want of love for my country; but because it is my deliberate and firm conviction that in no other way can our free institutions be saved. It will be better for *all* parties to have the question completely settled *now;* and it does seem as if Divine Providence were wonderously over-ruling things for that result. . . .

### 5. LMC to Sarah Shaw,[12] Wayland, June 14, 1861

. . . The civil war is an awful thing; and we cannot possibly foresee what is to be the end of it. I suppose no sane person doubts that the North must eventually beat. But after we have conquered them, what are we to *do* with subjects whose character is so incongruous to ours, and who hate us, our institutions and our manners, with such an irreconcilable hatred? The worst of it is, a large number of them, probably a majority, if we could fairly ascertain the sentiments in many of the States, wish to remain under the U.S. government; and it becomes a duty to protect such citizens from the lawless violence of their own oligarchy. My prevailing wish is that they might *all* want to go out of the Union, and that they might *all* go out, and stay out. But God knows best, and his hand is obviously in this work. We are on the top of a giant wave, and it must drift us whithersoever He wills.

I am sorry the English press has maintained such a tone on the subject. It has a bad moral influence on people *here*. They seem to speak of the contest as if it were six of one and half dozen of the other. They say the North has no *cause* to fight for. Good Heavens! when we are fighting to have *any* government preserved to us! to be saved from utter anarchy! They tell us these States are like partners in business, and if a portion of the firm wants to dissolve the partnership, why not let them go? The comparison is not correct. We are a *consolidated* government, not mere partners, as long as suits any party. But granting that we *are* mere partners, how does the case stand? A. and B. form a partnership. A. is the most industrious partner, pays much the largest share of the expenses, and increases the business in every direction. Years pass on, and the firm grows rich. Then B. says to A. I want to quit you, and set up in business for myself. I shall take as much of the property as I please, and if you make any objection, I'll burn your house and manufactories to the ground, and rob all your ships. . . .

Ah, the poor slaves have so few friends, and so many enemies! In all this war, there seems to be no feeling for *them*. As "contraband" articles of *property*, a few may escape, friendless wanderers, to find a home where they can. But any master, who swears he is a Union-man, can have the chattels back again, to scourge at pleasure; and it is so easy for the chivalry to swear! . . .

### 6. LMC to Sarah Shaw, Wayland, August 11, 1861

. . . Amid the complicated relations in which we stand at this crisis, I do *not* think it would be politic for government to proclaim freedom to the slaves.

Events may ripen public opinion for such a measure, but it is not yet ripened. But according to my idea, no proclamation from government, and no official action of any sort, *is needed.* There are but two horns to the dilemma. If the runaway slaves who come to our camps and forts say their masters are avowed secessionists, why then the veriest pro-slavery hunker would not contend that we were under any constitutional obligation to send back their fugitive slaves. By their treason, they have obviously forfeited the protection of the Constitution. In such a case then, the slave should be told that he is free, and that he may work for the U.S. at the same wages other men receive.

If, on the other hand, the slave says his master is a Union man, the answer should be, "If your master comes to claim you, we have no legal power to protect you; but then we have no legal power to stop your going wherever you choose. You can go to Hayti, or to Cuba, or wherever you like."

The *reason* I would have them say this, is that military officers have *no* legal power to act in such cases. When a slave is claimed, a *civil process* is required to prove his identity, and to prove that the man who claims him did legally own him in the State he ran from. In forts and camps there is no proper tribunal to examine and decide in such cases, and military officers have no shadow of right to proceed without due process of law. The consequence is, that our army is not bound, in any case, to send back a fugitive; and if, wherever our soldiers went, their uniform practice showed that slaves seeking protection under the banner of the U.S. *never were* sent back, the instinct for freedom would settle the matter for itself, and the government would have no *need* to issue a proclamation. It might all be done quietly, without violating any existing legal obligation, and without exciting any disunity of parties. At least, so it seems to *me.* . . .

### 7.  LMC to John Greenleaf Whittier, Wayland, September 10, 1861

. . . Nothing on earth has such effect on the popular heart as Songs, which the soldiers would take up with enthusiasm, and which it would thereby become the fashion to whistle and sing at the street-corners. "Old John Brown, Hallelujah!" is performing a wonderful mission now. Where the words came from, nobody knows, and the tune is an exciting, spirit-stirring thing, hitherto unknown outside of Methodist Conventicles. But it warms up soldiers and boys, and the air is full of it; just as France was of the Marseillaise, whose author was for years unknown.

If the soldiers only *had* a Song, to some spirit-stirring tune, proclaiming what they went to fight for, or *thought* they went to fight for,—for home, country, and liberty; and indignantly announcing that they did *not* go to hunt slaves, to send back to their tyrants poor lacerated workmen, who for years had been toiling for the rich without wages; if they *had* such a song, to a tune that excited them, how rapidly it would educate them!

Ballads, too, told in your pictorial fascinating style, would do a great work at this crisis. If you see returned soldiers, you will have plenty of subjects suggested. Dr. Furness wrote me that a young friend of his was a volunteer in a wealthy aristocratic company, that went from Philadelphia. They returned much worked up about slavery. The young man told Dr. F. that he one day met a rude, rough man, a corporal, crying right out, blubbering like a schoolboy. When asked what was the matter, he replied, "They've just sent a poor fellow back into slavery. I didn't leave my home to do such work as *this;* and I won't do it. I come here to fight for the country and the flag; not to hunt slaves; and if the Col. orders any more such work, I'm afraid I shall shoot him."

Another who was ordered on picket-duty, of course at *unusual* risk of his life, was told that while he was sentinel, if any *slave* attempted to pass the lines he must turn him back. He replied, "*That* is an order I will not obey." Being reminded of his duty to obey orders, he replied "I know the penalty I incur, and am ready to submit to it. But I did not enlist to do *such* work, and I *will* not do it." The officers being aware that his feeling would easily become contagious, *modified* the order thus: "If anybody tried to pass, ascertain that *all's right* before you allow them to pass." That night, the moon shone brightly, and the sentinel on duty saw a moving in the bushes before him. "Who goes there? Answer quickly!" Up rose a small ebony man. "Who are you?" "A Fugitive." "Are you *all right?*" "Yes, massa." "Then run quick."

Another time, a lordly Virginian rode up to the U.S. lines, with a pass to the other side. He curled his lip contemptuously, when a U.S. sentinel barred the course of his stylish chariot. "Where's your pass?" The Virginian, scorning to acknowledge authority from a "greasy mechanic" of the North, did not deign to make any reply, but motioned to the slave, who was driving his barouche, to deliver the paper to the soldier. The slave dismounted and gave the sentinel the required pass. The sentinel seized him, and by a quick motion set him twirling down the hill, at the bottom of which were marshalled the U.S. forces. "Now *you* can turn back," said the sentinel. "But I obtained an order allowing me to pass. How dare you hinder me?" "Where *is* your order?" "My servant just gave it to you." "Oh, that was an order to pass only *one*, and he has already gone with it."

The Virginian swore roundly, and called vociferously to his slave to come back. The bewildered slave attempted to do so, but the mischievous sentinel put his musket across the path. "Show the paper!" shouted the master. The slave did so. The sentinel read it, and coolly replied, "This is a pass *from* Norfolk. You must obtain another pass to go *to* Norfolk." And so the haughty Southerner was obliged to guide his own horses back again, whence he came.

Friend Whittier, it is impossible to exaggerate the good effect of such things as these, if put into the form of popular ballads. . . .

### 8. LMC to Lucy Searle, Wayland, October 11, 1861

. . . I did not mean to talk so much about public affairs; but this imbecile, pro-slavery government does try me so, that it seems as if I *must* shoot somebody. Willis is out again with a florid description of Mrs. Lincoln's autumn bonnet, called "The Princess." "Rose-colored velvet, with guipine medallions, trimmed with black thread lace, put on full, and this again trimmed on the edge with a deeper fringe of minute black marabout and ostrich feathers. &c &c. . . ."[13]

So *this* is what the people are taxed for! to deck out this vulgar doll with foreign frippery! And oppressed millions must groan on, lest her "noble native State" should take offence, if Government made use of the beneficient power God has so miraculously placed in its hands. To *see* these things, and have no power to *change* them, to see the glorious opportunity so *near*, yet slipping away, leaving the nation to sink deeper and deeper into the abyss of degradation—this is really the torment of Tantalus. . . . [14]

### 9. LMC to George W. Julian,[15] Wayland, January 30, 1862

. . . I suppose our fathers did really believe that slavery would be short-lived in this country; yet when my reverence for them leads me to make this excuse, I never can forget the ugly fact that they legislated for the continuance of the African Slave Trade twenty years. The fact is, they were determined to have a *Union*, on *any* terms; and the South then, as now, were imperious and unprincipled in their demands. The wise and good men of that time adopted a great fallacy, when they supposed that *any* compromise of moral principles *could* be transitory in its effects. Our politicians, with few exceptions, have gone on ever since in the same path; and whether our crooked ways will ever be made straight, God alone knows. Only seven generations have passed away since the noble band of Puritans in the May-Flower made their memorable Covenant with God: "As the Lord's free people, we will walk in all his ways made known, or to be known to us, according to our best endeavors, *whatever it may cost us.*" Only seven generations! and now how difficult it is to find a man who really *believes* in principles; in other words, who *really* believes in God! If there had been anything like a general state of moral healthfulness in the Free States, they would have long ago insisted upon calling a Convention of the people to modify the Constitution. But Alas! the same year that witnessed the landing of those sturdy freemen of the Lord in the May Flower, witnessed the landing of negro slaves to wait upon the "vagabond gentlemen," who settled Virginia. It was a mysterious Providence, that brought these two antagonistic elements in juxta position in this grand new field of human progress. If we could only get *rid* of the virus infused throughout the blood of our body politic! But it is not an excrescence to be cut off; it has infected the whole system with disease. If all the Slave States had seceded, the prospects for freedom would be hopeful; but I fear the *Union* slaveholders are dragging us all down to ruin. . . .

### 10. LMC to William P. Cutler,[16] Wayland, July 10, 1862

. . . I see much in the present Congress to inspire me with hope that there is vitality enough left among us to save our free institutions. I have a genuine, practical *belief* in *Freedom;* and it grieves me to see what a mere abstraction, what a "glittering generality," it is in many minds. I also believe in *labor,* and prove my faith by my works. Few women, who pass for "respectable," have done so large a share of manual labor; and I shall continue to do it while my strength lasts; because I reverence usefulness far more than I do gentility. Nothing Senator Wilson has said has inspired me with so much respect for him, as his Speech, "Are Working Men Slaves?"[17] Think of those lordly aristocrats of the South declaring that the position of Northern workingmen was no higher than that of their slaves, when they had before them in Congress those two specimens of Northern working men, Wilson and Banks![18] A South Carolinian told me, in a sneering tone, some years ago, "I pity you Northern women. You are mere beasts of burden." I replied, "For my own part, I had rather be a beast of *burden,* than a beast of prey." . . .

What can we do with the slaves? is a foolish question. "Take them away from Mr. Lash and place them with Mr. Cash" settles that imaginary difficulty. But what can we do with their *masters* is a much more difficult problem to solve. Of course, the substitution of free institutions for slave labor would change the moral and intellectual condition of the whole Southern people, in a few generations. But in their transition state, what a troublesome and dangerous set they will be to deal with! They talk about *slaves* being unfit to be trusted with legislation; doubtless it is true; but it seems to me that *slaveholders,* by the inevitable necessity of their position, are rendered even *more* unfit to legislate for free men. . . .

For myself, I have no prejudice against color. I do not claim it as any merit, or apologize for it as any defect. I was simply born without it. I naturally and habitually forget it, just as I unconsciously ignore all conventional distinctions of rank. I have a few colored acquaintance, who rank very high in my estimation for intelligence, culture, and fine manners. What they *are* I believe that multitudes of them *might be,* under favorable influences. I know one dark brown girl, whose handsome face absolutely *flashes* light when the inferiority of her race is alluded to. I have sometimes watched her, when her nostrils expanded proudly, and her well-shaped mouth expressed a beautiful disdain of such insults, and she seemed to me queenly enough for a model of Cleopatra. And such vulgar, shallow fools as some of them are, who consider it a degradation to be seated by her side! Really, the contrast is sometimes ludicrously to their disadvantage; but they, encased in a seven-fold armor of prejudice and self-conceit, are all unconscious of their inferiority. The superiority of this girl is to be ascribed to the fact that she was never a slave, that her parents were never slaves, and that her grandfather amassed sufficient property to enable his descendants to overcome the formidable obstacles in the way of their intellectual culture. Looking at that girl, and reading the intelligent productions of her pen, I recognize the possibilities of improvement now damned up in the souls of her oppressed people, and our long-continued guilt, as a nation of oppressors and accomplices, seems to me so immeasurable, that I hardly dare to hope that God will save our national existence. The worst part of it is the perpetual *lie* we have been enacting before God and the world. Mohammedans say there are seven hells, each deeper than the other, and that the *lowest* is for *hypocrites.* Other nations have been bad enough. It ill becomes England to profess to be shocked by "American barbarities," considering how many heads of English rebels have been stuck upon poles for birds to peck at, the skulls remaining a ghostly spectacle to the passers by; proclaiming, Thus England deals with rebels! If they say *that* was in olden time, what excuse have they for *Hindoo* rebels shot from the mouths of cannon, a mangled mass? It is a very observable fact that it is only the necessary results of war in the action of the *Free* States, that affects English nerves so unpleasantly. The barbarities of *slaveholders,* unknown in any *civilized* warfare, are ignored by them. The fact is, they want to split this nation asunder. They are *encouraging* the rebels to hold out, by proclaiming, through their press, that if they only keep on fighting a while longer, it will become a duty to recognize them.

But mean and selfish as England has shown herself at this crisis, candor compels me to admit that *we* deserve a place in that seventh pit *rather* more than *she* does. We have made such loud and large *professions!* We have so vaunted ourselves as the guardians of *freedom!* And, alas! behind our president's chair, behind the seats of Congress, in the pulpits with our preachers, on the platform with our Fourth-of-July orators, stood the ghost of the slave, saying by his mute presence, more emphatically than words could utter it, "Oh, ye *hypocrites.*" For more than thirty years, I have seen that ghost *everywhere;* and what a mockery it made of our grandiloquent boastings! . . .

11. LMC to Sarah Shaw, Wayland, October 30, 1862

. . . As for the President's Proclamation, I was thankful for it, but it excited no enthusiasm in my mind. With my gratitude to God was mixed an under-tone of sadness that the moral sense of the people was so low, that the thing could not be done nobly. However we may inflate the emancipation balloon, it will never ascend among the constellations. The ugly fact cannot be concealed from history that it was done reluctantly and stintedly, and that even the degree that was accomplished was done selfishly; was merely a war-measure, to which we were forced by our own perils and necessities; and that no recognition of principles of justice or humanity surrounded the politic act with a halo of moral glory. This war has furnished many instances of *individual* nobility, but our *national* record is mean. Another reason why my joy at the Proclamation was not exulting and exuberant was that it was not to go into effect immediately. It was nothing to wait three months longer, after waiting more than thirty years, but I had misgivings about what might *occur* between now and the 1'st of Jan. It gives ample time for our town traitors and their blinded tools to cooperate with the slaveholders, aided by Seward and McClellan. Everywhere I see signs that the subtle poison is working. The educated are saying, "A republican government has proved weak for times of war; better have a Dictator, and done with it." The ignorant masses are saying, "Let us have peace on *any* terms." . . .

12. LMC to Sarah Shaw, [after April 15, 1865]

. . . The assassination of our good President, shocked and distressed me. Yet I have been so deeply impressed by the wonderful guidance of Providence during this war, that five minutes after I heard the sad news, I said, "Dreadful as this is perhaps it is only another of the wonderful manifestations of Providence. The kind-hearted Abraham, was certainly in danger of making too easy terms with the rebels. Perhaps he has been removed, that he might not defeat his own work, and that another, better calculated to carry it to a safe and *sure end,* might come into his place." I have all along said, that nothing could happen which would shake my faith, that God was not going to *destroy* this nation, but only to mould it *anew* for the performance of a great work in the world. The murder of the President did not shake that faith for an instant; and I thought *nothing* could shake it. But I found I was like the woman who "trusted in Providence till the breeching broke," when the horse was running away. The news of Sherman's negotiations with Johnson filled me with dismay and indignation. It looks like downright treachery to the U.S. I suppose they will "hugger-mugger" it up; but it will take a *good deal* to convince *me,* that it was not something worse than an error in judgment. I think nothing since the war commenced has excited me so much. It made me use language quite too muscular for polite circles. When Fredrika Bremer was reminded that certain strong words were not deemed proper by well-bred people, she replied, "When I am very much incensed I *must swear*."[19] Our new President in some respects resembles Andrew Jackson. He has impressed me quite favorably. He *seems* to have honesty, and sincerity. His being Southern born is a favorable circumstance, and the fact that he belonged to the class of "poor whites" will, I think, have quite an important influence in bringing over that class. Andrew Johnson could not have been *elected* President, but Providence has placed that responsible trust in his hands, and perhaps he will better finish the work, his upright, and careful predecessor began, and carried forward so well. . . .

13.  Lydia Maria Child, "Advice from an Old Friend," *The Freedmen's Book* (Boston, 1865), pp. 269–76

For many years I have felt great sympathy for you, my brethren and sisters, and I have tried to do what I could to help you to freedom. And now that you have at last received the long-desired blessing, I most earnestly wish that you should make the best possible use of it. I have made this book to encourage you to exertion by examples of what colored people are capable of doing. Such men and women as Toussaint l'Ouverture, Benjamin Banneker, Phillis Wheatley, Frederick Douglass, and William and Ellen Crafts, prove that the power of *character* can overcome all external disadvantages, even that most crushing of all disadvantages, Slavery. Perhaps few of you will be able to stir the hearts of large assemblies by such eloquent appeals as those of Frederick Douglass, or be able to describe what you have seen and heard so gracefully as Charlotte L. Forten does. Probably none of you will be called to govern a state as Toussaint L'Ouverture did; for such a remarkable career as his does not happen once in hundreds of years. But the Bible says, "He that ruleth his own spirit is greater than he that ruleth a kingdom"; and such a ruler every man and woman can become, by the help and blessing of God. It is not the *greatness* of the thing a man does which makes him worthy of respect; it is the doing *well* whatsoever he hath to do. In many respects, your opportunities for usefulness are more limited than those of others; but you have one great opportunity peculiar to yourselves. You can do a vast amount of good to people in various parts of the world, and through successive generations, by simply being sober, industrious, and honest. There are still many slaves in Brazil and in the Spanish possessions. If you are vicious, lazy, and careless, their masters will excuse themselves for continuing to hold them in bondage, by saying: "Look at the freedmen of the United States! What idle vagabonds they are! How dirty their cabins are! How slovenly their dress! That proves that negroes cannot take care of themselves, that they are not fit to be free." But if your houses look neat, and your clothes are clean and whole, and your gardens well weeded, and your work faithfully done, whether for yourselves or others, then all the world will cry out, "You see that negroes *can* take care of themselves; and it is a sin and a shame to keep such men in Slavery." Thus, while you are serving your own interests, you will be helping on the emancipation of poor weary slaves in other parts of the world. It is a great privilege to have a chance to do extensive good by such simple means, and your Heavenly Father will hold you responsible for the use you make of your influence.

Your manners will have a great effect in producing an impression to your advantage or disadvantage. Be always respectful and polite toward your associates, and toward those who have been in the habit of considering you an inferior race. It is one of the best ways to prove that you are not inferior. Never allow yourselves to say or do anything in the presence of women of your own color which it would be improper for you to say or do in the presence of the most refined white ladies. Such a course will be an education for them as well as for yourselves. When you appoint committees about your schools and other public affairs, it would be wise to have both men and women on the committees. The habit of thinking and talking about serious and important matters makes women more sensible and discreet. Such consultations together are in fact a practical school both for you and them; and the more modest and intelligent women are, the better will children be brought up.

Personal appearance is another important thing. It is not necessary to be rich in order to dress in a becoming manner. A pretty dress for festival occasions will last a long while, if well taken care of; and a few wild-flowers, or bright berries, will ornament young girls more tastefully than jewels. Working-clothes that are clean and nicely patched always look respectable; and they make a very favorable impression, because they indicate that the wearer is neat and economical. And here let me say, that it is a very great saving to mend garments well, and before the rents get large. We thrifty Yankees have a saying that "a stitch in time saves nine"; and you will find by experience that neglected mending will require more than nine stitches instead of one, and will not look so well when it is done.

The appearance of your villages will do much to produce a favorable opinion concerning your characters and capabilities. Whitewash is not expensive; and it takes but little time to transplant a cherokee rose, a jessamine, or other wild shrubs and vines that make the poorest cabin look beautiful; and, once planted, they will be growing while you are working or sleeping. It is a public benefit to remove everything dirty or unsightly, and to surround homes with verdure and flowers; for a succession of pretty cottages makes the whole road pleasant, and cheers all passers by; while they are at the same time an advertisement, easily read by all men, that the people who live there are not lazy, slovenly, or vulgar. The rich pay a great deal of money for pictures to ornament their walls, but a whitewashed cabin, with flowering-shrubs and vines clustering round it, is a pretty picture freely exhibited to all men. It is a public benefaction.

But even if you are as yet too poor to have a house and garden of your own, it is still in your power to be a credit and an example to your race: by working for others as faithfully as you would work for yourself; by taking as good care of their tools as you would if they were your own; by always keeping your promises, however inconvenient it may be; by being strictly honest in all your dealings; by being temperate in your habits, and never speaking a profane or indecent word,—by pursuing such a course you will be consoled with an inward consciousness of doing right in the sight of God, and be a public benefactor by your example, while at the same time you will secure respect and prosperity for yourself by establishing a good character. A man whose conduct inspires confidence is in a fair way to have house and land of his own, even if he starts in the world without a single cent.

Be careful of your earnings, and as saving in your expenses as is consistent with health and comfort; but never allow yourself to be stingy. Avarice is a mean vice, which eats all the heart out of a man. Money is a good thing, and you ought to want to earn it, as a means of improving the condition of yourselves and families. But it will do good to your character, and increase your happiness, if you impart a portion of your earnings to others who are in need. Help as much as you conveniently can in building churches and school-houses for the good of all, and in providing for the sick and the aged. If your former masters and mistresses are in trouble, show them every kindness in your power, whether they have treated you kindly or not. Remember the words of the blessed Jesus: "Do good to them that hate you, and pray for them which despitefully use you and persecute you."

There is one subject on which I wish to guard you against disappointment. Do not be discouraged if freedom brings you more cares and fewer advantages than you expected. Such a great change as it is from Slavery to Freedom cannot be completed all at once. By being brought up as slaves, you have formed some bad habits, which it will take time to correct. Those who were formerly your masters have acquired still worse habits by being brought up as slaveholders; and they cannot be expected to change all at once. Both of you will gradually improve under the teaching of new circumstances. For a good while it will provoke many of them to see those who were once their slaves acting like freemen. They will doubtless do many things to vex and discourage you, just as the slaveholders in Jamaica did after emancipation there. They seemed to want to drive their emancipated bondmen to insurrection, that they might have a pretext for saying: "You see what a bad effect freedom has on negroes! We told you it would be so!" But the colored people of Jamaica behaved better than their former masters wished them to do. They left the plantations where they were badly treated, or poorly paid, but they worked diligently elsewhere. Their women and children raised vegetables and fowls and carried them to market; and, by their united industry and economy, they soon had comfortable little homes of their own.

I think it would generally be well for you to work for your former masters, if they treat you well, and pay you as much as you could earn elsewhere. But if they show a disposition to oppress you, quit their service, and work for somebody who will treat you like freemen. If they use violent language to you, never use impudent language to them. If they cheat you, scorn to cheat them in return. If they break their promises, never break yours. If they propose to women such connections as used to be common under the bad system of Slavery, teach them that freedwomen not only have the legal power to protect themselves from such degradation, but also that they have pride of character. If in fits of passion, they abuse your children as they formerly did, never revenge it by any injury to them or their property. It is an immense advantage to any man always to keep the right on his side. If you pursue this course you will always be superior, however rich or elegant may be the man or woman who wrongs you.

I do not mean by this that you ought to submit tamely to insult or oppression. Stand up for your rights, but do it in a manly way. Quit working for a man who speaks to you contemptuously, or tries to take a mean advantage of you, when you are doing your duty faithfully by him. If it becomes necessary, apply to magistrates to protect you and redress your wrongs. If you are so unlucky as to live where the men in authority, whether civil or military, are still disposed to treat the colored people as slaves, let the most intelligent among you draw up a statement of your grievances and send it to some of your firm friends in Congress, such as the Hon. Charles Sumner, the Hon. Henry Wilson, and the Hon. George W. Julian.

A good government seeks to make laws that will equally protect and restrain all men. Heretofore you had no reason to respect the laws of this country, because they punished you for crime, in many cases more severely than white men were punished, while they did nothing to protect your rights. But now that good President Lincoln has made you free, you will be legally protected in your rights and restrained from doing wrong, just as other men are protected and restrained. It is one of the noblest privileges of freemen to be able to respect the law, and to rely upon it always for redress of grievances, instead of revenging one wrong by another wrong.

You will have much to put up with before the new order of things can become settled on a permanent foundation. I am grieved to read in the newspapers how wickedly you are still treated in some places; but I am not surprised, for I knew that Slavery was a powerful snake, that would try to do mischief with its tail after its head was crushed. But, whatever wrongs you may endure, comfort yourselves with two reflections: first, that there is the beginning of a better state of things, from which your children will derive much more benefit than you can; secondly, that a great majority of the American people are sincerely determined that you shall be protected in your rights as freemen. Year by year your condition will improve. Year by year, if you respect yourselves, you will be more and more respected by white men. Wonderful changes have taken place in your favor during the last thirty years, and the changes are still going on. The Abolitionist did a great deal for you, by their continual writing and preaching against Slavery. Then this war enabled thousands of people to see for themselves what a bad institution Slavery was; and the uniform kindness with which you treated the Yankee soldiers raised you up multitudes of friends. There are still many pro-slavery people in the Northern States, who, from aristocratic pride or low vulgarity, still call colored people "niggers," and treat them as such. But the good leaven is now fairly worked into public sentiment, and these people, let them do what they will, cannot get it out.

The providence of God has opened for you an upward path. Walk ye in it, without being discouraged by the brambles and stones at the outset. Those who come after you will clear them away, and will place in their stead strong, smooth rails for the steam-car called Progress of the Colored Race.

John Esten Cooke, circa 1861

# John Esten Cooke
# (1830–1886)

"I can't compose, I can't think of anything but Virginia's degradation."
So confessed John Esten Cooke on March 6, 1861.[1] Coming from one
of the South's most distinguished writers, it was a striking admission.
Like so many others, Cooke feared the loss of his creative wellsprings,
feared that "writing is a lost art with me," but he never stopped compos-
ing.

Born in Virginia, Cooke had achieved prominence for his romances
set in pre-Revolutionary times. With *The Virginia Comedians* (1854) and
*Henry St. John, Gentleman* (1859), Cooke established himself in the
South and also gained the attention of Northern critics, particularly the
powerful George and Evert Duyckinck. His romances were criticized for
weak plots and thinly drawn characters, but they expressed Cooke's longing for a golden age of Virginia history, an age he viewed as characterized
by the perfect intermingling of democracy and aristocracy among Cava-
lier descendants. Cooke longed as well for progressive changes in antebellum Virginia. In *Ellie: or, the Human Comedy* (1855) he shifted from
romance to social criticism but his readership ignored him. On the eve of
war, his writing career took another turn as he decided to sacrifice social
and artistic relevance for commercial success. These shifts have led one
modern critic to describe Cooke as an "archetype of the tortured liberal
which the South has fathered for generations."[2]

It was one thing to criticize the South from within; quite another to
withstand assault from without. Cooke had no trouble wielding sword
along with pen; he was most likely, according to one scholar, "the best-
known novelist to see active service in the Civil War."[3] At First Manassas, Sergeant Cooke commanded a gun. Later, he was a first lieutenant

with J.E.B. Stuart's staff. Eventually he was promoted to captain. Though internal politics probably kept him from advancing any further, he served for four years and was present at Appomattox.

Situated with the Army of Northern Virginia on the Rappahannock, just below Fredericksburg, Cooke found a way to fuse his military and literary ambitions. When a new weekly, *The Southern Illustrated News,* was launched in Richmond in September, 1862, Cooke was ready to contribute. The editors knew they were taking a chance introducing the paper at that time: "The minds of men are too pre-occupied by the stirring events of the hour to be amused with the situations of the novelist or beguiled by the fancies of the poet."[4] But the editors also knew that literature could be tied to war in powerful, transformative ways.

In the winter and spring of 1862–63, Cooke wrote a column entitled "Outlines from the Outpost." Though the byline carried the pseudonym Tristan Joyeuse, most readers knew the author's identity. The first sketch appeared on January 31, 1863; the last of this series, on October 10, 1863. Part journalism, part propaganda, these pieces tried to give readers a sense of the exploits of Confederate leaders and common soldiers. The series began with a multi-part treatment of Stonewall Jackson, which became the basis of Cooke's enormously popular *Life of Stonewall Jackson* published later that year in Richmond. From there, Cooke wrote about other Confederate heroes—Jennings Wise, William Downs Farley, John Pelham, John S. Mosby, and P.G.T. Beauregard, to name a few—and about the hardship and camaraderie of daily life in camp. He never managed in these "Outlines" to capture what in his diary he called "the wild, tragic, loathsome Chaos" of war, but that was not his goal.[5] Rather, his essays probed one corner of the cult of Confederate superiority; they forced readers to consider the meaning and mythos of the war even as it raged.

Not everyone was pleased with Cooke's perspective. He received numerous letters challenging his choice of heroes and questioning his objectives. In the final sketch, Cooke responded to his critics. Bitter and besieged, he turned against his readers. They had no right, he thought, to probe beneath the texts into the intentions of the author. The dominant metaphor for writing used in that piece was primarily a military one— essays were either heavy guns or light field artillery, readers were lurking scouts. "The Batteries of Joyeuse" was a momentary outburst by a writer who learned in war that words can pierce like bullets, that meaningful writing exacted a price on both reader and author.

After the war, Cooke suppressed his anger and once again sought a widespread readership. As of 1867, he hoped "to become *the* writer of the South yet!"[6] For a brief time, he seemed on the verge of success. *Surry of Eagle's Nest* (1866) was one of the earliest and most successful Civil War novels among Northern as well as Southern readers; *Wearing of the Gray: Being Personal Portraits, Scenes and Adventures of the War* (1867) was an equally popular memoir. Blurring history and fiction, Cooke, in rapid succession, published *Hilt to Hilt* (1869), *Mohun* (1869), *Hammer and Rapier* (1870), and *Life of Gen. Robert E. Lee* (1871). With battles ended, words poured forth. Bodies were in the grave, but myths were in the air. And while, in order to sell books, Cooke tempered his wartime antagonism to the North, an antagonism evident in "Some Celebrated Yankees," he continued to spread in all directions myths of long lost bucolic lands and descending hordes. He never became the writer of the South, but he died one of the premier writers of the Confederacy.

### 1. "Describes the Den of Joyeuse," *Southern Illustrated News,* January 31, 1863

I intend these "Outlines" to embrace, you see, friend Hector, my reveries, my recollections, and my dreams.

When I saw you last you complained that we had not corresponded for a lengthy time, and told me that you missed the sight of my handwriting, no less than my "old familiar face."

In fact, we had not met before for many months, and months are years now, when we live so fast: when the fiery breath of war makes the pulses beat so quick, and the heart to thrill with such a host of thoughts and emotions. You had gone through all the vicissitudes of war beyond the Alleghenies, and accompanied the hero of the Shenandoah—famed forever!—in his great campaigns of the Valley: while I had served, an unknown soldier, under Beauregard, that other peerless captain, in his famous movements, and the battle yonder, which made the second combat on the same arena of Manassas, seem so strange to me, and full of such weird meaning.

Then from the Valley, and the banks of the Potomac, came the corps in which we served, to the fierce battles around Richmond, where they mingled like two streams and fell upon the foe, and scattered him, despite his trebly guarded lines, and mighty forces.

Step by step we approached each other—and our meeting came at last.

Do you remember when and where that meeting was, old friend of many years? . . .

Your last request was that you might hear from me—and now you are going to. The only query has been, what shall I write you? That we have beat the

Yankees here or there?—that somebody is defeated, and the war thus short-ened?

You read all that in the newspapers—the story of the battles, with their woe-ful list of "casualties," and the great or small result. You would rather have, I think, some dispatches wholly un-"official"—some lines about your friend in private character—how he lives, what he thinks, above all, what he remembers.

A step more:—you would not be averse, I think, to have, with these details and recollections, something of his reveries and dreams. Not his dreams alone of this strange and tragic war—not his recollections only of the gay or sombre scenes he has witnessed, the vicissitudes through which a kind and gracious Providence has led him safely, sending to the right or left the fatal bullet or the hideous projectile. You would like to know, too, if I'm not mistaken, some-thing of his reveries on other things,—of the inner life of the heart and mem-ory.

In the pine woods of Charles City, after those great battles, where you did your soldier's duty with such honor, you would have welcomed,—would you not?—a leaf of this description from your old true friend.

I think, Hector, that the "burnished brand" might have left the waist, as you reclined against some haughty pine to read my idle lucubrations—that the uni-form might have been unfastened—and even the fiery pipe have gone out!

It is, thus, not only some outlines of my material surroundings that I design—I shall speak too of my dreams.

You dream a good deal on the outpost—now, when the beaten foe and the wintry wind, if not the clarions, "sing truce": when all is quiet along the lines, and the drum is hushed, and the bugle sounds no more.

"In summer when the days were long," as says the ditty, we had a lively time at that most exciting if not exhilarating of sports, Yankee hunting. (I had a splendid fox hunt the other day, but it is nothing to it.) Now, however, when the winds of January sigh or roar, amid the pines—when the days are short, and the *nights* are long—you think instead of acting, and live in a tent instead of a saddle.

These long evenings tend to dreams—to memories of the past, and reveries of the future hours—and this, you know, friend Hector, is my old, old weak-ness.

I do my dreaming, in a smoke-embrowned tent, by a good wood fire, assisted by a pipe—your true dreamer always smokes—and this is the fashion I pur-sue. . . .

And now, good Captain Hector, since I have told you so many important things, I will close my portfolio, and return to my favorite pursuit of idleness. Writing is nearly a lost art with me: I scribble little—I who formerly betook myself not infrequently to the noble occupation of the penman.

Placing my feet upon the beam of my chimney—which does not smoke—I go away from the present "place and time," into other scenes in long gone years—or plunging my regards into the depths of my fire, ask "Where is Hector now?"

Is he smoking that same fiery "Powhatan" which he had carried with him through the campaigns of the mountains—sitting by a fire meanwhile, and chatting the long hours away, with merry comrades? Or is he on the outpost too, but picketing in front of the enemy, while he listens to the sad sigh of the pines?

Wherever he is, whatever he does, his friend, now musing, wishes him health and happiness.

Take the Joyeuse motto, Hector, for your banner, and your shield. That motto looks to the end of this mad war, and peace and independence in the Land of Lands.

That motto is—ESPERANCE!

2. "Stonewall Jackson, and the Old Stonewall Brigade,"
*Southern Illustrated News*, February 7, 1863

... I never knew him by any other name than that which the brave and noble Bee bestowed on him when he said, "Yonder stands Jackson like a stone wall." That name of "Stonewall" thenceforth clung to him, and never will leave him, while the grass grows and the water runs. It represents his character and genius in the popular mind, and will descend upon the pages of history, and to children's children, as the name by which he was baptized, in fire and blood, upon the hard-fought field of Manassas.

And now let me tell you where I saw him first, how he impressed me, and what an humble soldier of the great Southern army thinks of the famous General.

I write in no hero-worship spirit here or elsewhere, I assure you; for I am constitutionally incapable of worshipping any human being—even though he be a hero of the most approved description, and the utmost celebrity. My father told me once, with a smile, that "he did not like 'great men,' and always avoided them." His meaning doubtless was, that the native bent of his temperament not only made it impossible for him to

"Crook the pregnant hinges of the knee,
That thrift might follow fawning"—

not only rendered it repugnant to his self-respect to seek out and pay court to any one, but even to *appear* to act the courtier, by joining the obsequious throng.

I think I was born with the same unfortunate trait. I never could court any-

body. I never could stand hat in hand, awaiting the Olympian nod—or bend the
back, or make profound obsequious obeisance before his Lordship or his
Celebrity. In fact I hate the courtier, and the hero-worshipper, in all his ways:
He and myself are alien to each other, and sworn enemies.

And yet I have the faculty of reverence for real worth, largely developed. I
never worshipped hero yet—but I take my hat off and bow low to a great and
noble soul like Jackson. He is a true "soldier of the Cross" no less than the
valiant leader of our armies—and in his person centre the most conspicuous
virtues of the patriot and the Christian. They speak of his eccentricities, his
awkwardness, his shy odd ways, and many singularities. Let these be granted.
There is beneath all this in the soul of the man, a grandeur and nobility, a childlike purity and gracious sweetness, mingled with the indomitable will, which
make him what I call him—a real hero. . . .

The appearance of the famous General was not imposing. He wore that old
sun-embrowned uniform once gray, which his men are so familiar with, and
which has now become historic. To call it sun-embrowned is scarcely to
describe, however, the extent of its discoloration. It was positively scorched
by sun—had that dingy hue, the product of sun and rain, and contact with the
ground which is so unmistakable. A soldier from Franklin street, in his fine
new, braided uniform, would have scarcely deigned to glance at the wearer of
such a coat, and would have elbowed its possessor from the pavement with
extreme disdain;—but the men of the old Stonewall Brigade, loved that coat;
and admired it, and its owner, more than all the holiday uniforms and holiday
warriors in the world. The cap of the General matched the coat—if anything
was still more faded. The sun had turned it quite yellow indeed, and it tilted
over the wearer's forehead, so far as to make it necessary for him to raise his
chin, in looking at you. He rode in his peculiar foreward-leaning fashion, his
old rawboned sorrel, gaunt and grim—but like his master, careless of balls and
tranquil in the loudest hurly burly of battle.

Moving about slowly and sucking a lemon (Yankee spoil, no doubt) the celebrated General Stonewall looked as little like a general as possible. There was
nothing of the "pride, pomp, and circumstance of glorious war" about him, as
my outline sketch established. He had the air rather of a spectator than an
actor—and certainly no one would have taken him for the idolized leader of a
veteran army, then engaged in the battle to decide the fate of the Confederate
Capital. His dispositions had been made—his corps had closed in like an iron
arm around the enemy—and having led them into action, marching at their
head, on foot, like a simple captain, he now appeared to await the result with
entire calmness, almost with an air of indifference, trusting to a higher
Power—to the Lord of hosts who had given him victory so often.

Such would have been the impression of a casual observer. But a closer
glance easily penetrated this apparent tranquility and carelessness. The trust in

God, and utter reliance on his Will was surely there—but no apathetic calmness. The blaze of the eye beneath the yellow cap was unmistakable—there plainly was a soul on fire with deep feeling, and the ardor of battle. A slumbering volcano clearly burned beneath that face so calm and collected—the fire of Ney or Murat held in leash and waiting. . . .

As the fire grew hotter and hotter, as the enemy's position became more desperate, it seemed to interest the General more and more. He rode to the right or left—between the guns—to the front within their line of fire—but always with his air of utter calmness. "As calm as a May morning" scarcely conveys the idea. He advanced amid the screaming projectiles, making the air hideous with their discordant voices, amid plunging round shot, and bursting shells,—with the supreme indifference of one who felt that he bore a charmed life, and could not be harmed:—and no less that our cause must triumph. The bravest men become aroused, and excited at such moments;—but I saw no trace of any such emotion in the General's bearing. His countenance, as revealed, in the darkness, by the glare of the cannon flash,—as afterwards when, the enemy having retired, we advanced to his fire, kindled along the road—was immovable as before. The slumbering volcano was there, doubtless—but from the moment when I saw him first, when his corps had just gone in, and he sat upon a log, by the old Cold Harbor house, writing a dispatch—to the end of the battle, when the burning brushwood showed his face, I saw nothing but indomitable resolution and calmness.—I doubt not he was leaning upon a stronger arm than man's, and had left the event to the God of Battles.

I describe the great General as I saw him. I have never seen him strongly moved—though often in action. There is, however, no room to doubt the fury of the volcano within him, when it once breaks forth. Those who have been with him upon such occasions, declare that he becomes the genius of battle incarnate. Let the moment of extreme peril come, when the foe is pressing him hard, and endeavoring to hem him in, and destroy him. From the calm, collected spectator, so to speak, he becomes the fiery leader. Passing like a thunderbolt along the front he is everywhere in the thickest of the fight, holding his lines steady, however galling the fire, and rallying his men to the charge where the danger is greatest and the pressure heaviest.

His men are fond of telling how he expressed himself at Slaughter Mountain and elsewhere, saying to no one "*Go* on!" but "*Come* on!" They describe to you, how the eye flashed, the cheek flushed hot, the voice so low and calm on ordinary occasions, rose to loud and strident tones, as it called like a clarion, to the charge. At such moments, they tell you, "Old Stonewall," as they call him, cannot be recognized. The ice has turned to fire, the tranquil bearing to devouring excitement; and he leads the onslaught with the fury of a tiger, rushing on his prey.

Woe to the enemy who has to deal with General Stonewall at such moments—they are as stubble before the fire. The "red right arm" is carrying out the deep scheme of the powerful brain, and the possibility of a failure never seems to cross his mind. All energies of soul and sense are combined and concentrated in the stubborn and unfaltering struggle:—the flag of the Republic must be borne aloft in triumph tho' the dearest and most precious blood of the Southern land be poured forth like water. He does not spare his own. Where the great cause takes his men, he leads. The humblest private risks no danger which is not shared by his Commander. To him the cause is all—worth many noble lives—and he is ready to lay down his own.

To follow General Stonewall at such moments is a thing to tell to children's children:—and the flush of remembered triumph will overspread the bronzed cheek of the veteran who tells the story. It was then the bayonet charge was made, and the foe, however obstinate, scattered to the winds. For when General Jackson charges with the bayonet, the hour has struck—the struggle is decided. The field may be strewn with flower and pride of the whole South, but the red cross flag is floating still.

> "Ah maiden! wait and watch and yearn
> For news of Stonewall's band;
> Ah, widow! read, with eyes that burn
> That ring upon thy hand!
> Ah wife! sew on, pray on, hope on,
> Thy life shall not be forlorn—
> The foe had better ne'er been born,
> Than get in Stonewall's way!"

### 3. "The Sorrows of Fairfax," *Southern Illustrated News*, March 7, 1863

Manassas—Centreville—Fairfax—Vienna! What memories and emotions do those words excite in the hearts of the old soldiers of Beauregard!

When I saw it in the early months of the war the whole region was beautiful—a virgin land untouched by the foot of war. The legions who were to trample it and efface all its flowers, still hovered and hesitated on the banks of the Potomac; and the wildest imagination could scarcely have conceived of the sombre fate which awaited it. It was a smiling country full of joy and beauty—where garners were full and faces happy;—where "ancient peace" had erected its altars, and presided over sunny fields. . . .

A land which the hot breath of war had never scorched—where the tramp of cavalry had never resounded—the wheels of artillery had never rumbled;—where the roar of cannon and the rattle of musketry, had never yet come to startle the echoes, or awake the old "sleepy Hollow" from its reveries and dreams.

What dreamer ever fancied its future—ever thought it possible that this summer land, all flowers and sunshine and peace, would become as Golgotha, "the place of skulls"—a Jehoshaphat full of dead men's bones?

But even then the fiat had gone forth—the shadow of fate was moving on the face of the dial. The hour was approaching when all this rural happiness would be overthrown, and trodden under foot; when the inhabitants were to fly from a base and brutal foe—when the family altar would be toppled down, and the very churches fall a prey to worse than vandals.

Opposing columns were to advance over the smiling fields, in pursuit or retreat—the soil was to be furrowed by the wheels of cannon or supply trains;—the forage to be gleaned for the horses of troopers—and the woods and fences were to kindle the camp fire. All its flowers, its springing grasses, its budding forests, were to disappear. The old era of tranquility was to pass away, and a hideous spirit of destruction to rush in. The war dogs, held in leash, with difficulty at Washington, were to circle and trample and hunt for their prey—until they found the Southern wolf at Manassas and were torn by him!

When I visited Centreville and Fairfax, in 1862, when the region had become a highway for two great armies,—and when those two places were like bare, dead trees on that highway—I could scarcely believe that the grass was ever green or the forests ever grew there:—that the villages were ever surrounded by emerald fields. . . .

There was something . . . romantic and interesting . . . which came in due time, and impressed me deeply with respect and admiration. It has never been told: but many persons know it. I wish I could speak of it adequately—but I can only tell briefly how a young and shrinking lady—a "Simple girl"—rose perforce of a fearless heart, to the height of a great occasion, and a critical responsibility. This young and inexperienced girl, on the morning of the 17th of July, heard the Federal officers discussing their plans as they sat at her father's table—unwelcome guests;—and among many other things, overheard their scheme of raising the Confederate flag in the approaching battle. The true heart of the gently-nurtured modest girl throbbed at this vile and infamous device; her fears were forgotten, her resolution taken;—and procuring from the Yankee general a pass to visit her relations in the country, she rode through the enemy's lines to General Ewell at Bull Run, and communicated the intelligence which proved of such vital importance in the battle. Such was the act of a young Virginia lady—one of a people whose *men* can be conquered by the Yankee! I believe, if the men of the South were all slain, the women would continue the war! And this high-souled maiden would not be the last in the field, I fancy. For the present generation, and the generations to come, I say, in the words of Beauregard to the 8th Georgia regiment—"History shall never forget you!" . . .

I shall not soon forget how forlorn [Fairfax] looked, one December day, of 1861, when I accompanied some infantry, cavalry and artillery on a scout to Annandale. Forlorn of the forlornest was Fairfax then—the ruin of itself. All the grace, all the charm, all the freshness, and air of home comfort had departed. It was stripped and bare; almost uninhabited, and an "abode of owls." Had a raven croaked from the riven trees, or a wolf growled at me from the deserted tavern, neither sound would have appeared remarkable. As the hoofstrokes of the cavalry rattled on the hard street, and the artillery carriages rumbled, the echoes which they aroused, seemed unused to such disturbance, and died away quickly in the December air.

All was desolate; every house dismantled—even those of such inhabitants as had received safeguards. "The treacherous dealers had dealt treacherously: yea, the treacherous dealers had dealt very treacherously." The beauty of the hamlet, perched "on the head of the fat valley" had been "a fading flower, and as the hasty fruit before the summer." But "the drunkards of Ephraim" were Yankee soldiers,—and they, like the town, quickly faded and passed away:—exceedingly crabbed fruit, ground in the cider-press of Southern wrath, and giving forth worthless blood!

So I looked at the old town sadly, and lamented its fate. . . . Since that time the place has been occupied, almost always, by the enemy, and has felt his heavy hand laid on it. But the hour approaches in which it will be delivered. . . . Its youth shall be renewed as the eagle's:—and the red cross flag shall yet float over Fairfax, famed in history forever, and triumphant over all foes—again smiling in fresh beauty and the charm of peaceful years!

### 4. "Some Celebrated Yankees," *Southern Illustrated News,* April 11, 1863

What a hard time the Yankee generals have had in Virginia.

I have been sitting in my tent this morning with the snow falling without, but a good log fire blazing within, thinking of the unhappy careers of these distinguished gentlemen. They, one and all, ran a-tilt against Virginia, *nutrix leonum,* and her cubs dealt with them after such a fashion that they retired precipitately and never wished to try it any more.

An unknown soldier of the Southern army, I have had the honor to occupy one fifty thousandth part, let us say, of the thoughts of these great warriors—proud reflection! They have been after me, and I, more frequently still, after them, in something like thirty battles and skirmishes—and we have many recollections in common. Thus I take a personal interest in them, as it were: regard them not in the light of aliens or strangers—and to-day have spent an idle hour in recalling their virtues, their excellence, their glory and their unhappy reverses.

How those reverses must have tried their heroic minds!—tested to the utmost the sublime spirit of patience in their souls! The trials of Job were reproduced in the nineteenth century, and the lamentations of Jeremiah have been equalled!

As I sit and muse, I seem to see the mighty forms defile before me in a woeful line, with headless bodies, wrapped in their mantles, and an air of "woes unnumbered" in the very stride of the great phantoms, on their way toward the Stygian river. I fancy that their bearing is reproachful as they pass—full of the sense of undeserved misfortune, and an unjust obloquy, for did they not, one and all, explain completely the little accidents which negatived their triumphs—how, after "gaining a material advantage" in every instance, they were forced to "execute a movement to the rear," by this or that misunderstanding between this or that official at the seat of government? Alas! their great King Abraham I. would hear of no such talk—he chopped off their heads, and sent them to the Stygian river.

Mighty forms! Let an humble opponent record your names and celebrate your virtues. . . .

Last of all the great headless phantoms is General Burnside. The Young Napoleon [George McClellan] turned up again, and got whipped at Sharpsburg,—he declined advancing thereafter, and was decapitated. King Abraham—the mysterious decapitator of triumphant generals—politely took off his head, this time "positively without reserve:"—and the army of the Potomac was entrusted to General Burnside. This warrior was famous as the leader of the advance at the first battle of Manassas, where the South was so badly whipped. But his chief distinction was at Roanoke Island. Here with 15,000 men he had defeated 1500—and henceforth was a hero of immense fame. Called now to command the army of the Potomac, he betrayed a strange unnational modesty and distrust, piteously clamoring for "orders" what to do. His cry was responded to. The King of the Gorillas, with triumphant humor, discharged upon him this "order"—*"Do anything you choose, but do something! Do something!"* Could a request so complimentary to his faculties be denied—could Burnside hesitate? But he did. "I can't handle an army so large," said the worthy general. *Do something!* "I distrust by ability and would rather—" *Do something!* "I cannot cross the Rappahannock in face of—" *Do something!* "I am certain to be defeated by Lee if I—" *Do something!* The inexorable "Do something" pursued the unhappy general—and driven to desperation, he proceeded immediately to do it. He crossed his army at Fredericksburg—got terribly whipped—came back—and was decapitated! When last heard from, both he and his illustrious predecessor were making a pilgrimage through the New England States—and patting little children on the head, in the public schools. But these are only the phantasmagoria of their real selves. The actual personages are long since dead—headless and on their way to the land of Oblivion.

"Fighting Joe Hooker" rules now over the army of the Potomac—and Lee and Longstreet and Stuart, and the awful Stonewall, are waiting to demolish him in his turn. "He too shall go"—as says the poet—to that bourn from which no Yankee generals, with a few exceptions, ever return. The light of the great "Fighting Joe" shall be extinguished—his hat shall cruelly be knocked over his eyes—and he shall return to Washington, going and weeping,—maligning the day he ever undertook the "On to Richmond" journey. This appears like rhetoric, but it is only prediction—or rather statement of the coming event. "Fighting Joe" shall go as went his great fore *runners:*—headless he shall totter on, upon that dreary road, toward the refuge of Unfortunates, from which no howl of anguish ever pierces upper air, and where the bloody instincts of these terrible warriors will have no object but themselves. If like the famous cats of Kilkenny they devour each other, who will weep?

Then when "Fighting Joe Hooker" is down among the dead men—there will be seen the most terrible of spectacles to Southern eyes. Bankrupt of generals, and fired by the genius of battle, King Abraham himself will don the nodding plume, and buckle on the panoply of war. Captain-General Lincoln will take the head of the army—with Lincoln, Jr., in command of the grand advance. With the great motto of the republic "Booty and Beauty" upon his standard—with "The war shall end in ninety days" inscribed on every guidon—General Abraham, with a prefatory jest, shall advance upon the quaking troops of Lee, and Longstreet, Jackson and Stuart. Those unfortunate rebels shall thereupon tremble in their cavalry boots—put their heads together in counsel—and repelling the thought of surrendering at discretion—impelled alone by the fury of despair—oppose their fated followers, and themselves to the vengeance of the Gorilla King. The lines shall be drawn up for battle—Gen. Abraham, attended by his glittering staff, shall ride forth to the front, and make a joke—the signal gun shall roar—and the last great battle of the war shall then begin with hitherto unheard of fury.

From the awful picture thus evoked from the realms of imagination, the mind recoils with horror. King Abraham charging at the head of his victorious legions, and joking even in the heat of battle, is a thought too terrific to dwell upon. Let us hope that this is only imagination:—that a foe so frightful will not fall upon our weary and shattered columns, worn out and disheartened by so long a series of reverses: and that if the great Abraham is to join the headless procession, his ugly visage will be removed by his own betrayed countrymen—by the men whose rights he has denied, whose persons he has immersed in his loathsome bastiles, whose sons and brothers he has murdered upon Southern battle-fields—by that nation which the whole world despises now, because they regard this Buffoon as its type.

As I muse, the poor phantoms slink away like ghosts at cock-crow. They fade into mist—and are gone. Farewell noble souls! Mighty shades of the departed! Farewell Scott and McDowell, Patterson and Fremont! Farewell Wagonless Banks, Material-Advantage McClellan; farewell back-seeing Pope, and Do-Nothing Burnside! You did your best but fate was hard for you—you thought you were masters in the art of war, but the masters' masters were at hand! In your tombs you have little to console you—and your ghosts flit restless through that world which laughs at you. For you fought for a cause which the world declares infamous—for a government which has sounded all the depths and shoals of dishonor.

You were trained in arms, and some of you contended not unmanfully—but an Unseen Hand broke the sword in your grasp, and dragged down your banners to the dust. That Hand was the hand of the God of battles, who has strengthened the right, and visited the wrong-doer—who has swept you away, poor puppets of the hour!—and will overthrow all who succeed you!

### 5. "A Day with Beauregard," *Southern Illustrated News*, June 20, 1863

In December, 1861, chancing to be at the headquarters of one of our most eminent Generals, near Centreville, I spent a day with Gen. Beauregard; and perhaps some personal details relating to this great soldier will not prove uninteresting.

The interest almost universally felt in such familiar details is natural, and assuredly not unworthy or ignoble. A foreign writer published, some time since, a series of articles entitled "Great Men in Their Dressing Gowns;" and I am sure these "undress" personal sketches of the celebrated men of antiquity proved interesting to all readers. Men like to know how the distinguished individuals of their species "lived and moved" and looked—the habits which characterized them, and "what manner of men they were." When this sentiment takes the Boswellian form, it certainly becomes a mean and "hero-worshipping" trait—than which nothing is more repulsive and despicable. But the line of demarcation between the two sentiments is broad and distinct. None but the parasite in spirit will mistake it. The one feeling is natural, commendable—experienced by the best and proudest gentleman of the land. The other is petty, contemptible—experienced only by the sychophant, or those with the spirit of the sychophant.

For myself, I like to be told that the first Caesar—that "foremost man of all this world"—was delicate, thin, and pale; that he concealed his baldness with thin leaves of the laurel-crown; that he was a fine gentleman, a veritable fop of antiquity, indeed, and always traveled with his dressing-case, and unguents, and perfumes. I understand his career more correctly, when I know that in Gaul, while incessantly in the saddle, crossing rivers, fighting daily battles, and conducting with immense energy his great campaigns, he was pale, worndown, almost fainting under constant attacks of epilepsy. The foppish habits, the pallor, the thin cheeks, throw out in strong relief the mighty intellect and indomitable spirit, even then designing the downfall of the Republic, and reveal the "great Julius" as he mutably lived and moved before the eyes of his contemporaries.

That Napoleon had that statuesque head which Phidias delighted to produce in marble—that he took snuff from his waistcoat pocket in profusion—that he murmured, "These be Scythians indeed!" before burning Moscow—these are not idle or unprofitable details to him who strives to pierce the veil of mystery which envelopes a great individuality.

How Shakespeare looked, and dressed, and spoke, would, I think, be far more interesting to the Anglo-Saxon race than many dignified histories of wars and revolutions, with all the combats, treaties, protocols and "official documents" set forth at large. Suppose an old journal of Ben Johnson, or Francis Beaumont, was discovered, and you read: "To day spent an hour or more in conversation with Mr. William Shakespeare, who was clad in a new doublet of blue taffeta, which became his figure rarely. He told me he had become addicted to his pipe and the Virginia weed—had been planning a new drama, with an odd, fat knight, to be called 'Sir John Falstaff,' as the principal character—a bully, cut-purse, royster and friend of Prince Harry. . . ." I am sure that these leaves of an imaginary diary would be eagerly bought for many times their weight in gold, and that the first gentlemen of Great Britain would contend for their possession.

Between Caesar and Gen. Beauregard there is a long distance—but Beauregard is not one of the least prominent figures in our great revolution. . . . I recall his appearance with perfect distinctness, despite the thousand scenes and personages encountered since that time. He wore a uniform coat of the old United States army color and fashion—dark blue, with a double row of gilt buttons, and a stiff collar. This garment was buttoned closely from top to bottom, and defined a close set, muscular and vigorous chest. From the upper edge protruded a tall "standing collar," the fashion ten years ago—and the head was surmounted by a plain military cap, with a stiff brim, extending straight in front. He wore plain brown citizen's pantaloons, kept his hands in his pockets, and neither in appearance or attitude were there any indications of his rank.

The face was, however, an exception. Upon the broad brow and firm mouth, shaded by a heavy dark mustache, command had ineffaceably stamped its seal. . . . If ever "iron nerve" was written on human physiognomy it was there. It was impossible to doubt the fighting qualities of the man with that musculur, close-set lower face—or to imagine the peril which could ever make him lose "heart of hope." The rest of the countenance was gaunt, hard, somewhat melancholy—French, as I have said, in character, and that of a born soldier. In the complexion you read the Southern Creole descent of the General—it was brunette, sallow; and had been bronzed by sun and wind. Something of the pallor too, of care and watching. I discerned that bloodless hue which not seldom accompanies heavy responsibility and earnest toil to achieve great objects. For, believe me, the position of the leader of an army is not a bed of roses, and the bloom of youth and tranquil hours soon fades from the cheeks which are hollowed by the anxieties of command.

I have omitted one feature which is important to most men's countenances—in General Beauregard's was the most remarkable of all. His eyes were very striking. Large, melancholy, with the lids drooping, and somewhat inflamed—dark, sleepy, dreamy, their expression impressed you profoundly. It was the eye of the bloodhound, with his fighting instincts asleep, but ready at any moment to burst forth and overwhelm all opposition. It was impossible not to be struck with this resemblance—the idea of the bloodhound rose unconsciously to the mind as you gazed, and I have never been able to eradicate the impression. I do not mean to say that there was any *ferocity* at all in the glance of these large, slumbrous eyes, or one particle of that blood-thirsty instinct which we attach to the animal in question. But if ever "fight" was plain in any look—obstinate, pertinacious, desperate "fight"—it was plain in General Beauregard's. . . .

I had heard stories of his cuteness, his frigid repulse of all familiarity, his military brevity in conversation, and his moody, melancholy, unsocial demeanor. Stray correspondents of newspapers had drawn a curious figure for the public, and labelled it "Beauregard"—the figure of a solitary, sombre, musing individual—much addicted to attitudinizing and playing the "distinguished man"—fond of wrapping his cloak around him, and folding his arms and turning away moodily whenever he was spoken to—as having no thoughts in common with those around him, and absorbed in the mighty schemes of his gigantic and profound intellect. This, I say, was the popular caricature I had seen of General Beauregard—in this striking attitude he had appeared before my eyes and the eyes of the country—and lo! a few hours with the real personage toppled down all the fine fancies of Messieurs, the Correspondents, completely! Instead of a mock hero of tragedy, with scowls and mutterings, stalking about in his cloak, without addressing any one—I saw before me a modest and courteous gentlemen of the simplest demeanor, and apparently asking nothing better than to have some kind friend make him laugh.

For the General actually laughed, and when he laughed, strangely enough, he seemed to enjoy himself and to go through the ceremony without one thought of the tragedy-hero character! Standing on the portico of the small country house, or eating his dinner with simple, mundane enjoyment, like a common mortal, he seemed to be completely oblivious that he was "Beauregard, the Great Tragedian," and took his part in the conversation with an air of the utmost modesty and courtesy, losing no opportunity, I have said, to relax, by laughter, the weary facial muscles, which had settled into something like grimness and melancholy from "long thoughts" and great anxieties. . . .

Not as the soldier, but as the man, would I speak of General Beauregard. What the soldier has done is on record: what the man was like, remains to be told on some stray leaf like this. . . . I have referred to the tragic character of the letter writers—to "Beauregard, the Great Tragedian," who was supposed to be playing "Lara," or some other sombre, mysterious, scowling part at Manassas—the part of the romantic heroes of Byron or Schiller, above all human emotion, and unmoved by fate itself. . . . I have traced in outline the figure of the General as I saw him, and I think my sketch is truthful. The nervous figure—the gaunt, French, fighting, brunette countenance—the slumbrous, bloodhound eye—the grave politness—the kindly, simple bearing; wholly free from all assumption—these were the parts I noted in General Beauregard. They will stamp his personal individuality on the pages of history, where he will live, imperishably connected with the first great battle of Manassas—that battle which sums up a period, and meets us on the threshold of our Revolutionary annals—grim, disastrous, bloody—and eloquent yet with the groans of agony and the shout of triumph, as the northern hordes went down before the Southern bayonet.

### 6. "The Batteries of Joyeuse," *Southern Illustrated News*, October 10, 1863

Every writer, I suppose, could contribute his chapter to the 'Curiosities of Literature.'

The world seems to regard authors of all descriptions as public property—their works, whether elaborate and ambitious, or slight and transitory, whether heavy guns or light field artillery, popping here and there, and soon silenced and forgotten—as a species of goods and chattels, of real or unreal estate, in which everybody has his interest. An old acquaintance of mine told me that he once met a stranger in a bookstore, who was glancing at a volume by Washington Irving. 'A great author, sir!' said the stranger, 'a very great author, indeed! I regard his fame as the public property of the nation; and, being lately in the neighborhood of "Sunnyside," I called on Mr. Irving to get my *dividend!*'

There is property in shinplasters, as in thousand dollar bonds—in scribblers as in famous authors, argues the world. And immediately the position and character of the light artillery is reconnoitered as assiduously as though the guns were hundred pounders.

These reconnaisances are effected by letters often—sometimes by the accomplished scouts in person. Their letters are complimentary or the reverse—their visits are agreeable, or the contrary—but they come.

In vain does the poor author turn and wind like a fox, with a pack of hounds on his track; they will run him down. In vain does he attempt to mask his light field artillery—some lurking scout will spy his weakness, and pluck out the heart of his mystery. The *nom de plume* does not save him. By that masterly maneuvre he thinks to outgeneral the scouts—to throw the persistent enemy on another scent—and he argues upon the advantages of the proceeding in question, with apparent good sense. 'Have I written in past times—says the author—a romance which the world took a fancy to? wo to me if I affix my name to the new MS!—'Blank is deteriorating,' a discerning public will sigh; 'it is sad to see an author thus writing himself out!' Do I compose an historical work on the war—a book describing the performances of various corps and commanders, some anonymous correspondent will write me a letter straightway, and thunder apothegms down on my head, because I give Jones more credit than Smith in the affair, and omit all mention of Brown and Robinson!'

Thus argues the poor writer in favor of the *nom de plume*, and he adopts that convenient mask with joyful ardor, and a sentiment of cheap victory over his foes. He writes a chapter under his *nom de plume*, publishes the articles in a journal or magazine—and then the 'Pleasures of Literature' begin to shower down on him. By letters and visits is he made to understand that he is found out at once, and that he and his writings, whether thousand dollar bonds or shinplasters; whether heavy metal rifle-guns, or smooth bore six-pounders, are public property. . . .

John William De Forest, 1868

# John William De Forest
## (1826–1906)

Of all writers at the time, John De Forest saw the most action as a Civil War soldier. By his account, including service in war and peace, "I was six and a half years under the colors. I was in three storming parties, six days of field engagements, and thirty-seven days of siege duty, making forty-six days under fire." Through it all he kept writing: letters home, journal entries, essays for literary magazines, the beginnings of a novel. Ten years after the war, William Dean Howells, editor of the *Atlantic Monthly* praised De Forest as "the first to treat the war really and artistically."[1]

Nothing he had published before the war suggested such acclaim. Sickly as an adolescent, the New Haven native spent much time traveling abroad. He sampled assorted spas and water-cures in hopes of revitalizing his health. On the eve of the Civil War, De Forest's literary output consisted of his *History of the Indians of Connecticut from the Earliest Known Period to 1850* (1851), two travel books, *Oriental Acquaintance* (1856) and *European Acquaintance* (1858), and two novels, "Witching Times" (serialized in *Putnam's Monthly Magazine* beginning in 1856) and *Seacliff* (1859). Only this last work received any attention; a reviewer in the *Atlantic Monthly* praised it as a "very readable novel, artful in plot, effective in characterization, and brilliant in style."[2]

Just months prior to the firing on Fort Sumter, De Forest was in Charleston, South Carolina, visiting his wife, whose father was a professor at Charleston Medical College. In an essay titled "Charleston Under Arms," he assessed the mood of the region. He condemned the South for laboring under assorted delusions, but he did so without deriding Southerners. Charleston was a "persuaded, self-poised community," just like Boston only on the opposite side of the slavery question. In the essay, De Forest found his voice as narrator and reporter. By turns ana-lytical and sardonic, De Forest would continue throughout the war to probe the dimensions of conflict he first observed here: "fighting was a sober, sad subject; and yet at times it took a turn toward the ludi-crous."[3]

"Charleston Under Arms" appeared in April 1861. On January 1, 1862, De Forest was commissioned a captain of Company I of the Twelfth Connecticut. As with so many other chronically ill young men, war provided De Forest with an opportunity to refashion himself into an energetic and fearless officer. His writings reveal considerable talents as observer, story-teller, and scene-setter. He was no blind patriot and he never lost sight of his "character as novelist." If anything, there is too much posturing, too heavy a persona, in the material that came out of his experiences during the war. But he never flinched from trying to describe the ambiguities and uncertainties of human behavior and that is what con-tinues to give this work such vitality.

Though late in his life, De Forest began to assemble his writings from the Civil War and Reconstruction, which were not published until after World War II. In addition to *A Volunteer's Adventures: A Union Captain's Record of the Civil War* (1946), De Forest's experiences as Freedmen's Bureau agent in Greenville, South Carolina are recounted in *A Union Officer in the Reconstruction* (1948). De Forest's non-fiction prepared the way for his fiction: with *Miss Ravenel's Conversion from Secession to Loy-alty* (1867), he achieved the literary fame that had eluded him until then. William Dean Howells applauded the work, and even Henry James, who thought it a poorly constructed novel, praised it for its realistic depiction of war.[4]

The fame did not last. *Miss Ravenel's Conversion* sold poorly and De Forest turned away from realism. Through the 1870s, he published nearly a novel a year, works that have garnered far more attention in our time than in his. In 1898, a reporter from the *New York Times* visited De Forest, whose "name suggests little to the reader now," yet "thirty years ago he was a famous writer, as famous as any in America in his time." By the end of the century, De Forest had abandoned fiction. He devoted him-self to the study of ethnology. His focus, however, was not on the char-acteristics of blacks and whites, as one might have expected from a New England intellectual who spent much time in the South. Rather, he was looking back at the historical origins of his own people.[5]

In 1902, De Forest applied for a Civil War pension. He lived alone in a third-floor room at the Hotel Garde in New Haven. Indigent and failing in health, he was awarded $12 a month by the Pension Board. "I am closing up my literary life," he declared.[6] For a writer, that meant closing up life itself. He declined rapidly and died in his son's home on July 17, 1906. He rests in Grove Street Cemetery in New Haven, his place marked by a tombstone bearing saber and pen.

### 1. *A Volunteer's Adventures: A Union Captain's Record of the Civil War* (New Haven, 1946)[7]

#### STEAM TRANSPORT *FULTON*, MARCH 6, 1862

... Personally I am more comfortably situated than I expected to be. I have got out of the hole where I was lodged at first, and am in a tolerable stateroom beside the stairway, only objectionable as being too near the boiler and also not quite large enough for three. Even the soldiers are much better accommodated than I supposed when I last wrote you; there is room enough below for every man to stretch himself at full enough in his blanket or overcoat. Some of them were comically surprised and indignant when they learned that they were not to be made free of the afterpart of the ship. "That's a pooty way to treat a poor soldier!" whines one gawky lout as the sergeant of the guard, an old regular, routed him out of a seat on the quarter-deck and hustled him forward.

Not a woman on board; the ship is as the world was before Eve was created; the most jealous of wives need not be afraid to have her husband here. I am as indolent as passengers usually are; I cannot even study my drill book and the regulations. I smoke like a Turk; I walk the deck till the broiling sun sends me up to the breezy top of the wheelhouse; I load my revolver and shoot at gulls or floating tufts of seaweed; in my best estate I play at checkers on the quarter-deck. The cabin is so hot and close that it is not pleasant to linger there.

The general indifference to our future is curious and makes me wonder if we are beginning to be heroes. Nobody knows where we are ultimately going, and nobody appears to care. We vaguely expect to follow Porter's mortar fleet and occupy some place which has been shelled into submission.[8] It seems impossible as yet to believe that we peaceful burghers are going to fight. You must not suppose that this tremulous handwriting results from terror of coming battle. It is merely the ship's engine shaking the table.

#### SHIP ISLAND, MARCH 15, 1862

Why were we born! Just imagine a regiment landing on a desert island without baggage wagons and horses, without tents enough, and without even a tent pin to kindle a fire with! Every day I detail from a quarter to three quarters of my company to collect wood for cooking; and this wood they must bring on their backs a distance of two, three, and four miles. We have no cook-tent, and no lumber wherewith to build cook houses, so that I must store all the rations of my company in my own tent. Consequently I am encumbered with boxes of hardbread, and dispense a nutritious perfume of salt pork, salt beef, onions, potatoes, vinegar, sugar and coffee. . . .

A southerly gale commenced and by afternoon blew violently. . . . By nightfall the gale became a thunderstorm which deluged the camp and upset many tents. The pins of mine pulled out of the wet sand as if it had been butter, and the whole thing went prostrate with a hateful soft *swish*. As raising it in that tempest was out of the question, I plunged into the tent of a neighboring captain and slept on his floor. No harm resulted to health and very little to property. This reminds me to say that the general sanitary condition on the island is wonderfully good. The Ninth and Twenty-sixth have not had a death during their four-months' stay, so that if we hold on here and let the Rebs alone we may all become centenarians.

Three Western regiments joined us lately, making ten regiments now on the island besides a troop of cavalry and a battery of artillery, in all above nine thousand men. Nearly every day there are arrivals of transports, mortar boats, gunboats and ships of war. The naval officers tell us that this is to be a large expedition, and that there will be fully twenty-two thousand men of the land forces alone. If this is true, I infer that we are going to New Orleans, and that we are not likely to start immediately.

Today we have for the time seen the mainland distinctly; it is a low, far-stretching coast, apparently covered with forests. A mirage lifts it in the air so that there is a bar of steel-color between the verdure and the yellow waters of the Sound; and this same atmospheric magic must enable the Mississippians to study our array of masts and smoke funnels; all the same we are twenty miles asunder.

We are in the rainy season now, and the mornings are chilly. I have a chance to know this, for we get up at sunrise. Then the *reveille* beats; the men turn out under arms; the three commissioned officers look on while the first sergeant calls the roll; the muskets are stacked and the men break ranks. At half past six we breakfast; from seven to eight there is company drill; from half past nine to half past ten, more company drill; at twelve, dinner, which means soup and hardtack; from four to six, battalion drill; at half past six, hardtack, pork and coffee; at nine, another roll call; at a quarter past nine, lights out. It is a healthy, monotonous, stupid life, and makes one long to go somewhere, even at the risk of being shot.

SHIP ISLAND, APRIL 6, 1862

... Man is a brave animal, at least when danger is distant. Nine out of ten of our invalids got well as soon as they heard that we were to fight. None of my company wanted to stay behind, although five years on the sick list and one of them could scarcely hobble. As for myself, my only fear was lest my men should disgrace me and the regiment by running away; and I loaded my revolver with the grim intention of shooting the first dastard who should start for the rear. Of course, if ever bullets begin to whistle about me, I may set the example of poltroonery. That suspicion really alarms me more than anything else. "Let not him that putteth on his armor boast himself." ...

You would perhaps like a sketch of General Butler.[9] Three of us Twelfth officers called upon him apropos of rations, and in my character of novelist I made a study of him. He is not the grossly fat and altogether ugly man who is presented in the illustrated weeklies. He is stoutish but not clumsily so; he squints badly, but his eyes are very clear and bright; his complexion is fair, smooth and delicately flushed; his teeth are white and his smile is ingratiating. You need not understand that he is pretty; only that he is better looking than his published portraits.

He treated us very courteously and entered into the merits of our affair at length, stating the *pros* and *cons* from the army regulations like a judge delivering a charge, and smiling from time to time after the mechanical fashion of Edward Everett, as if he meant to make things pleasant to us and also to show his handsome teeth.[10] On the whole he seemed less like a major general than like a politician who was coaxing for votes. The result of the interview was that we got the desired order and departed with a sense of having them flattered.

Yesterday I called on General Phelps, the chief of our brigade.[11] He is a swarthy, grizzled six-footer, who looks all the more giant-like because of a loose build and a shambling carriage, and says unexpected things in a slow, solemn humoristic way.

"Come in, Captain; what's the news?" he drawled, rather satirically as I thought; for how can a captain tell a general anything?

When I replied that I had heard nothing but vague and absurd reports about possible movements, he smiled as if approving my incredulity, or my reticence, and said, "Sit down, Captain; what do you want?"

I explained that I merely wanted some blanks for my property returns from the brigade quartermaster; but he kept me nearly half an hour, talking much about drill and discipline and more about the South. He hates the Rebels bitterly, not so much because they are rebellious as because they are slaveholders, for he is a fervid abolitionist. He would not hearken with patience to the faint praise which I accorded them for their audacity and courage. His face flushed, and he replied in an angry snarl, "What have they done? They brag enormously and perform next to nothing. Their deeds fall so far below their words that they are nothing less than ridiculous." . . .

NEW ORLEANS, APRIL 30, 1862

Well, the forts have been captured, and New Orleans also. . . . I shall probably astonish you when I say that we did not find the bombardment magnificent nor even continuously interesting. It was too distant from us to startle the senses and too protracted to hold our attention. We could hear a continuous uproar of distant artillery; we could see clouds of smoke curling up from behind the leafage which fringed the river; and on the first day, when we were near the scene of action, we could see vessels lying along the low banks. Also, if we climbed up to the crosstrees, the forts were visible beyond a forested bend. Then we were ordered to the head of the passes, seven miles below; and there we lay for a week, gradually losing our interest in the combat.

We smoked and read novels; we yawned often and slept a great deal; in short, we behaved as people do in the tediums of peace; anything to kill time. Once or twice a day we got a rumor from above that the bombing was doing wonders, or that it was doing nothing at all. Now and then a blazing fireship floated by us, lighting red the broad, swift, sublime river, and glowing away southward. . . .

NEW ORLEANS, MAY 2, 1862

We had a charming sail from Fort Jackson to New Orleans through scenery which surpasses the Connecticut River valley and is not inferior to that of the Hudson, though quite different in character.

It is a continuous flat, generally below the level of the Mississippi, but richly beautiful and full of variety. The windings of the mighty river, the endless cypress forests in the background, the vast fields of cane and corn, the abundant magnolias and orange groves and bananas, the plantation houses showing white through dark-green foliage furnished an uninterrupted succession of lovely pictures. Of course the verdure was a fascinating novelty to men who came last from the white sands of Ship Island, and previously from the snows of New England.

Apparently this paradise had been nearly deserted by its inhabitants. Between Fort Jackson and Chalmette, a few miles below New Orleans, we saw hardly fifty white people on the banks, and the houses had the look of having been closed and abandoned. Even the Negroes were far from being as numerous as we had expected. None of the whites signalled to us, or took any other notice of us, or seemed to see us. One elderly man, driving northward with a rockaway full of women, kept along with us for a quarter of a mile or so, without once turning his white-bearded face toward us.

The blacks, as might be expected, were more communicative and more friendly. They gathered to stare to us, and when there were no whites near, they gave enthusiastic evidence of good will, dancing at us, waving hats or branches and shouting welcome. One old mauma, who spoke English and had perhaps once been "sold down de ribber," capered vigorously on the levee, screaming, "Bress de Lawd! I knows dat ar flag. I knew it would come. Praise de Lawd!"

Perhaps some of the planters had fled the region in fear of a slave insurrection; but, as we had learned at Fort Jackson, they had another reason for seeking a place of safety. The fleet had come up the river like an angel of destruction, hurling shells and broadsides into thickets which sheltered ambuscades, and knocking to pieces dwellings occupied by guerrillas. Seventeen miles below New Orleans it pitched into Fort Leon, and sent the garrison flying across the flats to the cypress forest. Then the town surrendered, and with it all the fortifications in the vicinity, while the Rebel troops scurried up the river. . . .

CARROLLTON, LOUISIANA, MAY 14, 1862

. . . The poverty of the once flourishing city of New Orleans is astonishing. I have seen nothing like its desolation since I quitted the deserted streets of Venice, Ferrara and Pisa. Almost the only people visible are shabby roughs and ragged beggars. Many poor Irish and Germans hang about our regiments begging for the refuse of our rations. The town is fairly and squarely on the point of starvation. No one denies now that our blockade has been effective; it kept out everything, even to the yellow fever. General Butler has commenced distributions of food; and it is possible that industry will recover within a few weeks from the fright of the threatened bombardment; but it will be years before it quite recovers from all the effects of this stupid rebellion.

Unless work is soon found for these people, I do not see how famine can be averted. Flour ranges from twenty-three to thirty dollars a barrel; Irish potatoes, eight dollars a bushel; sweet potatoes, undiscoverable. Mess beef, which the quartermaster holds at thirteen dollars a barrel, sells in the city at thirty. The country people charge us ten cents a quart for milk and seventy-five cents a dozen for eggs. A common broom, worth a quarter of a dollar at the North, fetches here a quarter of an eagle; a tin teapot, worth sixteen cents in Connecticut, costs seventy-five cents in Louisiana. Apparently, if the South should be corked up and left to itself, it would very soon turn savage and go naked.

Already it is verging on the barefooted stage; common soldiers' shoes sell for eight dollars; cavalry half-boots for twenty and thirty.

Of course these prices represent the depreciation of Confederate money as well as the scarcity of merchandise. Specie there was none before we arrived; nothing but shinplasters of fifty contemptible descriptions; a worse state of things than in bankrupt Austria. Louisiana small change consists of five-cent tickets for omnibuses, barrooms and shaving shops. Shortly after our landing my first sergeant bought some tobacco for the company and paid in gold and silver. The shopkeeper, a German woman, caught up a quarter of a dollar, kissed the eagle on it and said, "That's the bird for me. Why didn't you men come long ago?"

Negroes have depreciated as much as any other Southern circulating medium. They straggle into camp daily, more than we know what to do with. I have one named Charley Weeks, a bright and well-mannered mulatto, evidently a pet household servant, and lately chattel to one General Thompson of the departed Rebel army.[12] He has a trunk and two suits of broadcloth, besides his workaday clothes. I have established him in my cooking tent and promised him my sublime protection, which is more effective here now than it would have been three weeks ago.

### CAMP PARAPET, JUNE 15, 1862

... I begin to despair of finding a chance to fight unless there is another war after this one.

Singular as it may seem, this is a disappointment. Nearly every officer and the majority of the men would prefer to go up the river, taking the certainty of hard fare and hard times generally, with a fair likelihood of being killed or wounded, rather than stay here drilling and guard mounting in peace. When the long roll beat for the Seventh Vermont to start forward, they hurrahed for ten minutes while we sulked over their luck and their exultation, not even giving them a cheer as they marched by us to embark. Meanwhile we sniff at the Thirteenth Connecticut as a dandy corps which has never lived out of doors and is only fit to stand guard around General Butler. We believe that we could whip it in a fight, and we know that we could beat it in battalion drill. And so on, through a series of grumblings and snarlings, all illustrative of human nature. . . .

The Twelfth also has contrabands, fully sixty in number, some of them nurses and laborers at the hospital, others servants to officers, the remainder company cooks. Two of them carry my written protections in their pockets. Who said John Brown was dead? There are six hundred thousand John Browns now in the South. The old enthusiast is terribly avenged. The rotten post of slavery is getting a rousing shake.

The officer of the guard tells me that outside of his picket there is a camp, or rather bivouac, of one hundred and fifty Negroes, lately arrived from the other bank of the river. Their owner (a thousand-hogshead man) got into a rage about something, perhaps their insubordination, ordered them off the plantation and bade them go to the devil. Also there is a great floating population of blacks; men and women and pickaninnies streaming daily into the camp and sticking there until they are expelled as "unemployed persons"; a burden to the soul of our brigade provost marshal and a subject of intense commiseration to our general. . . .

### CAMP PARAPET, JUNE 29, 1862

. . . There was a little fight up the river a few days ago. A party of guerillas ambuscaded a company of Vermonters, killed or wounded thirteen men, and scampered off. This is the only skirmish which has occurred within forty miles of here since New Orleans surrendered. I had no idea until lately what a Quakerly business war could be. You need not fear but what the Twelfth will have a peaceful and inglorious campaign. Beauregard would be an idiot to venture into this narrow belt between the river and the swamps to attack our strong line of fieldworks under a flanking fire from gunboats and frigates. This is the only country I ever saw except Holland where the water commands the land. A ship in the river looks to us as if it were on a hill. . . .

### CAMP PARAPET, JULY 13, 1862

. . . As to the Negroes, they are all on our side, although thus far they are mainly a burden. In spite of indirect discouragements they are continually quitting the plantations and swarming to us for protection and support. Lieutenant Potter, our brigade provost marshal, has on his roll seven hundred of them, all living in or about the camp and drawing rations. Potter wishes they were on the coast of Guinea, and sulkily asks General Phelps what he shall do with them.

"I don't know," squalls the brigadier, as much bothered by the "inevitable nigger" as if he were not an abolitionist. If he had his own way, doubtless, he would raise black battalions; indeed, he has already asked one of our captains if he would be willing to command a colored regiment; whereupon the captain replied that he wouldn't. . . .

We wish we were on the Potomac or the Rappahannock. Why does not the president send out some of the new regiments to guard subjugated Louisiana, and so set us drilled fellows free for active service? One does not want to go

into the army merely to return home without seeing a battle. Besides, there are
no promotions; nobody is killed and nobody gets scared into resigning; there
is not a chance for a captain to become a field officer. . . .

CAMP PARAPET, AUGUST 6, 1862

The truth is (although you must not publish it) that the division has run down
terribly in numbers. There is a constant drain on troops in the field, much heav-
ier than a civilian would suppose. Something like one fifth of the men who
enlist are not tough enough nor brave enough to be soldiers. A regiment reaches
its station a thousand strong; but in six months it can only muster six or seven
hundred men for marching and fighting duty; the rest have vanished in various
ways. Some have died of hardship, or disease, or nostalgia; as many more have
been discharged for physical disability; others are absent sick, or have got fur-
loughs by shamming sickness; others are on special duty as bakers, hospital
nurses, wagoners, quartermasters' drudges, etc.; a few are working out sentences of court-martial. Thus your division of fifteen thousand men has
dropped to ten thousand or perhaps eight thousand effectives. The companies
have each lost one if not two of their original three officers. There you have
our history.

Meantime the government is raising new organizations, instead of filling up
the old ones; and to make matters as bad as possible it is putting its green regiments into the hands of green officers. To be effective, troops must have drill
and discipline; and the only way to give them these qualities is to give them
commanders who know their business; why shouldn't even a politician understand that?

Our whole system of raising an army is wrong; we ought to raise it by draft,
by conscription. Then our governors, instead of appointing officers who can
merely electioneer, could appoint such as have learned how to command. The
South has resorted to conscription, and it will beat us if we don't follow suit.
With a far inferior population it can levy soldiers faster than we can, and it can
put them under experienced colonels and captains.

What is it but drafting which has enabled it of late to resume the offensive?
Here is Breckinridge[13] invading Louisiana; losing the battlefield, to be sure, but
still awing us out of Baton Rouge; and only a little while ago we held the river
up to Vicksburg. Where did Jefferson Davis get the materials for these new
armies? The whole secret of their numbers, and of their energy and effective-
ness too, is conscription.

But if I keep on you will know as much of war as I do, which would be very
improper in a woman and might lead to more rebellion.

## CAMP PARAPET, AUGUST 13, 1862

This is the rainy season here, but by no means a cool season. I cannot give you the temperature, for there is not a thermometer in the brigade; but in scorching and sweating a man's strength away it beats anything that I ever before experienced. Sitting in my tent, with the sides looped up all around, I am drenched with perspiration. I come in from inspection (which means standing half an hour in the sun) with coat and trousers almost dripping wet, and my soaked sash stained with the blue of my uniform. There is no letup, no relenting, to the heat. Morning after morning the same brazen sun inflames the air till we go about with mouths open like suffering dogs. Toward noon clouds appear, gusts of wind struggle to overset our tents, and sheets of rain turn the camp into a marsh, but bring no permanent coolness.

The night air is as heavy and dank as that of a swamp, and at daybreak the rotten odor of the earth is sickening. It is a land moreover of vermin, at least in this season. The evening resounds with mosquitoes; a tent hums with them like a beehive, audible rods away; as Lieutenant Potter says, they sing like canary birds. When I slip under my mosquito bar they prowl and yell around me with the ferocity of panthers.

Tiny millers and soft green insects get in my eyes, stick to my perspiring face, and perish by scores in the flame of my candle. Various kinds of brilliant bugs drop on my paper, where they are slain and devoured by gangs of large red ants. These ants rummage my whole habitation for rations, crawl inside my clothing and under my blanket at night, and try to eat me alive. I have seen many large "lightning bugs," such as the Cuban ladies sometimes wear in their hair. Also there are black grasshoppers two or three inches in length, with red and yellow trimmings to their jackets, the most dandified fellows of their species that I know of. . . .

## CAMP PARAPET, SEPTEMBER 2, 1862

Last evening I thought that Breckinridge had come, and that the Twelfth was about to fight its first battle. About nine o'clock scattering musket shots broke out on the picket line, running along the front from the river to the cypress swamp. Then, before I could buckle on sword and revolver, there was a yell from the sergeants of "Fall in!" followed by the long roll of all the regiments roaring sullenly through the damp night.

The rain had poured nearly all day, and the camp was a slop of mud and puddles. My men splashed through the sludge and halted on the little company parade, jabbering, reeling and scuffling. I saw at once what was the matter: payday had worked its usual mischief: one third of them were as drunk as pipers.

In my rage at their condition I forgot all about the enemy. I pushed and flung them into their places, and called them sots, and used other bad language. . . .

To comprehend this drunkenness you must understand that many of my men are city toughs, in part Irish; also that they are desperate with malaria, with the monotony of their life, and with incessant discomforts; finally, that intoxication in itself is not a military offence and not punishable. If you could look into our tents you would not wonder that consolation is sought for in whiskey. The never-ceasing rain streams at will through numerous rents and holes in the mouldy, rotten canvas. Nearly every night half the men are wet through while asleep unless they wake up, stack their clothing in the darkness, and sit on it with their rubber blankets over their heads, something not easy to do when they are so crowded that they can hardly move.

It must be added in fairness that intoxication is not confined to the soldiers. The officers are nearly as miserable, and are tempted to seek the same consolation. Lately a lieutenant reeled into my tent, dropped heavily on bed, stared at me for a minute as if to locate me, and said in a thick voice, "Capm, everybody's drunk today. Capm, the brigade's drunk."

### NEW ORLEANS, SEPTEMBER 22, 1862

. . . Yesterday's mail brought me a letter from the wife of one of my private soldiers. She had not heard from her husband for a month, and she wanted to know if he was in trouble or was dead. She had received nothing from him since he enlisted but one remittance of nine dollars. A mortgage on her house had been foreclosed; and as her husband is not a Connecticut man, the authorities of her township will not allow her the "family bounty"; hence she and her children are likely to be homeless as well as penniless.

I fear that she will get little aid from her husband. He is a mild, weak young fellow, easily led away by comrades, low-spirited under the slightest illness, given to cosseting himself with sutler's trash, and given also to seeking courage in whiskey. Thirteen dollars a month can easily be spent in these follies.

The letter is nicely written and correctly spelled; moreover, it is well phrased and loving and touching. It is full of her husband; full of adoration for the poor creature and of prayers for his unimportant safety; pious terrors lest he may have been drawn into evil ways; prayers to me that I will not conceal from her the possible worst; then declarations that the feeble lout is the best of husbands; it is no fault of his—no fault of Henry's—that his family suffers.

In short, here are four pages of pathos which make me want to call in Henry and kick him for not deserving them. Apparently a fairly educated and quiteworthy girl has married a good-looking youth of inferior nature and breeding who has not the energy to toil effectively for her, nor the affection to endure privations for her sake. I shall give the letter to him with a few words of earnest, epauletted counsel. It may stop him from drinking himself into the gutter twice after every payday, and from sickening himself with bushels of abominable gingerbread and shameless pie.

CAMP KEARNY, OCTOBER 10, 1862

Do you fancy the idea of my applying for the colonelcy of a colored regiment? Important people here advise it and promise to help me with recommendations. It would be a comfortable position, I suppose; but there are some obvious serious disadvantages. The colored troops will probably be kept near here and used to garrison unhealthy positions; they will be called on for fatigue duty, such as making roads, building bridges and draining marshes; they will be seldom put into battle, and will afford small chances of distinction.

Since writing the above I have talked on the subject with Colonel Deming, who is acting mayor of New Orleans and well informed concerning affairs at headquarters. I had decided to apply for a black regiment, and I wrote to him for an introduction to General Butler. Thereupon he sent for me, treated me to a fine dinner and gave me his views.

"I advise you," said he, "not to make your proposed application, for fear it might be successful."

Then he went into details concerning the character of the officers who would be associated with me, and the nature of the service that will be assigned to the Negro troops, which details I do not feel free to repeat. In short, he counselled me so urgently against the step that I have given it up and decided to fight my way on in the Twelfth, if it is ever to have any fighting.

I must tell you of an adventure of mine with one of the heroines of secession. On my way down to the city in the crowded, dirty cars, I saw behind me, standing, a lady in half-mourning, a pallid and meagre young woman, with compressed thin lips, sharp grey eyes and a waspish expression. Much doubting whether my civility would be well received, I rose and offered her my seat. She would not look at me; she just conceded me a quick shake of the head and a petulent shrug of the shoulders; then, pinching her pale lips, she stood glaring straight before her.

After waiting her pleasure a moment I resumed my seat. Presently a rather pretty lady opposite me (a young mother with kindly eyes and a cultured expression) took her little girl into her lap and beckoned the scowling heroine to the vacant place. She accepted it with lavish thanks, adding in a loud, ostentatious tone, "*I* wasn't going to take a seat from a Yankee. These cars used to be a fit place for ladies. Now niggers and Yankees crowd decent people out."

The lady with the kindly eyes threw me an apologetic glance which seemed to say, "I hope you did not hear." There ended the comedy; or was it a tragedy?. . .


NEAR THIBODEAUX, DECEMBER 7, 1862

I have received your comments on our Liliputian battle at Labadieville. You must understand that I took post in the front rank during the charge for a good reason. As my men had never been under fire before, I was afraid they might get startled and disorderd, and I wanted to set them an example in facing danger. I can trust them now and shall hereafter march in rear of the company, where a captain should be according to the drill book.

I have discovered why officers are in general braver than soldiers. The soldier is responsible for himself alone, and so is apt to think of himself alone. The officer is responsible for his company, and so partially forgets his own peril. His whole soul is occupied with the task of keeping his ranks in order, and it is only now and then that he takes serious note of the bullets and shells. It would demand a good deal of courage, I think, to be a mere looker-on in a battle.

An officer of the —th gave me an amusing account of the chaplain of his regiment; sitting his horse calmly in rear of the charging, yelling line and peering after it through his specs with an expression of enlightened curiosity; now glancing at the rolls of smoke which marked the Rebels' position and now at the tufts of dust thrown up by their shot; the whole man as bland and content as if he were in a prayer meeting. He is a terrible forager, this valiant young son of the prophets. He makes frequent pilgrimages after provisions for his flock and helps personally towards devouring the substance of the enemy. Some days ago he presented himself at regimental headquarters and said, "Colonel, the health of this battalion requires sweet potatoes, and I should like permission to take up a contribution. By the way, it is Sunday, I believe. If I get back early enough, I shall preach this afternoon."

Off he went with a couple of soldiers, impressed a plough and a pair of mules at a plantation, and returned with a load of vegetables.

But we have nearly worn out the foraging business. The land for miles is as bare of pigs as if a legion of devils had run away with them all. Meantime I am nourished at a moderate cost in an honest fashion. One of my men has been detailed as guard over two large plantations, his duty being to drive off plunderers and to make the Negroes get in the sugar crop. The owners are humbly thankful for his protection; they have given him a pony, a hogshead of sugar and a barrel of syrup; and they allow him to bring me poultry at fair prices and vegetables for nothing.

Having been paid off lately, I am able to purchase, and we live well. Occasionally there is a hiatus; for instance, our sweet potatoes and turnips and cabbages arrived late this morning; consequently we had nothing for dinner but bread and roast turkey. But "accidents will happen in the best regulated families."

PORT HUDSON, JULY 10, 1863

Excuse this woefully soiled paper. It is as clean as it can be after having been treasured for a week in the dirty pocket of a very dirty captain. You can hardly imagine how unclean and ragged our regiment is, officers as well as soldiers. On all sides I can see great patches of bare skin showing through tattered shirts and trousers. I have but one suit, and so cannot wash it. My pantaloons will almost stand alone, so stiff are they with a dried mixture of dust, mud, showers and perspiration.

I look forward with longing unutterable to the day when I shall be able to substitute decent clothing for the whole foul encumbrance. I am far less out of humor with my wretched food which has consisted for weeks of little else than fried or boiled doughballs with an occasional seasoning of blackberries or of a minute slice of rusty bacon. It is rather surprising that under such circumstances we of the Twelfth are fairly healthy and show few men on the sick list compared with some other regiments. In killed and wounded we have been lucky, losing but little over a hundred out of about four hundred, while the Eighth New Hampshire and Fourth Wisconsin have been nearly exterminated. . . .

BRASHEAR CITY, LOUISIANA, JULY 29, 1863

. . . The heat is tremendous. Flies are thicker than in Egypt, and mosquitoes thicker than in Guilford. But it is astonishing how healthy and contented our bronzed veterans are. They build themselves hovels of rails and boards, bake under them like potatoes in hot ashes, and grumble at nothing but the lack of tobacco. A soldier is not a hero in fighting alone; his patience under hardship, privation and sickness is equally heroic; sometimes I feel disposed to put him on a level with the martyrs. . . .

VERMILION BAYOU, LOUISIANA, OCTOBER 10, 1863

. . . We forage like the locusts of Revelation. The Western men plunder worse than our fellows. It is pitiful to see how quickly a herd of noble cattle will be slaughtered. Our Negro servants bring in pigs, sheep and fowls, whether we bid it or forbid it. Of course, after the creatures are dead and cooked, we eat them to save them, for wasting food is prejudicial to military discipline.

It is curious how honest these looting darkeys are toward their employers; I never knew one of them to steal anything from a Union officer or soldier. They say that they used to feel free to rob their old masters, but it would be wrong to rob a man who hires them and pays them wages. . . .

NEAR BERRYVILLE, VIRGINIA, SEPTEMBER 8, 1864

I wish you could understand how difficult I find it to write even one letter. Since mailing my last I have had no baggage but my overcoat and rubber blanket. This half-sheet of foolscap was begged from a brother captain who begged the whole sheet from the adjutant general of our brigade. The ink was loaned me by another officer, and I hope somebody else will give me an envelope. The pen, thank Providence, is mine, and I still possess one postage stamp. . . .

### 2. "The First Time Under Fire," *Harper's New Weekly Magazine* 29 (September 1864): 475–82

We had lain for ten days within hearing of the bombardment of Fort Jackson, within sight of the bursting shells and of the smoke of that great torment, but still we had not as a regiment been under fire. We were the first troops to reach conquered New Orleans; but we had never yet heard the whistling of balls, excepting in a trifling skirmish on Pearl River, where five of our companied received a harmless volley from forty or fifty invisible guerrillas. About all that we knew of was the routine of drill and guard duty, and the false night alarms with which our brigadier used to try us and season us. No, I am mistaken: we did know what it was to suffer; to wilt under a Southern sun, and be daubed with Louisiana mud; to be sick by hundreds and die by scores. But now we were to quit garrison duty behind the great earth-works of Camp Parapet, and go into offensive operations. Lieutenant Godfrey Weitzel of the Engineers, the chief military adviser of General Butler, had lately been created Brigadier-General, and the extenuated forces of the department were exhausted to furnish him with a brigade suitable to the execution of the plans which he proposed.[14]

Weitzel did not want the Twelfth Connecticut. It was generally believed that the regiments which garrisoned Camp Parapet were not only sickly but broken in spirit and undisciplined. Sickly I have admitted that we were; but not broken in spirit, except so far as that life, from constant misery, had come to seem hardly desirable, and death, by constant presence, had lost its terrors; while, as to the third charge, I can neither broadly admit nor squarely deny it. . . .

On the 24th of October, 1862, [the brigade] embarked on some small river steamers, and, convoyed by three gun-boats, sailed one hundred miles up the

Mississippi, landing the following day near the once flourishing little town of Donelsonville. Donelsonville is on the right or western bank, astride of the Bayou Lafourche, which is one of the numerous outlets of the Mississippi, and carries off a considerable body of water through the rich district of Lafourche Interieur. The place was in ruins, shattered by shells and half burned—a punishment which had fallen upon it for firing on Farragut's gun-boats.[15] Our regiment slept on the floor of a church, and I ate my supper off a tombstone in the cemetery. At six in the morning, leaving the First Louisians to hold Donelsonville, we commenced our march, following the bayou in a westerly and then in a southerly direction, one regiment of infantry and one company of cavalry on the right bank, the remainder of the brigade on the left bank. Communication was secured by two gigantic Mississippi flat-boats, easily convertible into a pontoon-bridge, which were towed down the current by mules and contrabands.

This was the first night that our regiment passed out of doors. I thought I never should get to sleep. I had a bed of cornstalks, but I believed I was roughing it. It was the dreadful exposure to the night air which worried me, and not the proximity of hostile balls and bayonets. And when I was aroused at five in the morning to continue the march, I actually felt more fearful of being broken down by want of proper rest than of being shot in the approaching engagement. How mistaken our mothers were when they warned us against exposure to night air, and sleeping in damp clothing, and going with wet feet! Judging from a two-years' experience of almost constant field-service, I aver that these things are wholesome and restorative. It does not require a strong constitution to stand them; it is sleeping inside of walls which ought properly to be called exposure, and which demands a vigorous vitality; and it is the crowning triumph of civilization that it enables humanity to do this without extermination. I have a screed to deliver some day on this subject to a misguided and house-poisoned public. . . .

The troops marched as loosely as usual, in the road, on the levee, and all over the lots, taking advantage of every possible cut-off, and presenting an extraordinary contrast to the rank-and-file regularity of movement which the same regiments were brought to after six or eight months more of field duties. We passed pretty, flourishing plantations, and endless flats of waving green sugar-cane. The roads were vacant of vehicles; not an individual of the dominant white race showed his face; but crowds of negroes rushed out with the tumultuous simple acclamations of joy. It was "God bless you, massas!—Oh, de Lord's name be praised!—We knowed you'd come!—I'se a gwine 'long with you." And go with us they did by hundreds, ready to do anything for us, and submitting uncomplainingly to the trickeries and robberies which were practiced upon them by the jokers and scape-graces of the brigade. Looking ahead down the longer stretches of the winding bayou, we could occasionally see the parti-colored flags of the signal corps waving from some conspicuous angle of the levee, as they sent back in silent messages the discoveries of the advanced scouts. As on the day previous, we came across a freshly-deserted bivouac of the rebels, and we learned from the negroes that they numbered about five hundred, chiefly cavalry or mounted infantry. I, for one, expected no engagement, not knowing that these troopers were hastening to join a force of about two thousand infantry and artillery which General Mouton had collected at Thibodeaux, the capital of the Lafourche district.[16] Moreover our regiment formed the rear of the column, and I, as officer of the day, marched with the rear-guard of the regiment, so that I seemed to be far away from all chances of battle.

Then came a story that the fighting had been going on in front for more than an hour, and that the Thirteenth Connecticut had already lost seventy men; which, by-the-way, was only one of the numerous false rumors that fly broadcast like grape-shot through every combat; the losses being trifling up to this time, and the Thirteenth not having yet been engaged. . . .

When we received orders to move forward I obtained permission of the colonel to quit the rear-guard and take command of my company. With drums beating, fifes screaming, and banners floating, we hurried on, listening to the slow dropping of artillery two miles distant. I was anxious, but so far only for my men, not knowing how they would behave in this their first battle. I commenced a rough and ready joking with them, not because I was gay, but because I wanted them to be gay. I have forgotten what I said; it was poor, coarse fun enough probably; but it answered the purpose.

Well, the light-hearted, reckless, yet steady countenances of the company, and of the whole regiment, was all that one could desire. We found the pontoon-bridge in position, and the two howitzers which protected it firing slowly, while an unseen rebel battery answered it with equal deliberation. Here we first came under fire, and here I first saw a wounded man. In a country carriage, upheld by two negroes, was some sufferer, his knee crushed by a shot, his torn trowsers soaked with a dirty crimson, his face a ghastly yellow, and his eyes looking the agony of death. I did not want my men to see the dismaying spectacle, and called their attention to something, I have forgotten what, which was passing on the other side of the bayou. As we rushed down the inner slope of the levee an amazingly loud, harsh scream passed over us, followed by a sharp explosion and a splashing in the water. I was not alarmed, but rather relieved and gratified. If they can't aim better than that, I simply thought they are welcome to fire all day. Then came another shell, striking close to the crowded bridge and spattering the men, but without deterring the thirsty ones from stopping to fill their canteens. It was wonderfully fine practice, considering that they were aiming at us from behind the levee, half a mile down the stream, where the fellows who worked the guns could not see us. I remember that my chief anxiety while crossing was lest I should wet my feet in the sloppy bottom of the flat-boat. The terror of battle is not, I think, an abiding impression, but one that comes and goes like throbs of pain; and this is especially the case with veteran soldiers, who have learned to know when there is danger and when there is not; the moment an instantaneous peril has passed they are as cool as if it had never approached. But on the present occasion, I repeat, I was not oppressed by any feeling which could be called even alarm. I was buoyed up by the physical excitement of rapid movement, by my anxiety that my company should do well, and by my ignorance of the profounder, the really tremendous horrors into which battle may develop. A regiment of well-drilled greenhorns, if neatly brought into action, can charge as brilliantly as veterans. . . .

As we approached the edge of the wood nearest the enemy they caught sight of us, and a shell screamed over our heads, passing through the lower branches and sending down a shower of leaves. Nearly the whole regiment bowed low and gracefully but without halting or breaking. Stepping to the front, I turned around and laughed at my men saying, "I beg your pardon for not bowing when you did; the truth is, I did not think of it until it was too late." This was pure bravado, not characteristic of me, I hope, but suggested by the fear that my new soldiers were getting frightened, and intended to restore their spirits. Poor as the joke was it actually made them laugh, so slight was their anxiety, if any.

The shells came fast now, a majority of them screeching over the colors, at which they were evidently aimed. Not only were the four guns directly in front of us booming rapidly, but Sim's battery, half a mile down the bayou, and on the other side, was pitching his iron about us at a venture. Meantime our own two howitzers, the only ones as yet brought into action by Weitzel, had ceased firing, so as not to interfere with our advance. I remember that this damped my spirits at the time, although it was of course absolutely necessary. Each shot came lower than the last, and I thought calmly, they will hit something soon. I did not attempt to dodge. I reflected that a missile would hit me about the same time that I should hear it. I believed that the eyes of all my soldiers were upon me (whereas they were probably looking only for the enemy); and so, for reason's sake and example's sake, I kept my head steadfast. It cost me no great effort. I had no nervous inclination to duck, no involuntary twitching or trembling; I was not aware of any painful quickening of the pulse; in short, I was not frightened. I thought to myself, it is very possible that they will hit me, but I hope not, and I think not. It seemed to me the most natural thing in the world that others should be killed, and that I should not. I have suffered more in every engagement since than I did in this first trial. It is a frequent, it is the usual experience. . . .

We were just entering a large open field, dotted by a few trees and thorn-bushes, with a swamp forest on the right and the levee of the bayou on the left, when the rebels gave us their musketry. It was not a volley, but a file fire—it was a long rattle like that which a boy makes in running with a stick along a picket-fence, only vastly louder; and at the same time the sharp, quick *whit whit* of bullets chippered close to our ears. In the field little puffs of dust jumped up here and there; on the other side of it a long, low blue roll of smoke curled upward; to the right of it the gray smoke of the artillery arose in a thin cloud; but no other vestige of an enemy was visible.

About this time the First Lieutenant of Company D was surprised at seeing two of his men fall down and roll over each other. To his mind they seemed to be struggling which should get undermost, and thus find shelter from the bul-lets. "Get up! get into the ranks!" he commanded, hitting the uppermost with the flat of his sabre. One of them silently pointed to a bloody hole in his trow-sers and lay quiet; the other rose with a mazed air, looked about for his rifle, picked it up and ran after the company. A bullet had struck this man's piece, dashed it against him with such force as to knock him down, glanced, and passed through the thigh of his comrade.

The First Lieutenant of Company G had his hand on the shoulder of a lag-gard, pushing him forward into the ranks, when a fragment of a shell struck the man in the breast, passing downward through his body and killing him instantly. Private Judson of Company C flung up both hands with a loud scream and dropped dead with a ball in his heart. A shot through the foot disabled the left corporal of my company. A bullet struck the rifle of the man next to me in the rear rank, knocking it off his shoulder, end over end, several feet distant. Picking it up he showed me the now useless lock, and asked me what he should do. "Fetch it along," I said, "you may have a chance to use the bayonet; we shall be up there presently." Bringing it to a right-shoulder-shift he fell into his place and made the charge in that manner. On the right of me a sharp crash, as of dry bones broken by a hatchet, drew my attention, and, looking that way, I saw Edwards, one of the color-bearers, fall slowly backward, raising one hand to his mouth as the blood spurted from it; an "Oh!" of pain or alarm burst from his lips, and in his eyes there was a stare of woeful amazement.

I had expected that such sights as this would be most depressing and terrible. It was not so; it was not even painful; it hardly seemed unnatural; it only pro-duced a feeling of surprise. Kelley of the color guard, one of our Louisiana recruits, seized the Stars and Stripes from the fallen man's hand and bore them onward, calmly chewing his tobacco. . . .

The men fell into line again, and the dropping file fire had commenced in our ranks when I and every one near me heard distinctly a loud order to lie down. Down we went, all the more smartly, I think, because at that instant a shell flew between the colors with a deafening, hoarse screech as if the rebels had fired a brace of mad catamounts at us. I remember that I laughed at the nervous haste of my plunge, and that I saw one of my men laughing also as he went down, probably for similar reason. In my boyhood I have ducked the same way, and with very much the same laugh, in escaping from a particularly swift snow-ball.

"Forward!" we heard the Colonel shout; and springing up we advanced. It was our last stop. The men were excited, but not frightened. On they went, file-firing, straight toward the enemy, in the teeth of cannon and musketry. There was a heavy pressure from right to left toward the colors; some of my small men were crowded out of their places; we were three ranks deep instead of two. As little Sweeny dodged along the rear, trying to find a crack in the living, advancing wall to poke his gun through, one of my officers twice collared him and dragged him back to his place, saying, "What the — and — are you doing on the right of the company?"

"Lieutenant," was the ready answer, "I am up here purtectin' thim colors."

The swearing mania was irrepressible; nothing but oaths could express our feelings. I was not a profane man; I never swore at one of my company before that day; but at that moment I had a gift. In the rage of the charge, in the red presence of slaughter, it seemed as if every possible extremity of mere language was excusable, provided it would aid in gaining victory. A serious friend has asked me since if I did not think of eternity. Not once. I was anxious for nothing but to keep a steady line and to reach the enemy's position. I did not, as I previously supposed I should, urge my soldiers to fight desperately and fire rapidly. They were fighting well enough and firing fast enough. Nearly all that I said might be summed up as repetitions of the two orders, "Close up" and "Guide right." I even swore at one of the color corporals for being out of line, although the man had simply dropped back a pace in the process of loading. . . .

The field, I have said, was a quarter of a mile long. We had passed over one-half of it before I saw a single man of the hostile force; and their cannon I did not see at all, so well were they masked by shrubbery, although I could perceive the puffs of smoke which they gave out when discharged. Numbers of men in the regiment never laid eyes on a rebel during the whole action. The first troops that we caught sight of were probably the Lafourche militia, Mouton's reserve, which came down the cross-road on a run to reinforce the threatened position. As soon as they got in our front they commenced firing irregularly, without halting or forming, then broke suddenly in a panic, rushing into the thickets in their rear, and disappearing in a most rapid, harmless manner. This I did not see, for it happened opposite our right wing, and my eyes were set straight forward. But when we had got half across the field I became aware that the hostile battery had ceased firing; and immediately thereafter I perceived a crowd of men spring up from behind the fence in front of us, plunge across the road, and sweep into the forest, seeming to be actually jumping over each other in their haste, and looking, in their gray uniforms, like an immense flock of sheep swarming over a fence. At this sight our regiment raised a spontaneous yell of triumph, and quickened, if possible, the fury of its fire. . . .

One of the first men whom I beheld in the morning was Edwards, the color-bearer, whom I had seen fall with what I supposed to be a mortal wound, and who now presented himself to claim his colors, having understood that we were to have a second battle. The ball had actually passed through his head, entering the mouth, and coming out behind the left jaw. He simply complained that his mouth was very sore, and that he could eat nothing but soup. He was ordered back to hospital, being evidently too severely hit to do duty; and in fact he had a long illness, the fever of the hurt terminating in typhus. One of the most noticeable things in war is the heroism of the wounded.

Notwithstanding the great length at which I have described the combat of Labadieville, our regimental loss was but two killed and fourteen wounded. Its smallness was owing in part to the rapidity with which we advanced, and the consequent brevity of our exposure to fire, only an hour and twenty minutes elapsing from the time the first shell passed over us to the moment of reaching the fence. It did not seem, by-the-way, fifteen minutes. The entire loss of the brigade was less than ninety killed and wounded, of which about one-half fell to the share of the Eighth New Hampshire. . . .

Of all the combats that I have seen this one was the most scientific, orderly, comprehensible, and artistically satisfactory. I will venture one other military reflection. I think the success of our regiment in charging veterans in a strong position was owing very much to the file-fire which we kept up while advancing. In the first place, it supported the spirits of our men, who believed that they were doing as much damage as they received, and felt that they ought to be able to bear the trial as long as the enemy. In the second place, it killed the musketry of the rebels, who, unfortunately for their morale, I think, had for shelter a deep plantation ditch, which served them the purpose of a rifle-pit. Now a human being who has a cover in battle hates to put his head outside of it. As a proof that we actually did overwhelm and derange the hostile musketry, I may adduce the fact that we had only six men hit by bullets. The rebels lost very few, to be sure; but the fence above their heads was so tattered by our shot as to be a curiosity; and the prisoners said that, what with the whizzing of Min-iés and the flying of cypress splinters, the ditch was a most unpleasant position. I believe the manoeuvre of file-firing while advancing in battalion line to be quite a novelty. Notwithstanding frequent inquiries on the subject, I never yet heard of any other regiment having practiced it. An attacking line generally halts from time to time and delivers volleys, or advances at a right-shoulder shift, taking what the enemy sends without reply until the position to be seized is actually reached. All three of these methods, I admit, are sufficiently difficult of execution; but the one by which we carried our point at Labadieville is certainly the least trying to human nature. The difficulty is that it can not be put in practice except on level ground, where the rear rank can keep well closed up; and even then the leading men are in some danger of having their heads blown off by the muskets of their supporting comrades. For instance, I had my neck scorched at Labadieville by the fire of one of my own soldiers.

And now let us ascend from tactics to strategy. The plan of the campaign was that Weitzel should drive the enemy down the Lafourche to Thibodeaux; that Colonel Thomas, with the Eighth Vermont and a colored regiment, should flank them there by way of the railroad from New Orleans; and that the Twenty-first Indiana with a force of gun-boats should seize Brashear City, and cut off their retreat across the Atchafalaya. To bring all this about, Mouton ought to have fought a second battle with us at Thibodeaux, or at least to have retired with a decent degree of deliberation. But he had been too neatly whipped and too thoroughly frightened to do either. He made a desperate rush for Brashear City, deserted at every step by his Lafourche militiamen, and succeeded in crossing the Atchafalaya almost in sight of the intercepting force, which had been detained two days off the bar by a furious norther. As for us, we followed him in a most leisurely manner, fearing that he would do just what he did. And now for nearly six months—that is, until General Banks arrived to open his Teche campaign—was Weitzel military master of the fertile Lafourche country, and commander of the United States forces in all Louisiana west of the Mississippi.

Frederick Douglass, 1856 *(Courtesy of the University of New Mexico)*

# Frederick Douglass
## (1818–1895)

"The term negro is at this moment the most pregnant word in the English language." When Frederick Douglass, the most important and visible black man in America, made that pronouncement in 1863 he was laboring vigilantly to mold the nation's transition from slavery to freedom. His own transition had come decades earlier, in 1838, when the Maryland slave, then named Frederick Bailey, journeyed by ferry and train to New York. He stayed there long enough to await and marry fellow runaway Anna Murray before heading toward New England and changing his name to Douglass, a name he casually adopted, and misspelled, from Walter Scott's *Lady of the Lake*.

Self-taught, Douglass had a feel for words. The publication of his autobiographical *Narrative* in 1845 made him an international figure in the antislavery movement. In *My Bondage and My Freedom* (1855) and *The Life and Times of Frederick Douglass* (1881, 1892), he would again revise and update his story. Between 1847 and 1863, settled in Rochester, New York, he also edited and published a series of newspapers, variously called the *North Star, Frederick Douglass' Paper* and *Douglass' Monthly*.

Douglass was not only a writer but an orator, and we can not fathom his influence without trying to hear as well as see his words. In 1862, one reporter observed that "no printed sentences can convey any adequate idea of the manner, the tone of voice, the gesticulation, the action, the round soft, swelling pronunciation with which Frederick Douglass spoke."[1] He stood before packed auditoriums and testified as to what it was like to be a slave in America. He stood before huge congregations and pleaded for equality and justice for the black race. As the Civil War came, he was running out of patience with the tardiness of progress and growing angrier by the day.

"The awful and sublime crisis in our national affairs," Douglass proclaimed, "swallows up all other subjects." From the start of the war, Douglass pressed Lincoln to make the cause of the slave a priority. When the administration failed to act on emancipation, Douglass vilified the moral and social hypocrisy of the Union cause. When the administration refused to allow blacks to fight for their own cause, Douglass beseeched the Commander-in-Chief to call "the iron arm of the black man" into service. (Douglass's son Lewis served as first sergeant major of Robert Gould Shaw's Fifty-fourth Massachusetts Volunteers.) When the administration denied equal pay to black soldiers, Douglass denounced the injustice. And when the administration hesitated in formulating a post-emancipation policy, Douglass campaigned for equal rights.[2]

The years of Civil War would, in retrospect, turn out to be the last of Douglass's best years, years of struggle to be sure, but of exhilaration and triumph as well. "I had reached the end of the noblest and best part of my life," he would later claim.[3] In 1872, the orator's Rochester home burned to the ground, and that event served as part symbol and part cause of Douglass's own implosion. Resettling in Washington, Douglass sought political appointment, but Hayes and Garfield gained more from the famous black American than Douglass was able to gain from them. For a time, Douglass lost his identity as an outsider and critic lobbying for the welfare of the freedmen in America.

In the 1890s, he rose from the ashes of disappointment and confusion. He spoke on behalf of black suffrage and its benefit to the nation. He joined Ida Wells in denouncing the wave of Southern lynchings. He renewed his advocacy of women's rights. He supported Booker T. Washington's emphasis on self-help and self-education, telling blacks to "measure yourselves from the depths from which you have come."[4] And he again told his story, bringing his autobiography up to date, positioning himself as an example of what was possible for all men and women.

"There are moments in the lives of most men when the doors of their souls are open, and, unconsciously to themselves, their true characters may be read by the observant eye."[5] Throughout the war, Douglass kept the doors to his soul wide open. His words helped give birth to a newly constituted American Republic. His words reach forth and pull us back, forcing us to imagine what was, what is, and what might still be.

1. "Hope and Despair in These Cowardly Times," An Address
Delivered in Rochester, New York, April 28, 1861[6]

We meet here again after another week of deep, intense, heartfelt, widespread and thrilling excitement. I have never spent days so restless and anxious. Our mornings and evenings have continually oscillated between the dim light of hope, and the gloomy shadow of despair. We have opened our papers, new and damp from the press, tremblingly, lest the first line of the lightning should tell us that our National Capital has fallen into the hands of the traitors and murderers who have bound themselves as with an oath to break up our National Government.

The thing you and I want, most of all, to know, concerning this mighty strife, is yet far from us. We cannot see the end from the beginning. Our profoundest calculations may prove erroneous, our best hopes disappointed, and our worst fears confirmed. We live but to-day, and the measureless shores of the future are wisely hid from us. And yet we read the face of the sky, and may discern the signs of the times. We know that clouds and darkness, and the sounds of distant thunder mean rain. So, too, may we observe the fleecy drapery of the moral sky, and draw conclusions as to what may come upon us. There is a general feeling amongst us, that the control of events has been taken out of our hands, that we have fallen into the mighty current of eternal principles—invisible forces, which are shaping and fashioning events as they wish, using only as instruments to work out their own results in our National destiny.

I cannot claim to speak on this great movement of the great North, as one of the privileged class of the American people. I take my place cheerfully, with the enslaved and proscribed in the land, and from their humble and lowly position. I wish to view the events now transpiring, and rightly interpret their significance as affecting the oppressed and enslaved.

Nevertheless, I am not indifferent, but profoundly solicitous for the character, growth and destiny of this American republic, which but for slavery, would be the best governed country in the world. While, therefore, I may speak as a man, and view the great subject which now comes before us, as one of the oppressed, I can also speak as an American. All that I have and am, are bound up with the destiny of this country. When she is successful, I rejoice; when she is prosperous, I am happy; and when she is afflicted, I mourn with her as sincerely as any other citizen, for though not yet taken into full communion with her, I still feel she is my country, and that I must fall or flourish with her. But what of this war? What does it mean? And what results will it finally arrive at?

We all know what the rebels and traitors mean. They mean the perpetuity, and supremacy of slavery. They mean that the slave power shall control and administer the American government now and forever, or else that the government shall be destroyed, and that another shall be put in its place, of which slaveholders shall have absolute control; they mean in a word to have Washington, and to drive the present government away.

Once in possession of the machinery of the Federal Government they would place their iron yoke upon the necks of freemen, and make the system of Slavery the great and all commanding interest of the whole country. With their success the historian may record the decline and fall of American Liberty and Civilization, the banishment and proscription of free speech and free press, and the domination of a proud, selfish, cruel and semi-barbarous oligarchy—whose argument are bowie-knives, slingshot and revolvers.

It is this purpose that animate all their movements. The war on their part is for a government in which Slavery shall be National, and freedom no where, in which the capitalist shall own the Laborer. And the white non-slaveholder a degraded man—to be classed, as such men are now classed all over the South, as "poor white trash."

But what does the war mean to the North? This inquiry is far more important than any concerning the South, for the South can do nothing without the great North shall see fit to let her. I look upon the war as in the hands of the North. It should be made short or long, important or insignificant, as they shall and will determine.

There are many conflicting theories of the end in view of this war. To some it means the complete dissolution of the American Union, the absolute and final separation of the slaveholding States from the non-slaveholding States; a division of the national property, and an acknowledgment of the independence of the governments of the respective sections. To others it means simply the suppression of rebellion, and the establishment of things precisely as they were before the election of Mr. Lincoln, without any alterations of a single principle or inference of the old Union. To still another class, it means a national convention which shall reconstruct the Union upon a basis which shall remove the objections which the slaveholders have raised against the present one. While others see, or think they see, in it the complete humiliation of the slaveholders, and the abolition of slavery, and a strong federal government which will make successful resistance to its authority and power, useless if not improbable.

The complete dissolution of the Union will depend upon the will and ability of the government, and of the North that sustains it against the traitors and rebels of the South, who have attempted its destruction. It would be a most lame and impotent conclusion, after expending millions of treasure and rivers of blood, for the North to consent to a dissolution of the Union. Such a conclusion would be giving up the point contended for in the war, and would be a triumph of the South. It would brand the war as a useless and worthless war, and draw after it all the evils that the war was intended to avert and prevent. There are great natural as well as moral objections to such a termination of the conflict, which make it quite impossible.

All natural relations conspire to make the United States one country, under one government, and one general code of laws. Nature seems to have frowned upon separation, and welded the sections together so strongly as to defy permanent separation of the people who inhabit it. To the mighty rivers and fertile fields that bind it together, civilization, commerce and science flung over it a net-work of iron, making the sections one and indivisible. The great Mississippi river, father of waters, would look ill indeed in the possession of two rival nations. Dissolution is not a solution of our present troubles. . . . There can be no peace or unity in this country while slavery exists. Slavery is an enemy of free speech. It struck down Charles Sumner, and stained the floor of the Senate Chamber with his blood. The language of slavery is and always must be, "put out the light." The slaveholders know their vile institution will not bear discussion. All nature is opposed to slavery. The broad sunlight, the free roving winds, the blue o'erarching sky, and ocean's bounding billows, were all eloquent against the enslavement of man by his fellow man.

## 2. "The American Apocalypse," An Address Delivered in Rochester, New York, June 16, 1861

. . . Men have their choice in this world. They can be angels, or they may be demons. In the apocalyptic vision, John describes a war in heaven. You have only to strip that vision of its gorgeous Oriental drapery, divest it of its shining and celestial ornaments, clothe it in the simple and familiar language of common sense, and you will have before you the eternal conflict between right and wrong, good and evil, liberty and slavery, truth and falsehood, the glorious light of love, and the appalling darkness of human selfishness and sin. The human heart is a seat of constant war. Michael and his angels are still contending against the infernal host of bad passions, and excitement will last while the fight continues, and the fight will continue till one or the other is subdued. Just what takes place in individual human hearts, often takes place between nations, and between individuals of the same nation. Such is the struggle now going on in the United States. The slaveholders had rather reign in hell than serve in heaven. . . .

The strong and enduring power which anti-slavery truth naturally exercises upon the minds of men, when earnestly presented, is explained, as I have already intimated, not by the cunning arts of rhetoric, for often the simplest and most broken utterances of the uneducated fugitive slave, will be far more touching and powerful than the finest flights of oratory. The explanation of the power of anti-slavery is to be found in the inner and spontaneous consciousness, which every man feels of the comprehensive and stupendous criminality of slavery. There are many wrongs and abuses in the world that shock and wound the sensibilities of men. They are felt to be narrow in their scope, and temporary in their duration, and to require little effort for their removal. But not so can men regard slavery. It compels us to recognize it, as an ever active, ever increasing, all comprehensive crime against human nature. It is not an earthquake swallowing up a town or a city, and then leaving the solid earth undisturbed for centuries. It is not a Vesuvius which, belching forth its fire and lava at intervals, causes ruin in a limited territory; but slavery is felt to be a moral volcano, a burning lake, a hell on the earth, the smoke and stench of whose torments ascend upward forever. Every breeze that sweeps over it comes to us tainted with its foul miasma, and weighed down with the sighs and groans of its victims. It is a compendium of all the wrongs which one man can inflict upon a helpless brother. It does not cut off a right hand, nor pluck out a right eye, but strikes down at a single blow the God-like form of man. It does not merely restrict the rights, or lay heavy burdens upon its victims, grievous to be borne; but makes deliberate and constant war upon human nature itself, robs the slave of personality, cuts him off from the human family, and sinks him below even the brute. It leaves nothing standing to tell the world that here was a man and a brother. . . .

Slavery, like all other gross and powerful forms of wrong which appear directly to human pride and selfishness, when once admitted into the framework of society, has the ability and tendency to beget a character in the whole network of society surrounding it, favorable to its continuance. The very law of its existence is growth and dominion. Natural and harmonious relations easily repose in their own rectitude, while all such as are false and unnatural are conscious of their own weakness, and must seek strength from without. Hence the explanation of the uneasy, restless, eager anxiety of slaveholders. Our history shows that from the formation of this Government, until the attempt now making to break it up, this class of men have been constantly pushing schemes for the safety and supremacy of the class system. They have had marvelous success. They have completely destroyed freedom in the slave States, and were doing their best to accomplish the same in the free States. He is a very imperfect reasoner who attributes the steady rise and ascendency of slavery to anything else than the nature of slavery itself. Truth may be careless and forgetful, but a lie cannot afford to be either. Truth may repose upon its inherent strength, but a falsehood rests for support upon external props. Slavery is the most stupendous of all lies, and depends for existence upon a favorable adjustment of all its surroundings. Freedom of the speech, of the press, of education, of labor, of locomotion, and indeed all kinds of freedom, are felt to be a standing menace to slavery. Hence, the friends of slavery are bounded by the necessity of their system to do just what the history of the country shows they have done—that is, to seek to subvert all liberty, and to prevent all the safeguards of human rights. They could not do otherwise. It was the controlling law of their situation.

Now, if these views be sound, and are borne out by the whole history of American slavery, then for the statesman of this hour to permit any settlement of the present war between slavery and freedom, which will leave untouched and undestroyed the relation of master and slave, would not only be a great crime, but a great mistake, the bitter fruit of which would poison the life blood of unborn generations. No grander opportunity was ever given to any nation to signalize, either its justice and humanity, or its intelligence and statesmanship, than is now given to the loyal American people. We are brought to a point in our National career where two roads meet and divert. It is the critical moment for us. The destiny of the mightiest Republic in the modern world hangs upon the decision of that hour. If our Government shall have the wisdom to see, and the nerve to act, we are safe. If it fails, we perish, and go to our own place with those nations of antiquity long blotted from the maps of the world. I have only one voice, and that is neither loud nor strong. I speak to but few, and have little influence; but whatever I am or may be, I may, at such a time as this, in the name of justice, liberty and humanity, and in that of the permanent security and welfare of the whole nation, urge all men, and especially the Government, to the abolition of slavery. Not a slave should be left a slave in the returning footprints of the American army gone to put down this slaveholding rebellion. Sound policy, not less than humanity, demands the instant liberation of every slave in the rebel States.

### 3. FD to Samuel J. May,[7] Rochester, August 30, 1861

... It now seems to me that our Government has resolved that no good shall come to the Negro from this war, and that it means by every means in its power to convince the slaveholders that slavery is safer in than out of the union—that the slaveholding rebel is an object of higher regard than is his humble slave. The hope that the war would finally become an abolition war has been dissipated and men are now preparing for another attempt to preserve the liberty of the white man at the expense of that of the black. I have tried to be hopeful and do still try to be so—but I confess that it seems much like hoping against hope. What I feared would result from sudden success has come from defeat. The Government defeated seems as little disposed to carry the war to the abolition point as before. Who would have supposed that General Banks would have signalized the first week of his campaign on the Potomac by capturing slaves and returning them to their masters? He has done less to punish the rebels than to punish their victims. . . . Looking at the government in light of these and similar examples, and the fact that the government consents only that Negroes shall smell powder in the character of cooks and body servants in the army, my anti-slavery confidence is blown to the winds. I wait and work relying more upon the stern logic of events than upon any disposition of the Federal army towards slavery.

When I join any movement such as I suppose contemplated, I must have a country or the hope of a country under me—a government around me—and some flag of a Northern or Southern nation floating over me. The Negro can do much, but he can not hope to whip two nations at once. Not even the allowance that the Government at Washington would wink at a John Brown movement could induce me to join it. Nothing short of an open recognition of the Negro's manhood, his rights as such to have a country, to bear arms, and to defend that country equally with others would induce me to join the army in any capacity. I am sick of seeing mere isolated, extemporaneous insurrections the only result of which is the shooting and hanging of the few brave men who take part in them—and not being willing to take the chances of such an insurrection myself I could not advise any one else to take part in them. Whenever the government is ready to make the war, a war for freedom and progress and will receive the service of black men on the same terms upon which it receives that of other men I pledge myself to do one man's work in supplying the Government. . . .

### 4. "Fighting the Rebels with One Hand," An Address Delivered in Philadelphia, Pennsylvania, January 14, 1862

. . . I am to speak to you to-night of the civil war, by which this vast country— this continent is convulsed. The fate of the greatest of all modern republics trembles in the balance. "To be, or not to be—that is the question."[8] The lesson of the hour is written down in characters of blood and fire. We are taught, as with the emphasis of an earthquake, that nations, not less than individuals, are subjects of the moral government of the universe, and that flagrant, long continued, and persistent transgression of the laws of this Divine government will certainly bring national sorrow, shame, suffering and death. Of all the nations of the world, we seem most in need of this solemn lesson. To-day we have it brought home to our hearths, our homes, and our hearts.

Hitherto, we have been content to study this lesson in the history of ancient governments and nationalities. To-day, every thoughtful American citizen is compelled to look at home. Egypt, Palestine, Greece and Rome *all* had their warnings. They disregarded them, and they perished. To-day, we have our warning, not in comets blazing through the troubled sky, but in the terrible calamity of a wide-spread rebellion enacted before our eyes. The American Republic is not yet a single century from the date of its birth. Measuring its age by that of other great nations, our *great* Republic—for such it truly is—great in commerce, great in numbers, great in mechanical skill, great in mental, moral and physical resources, great in all the elements of national greatness—fills but a speck on the dial plate of time, and stands within the inner circle of childhood. In the brief space of three quarters of a century, this young nation, full of promise and the hope of political liberty throughout the world, rose from three millions to thirty millions. Its mighty heart beats with the best blood of all nations. It was literally sown in weakness and raised in power. It began life in toil and poverty, and up to the present moment, it is conspicuous among the nations of the earth for opulence and ease. In the fullness of our national strength and glory, we had already begun to congratulate ourselves upon the wisdom and stability of our Government. When all Europe, a few years ago, was convulsed with revolution and bloodshed, America was secure, and sat as a queen among the nations of the earth, knowing no sorrow and fearing none.

To-day, all is changed. The face of every loyal citizen is sicklied over the pale cast of thought. Every pillar in the national temple is shaken. The nation itself has fallen asunder in the centre. A million of armed men confront each other. Hostile flags wave defiance in sight of the National Capital during a period of six long and anxious months. Our riches take wings. Credit is disturbed, business is interrupted, national debt—the mill-stone on the neck of nations—and heavy taxation, which breaks the back of loyalty, loom in the distance. As the war progresses, property is wantonly destroyed, the wires are broken down, bridges demolished, railroads are pulled up and barricaded by fallen trees; still more and worse, the great writ of *habeas corpus* is suspended from necessity, liberty of speech and of the press have ceased to exist. An order from Richmond or Washington—one stroke of the pen from Davis or Lincoln sends any citizen to prison, as in England, three centuries ago. British subjects were sent to the Tower of London. A hateful system of espionage is in process of formation, while war and blood mantles the whole land as with the shadow of death. We speak and write now by the forbearance of our rulers, not by the sacredness of our rights. I speak this not in complaint; I admit the necessity, while I lament it. The scene need not be further portrayed. It is dismal and terrible beyond all description. We have it burnt upon our very souls. I will not mock you by further painting that scene. . . .

We have made the mistake—the great and deplorable mistake of supposing that we could sow to the wind without reaping the whirlwind. We have attempted to maintain our Union in utter defiance of the moral Chemistry of the universe. We have endeavored to join together things which in their nature stand eternally asunder. We have sought to bind the chains of slavery on the limbs of the black man, without thinking that at last we should find the other end of that hateful chain about our own necks.

A glance at the history of the settlement of the two sections of this country will show that the causes which produced the present rebellion, reach back to the dawn of civilization on this continent. In the same year that the *Mayflower* landed her liberty-seeking passengers on the bleak New England shore, a Dutch galliot landed a company of African slaves on the banks of the James river, Virginia. The *Mayflower* planted liberty at the North, and the Dutch galliot slavery at the South. There is the fire, and there is the gunpowder. Contact has produced the explosion. What has followed might have been easily predicted. Great men saw it from the beginning, but no great men were found great enough to prevent it.

The statesmanship of the last half century has been mainly taxed to perpetuate the American Union. A system of compromise and concessions has been adopted. A double dealing policy—a facing both-ways statesmanship, naturally sprung up, and became fashionable—so that political success was often made to depend upon political cheating. One section or the other must be deceived. Before railroads and electric wires were spread over the country, this trickery and fraud had a chance of success. The lightning made deception more difficult, and the Union by compromise impossible. Our Union is killed by lightning. . . .

I have often been asked since this war began, why I am not at the South battling for freedom. My answer is with the Government. The Washington Government wants men for its army, but thus far, it has not had the boldness to recognize the manhood of the race to which I belong. It only sees in the slave an article of commerce—a contraband. I do not wish to say aught against our Government, for good or bad; it is all we have to save us from anarchy and ruin; but I owe it to my race, in view of the cruel aspersions cast upon it, to affirm that, in denying them the privilege to fight for their country, they have been most deeply and grievously wronged. Neither in the Revolution, nor in the last war did any such narrow and contemptible policy obtain. It shows the deep degeneracy of our times—the height from which we have fallen—that, while Washington, in 1776, and Jackson, in 1814, could fight side by side with negroes, now, not even the best of our generals are willing so to fight. Is McClellan better than Washington? Is Halleck better than Jackson? . . .

Now, what is the remedy for all this? The answer is ready. Have done at once and forever with the wild and guilty phantasy that any one man can have a right of property in the body and soul of another man. Have done with the now exploded idea that the old Union, which has hobbled along through seventy years upon the crutches of compromise, is either desirable or possible, now, or in the future. Accept the incontestible truth of the "irrepressible conflict." It was spoken when temptations to compromise were less strong than now. Banish from your political dreams the last lingering adumbration that this great American nation can ever rest firmly and securely upon a mixed basis, part of iron, part of clay, part free, and part slave. The experiment has been tried, and tried, too, under more favorable circumstances than any which the future is likely to offer, and has deplorably failed. Now lay the axe at the root of the tree, and give it—root, top, body and branches—to the consuming fire. You have now the opportunity.

> "There is a tide in the affairs of men
> Which, taken at the flood, leads on to fortune
> Omitted, all the voyage of ther lives
> Is bound in shallows and in miseries.
> On such a full sea are we now afloat.
> We must take the current when it serves,
> Or lose our ventures."[9]

To let this occasion pass unimproved, for getting rid of slavery, would be a sin against unborn generations. . . .

## 5. "The Black Man's Future in the Southern States," An Address Delivered in Boston, Massachusetts, February 5, 1862

. . . I have studied slavery and studied freedom on both sides of Mason and Dixon's line. Nearly twenty-two years of my life were spent in Slavery, and more than twenty-three have been spent in freedom. I am of age in both conditions, and there seems an eminent fitness in allowing me to speak for myself and my race. If I take my stand to-night as I shall do, with the down-trodden and enslaved, and view the facts of the hour more as a bondman than as a freeman, it is not because I feel no interest in the general welfare of the country. Far from it.

I am an American citizen. In birth, in sentiment, in ideas, in hopes, in aspirations, and responsibilities. I am an American citizen. According to Judge Kent[10] there are but two classes of people in America: they are citizens and aliens, natives and foreigners. Natives are citizens—foreigners are aliens until naturalized.

But I am not only a citizen by birth and lineage. I am such by choice.

I once had a very tempting offer of citizenship in another country; but declined it because I preferred the hardships and duties of my mission here. I have never regretted that decision, although my pathway has been anything than a smooth one; and to-night, I allow no man to exceed me in the desire for the safety and welfare of this country. And just here do allow me to boast a little.

There is nothing in the circumstances of the present hour, nothing in the behavior of the colored people, either North or South, which requires apology at my hands. Though everywhere spoken against, the most malignant and unscrupulous of all our slanderers have not, in this dark and terrible hour of the nation's trial dared to accuse us of a want of patriotism or loyalty. Though ignored by our friends and repelled by our enemies, the colored people, both North and South, have evinced the most ardent desire to serve the cause of the country, as against the rebels and traitors who are endeavoring to break it down and destroy it. That they are not largely represented in the loyal army, is the fault of the Government, and a very grievous fault it is. Mark here our nation's degeneracy. Colored men were good enough to fight under Washington. They are not good enough to fight under McClellan. They were good enough to fight under Andrew Jackson. They are not good enough to fight under Gen. Halleck. They were good enough to help win American independence but they are not good enough to help preserve that independence against treason and rebellion. They were good enough to defend New Orleans but not good enough to defend our poor beleaguered Capital. I am not arguing against, not condemning those in power, but simply stating facts in vindication of my people; and as these facts stand, I do say that I am proud to be recognized here as an humble representative of that rejected race. Whether in peace or war, whether in safety or in peril, whether in evil report or good report, at home or abroad, my mission is to stand up for the down-trodden, to open my mouth for the dumb, to remember those in bonds as bound with them. . . .

The field is ripe for the harvest. God forbid that when the smoke and thunder of this slaveholding war shall have rolled from the troubled face of our country it shall be said that the harvest is past, the summer is ended and we are not saved. . . .

Why, O why, should we not abolish slavery now? All admit that it must be abolished at some time. What better time than now can be assigned for that great work? Why should it longer live? What good thing has it done that it should be given further lease of life? What evil thing has it left undone? Behold its dreadful history! Saying nothing of the rivers of tears and streams of blood poured out by its 4,000,000 victims—saying nothing of the leprous poison it has diffused through the life blood of our morals and our religion—saying nothing of the many humiliating concessions already made to it—saying nothing of the deep and scandalous reproach it has brought upon our national good name—saying nothing of all this, and more the simple fact that this monster Slavery has eaten up and devoured the patriotism of the whole South, kindled the lurid flames of a bloody rebellion in our midst, invited the armies of hostile nations to desolate our soil, and break down our Government, is good and all-sufficient cause for smiting it as with a bolt from heaven. If it is possible for any system of barbarism to sign its own death warrant, Slavery by its own natural working, is that system. All the arguments of conscience, sound expediency, national honor and safety unite in the fiat—let it die the death of its own election. . . .

It is one of the strangest and most humiliating triumphs of human selfishness and prejudice over human reason, that it leads men to look upon emancipation as an experiment, instead of being, as it is, the natural order of human relations. Slavery, and not Freedom, is the experiment; and to witness its horrible failure we have to open our eyes, not merely upon the blasted soil of Virginia and other Slaves States, but upon a whole land brought to the verge of ruin.

We are asked if we would turn the slaves all loose. I answer, Yes. Why not? They are not wolves nor tigers, but men. They are endowed with reason—can decide upon questions of right and wrong, good and evil, benefits and injuries—and are therefore subjects of government precisely as other men are.

But would you have them stay here? Why should they not? What better is here than there? What class of people can show a better title to the land on which they live than the colored people of the South? They have watered the soil with their tears and enriched it with their blood, and tilled it with their hard hands during two centuries; they have leveled its forests, taken out the obstructions to the plow and hoe, reclaimed the swamps, and produced whatever has made it a goodly land to dwell in, and it would be a shame and a crime little inferior in enormity to Slavery itself if these natural owners of the Southern and Gulf States should be driven away from their country to make room for others—even if others could be obtained to fill their places. . . .

My friends, the destiny of the colored American, however this mighty war shall terminate, is the destiny of America. We shall never leave you. The allotments of Providence seem to make the black man of America the open book out of which the American people are to learn lessons of wisdom, power, and goodness—more sublime and glorious than any yet attained by the nations of the old or the new world. Over the bleeding back of the American bondman we shall learn mercy. In the very extreme difference of color and feature of the negro and the Anglo-Saxon, shall be learned the highest ideas of sacredness of man and the fullness and protection of human brotherhood.

## 6. "The Slaveholders' Rebellion," An Address Delivered at Himrod's, New York, July 4, 1862

Never was this national anniversary celebrated in circumstances more trying, more momentous, more solemn and perilous, than those by which this nation is now so strongly environed. We present to the world at this moment, the painful spectacle of a great nation, undergoing all the bitter pangs of a gigantic and bloody revolution. We are torn and rent asunder, we are desolated by large and powerful armies of our own kith and kin, converted into desperate and infuriated rebels and traitors, more savage, more fierce and brutal in their modes of warfare, than any recognized barbarians making no pretensions to civilization.

In the presence of this troubled and terrible state of the country, in the appalling jar and rumbling of this social Earthquake, when sorrow and sighing are heard throughout our widely extended borders, when the wise and brave men of the land are everywhere deeply and sadly contemplating this solemn crisis as one which may permanently decide the fate of the nation I should greatly transgress the law of fitness, and violate my own feelings and yours, if I should on this occasion attempt to entertain you by delivering anything of the usual type of our 4th of July orations. The hour is one for sobriety, thoughtfulness and stern truthfulness. When the house is on fire, when destruction is spreading its baleful wings everywhere, when helpless women and children are to be rescued from devouring flames a true man can neither have ear nor heart for anything but the thrilling and heart rending, cry for help. Our country is now on fire. No man can now tell what the future will bring forth. . . .

The past may be dismissed with a single word. The claims of our fathers upon our memory, admiration and gratitude, are founded in the fact that they wisely, and bravely, and successfully met the crisis of their day. And if the men of this generation would deserve well of posterity they must like their fathers, discharge the duties and responsibilities of their age. . . .

I hold that this conflict is the logical and inevitable result of a long and persistent course of national transgression. . . . The date of the Missouri Compromise forms the beginning of that political current which has swept us on to this rebellion, and made the conflict unavoidable. From this dark date in our nation's history, there started forth a new political and social power. Until now slavery had been on its knees, only asking time to die in peace. But the Missouri Compromise gave it a new lease of life. It became at once a tremendous power. The line of thirty-six degrees, thirty minutes, at once stamped itself upon our national politics, our morals, manners, character and religion. From this time there was a south side to everything American, and the country was at once subjected to the slave power, a power as restless and vigilant as the eye of an escaping murderer. We became under its sway an illogical nation. Pure and simple truth lost its attraction for us. We became a nation of Compromisers. . . .

This slavery begotten and slavery sustained, and slavery animated war, has now cost this nation more than a hundred thousand lives, and more than five hundred millions of treasure. It has weighed down the national heart with sorrow and heaviness, such as no speech can portray. It has cast a doubt upon the possibility of liberty and self Government which it will require a century to remove. The question is, shall this stupendous and most outrageous war be finally and forever ended? or shall it be merely suspended for a time, and again revived with increased and aggravated fury in the future? Can you afford a repetition of this costly luxury? Do you wish to transmit to your children the calamities and sorrows of to-day? The way to either class of these results is open to you. By urging upon the nation the necessity and duty of putting an end to slavery, you put and end to the war, and put an end to the cause of the war, and make any repetition of it impossible. But, just take back the pet monster again into the bosom of the nation, proclaim an amnesty to the slaveholders, let them have their slaves, and command your services in helping to catch and hold them, and so sure as like causes will ever produce like effects, you will hand down to your children here, and hereafter, born and to be born all the horrors through which you are now passing. I have told you of the great national opportunities in the past[;] a greater [one] than any in the past is the opportunity of the present. If now we omit the duty it imposes, steel our hearts against its teachings, or shrink in cowardice from the work of to-day, your fathers will have fought and bled in vain to establish free Institutions, and American Republicanism will become a hissing and a by-word to a mocking earth.

## 7. "The Day of Jubilee Comes," An Address Delivered in Rochester, New York, December 28, 1862

This is scarcely a day for prose. It is a day for poetry and song, a new song. These cloudless skies, this balmy air, this brilliant sunshine, (making December as pleasant as May,) are in harmony with the glorious morning of liberty about to dawn upon us. Out of a full heart and with sacred emotion, I congratulate you my friends, and fellow citizens, on the high and hopeful condition, of the cause of human freedom and the cause of our common country, for these two causes are now one and inseparable and must stand or fall together. We stand to-day in the presence of a glorious prospect. This sacred Sunday in all the likelihoods of the case, is the last which will witness the existence of legal slavery in all the Rebel slaveholding States of America. Henceforth and forever, slavery in those States is to be recognized, by all the departments [of] the American Government, under its appropriate character, as an unmitigated robber and pirate, branded as the sum of all villainy, an outlaw having no rights which any man white or colored is bound to respect. It is difficult for us who have toiled so long and hard to believe that this event, so stupendous, so far reaching and glorious is even now at the door. It surpasses our most enthusiastic hopes that we live at such a time and are likely to witness the downfall, at least the legal downfall of slavery in America. It is a moment for joy, thanksgiving and Praise. . . .

Slavery has existed in this country too long and has stamped its character too deeply and indelibly, to be blotted out in a day or a year, or even in a generation. The slave will yet remain in some sense a slave, long after the chains are taken from his limbs, and the master will retain much of the pride, the arrogance, imperiousness and conscious superiority, and love of power, acquired by his former relation of master. Time, necessity, education, will be required to bring all classes into harmonious and natural relations. . . .

Law and the sword can and will, in the end abolish slavery. But law and the sword cannot abolish the malignant slaveholding sentiment which has kept the slave system alive in this country during two centuries. Pride of race, prejudice against color, will raise their hateful clamor for oppression of the negro as heretofore. The slave having ceased to be the abject slave of a single master, his enemies will endeavor to make him the slave of society at large. . . . [T]he friends of freedom, the men and women of the land who regard slavery as a crime and the slave as a man will still be needed even after slavery is abolished.

## 8. "January First, 1863," *Douglass' Monthly*, January 1863

The first of January, which is now separated from us only by a few days and hours, is probably looked forward to with an intense and all surpassing interest, by all classes of the American people and from the most opposite reasons and motives. The slave hopes to gain his liberty, the slaveholders fear the loss of Slaves, and northern doughfaces fear the loss of political power. It is a pivotal period in our national history—the great day which is to determine the destiny not only of the American Republic, but that of the American Continent. Far off in the after coming centuries, some Gibbon[11] with truthful pen, will fix upon that date, as the beginning of a glorious rise, or of a shameful fall of the great American Republic. Unquestionably, for weal or for woe, the first of January is to be the most memorable day in American Annals. The fourth of July was great, but the first of January, when we consider it in all its relations and bearings, is incomparably greater. The one had respect to the mere political birth of a nation, the last concerns the national life and character, and is to determine whether that life and character shall be radiantly glorious with all high and noble virtues, or infamously blackened, forevermore, with all the hell darkened crimes and horrors which attach to Slavery—it is whether our national life shall be to ourselves and the world, a withering curse or a benediction of all national blessedness for ages to come. We may well stay before it and amplify it. It is an occasion which can happen but seldom in the life of any nation. It is not the creation of individual design and calculation, but the grand result of stupendous, all controlling, wide sweeping national events. Powerful as Mr. Lincoln is, he is but the hands of the clock. He cannot change the pivotal character of the day. The word has gone forth—and no system of balancing of props here, or weight there, can possibly anchor the national ship in anything like a stationary position after the first of January. From that day, her ample form will swing round, her towering rails will be swelled by the trade winds of the Almighty and she will either be wafted off gloriously to the open sea, on a prosperous voyage, or furiously driven by rebellious gales upon the sharp and flinty rocks only to mark the place of danger to other and aftercoming voyagers. We repeat, there is no escape. The tide is reached which must be taken at the flood.—For the present the Angel of Liberty has one ear of the nation and the demon of Slavery the other. One or the other must prevail on the first of January. The national head swings, pendulum like, now to the one side and now to the other. Alas, no man can tell which will prevail—and we are compelled to wait, hope, labor and pray. . . .

### 9. "The Proclamation and the Negro Army," An Address Delivered in New York, New York, on February 6, 1863

. . . Born and reared as a slave, as I was, and wearing on my back the marks of the slavedriver's lash, as I do, it is natural that I should value the Emancipation Proclamation for what it is destined to do for the slaves. I do value it for that. It is a mighty event for the bondman, but it is a still mightier event for the nation at large, and mighty as it is for both, the slave and the nation, it is still mightier when viewed in its relation to the cause of truth and justice throughout the world. It is in this last character that I prefer to consider it. . . .

It is again objected to this Proclamation that it is only an ink and paper proclamation. I admit it. The objector might go a step further, and assert that there was a time when this Proclamation was only a thought, a sentiment, an idea—a hope of some radical Abolitionist—for such it truly was. But what of it? The world has never advanced a single inch in the right direction, when the movement could not be traced to some such small beginning. The bill abolishing Slavery, and giving freedom to eight hundred thousand people in the West Indies, was a paper bill. The Reform bill, that broke up the rotten borough system in England, was a paper bill. The act of Catholic Emancipation was a paper act; and so was the bill repealing the Corn Laws. Greater than all, our own Declaration of Independence was at one time but ink and paper. The freedom of the American colonies dates from no particular battle during the war. No man can tell upon what particular day we won our national independence. But the birth of our freedom is fixed on the day of the going forth of the Declaration of Independence. In like manner aftercoming generations will celebrate the first of January as the day which brought liberty and manhood to the American slaves. How shall this be done? I answer: That the paper Proclamation must now be made iron, lead and fire, by the prompt employment of the negro's arm in this contest. I hold that the Proclamation, good as it is, will be worthless— a miserable mockery—unless the nation shall so far conquer its prejudice as to welcome into the army full-grown black men to help fight the battles of the Republic....

Do you ask me whether black men will freely enlist in the service of the country? I tell you that that depends upon the white men of the country. The Government must assure them of protection as soldiers, and give them a fair chance of winning distinction and glory in common with other soldiers. They must not be made the mere hewers of wood and drawers of water for the army. When a man leaves home, family, and security, to risk his limbs and life in the field of battle, for God's sake let him have all the honor which he may achieve, let his color be what it may. If, by the fortunes of war he is flung into the hands of the Rebels, let him be assured that the loyal Government will not desert him, but will hold the Confederate Government strictly responsible, as much for a black as for a white soldier. Give us fair play, and open here your recruiting offices, and their doors shall be crowded with black recruits to fight battles of the country. Do your part, my white fellow-countrymen, and we will do ours.... The colored man only waits for honorable admission into the service of the country. They know that who would be free, themselves must strike the blow, and they long for the opportunity to strike that blow....

I know the colored men of the North; I know the colored men of the South. They are ready to rally under the stars and stripes at the first tap of the drum. Give them a chance; stop calling them "niggers," and call them soldiers. Give them a chance to seek the bubble reputation at the cannon's mouth.[12] Stop telling them they can't fight, and tell them they can fight and shall fight, and they will fight, and fight with vengeance. Give them a chance....

### 10. "The Present and Future of the Colored Race in America," An Address Delivered in Brooklyn, New York, May 15, 1863

... All the circumstances of the hour plead with an eloquence, equaled by no human tongue, for the immediate solution of this vital problem. 200,000 graves.—A distracted and bleeding country plead for this solution. It cannot be denied, nobody now even attempts to deny that, the question, what shall be done with the negro, is the one grand cause of the tremendous war now upon us, and likely to continue upon us, until the country is united upon some wise policy concerning it. When the country was at peace and all appeared prosperous, there was something like a plausible argument in favor of leaving things to their own course. No such policy avails now. The question now stands before us as one of life and death. We are encompassed by it as by a wall of fire. The flames singe and burn us on all sides, becoming hotter every hour.

Men sneer at it as the "nigger question," endeavoring to degrade it by misspelling it. But they degrade nothing but themselves. They would much rather talk about the Constitution as it is, and the Union as it was, or about the Crittenden,[13] or some other impossible compromise, but the negro peeps out at every flash of their rhetorical pyrotechnics and utterly refuses to be hid by either fire, dust or smoke. The term negro is at this hour the most pregnant word in the English language. The destiny of the nation has the negro for its pivot, and turns upon the question as to what shall be done with him. Peace and war, union and disunion, salvation and ruin, glory and shame all crowd upon our thoughts the moment this vital word is pronounced.

You and I have witnessed many attempts to put this negro question out of the pale of popular thought and discussion, and have seen the utter vanity of all such attempts. It has baffled all the subtle contrivances of an ease loving and selfish priesthood, and has constantly refused to be smothered under the soft cushion of a canting and heartless religion. It has mocked and defied the compromising cunning of so-called statesmen, who would have gladly postponed our present troubles beyond our allotted space of life and bequeath[ed] them as a legacy of sorrow to our children. But this wisdom of the crafty is confounded and their counsels brought to naught. A divine energy, omniscient and omnipotent, acting through the silent, solemn and all pervading laws of the universe, irresistible, unalterable and eternal, has evermore forced this mighty question of the negro upon the attention of the country and the world.

What shall be done with the Negro? meets us not only in the street, in the Church, in the Senate, and in our State Legislatures; but in our diplomatic correspondence with foreign nations, and even on the field of battle, where our brave sons and brothers, are striking for Liberty and country, or for honored graves.

This question met us before the war; it meets us during the war, and will certainly meet us after the war, unless we shall have the wisdom, the courage, and the nobleness of soul to settle the status of the negro, on the solid and immovable basis of eternal justice.

I stand here to-night, to advocate what I conceive to be such a solid basis, one that shall fix our peace upon a rock. Putting aside all the hay, wood and stubble of expediency, I shall advocate for the negro, his most full and complete adoption into the great national family of America. I shall demand for him the most perfect civil and political equality, and that he shall enjoy all the rights, privileges and immunities enjoyed by any other members of the body politic. I

weigh my words and I mean all I say, when I contend as I do contend, that this
is the ONLY SOLID, AND FINAL SOLUTION of the problem before us. It
is demanded not less by the terrible exigencies of the nation than by the negro
himself, for the negro and the nation are to rise or fall, be killed or cured, saved
or lost together. Save the negro and you save the nation, destroy the negro and
you destroy the nation, and to save both you must have but one great law of
Liberty, Equality and fraternity for all Americans without respect to color. . . .

### 11. "Emancipation, Racism, and the Work Before Us," An Address Delivered in Philadelphia, Pennsylvania, December 4, 1863

. . . Abraham Lincoln will not go down to posterity as Abraham the Great, or
as Abraham the Wise, or as Abraham the Eloquent, although he is all three,
wise, great, and eloquent. [H]e will go down to posterity, if the country is
saved, as Honest Abraham; and going down thus, his name may be written anywhere in this wide world of ours side by side with that of Washington, without
disparaging the latter.

But we are not to be saved by the captain this time, but by the crew. We are
not to be saved by Abraham Lincoln, but by the power behind the throne,
greater than the throne itself. You and I and all of us have this matter in hand.
Men talk about saving the Union, and restoring the Union as it was. They
delude themselves with the miserable idea that that old Union can be brought
to life again. That old Union, whose canonized bones we so quietly inurned
under the shattered walls of Sumter, can never come to life again. It is dead,
and you cannot put life into it. The first shot fired at the walls of Sumter caused
it to fall as dead as the body of Julius Caesar when stabbed by Brutus. We do
not want it. We have outlived the old Union. We had outlived it long before
the rebellion came to tell us—I mean the Union under the old pro-slavery interpretation of it—and had become ashamed of it. The South hated it with our
anti-slavery interpretation, and the North hated it with the Southern interpretation of its requirements. We had already come to think with horror of the
idea of being called upon here in our churches and literary societies, to take up
arms and go down South, and pour the leaden death into the breasts of the
slaves, in case they should rise for liberty; and the better part of the people did
not mean to do it. They shuddered at the idea of so sacrilegious a crime. They
had already become utterly disgusted with the idea of playing the part of blood-
hounds for the slave-masters, and watch-dogs for the plantations. They had
come to detest the principle upon which the slaveholding States had a larger
representation in Congress than the free States. They had come to think that
the little finger of dear old John Brown was worth more to the world than all

the slaveholders in Virginia put together. What business, then, have we to fight for the old Union? We are not fighting for it. We are fighting for something incomparably better than the old Union. We are fighting for unity; unity of object, unity of institutions, in which there shall be no North, no South, no East, no West, no black, no white, but a solidarity of the nation, making every slave free, and every free man a voter.

Ralph Waldo Emerson *(By permission of the Houghton Library, Harvard University)*

# Ralph Waldo Emerson
## (1803–1882)

Emerson peered into the war and liked what he saw. War, he said, was "teacher," "instructor," "searcher," "magnetiser," and "reconciler." It disorganized but also organized; it threatened but also purged. Its origins, he thought, were not narrowly political, but organic, lodged from the beginning in hearts and heads and ways of living. Emerson the idealist welcomed war the realist. War was a grave and war was a poem. He became lyrical over the death all around him. He viewed the relationship between the individual and the state, between freedom and law, between innocence and sin. The war was "a new glass to see all old things through," and the philosopher from Concord refocused his sights.[1]

The most famous intellectual in America at the time of the Civil War, Emerson had started out confused and rebellious. Like his father he became a minister, but he resigned his pulpit in 1832 feeling that Unitarianism did not respond to the stirrings of the heart. In the next decade, he developed his ideas on the place of the individual in society. In *Nature* (1836) he encouraged readers to break free from the stranglehold of the past, from empirical science, and from artificial social arrangements, all of which had combined to fracture and blind mankind. He called for intuition and spontaneity, for a return to nature which meant feeling the "currents of the Universal Being circulate through me." "I am part or parcel of God," he proclaimed, an idea that scandalized most religious authorities.[2]

For twenty-five years he did not let up. In his oration "The American Scholar" (1837), he decried the dismemberment of individuals by society and called for a new life of the mind in America. In his "Divinity School Address" (1838), he came to Harvard, his alma mater, and denounced the impotence of the ministry, rejected the divinity of Christ, and attacked the place of miracles in Christianity; he would not be invited back for nearly thirty years. In "Self-Reliance" (1841), he issued a call for originality, even non-conformity. By the time he was done, he had followers. Some were also young New England men and women who gathered together, became known as Transcendentalists, and published a paper called *The Dial* (1840–44). Others were less devoted but greater in number, for when Emerson left the church he became a secular prophet who toured the country lecturing sold-out audiences on such topics as Culture, Education, and History.

He was a philosopher, a philosopher for whom life did not come easily. He grieved over the death of his first wife in 1831, his brother in 1836, and his five-year old son in 1842, grieved until he could only grieve that he could grieve no more—no wonder he could absorb the death all around him during the Civil War. He lamented his own iciness and inability to get close to others and often bristled at the idea of joining a reform association or utopian community—no wonder he embraced the war as a chance to come in from the frost and involve himself in the questions of his age. He offered harsh judgments, at times more in keeping with the opinions of conservative New England merchants than those of Transcendentalists—no wonder he continued to denounce Irishmen and Southerners, continued to lament the failure of his English friends to join the Union cause.

If Emerson the individualist and idealist had reservations about the machinery of war, Emerson the Unionist and realist celebrated the creation of a new order. Sometimes his meditations led him to employ a new language, a new way of thinking about the subject, as when he talks in scientific terms about measuring and calculating the effects of war. At other times, those meditations led him to rely on an old and familiar language, as when he thinks in terms of sin and redemption, or talks about having been "planted . . . on a law of nature."

The war stimulated Emerson's last burst of creative energy. He wrote extensively, both for his own eyes and for the eyes of others. He lectured widely, speaking on such topics as "American Nationality," "Courage," and "The Fortune of the Republic." He worked locally, supporting Concord's contribution to the war effort, and nationally, serving on a committee of visitation at West Point and traveling to Washington to meet Lincoln and the Cabinet. The man who once claimed he was "born a seeing eye, not a helping hand," now took a radical position on the question of emancipation and helped shape Administration policy and mold public opinion.[3]

It would be a mistake, however, to paint Emerson in only one hue as patriot and nationalist. At times he wondered whether "this mad war has made us all mad." And he was again driven inward and challenged to remember an earlier time by the death of two neighbors during the war. In 1862, Henry David Thoreau, aged forty-four, died of tuberculosis. Thoreau had opposed the Mexican War, and one can not help but wonder if teacher and disciple discussed the morality of the Civil War. And in 1864, Hawthorne died. Emerson was enraged by Hawthorne's friendship with Franklin Pierce, but in his journal he regretted waiting too long to "conquer a friendship" with the novelist. In November 1865, he expressed disappointment that his highest hopes for the outcome of the war had not been realized: "We hoped that in Peace, after such a war, a great expansion would follow in the mind of the country: grand views in every direction,—true freedom in politics, in religion, in social science, in thought. But the energy of the nation seems to have expended itself in the war, and every interest is found as sectional & timorous as before."[4]

Especially during the years of the Civil War, there was no separating the lines of friendship, memory, philosophy, politics, life and death. Wherever he turned, Emerson had to think about others and he had to think about self. He had been doing this for many years; when he retired from war he spent the last years of his life in a sun-drenched study, content in his solitude, gazing beyond the garden wall.

## 1. RWE, Journal GL,[5] 1861

The country is cheerful & jocund in the belief that it has a government at last. The men in search of a party, parties in search of a principle, interests & dispositions that could not fuse for want of some base,—all joyfully unite in this great Northern part, on the basis of Freedom. What a healthy tone exists! I suppose when we come to fighting, & many of our people are killed, it will yet be found that the bills of mortality in the country will show a better result of this year than the last, on account of the general health; no dyspepsia, no consumption, no fevers, where there is so much electricity, & conquering heart & mind.

## 2. RWE to Herman Grimm, Concord, June 27, 1861

. . . We are cleaning up America in these days to give you a better reception. You will have interested yourself to some extent, I am sure, in our perverse politics. What shall I say to you of them? 'Tis a mortification that because a nation had no enemy, it should become its own; and, because it has an immense future, it should commit suicide! Sometimes I think it a war of manners. The Southern climate and slavery generate a marked style of manners. The people are haughty, self-possessed, suave, and affect to despise Northern manners as of the shop and compting-room; whilst we find the planters picturesque, but frivolous and brutal. Northern labor encroaches on the planters daily, diminishing their political power, whilst their haughty temper makes it impossible for them to play a second part. The day came when they saw that the Government, which their party had hitherto controlled, must now, through the irresistible census, pass out of their hands. They decided to secede. The outgoing administration let them have their own way, and when the new Government came in, the rebellion was too strong for any repression short of vast war; and our Federal Government has now 300,000 men in the field. To us, before yet a battle has been fought, it looks as if the disparity was immense, and that we possess all advantages,—whatever may be the issue of first collisions. If we may be trusted, the war will be short,—and yet the parties must long remain in false position, or can only come right by means of the universal repudiation of its leaders by the South. . . .

### 3. RWE to James Eliot Cabot, Concord, August 4, 1861

. . . The war,—though from such despicable beginnings, has assumed such huge proportions that it threatens to engulf us all—no preoccupation can exclude, & no hermitage hide us—And yet, gulf as it is, the war with its defeats & uncertainties is immensely better than what we lately called the integrity of the Republic, as amputation is better than cancer. I think we are all agreed in this, and find it out by wondering why we are so pleased, though so beaten & so poor. No matter how low down, if not in false position. If the abundance of heaven only sends us a fair share of light & conscience, we shall redeem America for all its sinful years since the century began. At first sight, it looked only like a war of manners, showing that the southerner who owes to climate & slavery his suave, cool, & picturesque manners, is so impatient of ours, that he must fight us off. And we all admired them until a long experience only varying from bad to worse has shown us, I think finally, what a noxious reptile the green & gold thing was. Who was the French Madame who said of Talleyrand, "How can one help loving him he is so vicious?" But these spit such unmistakeable venom, that I think we are *désillusionnés* once for all. There is such frank confession in all they do, that they can have no secrets hereafter for us. Their detestation of Massachusetts is a chemical description of their substance, & if a state more lawful, honest, & cultivated were known to them, they would transfer to it this detestation. This *spiegato caratere* of our adversary makes our part & duty so easy. Their perversity is still forcing us into better positions than we had taken. Their crimes force us into virtues to antagonize them and we are driven into principles by their abnegation of them. Ah if we dared think that our people would be simply good enough to take & hold this advantage to the end!— But there is no end to the views the crisis suggests, & day by day. You see I have only been following my own lead, without prying into your subtle hints of ulterior political effects. But one thing I hope,—that 'scholar' & 'hermit' will no longer be exempts, neither by the country's permission nor their own, from the public duty. The functionaries, as you rightly say, have failed. The statesmen are all at fault. The good heart & mind, out of all private corners, should speak & save. . . .

## 4. RWE, Journal GL, 1861 and 1862

The misfortune of war is that it makes the country too dependent on the action of a few individuals, as the generals, cabinet officer, &c. who direct the important military movement & action of the great masses of citizens. . . .

August 5. The war goes on educating us to a trust in the simplicities, and to see the bankruptcy of all narrow views. The favorite pet policy of a district, the *épicier* party of Boston or N York, is met by conflicting *épicier* party in Philadelphia, another in Cincinnati, others in Chicago & St Louis, so that we are forced still to grope deeper for something catholic & universal, wholesome for all. Thus war for the Union is broader than any State policy, or Tariff, or Maritime, or Agricultural, or Mining interest. Each of these neutralizes the other. But, at last, Union Party is not broad enough, because of Slavery, which poisons it; and we must come to "emancipation with compensation to the Loyal States," as the only broad & firm ground. This is a principle. Every thing else is an intrigue. . . .

The War is a great teacher, still opening our eyes wider to some larger consideration. It is a great reconciler, too, forgetting our petty quarrels as ridiculous. . . . But to me the first advantage of the War is the favorable moment it has made for the cutting out of our cancerous Slavery. Better that war & defeats continue, until we have come to that amputation. . . . I suppose, if the war goes on, it will be impossible to keep the combatants from the extreme ground on either side. In spite of themselves, one army will stand for slavery pure; & the other for freedom pure. . . .

War the searcher, of character, the test of men, has tried already so many reputations, has pricked so many bladders. 'Tis like the financial crises, which, once in ten or twenty years, come to try the men & institutions of trade; using, like them, no ceremony, but plain laws of gravity & force to try tension & resistance. Scott. McDowell, Maclellan [*sic*], Frémont, Banks, Butler, & I know not how many more, are brought up, each in turn, dragged up irresistibly to the anthropometer, measured & weighed, & the result proclaimed to the universe.

With this dynamometer, & not so much that as *rack* to try the tension of your muscles & bones, standing close at hand, everybody takes the hint, drops much of brag & pretension, & shortens his speeches. The fop in the street, the beau at the ball feels the war in the air,—the examiner, the insatiate demand for reality,—& becomes modest and serious. The writer is less florid, the wit is less fantastical. The epicure & the man of pleasure put some check & cover on their amusements. Everybody studies retrenchment & economy.

Every body bethinks himself how he shall behave, if worst should come to worst. It will not always serve, or may not, to stand aloof & contribute money. Shall we carry on a war by subscription and politely? They will conquer who take up the bayonet, or leave their other business and apply themselves to the business of war.

The war searches character, & acquits those whom I acquit, whom life acquits, those whose reality & spontaneous honesty & singleness appear. Force it requires. 'Tis not so much that you are moral, as that you are genuine, sincere, frank, & bold. I do not approve those who give money, or give their voices for liberty, from long habit, & the feminine predominance of sentiment; but the rough democrat who hates Garrison, but detests these southern traitors. The first class will go in the right way, but they are devoured by sentiments, like premature fruit ripened by the worm. The "logic of events" has become a household word. . . .

The War is a new glass to see all our old things through, how they look. Some of our trades stand the test well. Baking & butchering are good under all skies & times. Farming, haying, & wood chopping don't go out of vogue. Meat & coal & shoes we must have; but coach painting & bronze matchholders we can postpone for a while yet. Yet the music was heard with as much appetite as ever, and our Quintettes had only to put the "Starspangled Banner" into the Programme, to gain a hurra beside; but the concert could have prospered well without. And so if the Union were beaten, & Jeff Davis ruled Massachusetts, these flutes & fiddles would have piped & scraped all the same, & no questions asked. It only shows that those fellows have hitched on their apple-cart to a star, & so it gets dragged by might celestial. They know that few have thoughts or benefits, but all have ears; that the blood rolls to pulsebeat & tune, that the babe rhymes & the boy whistles, & they throw themselves on a want so universal, and as long as birds sing, ballad singers will, & organ grinders will grind out their bread. . . .

## 5. RWE, Journal War, 1862

Visit to Washington. 31 January, 1862. . . . The President impressed me more favorably than I had hoped. A frank, sincere, well-meaning man, with a lawyer's habit of mind, good clear statement of his fact, correct enough, not vulgar, as described; but with a sort of boyish cheerfulness, or that kind of sincerity & jolly good meaning that our class meetings on Commencement Days show, in telling our old stories over. When he has made his remark, he looks up at you with great satisfaction, & shows all his white teeth, & laughs. . . . When I was introduced to him, he said, "O Mr Emerson, I once heard you say in lecture, that a Kentuckian seems to say by his air & manners, *"Here I am; if you don't like me, the worse for you."* . . .

With the South the war is primary; with the North it is secondary; secondary of course to their trade, then also to their pleasure. The theatres & concerts are filled as usual. . . .

## 6. RWE, "American Civilization," *Atlantic Monthly,* 10 (April 1862): 502–522

. . . At this moment in America the aspects of political society absorb attention. In every house, from Canada to the Gulf, the children ask the serious father,— "What is the news of the war to-day? and when will there be better times?" The boys have no new clothes, no gifts, no journeys; the girls must go without new bonnets; boys and girls find their education, this year, less liberal and complete. All the little hopes that heretofore made the year pleasant are deferred. The state of the country fills us with anxiety and stern duties. We have attempted to hold together two states of civilization: a higher state, where labor and the tenure of land and the right of suffrage are democratical; and a lower state, in which the old military tenure of prisoners or slaves, and of power and land in a few hands, makes an oligarchy: we have attempted to hold these two states of society under one law. But the rude and early state of society does not work well with the later, nay, works badly, and has poisoned politics, public morals, and social intercourse in the Republic, now for many years.

The times put this question,—Why cannot the best civilization be extended over the whole country, since the disorder of the less civilized portion menaces the existence of the country? Is this secular progress we have described, this evolution of man to the highest powers, only to give him sensibility, and not to bring duties with it? Is he not to make his knowledge practical? to stand and to withstand? Is not civilization heroic also? Is it not for action? has it not a will? "There are periods," said Niebuhr, "when something much better than happiness and security of life is attainable." We live in a new and exceptional age.

America is another word for Opportunity. Our whole history appears like a last effort of the Divine Providence in behalf of the human race; and a literal slavish following of precedents, as by a justice of the peace, is not for those who at this hour lead the destinies of this people. The evil you contend with has taken alarming proportions, and you still content yourself with parrying the blows it aims, but, as if enchanted, abstain from striking at the cause.

If the American people hesitate, it is not for want of warning or advices. The telegraph has been swift enough to announce our disasters. The journals have not suppressed the extent of the calamity. Neither was there any want of argument or of experience. If the war brought any surprise to the North, it was not the fault of sentinels on the watch-towers, who had furnished full details of the designs, the muster, and the means of the enemy. Neither was anything concealed of the theory or practice of slavery. To what purpose make more big books of these statistics? There are already mountains of facts, if any one wants them. But people do not want them. They bring their opinions into the world. If they have a comatose tendency in the brain, they are pro-slavery while they live; if of a nervous sanguineous temperament, they are abolitionists. Then interests were never persuaded. Can you convince the shoe interest, or the iron interest, or the cotton interest, by reading passages from Milton or Montesquieu? You wish to satisfy people that slavery is bad economy. Why, the "Edinburgh Review" pounded on that string, and made out its case forty years ago. A democratic statesman said to me, long since, that, if he owned the State of Kentucky, he would manumit all the slaves, and be a gainer by the transaction. Is this new? No, everybody knows it. As a general economy it is admitted. But there is no one owner of the State, but a good many small owners. One man owns land and slaves; another owns slaves only. Here is a woman who has no other property,—like a lady in Charleston I knew of, who owned fifteen chimney-sweeps and rode in her carriage. It is clearly a vast inconvenience to each of these to make any change, and they are fretful and talkative, and all their friends are; and those less interested are inert, and, from want of thought, averse to innovation. It is like free trade, certainly the interest of nations, but by no means the interests of certain towns and districts, which tariff feeds fat; and the eager interest of the few overpowers the apathetic general conviction of the many. Banknotes rob the public, but are such a daily convenience that we silence our scruples, and make believe they are gold. So imposts are the cheap and right taxation; but by the dislike of people to pay out a direct tax, governments are forced to render life costly by making them pay twice as much, hidden in the price of tea and sugar.

In this national crisis, it is not argument that we want, but that rare courage which dares commit itself to a principle, believing that Nature is its ally, and will create the instruments it requires, and more than make good any petty and injurious profit which it may disturb. There never was such a combination as this of ours, and the rules to meet it are not set down in any history. We want men of original perception and original action, who can open their eyes wider than to a nationality, namely, to considerations of benefit to the human race, can act in the interest of civilization. Government must not be a parish clerk, a justice of the peace. It has, of necessity, in any crisis of the State, the absolute powers of a Dictator. The existing Administration is entitled to the utmost candor. It is to be thanked for its angelic virtue, compared with any executive experiences with which we have been familiar. But the times will not allow us to indulge in compliment. I wish I saw in the people that inspiration which, if Government would not obey the same, it would leave the Government behind, and create on the moment the means and executors it wanted. Better the war should more dangerously threaten us,—should threaten fracture in what is still whole, and punish us with burned capitals and slaughtered regiments, and so exasperate the people to energy, exasperate our nationality. There are Scriptures written invisibly on men's hearts, whose letters do not come out until they are enraged. They can be read by war-fires, and by eyes in the last peril. . . .

### 7. RWE, "The President's Proclamation," *Atlantic Monthly*, 10 (November 1862): 638-642

In so many arid forms which States incrust themselves with, once in a century, if so often, a poetic act and record occur. These are the jets of thought into affairs, when, roused by danger or inspired by genius, the political leaders of the day break the else insurmountable routine of class and local legislation, and take a step forward in the direction of catholic and universal interests. Every step in the history of political liberty is a sally of the human mind into the untried future, and has the interest of genius, and is fruitful in heroic anecdotes. Liberty is a slow fruit. It comes, like religion, for short periods, and in rare conditions as if awaiting a culture of the race which shall make it organic and permanent. Such moments of expansion in modern history were the Confession of Augsburg, the plantation of America, the English Commonwealth of 1648, the Declaration of American Independence in 1776, the British emancipation of slaves in the West Indies, the passage of the Reform Bill, the repeal of the Corn Laws, the Magnetic Ocean-Telegraph, though yet imperfect, the passage of the Homestead Bill in the last Congress, and now, eminently, President Lincoln's Proclamation on the twenty-second of September. These are acts of great scope, working on a long future, and on permanent interests, and honoring alike those who initiate and those who receive them. These measures provoke no noisy joy, but are received into a sympathy so deep as to apprise us that mankind are greater and better than we know. At such times it appears as if a new public were created to greet the new event. It is as when an orator, having ended the compliments and pleasantries with which he conciliated attention, and having run over the superficial fitness and commodities of the measures he urges, suddenly, lending himself to some happy inspiration, announces with vibrating voice the grand human principles involved,—the bravoes and wits who greeted him loudly thus far are surprised and overawed: a new audience is found in the heart of the assembly,—an audience hitherto passive and unconcerned, now at last so searched and kindled that they come forward, every one a representative of mankind, standing for all nationalities.

The extreme moderation with which the President advanced to his design,— his long-avowed expectant policy, as if he chose to be strictly the executive of the best public sentiment of the country, waiting only till it should be unmistakably pronounced,—so fair a mind that none ever listened so patiently to such extreme varieties of opinion,—so reticent that his decision has taken all parties by surprise, whilst yet it is the just sequel of his prior acts,—the firm tone in which he announces it, without inflation or surplusage,—all these have bespoken such favor to the act, that, great as the popularity of the President has been, we are beginning to think that we have underestimated the capacity and virtue which the Divine Providence has made an instrument of benefit so vast. He has been permitted to do more for America than any other American man. He is well entitled to the most indulgent construction. Forget all that we thought shortcomings, every mistake, every delay. In the extreme embarrassments of his part, call these endurance, wisdom, magnanimity, illuminated, as they now are, by this dazzling success. . . .

"Better is virtue in the sovereign than plenty in the season," say the Chinese. 'Tis wonderful what power is, and how ill it is used, and how its ill use makes life mean, and the sunshine dark. Life in America had lost much of its attraction in the later years. The virtues of a good magistrate undo a world of mischief, and, because Nature works with rectitude, seem vastly more potent than the acts of bad governors, which are ever tempered by the good-nature in the people, and the incessant resistance which fraud and violence encounter. The acts of good government work at a geometrical ration, as one midsummer day seems to repair the damage of a year of war.

A day which most of us dared not hope to see, an event worth the dreadful war, worth its costs and uncertainties, seems now to be close before us. October, November, December will have passed over beating hearts and plotting brains: then the hour will strike, and all men of African descent who have faculty enough to find their way to our lines are assured of the protection of American law.

It is by no means necessary that this measure should be suddenly marked by any signal results on the negroes or on the Rebel masters. The force of the act is that it commits the country to this justice,—that it compels the innumerable officers, civil, military, naval, of the Republic to range themselves on the line of this equity. It draws the fashion to this side. It is not a measure that admits of being taken back. Done, it cannot be undone by a new Administration. For slavery overpowers the disgust of the moral sentiment only through immemorial usage. It cannot be introduced as an improvement of the nineteenth century. This act makes that the lives of our heroes have not been sacrificed in vain. It makes a victory of our defeats. Our hurts are healed; the health of the nation is repaired. With a victory like this, we can stand many disasters. It does not promise the redemption of the black race: that lies not with us: but it relieves it of our opposition. The President by this act has paroled all the slaves in America; they will no more fight against us; and it relieves our race once for all of its crime and false position. The first condition of success is secured by putting ourselves right. We have recovered ourselves from our false position, and planted ourselves on a law of Nature.

> "If that fail,
> The pillared firmament is rottenness,
> And earth's base built on stubble."

The Government has assured itself of the best constituency in the world: every spark of intellect, every virtuous feeling, every religious heart, every man of honor, every poet, every philosopher, the generosity of the cities, the health of the country, the strong arms of the mechanics, the endurance of farmers, the passionate conscience of women, the sympathy of distant nations,—all rally to its support. . . .

The war existed long before the cannonade of Sumter, and could not be postponed. It might have begun otherwise or elsewhere, but war was in the minds and bones of the combatants, it was written on the iron leaf, and you might as easily dodge gravitation. If we had consented to a peaceable secession of the Rebels, the divided sentiment of the Border States made peaceable secession impossible, the insatiable temper of the South made it impossible, and the slaves on the border, wherever the border might be, were an incessant fuel to rekindle the fire. Give the Confederacy New Orleans, Charleston, and Richmond, and they would have demanded St. Louis and Baltimore. Give them these, and they would have insisted on Washington. Give them Washington, and they would have assumed the army and navy, and, through these, Philadelphia, New York, and Boston. It looks as if the battlefield would have been at least as large in that event as it is now. The war was formidable, but could not be avoided. The war was and is an immense mischief, but brought with it the immense benefit of drawing a line, and rallying the Free States to fix it impassably,—preventing the whole force of Southern connection and influence throughout the North from distracting every city with endless confusion, detaching that force and reducing it to handfuls, and, in the progress of hostilities, disinfecting us of our habitual proclivity, through the affection of trade, and the traditions of the Democratic party, to follow Southern leading. . . .

[I]t is to be noted, that, in the Southern States, the tenure of land, and the local laws, with slavery, give the social system not a democratic, but an aristo-cratic complexion; and those States have shown every year a more hostile and aggressive temper, until the instinct of self-preservation forced us into war. And the aim of the war on our part is indicated by the aim of the President's Proclamation, namely, to break up the false combination of Southern society, to destroy the piratic feature in it which makes it our enemy only as it is the enemy of the human race, and so allow its reconstruction on a just and healthful basis. Then new affinities will act, the old repulsions will cease, and, the cause of war being removed, Nature and trade may be trusted to establish a lasting peace.

We think we cannot overstate the wisdom and benefit of this act of the Gov-ernment. The malignant cry of the Secession press within the Free States, and the recent action of the Confederate Congress, are decisive as to its efficiency and correctness of aim. Not less so is the silent joy which has greeted it in all generous hearts, and the new hope it has breathed into the world.

It was well to delay the steamers at the wharves, until this edict could be put on board. It will be an insurance to the ship as it goes plunging through the sea with glad tidings to all people. Happy are the young who find the pestilence cleansed out of the earth, leaving open to them an honest career. Happy the old, who see Nature purified before they depart. Do not let the dying die: hold them back to this world, until you have charged their ear and heart with this message to other spiritual societies, announcing the melioration of our planet.

> "Incertainties now crown themselves assured,
> And Peace proclaims olives of endless age."

Meantime that ill-fated, much-injured race which the Proclamation respects will lose somewhat of the dejection sculptured for ages in their bronzed coun-tenance, uttered in the wailing of their plaintive music,—a race naturally benevolent, joyous, docile, industrious, and whose very miseries sprang from their great talent for usefulness, which, in a more moral age, will not only defend their independence, but will give them a rank among nations.

## 8. RWE, Journal VA, 1862

It is curious how negligent the public is of the essential qualifications of its representatives. They ask if a man is a republican? Yes. Is he a man of talent? Yes. And is he honest, & not looking for an office or a bribe? Yes, he is honest. Well then choose him by acclamation, & they go home & tell their wives with great satisfaction what a good thing they have done. But they forget to ask the fourth question, not less important than either of the others, & without which the others do not avail;—*has he a will?* . . .

The Supreme Court under Southern dictation pronounced, that, "the negro had no rights which the white man was bound to respect." Today, by the rebellion, the same rule holds & is worked against the Southerner; "The rebel has no rights which negro or white man is bound to respect." The world is upside down when this dictum comes from the Chief Justice of the Supreme Court of the United States of America. . . .

The points that glowed a little in yesterday's conversation, were, that the North must succeed. That is sure, was sure for 30 or 60 years back, was in the education, culture, & climate of our people;—they are bound to put through their undertakings. The exasperations of our people by the treacheries & savageness of the Southern warfare are most wholesome disinfectants from the potent influence of Southern manners on our imagination. It was certain also that the Southerner would misbehave; that he will not keep his word; that he will be overbearing, rapacious. Slavery corrupts & denaturalizes people, as it has done Anna Barnard. There is no more probity in a slaveholder than truth in a drunken Irishman. Our success is sure. Its roots are in our poverty, our Calvinism, our schools, our thrifty habitual industry, in our snow, & east wind, & farm-life, & sea-life. These able & generous merchants are the sons & grandsons of farmers, & mechanics & sailors. . . .

I look on the Southern victories as I look at those of the Mussulman over Christendom due to fanaticism, to the petulance & valor of a people who had nothing else & must make a brilliant onset & raise here & there. But ideas & their slow massive might are irresistible at last. The few lessons which the first had to teach are learned by the last in one or two campaigns, but the last vegetates eternally. The other reaches its short acme & decomposes in a day; violence & cunning are no match for wisdom. For they must find dogmas that are not ridiculous, that none can travestie, but that still return immortal like the sky, how long soever you have hid yourself in cellars. . . .

A movement in an aristocratic state does not argue a deep cause. A dozen good fellows may have had a supper & warmed each other's blood to some act of spite or arrogance, which they talk up & carry out the next month, or one man, Calhoun or Rhett, may have grown bilious, & his grumble & fury are making themselves felt at the Legislature. But, in a Democracy, every movement has a deepseated cause. . . .

When we build, our first care is to find good foundation. If the surface be loose, or sandy, or springy, we clear it away, & dig down to the hard pan, or, better, to the living rock, & bed our courses in that. So will we do with the state. The War is serving many good purposes. It is no respecter of respectable persons or of worn out party platforms. War is a realist, shatters everything flimsy & shifty, sets aside all false issues, & breaks through all that is not real as itself, comes to organize opinions & parties, resting on the necessities of man, like its own cannonade comes crushing in through party walls that have stood fifty or sixty years as if they were solid. The screaming of leaders, the votes by acclamation of conventions, are all idle wind. They cry for mercy but they cry to one who never knew the word. He is the Arm of the Fates and as has been said "nothing prevails against God but God." Everything must perish except that which must live.

Well, this is the task before us, to accept the benefit of the War: it has not created our false relations, they have created it. It simply demonstrates the rottenness it found. We watch its course as we did the cholera, which goes where predisposition already existed, took only the susceptible, set its seal on every putrid spot, & on none other, followed the limestone, & left the granite. So the War. Anxious Statesmen try to rule it, to slacken it here & let it rage there, to not exasperate, to keep the black man out of it; to keep it well in hand, nor let it ride over old party lines, nor much molest trade, and to confine it to the frontier of the two sections. Why need Cape Cod, why need Casco Bay, why need Lake Superior, know any thing of it? But the Indians have been bought, & they come down on Lake Superior; Boston & Portland are threatened by the pirate; more than that, Secession unexpectedly shows teeth in Boston, our parties have just shown you that the war is already in Massachusetts, as in Richmond.

Let it search, let it grind, let it overturn, &, like the fire when it finds no more fuel, it burns out. The war will show, as all wars do, what wrong is intolerable, what wrong makes and breeds all this bad blood. I suppose that it shows two incompatible states of society, freedom & slavery. If a part of this country is civilized up to a clear insight of freedom, & of its necessity, and another part is not so far civilized, then I suppose that the same difficulties will continue; the war will not be extinguished; no treaties, no peace, no Constitutions can paper over the lips of that red crater.

Only when, at last, so many parts of the country as can combine on an equal & moral contract,—not to protect each other in polygamy, or in kidnapping, or in eating men,—but in humane & just activities,—only so many can combine firmly & durably.

I speak the speech of an idealist. I say let the rule be right. If the theory is right, it is not so much matter about the facts. If the plan of your fort is right it is not so much matter that you have got a rotten beam or a cracked gun somewhere, they can by & by be replaced by better without tearing your fort to pieces. But if the plan is wrong, then all is rotten, & every step adds to the ruin. Then every screw is loose, and all the machine crazy. The question stands thus, reconstruction is no longer matter of doubt. All our action now is new & unconstitutional, & necessarily so. To bargain or treat at all with the rebels, to make arrangements with them about exchange of prisoners or hospitals, or truces to bury the dead, all unconstitutional & enough to drive a strict constructionist out of his wits. . . . Then how to reconstruct. I say, this time, go to work right. Go down to the pan, see that your works turn on a jewel. Do not make an impossible mixture. Do not lay your cornerstone on a shaking morass that will let down the superstructure into a bottomless pit again. Leave slavery out. Since (unfortunately as some may think,) God is God, & nothing satisfies all men but justice, let us have that, & let us stifle our prejudices against commonsense & humanity, & agree that every man shall have what he honestly earns, and, if he is a sane & innocent man, have an equal vote in the state, and a fair chance in society.

And I, speaking in the interest of no man & no party, but simply as a geometer of his forces, say that the smallest beginning, so that it is just, is better & stronger than the largest that is not quite just.

This time, no compromises, no concealments, no crimes that cannot be called by name, shall be tucked in under another name, like, "persons held to labor," meaning persons stolen, & "held," meaning held by hand-cuffs, when they are not under whips.

Now the smallest state so formed will & must be strong, the interest and the affection of every man will make it strong by his entire strength, and it will mightily persuade every other man, & every neighboring territory, to make it larger, and it will not reach its limits until it comes to people who think that they are a little cunninger than the maker of this world & the consciences of men.

## 9. RWE, Journal War, 1862, 1863

Negro Soldiers[6]

If the war means liberty to you you should enlist. It does mean liberty to you in the opinion of /Jeff Davis/ the South/ for the South says, we fight to plant slavery as our foundation. And of course we who resist the South, are forced to make liberty of the negro our foundation. I speak for the forces above us those issues which are made for us over our heads, under our feet, paramount to our wills. If you will not fight for your liberty, who will? If you will not, why then take men as they are and the Universe of men will say you are not worth fighting for. Go & be slaves forever & you shall have our aid to make you such. You had rather be slave than freemen. Go to your own place.

Plainly we must have a worthy cause for such soldiers as we send to battle or they shall not go. Do you think such lives as this city & state have yielded up already, the children of this famed city, the children of our public schools, the children of Harvard College, the best blood of our educated counties, objects of the most romantic hope & love, poets & romancers themselves—I attended the funeral of one of them & heard with hearty assent the voice that said that the whole state of S Carolina was not worth that one life—that these precious young men Lander, Lowell, Putnam, Dwight, Willard, the voice will choke to name them are given up to bring back into the Capital of Washington the reckless politicians who had reeled out of it with threats to destroy it, or come back into it to rule again? Never. Better put gunpowder under its foundations & plough up the ground where its streets stand than they die for the disgraceful dynasty which had brought our freedom to be a lie & our civilization & wealth to dishonor as a partnership of thieves. No, they died for the largest & noblest sentiment, the largest interpretation that could be put on the meaning & action of the North, died for what an American might die for. . . .

And the Governor of the Commonwealth nobly spoke the sense of his people when he said we will enlist if you send us out for freedom & not if you send us out to return slaves. Whatever mean carpers & the owls & jackals who squeak & gibber to the contrary will say, he spoke the voice of patriot fathers & mothers who offered their sons & of the patriot youths who offered up themselves, when he said, see that the cause is clear & great, & you shall have them & us; but we go not to restore those falsehearted usurpers of the power of Union or the like of them to their places. God in his mercy forbid but to restore the spirit of the American constitution & not its forced and falsely construed letter, not to restore those men but to exclude & brand them forever & put upright sound men in their places not to maintain slavery but to maintain freedom & to limit & end slavery . . . at the earliest day as it was in the beginning is now & ever shall be.

My opinion may not interest you & I will not bore you with it, but such as it is it is myself & if you wish my aid it must be in conformity with my opinion. You ask me to fight, to send soldiers, to go myself. With all my heart, if your objects are mine. I will fight for freedom. I will not fight to secure any more power to slaveholders. They had already, as our history shows, far too much. I will not fight to force them to remain in the Union. I had rather they would go out. . . .

You cannot refine Mr. Lincoln's taste, or /clear his judgment/ extend his horizon/; he will not walk dignifiedly through the traditional part of the President of America, but will pop out his head at each railroad station & make a little speech, & get into an argument with Squire A. & Judge B. He will write letters to Horace Greeley, and any Editor or Reporter or saucy Party committee that writes to him, & cheapen himself. But this we must be ready for, and let the clown appear, & hug ourselves that we are well off, if we have got good nature, honest meaning, & fidelity to /popular/public/interest, with bad manners, instead of an elegant roué & malignant selfseeker. . . .

The difference between you and your enemies is eternal; it is the difference of motive. Your action is to build, & their action is to destroy; yours to protect and to establish the rights of men; and theirs to crush them. . . .

## 10. RWE to Thomas Carlyle,[7] Concord, December 8, 1862

. . . Here we read no books. The war is our sole & doleful instructor. All our bright young men go into it, to be misused & sacrificed hitherto by incapable leaders. One lesson they all learn—to hate slavery, *teterrima causa*.[8] But the issue does not yet appear. We must get ourselves morally right. Nobody can help us. Tis of no account what England or France may do. Unless backed by our profligate parties, their action would be nugatory, and, if so backed, the worst. But even the war is better than the degrading & descending politics that preceded it for decades of years, & our legislature has made great strides, and if we can stave off that fury of trade which rushes to peace at the cost of replacing the South in the *status ante bellum*, we can, with something more of courage, leave the problem to another score of years—free labor to fight with the Beast, & see if bales & barrels & baskets cannot find out that they pass more commodiously & surely to their ports through free hands, than through barbarians. . . .

## 11. RWE, Journal FOR, 1863

Country wants men. No want of men in the railroad cars, in Brighton market; in the city, in Washington street, men to see Booth, to see Cubas, to see the great organ, to fill Faneuil Hall. Everywhere, hosts of men. In the swarming population, the drain of the Army, and all the loss by war, is a drop in the bucket. But the country wants them, wants every body. To be sure, there are many that should not go,—those exempted by age, by infirmity, so held by peremptory engagements to their civil domestic or professional affairs, as that the loss of them out of these would be the greatest disaster. But for the multitude of young able men, there is not this necessity to stay. Let them go. "One omen is good, to fight for one's country." Every kind of man is wanted, every talent, every virtue; the artillerist, the horseman, sharpshooter, engineer, secret-service man, carpenter, teamster, clerk; the Good, to be the soul & religion of the camp; the bad, because to fight & die for one's country not covers, but atones for a multitude of sins. And what? will you send them to die with Winthrop, Lowell, Dwight, Shaw, Bowditch? Yes, when I consider what they have sealed & saved, freedom for the world; yes a thousand times yes. Young they were old; had only crowded 4 score into 30. It was well worth the inestimable sacrifice, or to blot out one generation were well. The War an exceptional struggle, in which the first combatants are met,—the highest principles against the worst. What a teacher! what a field! what results!

Now I well know how grave & searching this ordeal is, how it has taught courage! Anxiety of the youth, sensible, tender, from school, college, counting-room, with no experience beyond football game, or school-yard quarrel, now to leap on a battery, or a file of bayonets. He says, I know not how it will be with me; one thing is certain, I can well die,—O yes,—but I cannot afford to mis-behave. Dearest friends will know tomorrow, as the whole earth will know, whether I have kept faith with them. But the experience is uniform, that the gentle soul makes the firm hero after all. . . .

All decomposition is recomposition. What we call consumption is energetic growth of the fungus or whatever new order. War disorganizes, but it also organizes; it forces individuals & states to combine & act with larger views, & under the best heads, & keeps the population together, producing the effect of cities; for camps are wandering cities. . . .

My interest in my Country is not primary, but professional. I wish that war as peace shall bring out the genius of the men. In every company, in every town, I seek intellect & character; & so in every circumstance. War, I know, is not an unmitigated evil: it is a potent alternative, tonic, magnetiser, reinforces manly power a hundred & a thousand times. I see it come as a frosty October, which shall restore intellectual & moral power to these languid & dissipated populations.

### 12. RWE to Matilda Ashurst Biggs, Concord, April 8, 1863

. . . Our sky is very dark but the feeling is very general in the Union that bad as the war is it is far safer & better than the foregoing peace. Our best ground of hope now is in the healthy sentiment which appears in reasonable people all over the country, accepting sacrifices, but meaning riddance from slavery, &

from Southern domination. I fear this sentiment is not yet represented by our government or its agents in Europe, but it is sporadic in the country. Indeed the governments of both England & America are far in the rear of their best constituencies. In England, as shown in the resolution with which the government shuts its eyes to the building of ships of war in your ports to attack the Republic,—now in this spasm to throw off slavery. This unlooked for attitude of England is our gravest foreign disadvantage—But I have gone quite too far into these painful politics whose gloom is only to be relieved by the largest considerations. I rejoice in so many assurances of sound heart & clear perception as come to us from excellent persons in England,—among which I rank your letter chiefly;—and the significant sympathy of the Manchester workmen, which I wish had been better met. . . .

## 13. RWE to Benjamin and Susan Morgan Rodman, Concord, June 17, 1863

I have waited a week since I heard the heavy news from Port Hudson,—fearing to disturb you,—but do not like to wait longer. I believe I have read every syllable which the journals contain of William's heroic behavior & death at the head of his regiment, & with entire sympathy for, &, I fear, too true knowledge of the desolation the tidings will have brought to your house, however consoled by the cordial testimony which the Army sends home of the love & honor which attached to him in life & in death. I had kept up by frequent inquiries some knowlege of his whereabouts, & read the New Orleans correspondence with hope of quite happier news.—But this sacrifice which he has finished, I am sure, could not be a surprise to his thoughts, not to yours. The soldier & the soldier's father & mother must have rehearsed this dread contingency to themselves quite too often, not to know its face when it arrives.—And yet there can be no sufficient preparation.

His life, so fair & amiable from the childhood which I remember,—his manly form & qualities, promised a solid character & fortune. I dread to think how the change will darken your house,—hitherto the home of every friendly influence. Neither perhaps can any consideration of duty to country & mankind for a long time reconcile to this devastation in the family. And yet who dare say, amid all the greatness the war has called out, in the privatest & obscurest, as well as in eminent persons, that these calamities do not suddenly teach self-renouncement, & raise us to the force they require. I am sure your son's own devotion will arm you to surrender him.

I think daily that there are crises which demand nations, as well as those which claim the sacrifice of single lives. Ours perhaps is one,—and that one whole generation might well consent to perish, if, by their fall, political liberty & clean & just life could be made sure to the generations that follow. As you suffer, all of us may suffer, before we shall have an honest peace. . . .

## 14. RWE to Thomas Carlyle, Concord, September 26, 1864

. . . I have in these last years lamented that you had not made the visit to America, which in earlier years you projected or favored. It would have made it impossible that your name should be cited for one moment on the side of the enemies of mankind. Ten days' residence in this country would have made you the organ of the sanity of England & of Europe to us & to them, & have shown you the necessities and aspirations which struggle up in our Free States, which, as yet, have no organ to others, & are ill & unsteadily articulated here. In our today's division of Republican & Democrat, it is certain that the American nationality lies in the Republican party (mixed & multiform though the party be;) & I hold it not less certain, that, viewing all the nationalities of the world, the battle for Humanity is, at this hour, in America. A few days here would show you the disgusting composition of the party which within the Union resists the national action. Take from it the wild Irish element, imported in the last twenty five years into this country, & led by Romish priests, who sympathize, of course, with despotism, & you would bereave it of all its numerical strength. A man intelligent and virtuous, is not to be found on that side. Ah! how gladly I would enlist you with your thunderbolt, on our part! How gladly enlist the wise, thoughtful, efficient pens & voices of England! We want England & Europe to hold our people staunch to their best tendency. Are English of this day incapable of a great sentiment? Can they not leave cavilling at petty failures, & bad manners, & at the dunce part, (always the largest part in human affairs), and leap to the suggestions & fingerpointings of the gods, which, above the understanding, feed the hopes & guide the wills of men? This war has been conducted over the heads of all the actors in it: and the foolish terrors—"what shall we do with the negro?" "the entire black population is coming north to be fed," &c. have strangely ended in the fact, that the black refuses to leave his climate; gets his living *and* the living of his employers there, as he has always done; is the natural ally & soldier of the Republic, in that climate; now takes the place of 200,000 white soldiers; & will be, as this conquest of the country proceeds, its garrison, till peace, without slavery, returns. Slaveholders in London have filled English ears with their wishes & perhaps beliefs; and our people, generals & politicians, have carried the like, at first, to the war, until corrected by irresistible experience. I shall always respect War hereafter. The cost of life, the dreary havoc of comfort & time are overpaid by the Vistas it opens of Eternal Life, Eternal Law, reconstructing & uplifting Society,— breaks up the old horizon, & we see through the rifts a wider. The dismal Malthus, the dismal De Bow, have had their night. Our Census of 1860, and the War, are poems, which will, in the next age, inspire a genius like your own. . . .

Charlotte Forten *(Courtesy of the Moorland-Spingarn Research Center, Howard University)*

# Charlotte Forten
## (1837–1914)

Why did she go to Port Royal, South Carolina in 1862 to teach the freed slaves? On her twenty-fifth birthday, Charlotte Forten said it was to forget her desire for success—literary success, social success, success in the community of reform. In this way, her departure from Salem, Massachusetts, where she had taught school, attended lectures, and wrote poetry and occasional essays for antislavery periodicals, amounted to an admission of failure. She thought she would never possess the talent or fame of a Phillips, Stowe, Child, or Whittier. She knew she had the habits—the radical politics, the obsessive scrutiny of self, the physical ailments, the literary pretentions—but she suspected that she did not have the abilities. Maybe the burden of personal history was too great. The Fortens were the most distinguished and affluent of Philadelphia's free black community. The accomplishments of Charlotte's grandfather James Forten, who fought for the patriot cause during the Revolution and was a leader of the abolitionist community in the Quaker City, set a heroic standard that neither male nor female descendants felt they could possibly meet. In 1855, her father Robert had left for Canada; with the outbreak of Civil War, Charlotte too was on the move.

After an arduous journey that challenged her romantic notions of voyage at sea, she arrived at Port Royal on October 28, 1862. From that moment on, Forten became a student of nature and character. She turned to her journal as a creative outlet. The words she could not find in public ("words always fail me when I want them most") poured forth in private. Her journal served several functions: it became the canvas onto which she painted her impressions of life in the sea-islands, it kept her company, and it allowed her to confess her often mixed desires. She wanted desperately to believe that she had come South purely to help those less fortunate than herself, to make a contribution to the elevation of the black race. She prayed that her teaching would "fill up my whole existence to the exclusion of all vain longings," but it is those longings that make the journal an extraordinary document.[1]

She longed for beauty, and she found it in ancient moss-covered trees, the oaks and pines, and the crimson sunsets and gently blown sand. She desired romance, and she found it on long horseback rides with the white, married doctor of the First South Carolina Volunteers, rides that swelled her soul and the details of which were not always "writable." She sought heroes, and she found them in her meetings with Thomas Wentworth Higginson, Harriet Tubman, and Robert Gould Shaw. She prayed for liberation, her own as well as the slave's, and in the Southern heat she at times exulted over it. She longed to understand and help the newly emancipated slaves. That meant trying to force black residents of the Sea Islands into literary tropes, as when she wanted to hear some oarsmen sing Whittier's "Song of the Negro Boatman." Helping the freedmen also meant inspiring her students to achieve great things and introducing them to the middle-class values she believed they would need to get ahead. She was enraptured by black culture, by the stories of struggle and triumph and by the deep spirituality that permeated the lives of freed slaves.

What Forten wrote in her journal and what she wrote for publication were not the same. She took the scenes and details of her experience as recorded in her journal and, for her essays in the *Atlantic Monthly*, transformed them into literary works. These published essays were meant to give a Northern reading public confidence that the emancipated slaves were capable of "improvement." And thus Forten in her essays is at points less radical and open than Forten in her journals. One example will suffice. In her account of one Thanksgiving Day, Forten wrote in her essay that "Mrs. Gage told the people how the slaves in Santa Cruz had secured their liberation." The journal reads Mrs. Gage "told the people about the slaves in Santa Cruz, how they rose and conquered their masters, and declared themselves free, and no one dared to oppose them." There are other examples of shifts in content and tone between the journals and the essays that are worth examining—such as her accounts of her students or her depiction of Shaw—but this is only to say that Forten was an artist who transformed personal experience and memory into narrative history.

Forten never believed in her talent. One reason was external—the culture in which she lived would not let her. No matter how much she sought to escape categories, she was seen first as a black woman and only second, if at all, as a writer. When John Greenleaf Whittier commented that "I look upon her as one of the most gifted representatives of her class," he did not realize that he was qualifying Forten into oblivion. But another reason was internal, or perhaps this is only the way the external and cultural become personal. "I am disgusted with myself. I feel as if my life were a failure. Not one of its long-cherished aspirations has yet been fulfilled," she lamented after the war.[2] She continued to write, but her happiness and success ultimately came with her marriage to Francis Grimké, a former slave and Presbyterian minister, and her work on behalf of the Church. It is unfortunate that she was never allowed, and that she never allowed herself, to enjoy her considerable gifts.

## 1.   Charlotte Forten, *Journal*[3]

*Salem. June 22, 1862.* More penitent than ever I come to thee again, old Journal, long neglected friend. More than two years have elapsed since I last talked to thee.—Two years full of changes. A little while ago a friend read to me Miss Mullock's "Life for a Life." The Journal letters, which I liked so much, were at first addressed to an unknown friend. So shall mine be. What name shall I give to thee, oh *ami inconnu?* It will be safer to give merely an initial—A. And so dear A. I will tell you a little of my life, for the past two years. When I wrote to you last,—on a bright, lovely New Year's Day, I was here in old Salem, and in this very house. What a busy winter that was for me, I was assisting my dear Miss S. with one of her classes, and at the same time studying, and reciting at the Normal, Latin, French and a little Algebra. Besides I was taking German lessons. How was I not busy, dear A.? Yet it seems to me I was never so happy. I enjoyed life perfectly and all the winter was strong and well. But when Spring came my health gave way. First my eyesight failed me, and the German which I liked better than anything else, which it was a real luxury to study had to be given up, and then all my other studies. My health continuing to fail, I was obliged to stop teaching, and go away. . . . [W]ent to the water cure at Worcester, where the excellent Dr. R. did me a world of good—spiritually as well as physically.[4] To me he seems one of the best and noblest types of manhood I ever saw. In my heart I shall thank him always. Early in September, came back from W. and recommenced teaching, feeling quite well. But late in October had a violent attack of lung fever, which brought me very, very near the grave, and entirely unfitted me for further work. . . . I was obliged to return to P[hiladelphia]. A weary winter I had there, unable to work, and having but little congenial society, and suffering the many deprivations which all of our unhappy race must suffer in the so-called "City of Brotherly Love." What a mockery that name is! But over these weary months it is better to draw the veil and forget. . . .

  Went to Marblehead Beach. The tide was coming in, and never have I seen Old Ocean more gloriously beautiful. We had an afternoon of rare enjoyment;

and it seemed to me as if I really *could* not tear myself away. I think I should have stayed all night if any one would have stayed with me. It was too much happiness to sit upon the rocks, and see those breaking waves, again. As they receded, my whole soul seemed drawn away with them, then when they rushed back again upon the steadfast rocks my being thrilled, glowed, with joyous exultant life. Strange, strange, old sea, how something in the deepest depths of my nature responds to you, how the very fibres of my being seem to cling to you. But how can I describe the emotions you awake in me? Words cannot do it. They fail, and are worthless, absurd. Well, dear A. are you weary of my rhapsodizing? But, kind unknown, you will not tell me if you are. You will not blame nor laugh at me, but simply listen and be silent. . . .

*Sunday, July 6.* . . . Ah, friend of mine, I must not forget to tell you about a little adventure I met with to-day. I was boarding with Mrs. R.[,] a very good anti-slavery woman, and kind and pleasant as can be. Well, when I appeared at the dinner-table to-day, it seems that a *gentleman* took umbrage at sitting at the same table with one whose skin chanced to be "not colored like his own," and rose and left the table. Poor man! he feared contamination. But the charming part of the affair is that I with eyes intent upon my dinner, and mind entirely engrossed by Mr. Phillips' glorious words, which were still sounding in my soul, did not notice this person's presence nor disappearance.[5] So his proceedings were quite lost upon me, and I sh'd have been in a state of blissful ignorance as to his very existence had not the hostess afterward spoken to me about it, expressing the wish, good woman—that my "feelings were not hurt." I told her the truth, and begged her to set her mind at ease, for even had I have noticed the simpleton's behavior it w'ld not have troubled me. I felt too thorough a contempt for such people to allow myself to be wounded by them. This wise gentleman was an *officer in the navy,* I understand. An honor to his country's service isn't he? but he is not alone, I know full well. The name of his kindred is Legion,—but I defy and despise them all. I hope as I grow older I get a little more philosophy. Such things do not wound me as deeply as of yore. "When, when will these outrages cease?" often my soul cries out—"How long, oh Lord, how long?" . . .

*Sunday, August 17.* My twenty-fifth birthday. Tisn't a very pleasant thought that I have lived a quarter of a century, and am so very, very ignorant. Ten years ago, I hoped for a different fate at twenty-five. But why complain? The accomplishments, the society, the delights of travel which I have dreamed of and longed for all my life, I am now convinced can never be mine. If I can go to Port Royal, I will try to forget all these desires. I will pray that God in his goodness will make me noble enough to find my highest happiness in doing my duty. Since Mrs. J. has given me such sad accounts of the suffering of the poor freed people my desire of helping them has increased. It is but little I c'ld do, I know, but that little I w'ld do with all my heart. . . .

*At Sea. October 27*, Monday.—Let me see. Where am I? What do I want to write? I am in a state of utter bewilderment. It was on Wed. I rec'd the note. On Thursday I said "goodbye" to the friends that are so dear, and the city that is so hateful, and went to N.Y. . . . Enjoyed the sail down the harbor perfectly. The shipping is a noble sight. Had no symptoms of sea-sickness until eve. when, being seated at the table an inexpressibly singular sensation caused me to make a hasty retreat to the aft-deck, where by keeping perfectly still sitting on a coil of ropes spent a very comfortable eve. and had a pleasant conversation with one of the passengers. Did not get out of sight of land until after dark. I regretted that.

Went below for the night into the close ladies' cabin with many misgivings which proved not unfounded. Was terribly sea-sick that night and all the next morning. Did not reappear on deck till noon of the next day—Saturday. What an experience. Of all doleful, dismal, desperate experiences sea-sickness is certainly the dolefulest, dismalist, desperate-est! . . .

*Tuesday Night* [October 28]. . . .

To my great joy found that we were to be rowed by a crew of negro boatmen. . . . The row was delightful. It was just at sunset—a grand Southern sunset; and the gorgeous clouds of crimson and gold were reflected in the waters below, which were smooth and calm as a mirror. Then, as we glided along, the rich sonorous tones of the boatmen broke upon the evening stillness. Their singing impressed me much. It was so sweet and strange and solemn. "Roll, Jordan, Roll" was grand, and another

> "Jesus make de blind to see
> Jesus make de deaf to hear
> Jesus make de cripple walk
> Walk in, dear Jesus,"

and the refrain "No man can hender me." It was very, very impressive. I want to hear these men sing Whittier's "Song of the Negro Boatman." I am going to see if it can't be brought about in some way. . . . It is all a strange wild dream, from which I am constantly expecting to awake. But I can write no more now. I am tired, and still feel the motion of the ship in my poor head. Good night, dear A! . . .

*Wednesday, October 29*. . . . We went into the school, and heard the children read and spell. The teachers tell us that they have made great improvement in a very short time, and I noticed with pleasure how bright, how eager to learn many of them seem. The singing delighted me most. They sang beautifully in their rich, sweet clear tones, and with that peculiar swaying motion which I had noticed before in the older people, and which seems to make their singing all the more effective. . . . Dear children! born in slavery, but free at last? May God preserve to you all the blessings of freedom, and may you be in every pos-

sible way fitted to enjoy them. My heart goes out to you. I shall be glad to do
all that I can to help you. . . .

*Wednesday, November 5.* Had my first regular teaching experience, and to
you and you only friend beloved, will acknowledge that it was *not* a very pleasant one. Part of my scholars are very tiny,—babies, I call them—and it is hard
to keep them quiet and interested while I am hearing the larger ones. They are
too young even for the alphabet, it seems to me. I think I must write home and
ask somebody to send me picture-books and toys to amuse them with. . . .

*Thursday, November 13.* Was there ever a lovelier road than that through part
of my way to school lies? Oh, I wish you were here to go with me, *cher ami.* It
is lined with woods on both sides. On the one tall stately pines, on the other
the noble live oaks with their graceful moss drapery. And the road is captured
with those brown odorous pine leaves that I love so well. It is perfectly lovely.
I forgot that I was almost ill to-day, while sauntering along, listening to the
birds and breathing the soft delicious air. Of the last part of the walk, through
sun and sand, the less said the better. Talked to the children a little while to-
day about the noble Toussaint.[6] They listened very attentively. It is well that
they sh'ld know what one of their own color c'ld do for his race. I long to
inspire them with courage and ambition (of a noble sort) and high purposes. It
is noticeable how very few mulattoes there are here. Indeed in our school, with
one or two exceptions, the children are all black. A little mulatto child strayed
into the school house yesterday—a pretty little thing with large beautiful black
eyes and lovely long lashes. But so dirty! I longed to seize and thoroughly
cleanse her. The mother is a good-looking woman, but quite black. "Thereby,"
I doubt not, "hangs a tale." This eve. Harry, one of the men on the place, came
in for a lesson. He is most eager to learn, and is really a scholar to be proud of.
He learns rapidly. I gave him his first lesson in writing to-night, and his progress was wonderful. He held his pen almost perfectly right the first time. He
will very soon learn to write, I think. I must inquire who w'ld like to take lessons at night. Whenever I am well enough it will be a real pleasure to teach
them. . . .

*Sunday, November 23. . . .*
This eve. our boys and girls with others from across the creek came in and
sang a long time for us. . . . The effect of the singing has been to make me feel
a little sad and lonely to-night. A yearning for congenial companionship *will*
sometimes come over me in the few leisure moments I have in the house. 'Tis
well they are so few. Kindness, most invariable,—for which I am most grateful—I meet with constantly, but congeniality I find not at all in this house. But
silence, foolish murmurer. He who knows all things knows that it was for no
selfish motive that I came here, far from the few who are so dear to me. Therefore let me not be selfish now. Let the work to which I have solemnly pledged
myself fill up my whole existence to the exclusion of all vain longings. . . .

*Thursday, November 27.* . . . And what a significant fact it is that one may now sit here in safety—here in the rebellious little Palmetto State and read the "Liberator," and display it to one's friends, rejoicing over it in the fulness of one's heart as a very great treasure. It is fitting that we sh'ld give to this—the pioneer paper in the cause of human rights—a heart welcome to the land where, until so recently, those rights have been most barbarously trampled upon. We do not forget that it is in fact directly traceable to the exertions of the editor of this paper and those who have labored so faithfully with him, that the Northern people now occupy in safety the S.C. shore; that freedom now blesses it, and it is, for the first time, a place worth living in. This eve. commenced a long letter to Mr. Garrison. Composed partly of today's journalism, and partly of other things that I thought w'ld interest him. He can publish it in the "Liberator," if he thinks it worth printing, which I do not.[7] Truly this has been a delightful day to me. I recal[l] with pleasure the pleasant Thanksgiving days passed in N.E. in Mass., which I believe I am in the habit of considering as *all* N.E. But this has been the happiest, the most jubilant Thanksgiving day of my life. We hear of cold weather and heavy snow-storms up in the North land. But here roses and oleanders are blooming in the open air. Figs and oranges are ripening, the sunlight is warm and bright, and over all shines gloriously the blessed light of Freedom—Freedom forevermore! . . .

*Sunday, November 30.* . . . It is a very strange wild thing. I am quite in love with one of the children here—little Amaretta who is niece to our good Amaretta. She is a cunning little kittenish thing with such a gentle demure look. She is not quite black, and has pretty close hair, but delicate features. She is bright too. I love the child. Wish I cld take her for my own. Am in a writing mood to-night, and think I will give to you, my dearest A. a more minute description of the people around than I've yet given to anyone. I shall write down their names too, that I may remember them always. Don't know them thoroughly enough yet to say much about their characters. To begin with the older ones. First there is old Harriet. She is a very kind, pleasant old soul. Comes from Darien G. Her parents were Africans. She speaks a *very* foreign tongue. Three of her children have been sold from her. Her master's son killed somebody in a duel, and was obliged to "pay money" H. says. I suppose she means to give bail. And she and her children were sold to this place, to raise the money. Then there is her daughter Tillah. Poor creature, she has a dear little baby, Annie, who for weeks has been dangerously ill with whooping cough and fever. Our good Miss T. attends it, and does all that can be done, but the baby is still very ill. For Tillah's sake I hope it will get well. She is devoted to it night and day. T.'s husband is a gallant looking young soldier—a member of the black regiment. H.'s mother, Bella, is rather a querulous body. But who can blame her? She has had enough to try her sorely. One by one her children at a tender age have been dragged from her to work in the cotton fields. She herself has been

made to work when most unfit for it. She has had to see her own children cruelly beaten. Is it strange that these things sh'ld have embittered her? But she has
much of the milk of human kindness left her yet. She nurses her poor baby
faithfully, and often, old as she is, sits up the entire night with it. Harry is
another of her sons. I have told you, dear A., how bright, how eager to learn,
he is. His wife Tamar, is a good-natured easy soul. She has several nice little
children, and the baby—Mary Lincoln—as Mr. R. the Superintendent has
named her—is a very cunning little creature, an especial pet of ours. Celia is
one of the best women on the place. She is a cripple. Her feet and limbs were
so badly frozen by exposure that her legs were obliged to be amputated just
above the knees. But she manages to get about almost as actively as any of the
others. Her husband, Thomas, has been a soldier, and is now quite ill with
pneumonia. She has several children—Rose, who is our little maid, Olivia the
eldest, Dolly, a bright little thing who goes to school with me every morn, and
who likes to go. Lastly Aiken, whose proper name is Thomas. He is an odd
little fellow, very much spoiled. Amaretta, Celia's sister is our laundress and
cook. I like her very much. Then there is Wilhelmina, a mulatto (the others are
all black). She comes from Virginia, and speaks therefore quite intelligibly. She
is a good sensible woman, and both she and her husband Robt.,—who is one
of my night pupils—are most anxious for their three little ones to learn. Cupid
our major-domo, is as obliging as possible. A shrewd fellow, who knows well
what he is about. His wife Patience, is Tamar's sister, and lives across the creek
at Pollywana. Their children—two of them—come to our school. They are
good scholars. I do enjoy hearing Cupid and Harry tell about the time that the
Secesh had to flee. The time of the "gun shoot," as they call the taking of Bay
Point, which is opposite Hilton Head. It delights them greatly to recall that
time. Their master had the audacity to venture back even while the Union
troops were occupying Beaufort. H. says he tried to persuade him to go back
with him, assuring him that the Yankees w'ld shoot them all when they came.
"Bery well sur," he replied, "if I go wid you I be good as dead, so if I got the
dead, I might's well dead here as anywhere. So I'll stay and wait for the Yankees." He told me that he knew all the time that his master was not telling the
truth. Cupid says the master told the people to get all the furniture together and
take it over to Pollywana, and to stay on that side themselves, "so" says Cupid
"dey c'ld jus' swap us all and put us in de boat. And he told me to row Patience
and de chilens down to a certain pint, and den I c'ld come back if I choose."
"Jus' as if I was gwine to be sich a goat" adds Cupid, with a look and gesture
of ineffable contempt. The *finale* of the story is that the people left the premises
and hid themselves so that when the master returned not one of all his "faithful
servants" was to be found to go into slavery with him, and he was obliged to
return, a disappointed, but it is hoped, a wiser man. . . .

*Thursday, New Year's Day, 1863.* The most glorious day this nation has yet seen, *I* think. I rose early—an event here—and early we started, with an old borrowed carriage and a remarkably slow horse. . . . Walking on a little distance I found myself being presented to Col. Higginson, whereat I was so much overwhelmed, that I had no reply to make to the very kind and courteous little speech with which he met me. I believe I mumbled something, and grinned like a simpleton, that was all. Provoking, isn't it? that when one is most in need of sensible words, one finds them not. I *cannot* give a regular chronicle of the day. It is impossible. I was in such a state of excitement. It all seemed, and seems still, like a brilliant dream. . . . The exercises commenced. . . . Then the beautiful flags presented by Dr. Cheever's Church were presented to Col. H. for the Reg. in an excellent and enthusiastic speech, by Rev. Mr. French. Immediately at the conclusion, some of the colored people—of their own accord sang "My Country Tis of Thee." It was a touching and beautiful incident, and Col. Higginson, in accepting the flags made it the occasion of some happy remarks. He said that *that* tribute was far more effecting than any speech he c'ld make. He spoke for some time, and all that he said was grand, glorious. He seemed inspired. Nothing could have been better, more perfect. And Dr. R. told me afterward that the Col. was much affected. That tears were in his eyes. He is as Whittier says, truly a "sure man." The men all admire and love him. There is a great deal of personal megnetism about him, and his kindness is proverbial. . . . The Dress Parade—the first I have ever seen—delighted me. It was a brilliant sight—the lone line of men in their brilliant uniforms, with bayonets gleaming in the sunlight. . . . To me it was a grand triumph—that black regiment doing itself honor in the sight of the white officers, many of whom, doubtless "came to scoff." It was typical of what the race, so long down-trodden and degraded will yet achieve on this continent. . . . Ah, what a grand, glorious day this has been. The dawn of freedom which it heralds may not break upon us at once; but it will surely come, and sooner, I believe than we have ever dared hope before. . . .[8]

*Saturday, January 31.* . . . Deep green in the pines and "deep delicious blue" in the sky. Why is it that green and blue together are so lovely in Nature, and so unlovely elsewhere? In B. we spent nearly all our time at Harriet Tubman's otherwise "Moses."[9] She is a wonderful woman—a real heroine. Has helped off a large number of slaves, after taking her own freedom. She told us that she used to hide them in the woods during the day and go around to get provisions for them. Once she had with her a man named Joe, for whom a reward of $1500 was offered. Frequently, in different places she found handbills exactly describing him, but at last they reached in safety the Suspension Bridge over the Falls and found themselves in Canada. Until then she said, Joe had been very silent. In vain had she called his attention to the glory of the Falls. He sat perfectly still—moody, it seemed, and w'ld not even glance at them. But when she said, "Now we are in Can." he sprang to his feet—with a great shout and sang and clapped his hands in a perfect delirium of joy. So when they got out, and he first touched *free* soil, he shouted and hurrahed "as if he were crazy"—she said. How exciting it was to hear her tell the story. And to hear her sing the very scraps of jubilant hymns that he sang. She said the ladies crowded around them, and some laughed and some cried. My own eyes were full as I listened to her—the heroic woman! A reward of $10,000 was offered for her by the Southerners, and her friends deemed it best that she sh'ld, for a time find refuge in Can. And she did so, but only for a short time. She came back and was soon at the good brave work again. She is living in B[eaufort] now; keeping an eating house. But she wants to go North, and will probably do so ere long. I am glad I saw her—*very* glad. . . .

*Saturday, February 7*. . . . Another day, one of the black soldiers came in and gave us *his* account of the Expedition. No words of mine, dear A. can give you any account of the state of exaltation and enthusiasm that he was in. He was eager for another chance at "de Secesh." I asked him what he w'ld do if his master and others sh'ld come back and try to reenslave him. "I'd fight un Miss, I'd fight un till I turned to dust!" He was especially delighted at the ire which the sight of the black troops excited in the minds of certain Secesh women whom they saw. These vented their spleen by calling the men "baboons dressed in soldier's clothes, and telling them that they ought to be at work in their master's rice swamps, and that they ought to be lashed to death." "And what did you say to them?" I asked. "Oh miss, we only tell us 'Hole your tongue, and dry up!' You see we wusn't feared of *dem, dey cldn't hurt us now.* Whew! didn't we laugh to see dem so mad!" The spirit of resistance to the Secesh is strong in these men. . . .

*Thursday, February 19.* . . . Dr. R. . . . and I—had the loveliest horseback ride. Dear A. I can give you no idea of the ride homeward. I know only that it was the most delightful ride I ever had in my life. The young moon—just a silver bow—had a singular, almost violet tinge, and all around it in the heavens was a rosy glow, deepening every moment, which was wonderfully beautiful. I shall never forget how that rosy light, and the moon and stars looked to us as we caught them in glimpses, riding through the dark pines. How wild and unreal it all seemed and what happiness it was, as we rode slowly along to listen to the conversation of the dear friend who is always so kind, so full of noble sympathy, and of eager enthusiasm in the great work in which he is engaged. No wonder the soldiers love him so much, no wonder that, as Col. H. says, he has such a hold upon them. So that one of them said to him "Why Dr., don't you know there ain't a man in de regiment—but what *dotes his eyes on you.*" There is a magnetism about him impossible to resist. I can never be thankful enough that he came here. But oh, I do not want him to be ill, or to die. Most gladly w'ld I give my life that one so noble so valuable might be preserved. . . .

*Saturday, April 11....* Dr. and I rode on to Barnwell's which is the most beautiful place I have ever yet seen.... How shall I tell you, dear A. about our ride home first through an avenue of beautiful trees—mostly live oaks draped with moss—and then for miles and miles through the Pine Barrens. The air was soft, Italian, only a low faint murmur c'ld be heard among the pines,— hardly "the slow song of the sea." The ground was thickly carpeted with ferns of a most delicious green, and to crown all we found Azaleas of a deep pink color and perfect fragrance.... We rode through the Barrens. I think I never enjoyed anything so perfectly. I *luxuriated* in it. It was almost "too much, too much." Dr. R. and I had a long and interesting talk. How kind, how good he is! It is very pleasant to know he cared so much for me, even although I *know* he thinks far better of me than I deserve. The brightest and most delightful experience must come to an end, and at last but too soon we emerged from the Pine Barrens and came out into the shell road.... I sit composedly taking down notes; and shall now occupy myself with darning a pair of stockings for the doctor until something further occurs which is *writable*. Have no fear....

*Friday, May 1....* Sat a long time on the piazza listening to the low tones of the piano or the equally musical murmur of the wind in the tree tops, and think- ing of some loved ones who are far, far away. How old memories crowd around one on such nights as these! And how dreamy, strange and unreal the present seems. Here on the piazza of this old southern house I sit and think of friends a thousand miles away—of scenes that have past, never, never to return again. Shall I ever see the dear ones "up North" I wonder? Something answers "never" but for to-night at least, I will not listen to that voice. Here the fleas interpose. Farewell to all reminiscences. Now for tortures unendurable! Oh the *fleas!!* The fleas!!. The fleas!! . . .

*Thursday, July 2. . . .* I am perfectly charmed with Col. [Robert] S[haw].[10] He seems to me in every way one of the most delightful persons I have ever met. There is something girlish about him, and yet I never saw anyone more manly. To me he seems a thoroughly lovable person. And there is something so exqui- site about him. The perfect breeding, how evident it is. Surely he must be a worthy son of such noble parents. I have seen him but once, yet I really cannot help feeling a really affectionate admiration for him. We had a very pleasant talk on the moonlit piazza, and then went to the Praise House to see the shout. I was delighted to find that it was one of the very best and most spirited that we had had. The Col. looked and listened with the deepest interest. And after it was over, expressed himself much gratified. He said, he w'ld like to have some of the hymns to send home. I shall be only too glad to copy them for him. Old Maurice surpassed himself to-night in singing "The Talles' Tree in Par- adise." He got much excited and his gestures were really quite tragic. I c'ld see with what astonishment and interest our guests watched the old blind man. . . .

*Monday, July 6.* . . . I am more than ever charmed with the noble little Col. What purity, what nobleness of soul, what exquisite gentleness in that beautiful face! As I look at it I think "The bravest are the tenderest." I can imagine what he must be to his mother. May his life be spared to her! . . . Tonight, he helped me on my horse, and after carefully arranging the folds of my riding skirt, said, so kindly, "Good-bye. If I don't see you again down here I hope to see you at our house." . . .

*Monday, July 20.* For nearly two weeks we have waited, oh how anxiously for news of our regt. which went, we know to Morris Is. to take part in the attack on Charleston. To-night comes news oh, so sad, so heart-sickening. It is too terrible, too terrible to write. We can only hope it may not all be true. That our noble, beautiful young Colonel is killed, and the regt. cut to pieces! I cannot, cannot believe it. And yet I know it may be so. But oh, I am stunned, sick at heart. I can scarcely write. There was an attack on Fort Wagner. The 54th put in advance; fought bravely, desperately, but was finally overpowered and driven back after getting into the Fort. Thank Heaven! they fought bravely! And oh, I still must hope that our colonel, *ours* especially he seems to me, is not killed. But I can write no more to-night. . . .

*Friday, July 24.* To-day the news of Col. Shaw's death is confirmed. There can no longer be any doubt. It makes me sad, sad at heart. They say he sprang from the parapet of the fort and cried "Onward, my brave boys, onward"; then fell, pierced with wounds. I know it was a glorious death. But oh, it is hard, very hard for the young wife, so late a bride, for the invalid mother, whose only and most dearly loved son he was,—that heroic mother who rejoiced in the position which he occupied as colonel of a colored regiment. My heart bleeds for her. His death is a very sad loss to us. I recall him as a much loved friend. Yet I saw him but a few times. Oh what must it be to the wife and the mother. Oh it is terrible. It seems very, very hard that the best and the noblest must be the earliest called away. Especially has it been so throughout this dreadful war. . . .

*Sunday, July 26.* . . . My strength has failed rapidly of late. Have become so weak that I fear I sh'ld be easy prey to the fever which prevails here, a little later in this season. A few weeks since I stopped going to the church finding it impossible to drive there longer through the heat of the day, and opened a small school for some of the children from Frogmore in a carriage house on our place. Most of the children are crude little specimens. I asked them once what their ears were for. One bright-eyed little girl answered promptly "to put rings in." When Mrs. H. asked some of them the same question, they said "To put cotton in." One day I had been telling them about metals; how they were dug from the ground, and afterward in review, I asked "Where is iron obtained from?" "From the ground" was the prompt reply. "And Gold?"—"From the sky!" shouted a little boy. I have found it very interesting to give them a kind of object lesson with the picture cards. They listen with eager attention, and seem to understand and remember very well what I tell them. But although this has been easier for me than teaching at the church—where, in addition to driving through the hot sun to get there, I was obliged to exert my lungs far above their strength to make myself heard when more than a hundred children were reciting at the same time in the same room—yet I have found my strength steadily decreasing, and have been every day tortured by a severe headache. I take my good Dr.'s advice, therefore, and shall go North on a furlough—to stay until the unhealthiest season is over. . . .

*N.Y. Sunday, August 2.* . . . It seems so strange to be in a great city again. The Southern dream is over for a time. The real life of the Northland begins again— Farewell!

### 2. [Charlotte Forten] "Life on the Sea Islands," *Atlantic Monthly*, 13 (May and June 1864): 587–596; 666–676

It was on the afternoon of a warm, murky day late in October that our steamer, the United States, touched the landing at Hilton Head. A motley assemblage had collected on the wharf,—officers, soldiers, and "contrabands" of every size and hue: black was, however, the prevailing color. The first view of Hilton Head is desolate enough,—a long, low, sandy point, stretching out into the sea, with no visible dwellings upon it, except the rows of small white-roofed houses which have lately been built for the freed people. . . .

From Hilton Head to Beaufort the same long, low line of sandy coast, bordered by trees; formidable gunboats in the distance, and the gray ruins of an old fort, said to have been built by the Huguenots more than two hundred years ago. . . . A large building which was once the Public Library is now a shelter for freed people from Fernandina. Did the Rebels know it, they would doubtless upturn their aristocratic noses, and exclaim in disgust, "To what base uses," etc. We confess that it was highly satisfactory to us to see how the tables are turned, now that "the whirligig of time has brought about its revenges." . . . There were indications that already Northern improvements had reached this Southern town. Among them was a wharf, a convenience that one wonders how the Southerners could so long have existed without. The more we know of their mode of life, the more we are inclined to marvel at its utter shiftlessness.

Little colored children of every hue were playing about the streets, looking as merry and happy as children ought to look,—now that the evil shadow of Slavery no longer hangs over them. Some of the officers we met did not impress us favorably. They talked flippantly, and sneeringly at the negroes, whom they found we had come down to teach, using an epithet more offensive than gentlemanly. . . .

The next morning L. and I were awakened by the cheerful voices of men and women, children and chickens, in the yard below. We ran to the window, and looked out. Women in bright-colored handkerchiefs, some carrying pails on their heads, were crossing the yard, busy with their morning work; children were playing and tumbling around them. On every face there was a look of serenity and cheerfulness. My heart gave a great throb of happiness as I looked at them and thought, "They are free! so long down-trodden, so long crushed to the earth, but now in their old homes, forever free!" And I thanked God that I had lived to see this day. . . .

The first day of school was rather trying. Most of my children were very small, and consequently restless. Some were too young to learn the alphabet. These little ones were brought to school because the older children—in whose care their parents leave them while at work—could not come without them. We were therefore willing to have them come, although they seemed to have discovered the secret of perpetual motion, and tried one's patience sadly. But after some days of positive, though not severe treatment, order was brought out of chaos, and I found but little difficulty in managing and quieting the tiniest and most restless spirits. I never before saw children so eager to learn, although I had had several years' experience in New-England schools. Coming to school is a constant delight and recreation to them. They come here as other children go to play. The older ones, during the summer, work in the fields from early morning until eleven or twelve o'clock, and then come into school, after their hard toil in the hot sun, as bright and as anxious to learn as ever.

Of course there are some stupid ones, but these are the minority. The majority learn with wonderful rapidity. Many of the grown people are desirous of learning to read. It is wonderful how a people who have been so long crushed to the earth, so imbruted as these have been,—and they are said to be among the most degraded negroes of the South,—can have so great a desire for knowledge, and such a capability for attaining it. One cannot believe that the haughty Anglo-Saxon race, after centuries of such an experience as these people have had, would be very much superior to them. And one's indignation increases against those who, North as well as South, taunt the colored race with inferiority while they themselves use every means in their power to crush and degrade them, denying them every right and privilege, closing against them every avenue of elevation and improvement. Were they, under such circumstances, intellectual and refined, they would certainly be vastly superior to any other race that ever existed. . . .

In the evenings, the children frequently came in to sing and shout for us. These "shouts" are very strange,—in truth, almost indescribable. It is necessary to hear and see in order to have any clear idea of them. The children form a ring, and move around in a kind of shuffling dance, singing all the time. Four or five stand apart, and sing very energetically, clapping their hands, stamping their feet, and rocking their bodies to and fro. These are the musicians, to whose performance the shouters keep perfect time. The grown people on this plantation did not shout, but they do on some other plantations. It is very comical to see little children, not more than three or four years old, entering into the performance with all their might. But the shouting of the grown people is rather solemn and impressive than otherwise. We cannot determine whether it has a religious character or not. Some of the people tell us that it has, others that it has not. But as the shouts of the grown people are always in connection with their religious meetings, it is possible that they are the barbarous expression of religion, handed down to them from their African ancestors, and destined to pass away under the influence of Christian teachings. The people on this island have no songs. They sing only hymns, and most of these are sad. Prince, a large black boy from a neighboring plantation, was the principal shouter among the children. It seemed impossible for him to keep still for a moment. His performances were most amusing specimens of Ethiopian gymnastics. . . .

Thanksgiving-Day was observed as a general holiday. According to general Saxton's orders, an ox had been killed on each plantation, that the people might that day have fresh meat, which was a great luxury to them, and, indeed, to all of us. In the morning, a large number—superintendents, teachers, and freed people—assembled in the Baptist Church. It was a sight not soon to be forgotten,—that crowd of eager, happy black faces, from which the shadow of Slavery had forever passed. "Forever free! forever free!" those magical words of the Proclamation were constantly singing themselves in my soul. After an appropriate prayer and sermon by Mr. P., and singing by the people, General Saxton made a short, but spirited speech, urging the young men to enlist in the regiment then forming under Colonel Higginson. Mrs. Gage told the people how the slaves in Santa Cruz had secured their liberty. It was something entirely new and strange to them to hear a woman speak in public; but they listened with great attention, and seemed much interested. Before dispersing, they sang "Marching Along," which is an especial favorite with them. It was a very happy Thankgiving-Day for all of us. The weather was delightful; oranges and figs were hanging on the trees; roses, oleanders, and japonicas were blooming out-of-doors; the sun was warm and bright; and over all shone gloriously the blessed light of Freedom,—Freedom forevermore. . . .

[Christmas Day] the children of our school assembled . . . and we gave them the nice, comfortable clothing, and the picture-books, which had been kindly sent by some Philadelphia ladies. There were at least a hundred and fifty children present. It was very pleasant to see their happy, expectant little faces. To them, it was a wonderful Christmas-Day,—such as they had never dreamed of before. There was cheerful sunshine without, lighting up the beautiful moss-drapery of the oaks, and looking in joyously through the open windows; and there were bright faces and glad hearts within. The long, dark night of the Past, with all its sorrows and its fears, was forgotten; and for the Future,—the eyes of these freed children see no clouds in it. It is full of sunlight, they think, and they trust in it, perfectly. . . .

New-Year's Day—Emancipation-Day—was a glorious one to us. . . . Our friend took us over the camp, and showed us all the arrangements. Everything looked clean and comfortable, much neater, we were told, than in most of the white camps. An officer told us that he had never seen a regiment in which the men were so honest. "In many other camps," said he, "the colonel and the rest of us would find it necessary to place a guard before our tents. We never do it here. They are left entirely unguarded. Yet nothing has ever been touched." We were glad to know that. It is a remarkable fact, when we consider that these men have all their lives been *slaves;* and we know what the teachings of Slavery are. . . . To us it seemed strange as a miracle,—this black regiment, the first mustered into the service of the United States, doing itself honor in the sight of officers of other regiments, many of whom, doubtless, "came to scoff." . . . At Beaufort we took the row-boat for St. Helena; and the boatmen, as they rowed, sang some of their sweetest, wildest hymns. It was a fitting close to such a day. Our hearts were filled with an exceeding great gladness; for, although the Government had left much undone, we knew that Freedom was surely born in our land that day. It seemed too glorious a good to realize,—this beginning of the great work we had so longed and prayed for. . . .

Among the visitors present was the noble young Colonel Shaw, whose regiment was then stationed on the island. We had met him a few nights before, when he came to our house to witness one of the people's shouts. We looked upon him with the deepest interest. There was something in his face finer, more exquisite, than one often sees in a man's face, yet it was full of courage and decision. The rare and singular charm of his manner drew all hearts to him. He was deeply interested in the singing and appearances of the people. A few days afterwards we saw his regiment on dress-parade, and admired its remarkably fine and manly appearance. After taking supper with the Colonel we sat outside the tent, while some of his men entertained us with excellent singing. Every moment we became more and more charmed with him. How full of life and hope and lofty aspirations he was that night! How eagerly he expressed his wish that they might soon be ordered to Charleston! "I do hope they will give *us* a chance," he said. It was the desire of his soul that his men should do themselves honor,—that they should prove themselves to an unbelieving world as brave soldiers as though their skins were white. And for himself, he was like the Chevalier of old, "without reproach or fear." After we had mounted our horses and rode away, we seemed still to feel the kind clasp of his hand,—to hear the pleasant, genial tones of his voice, as he bade us goodbye, and hoped that we might meet again. We never saw him afterward. In two short weeks came the terrible massacre at Fort Wagner, and the beautiful head of the young hero and martyr was laid low in the dust. Never shall we forget the heart-sickness with which we heard of his death. We could not realize it at first,—we, who had seen him so lately in all the strength and glory of his young manhood.

For days we clung to a vain hope; then it fell away from us, and we knew that he was gone. We knew that he died gloriously, but still it seemed very hard. Our hearts bled for the mother whom he so loved,—for the young wife, left desolate. And then we said, as we say now,—"God comfort them! He only can." During a few of the sad days which followed the attack on Fort Wagner, I was in one of the hospitals in Beaufort, occupied with the wounded soldiers of the Fifty-fourth Massachusetts. The first morning was spent in mending the bullet-holes and rents in their clothing. What a story they told! Some of the jackets of the poor fellows were literally cut in pieces. It was pleasant to see the brave, cheerful spirit among them. Some of them were severely wounded, but they uttered no complaint; and in the letters which they dictated to their absent friends there was no word of regret, but the same cheerful tone throughout. They expressed an eager desire to get well, that they might "go at it again." Their attachment to their young colonel was beautiful to see. They felt his death deeply. One and all united in the warmest and most enthusiastic praise of him. He was, indeed, exactly the person to inspire the most loyal devotion in the hearts of his men. And with everything to live for, he had given up his life for them. Heaven's best gifts had been showered upon him, but for them he had laid them all down. I think they truly appreciated the greatness of the sacrifice. May they ever prove worthy of such a leader! Already, they, and the regiments of freedmen here, as well, have shown that true manhood has no limitation of color.

Daily the long-oppressed people of these islands are demonstrating their capacity for improvement in learning and labor. What they have accomplished in one short year exceeds our utmost expectations. Still the sky is dark; but through the darkness we can discern a brighter future. We cannot but feel that the day of final and entire deliverance, so long and often so hopelessly prayed for, has at length begun to dawn upon this much-enduring race. An old freedman said to me one day, "De Lord make me suffer long time, Miss. 'Peared like we nebber was gwine to git troo. But now we's free. He bring us all out right at las'." In their darkest hours they have clung to Him, and we know He will not forsake them.

"The poor among men shall rejoice
For the terrible one is brought to nought."

While writing these pages I am once more nearing Port Royal. The Fortunate Isles of Freedom are before me. I shall again tread the flower-skirted woodpaths of St. Helena, and the sombre pines and bearded oaks shall whisper in the sea-wind their grave welcome. I shall dwell again among "mine own people." I shall gather my scholars about me, and see smiles of greeting break over their dusk faces. My heart sings a song of thanksgiving, at the thought that even I am permitted to do something for a long-abused race, and aid in promoting a higher, holier, and happier life on the Sea Islands.

Nathaniel Hawthorne, photographed by Mathew Brady, 1862 *(Courtesy of the Library of Congress)*

# Nathaniel Hawthorne
## (1804–1864)

❧

On June, 28, 1860, after nearly seven years' absence, Nathaniel Hawthorne returned to America. Following several days of welcome-home dinners and parties (Emerson had friends over for strawberries and cream), Hawthorne, the renowned author of *Twice-Told Tales* (1837), *The Scarlet Letter* (1850), *The House of the Seven Gables* (1851), *The Blithedale Romance* (1852), and *The Marble Faun* (1860), resumed work at his home in Concord, Wayside Inn. For the next year, he struggled with his writing. He reworked some notebook sketches and published them, more for money than for art. He made several false starts on a new romance before abandoning the project. He often complained about his paper and his pens. But he knew the problem was with the craftsman and not with his tools. "Mentally and physically languid," Hawthorne drifted through time.[1]

The outbreak of war temporarily recharged his creative energies. His letters showed vitality and independence. He tweaked his dear English friends for supporting the Confederacy and he derided his abolitionist neighbors for their simplicity. He marveled at how war-spirit galvanized the nation and even proclaimed a desire to shoulder a musket himself. But he failed to see what would be gained from the slaughter and was more than willing to let the Confederacy go provided that the border states— Virginia, Maryland, Kentucky, and Missouri—remained with the Union. When, on March 6, 1862, he left with his publisher and friend William Ticknor on a trip to Washington, he hoped the change of scene would do him good and that he would get closer to the war that alone was able to stimulate his imagination.

Once in Washington, Hawthorne became part of a Massachusetts delegation that called at the White House and met Lincoln. He toured Harper's Ferry and Fortress Monroe, Newport News and Manassas. He studied George McClellan, and he saw the *Monitor*. He met Confederate prisoners. And he viewed the Cumberland, a frigate sunk by the *Merrimack*, with its three masts sticking out of the water, a tattered flag still flying. He wrote his son that he wished he could compose a song about the gallantry of the crew, which was reported to have continued firing even after the ship's decks were partially submerged. During the trip, Hawthorne kept a journal which he later destroyed ("In the way of manuscript," he told one correspondent in 1864, "I generally burn everything behind me like a retreating army").² But he came home eager to write.

Hawthorne returned to Concord on April 10; by May 7, he had completed the manuscript of "Chiefly About War-Matters" and mailed it to his publisher. As written, the essay was a searching meditation on the war, simultaneously patriotic and treasonous, lyrical and satirical. Hawthorne used the device of editorial footnotes to condemn the opinions of the narrator, identified only as "the peaceable man." James Fields, editor of the *Atlantic Monthly*, liked the piece, but asked Hawthorne to alter his description of Lincoln and not to call him "Uncle Abe." Hawthorne refused to change the section, but, with the warning that "you omit the only part of the article really worth publishing," allowed Fields to cut it.³ The excerpt that follows includes the original passages, which Fields ultimately published in 1871.

If Hawthorne's neighbors appreciated the artistry of "Chiefly About War-Matters," they did not say. But they could not contain themselves over a final literary act on Hawthorne's part, the dedication of *Our Old Home*, a collection of essays on England, published in 1863. Hawthorne dedicated the volume to Franklin Pierce, the former Democratic President of the United States who was a student with Hawthorne at Bowdoin College in the 1820s and who, in 1853, appointed him United States Consul at Liverpool and Manchester. Hawthorne had written Pierce's campaign biography, but his acknowledgment of the ex-President was intended not as a political statement but as a personal one. He offered the volume "as a slight memorial of a college friendship, prolonged through manhood, and retaining all its vitality in our autumnal years."

Hawthorne's commemoration of Pierce came at the moment that Pierce's reputation in the North was at its lowest. Proponents of the Union effort trusted few Northern Democrats during the war, and Pierce seemed especially suspect. In July 1863, Pierce addressed a crowd in New Hampshire on the benefits of peace and Union, this just after news of Gettysburg. And in the fall, newspapers reprinted a letter from Pierce to Jefferson Davis, written in 1860, that denounced the "madness

Northern abolitionists." Whatever Hawthorne thought of his friend's politics, and it is clear that he did not agree entirely on the benefits of Union, he stood by Pierce. Fields was concerned that the dedication would help sink the volume, but Hawthorne would not "merely on account of pecuniary profit and literary reputation, go back from what I have deliberately felt and thought it right to do. . . . I would gladly sacrifice a thousand or two of dollars rather than retain the good will of such a herd of dolts and mean-spirited scoundrels."[4]

The reactions from foes and friends must have disheartened the already weary author. Some book dealers threatened to boycott the volume; one abolitionist sent him a packet of anti-Pierce writings; Emerson tore the dedication page and letter out of his copy. When Hawthorne's sister-in-law, Elizabeth Peabody, attacked him for the dedication, she got back a blazing letter.

The Dedication, it turns out, concluded Hawthorne's literary life. He could no longer write Romance. His essays and letters on the war allowed him to probe irony and ambiguity, light and darkness, but it seemed too late in his career to continue along this road. A dedication had become a political act; writing had become more dangerous than ever. In the three-page dedication letter, Hawthorne wrote that he had wished to offer his friend a more substantial volume, but "the Present, the Immediate, the Actual, has proved too potent for me. It takes away not only my scanty faculty, but even my desire for imaginative composition, and leaves me sadly content to scatter a thousand peaceful fantasies upon the hurricane that is sweeping us all along with it, possibly, into a Limbo where our nation and its polity may be as literally the fragments of a shattered dream as my unwritten Romance."[5]

On May 18, 1864, on yet another brief journey in search of renewed health and vitality, with Franklin Pierce less than five feet away, Hawthorne succumbed to the potency of his nation's strife.

### 1. NH to Horatio Bridge,[6] Concord, May 26, 1861[7]

. . . The war, strange to say, has had a beneficial effect upon my spirits, which were flagging woefully before it broke out. But it was delightful to share in the heroic sentiment of the time, and to feel that I had a country—a consciousness which seemed to make me young again. One thing, as regards this matter, I regret, and one thing I am glad of;—the regrettable thing is, that I am too old to shoulder a musket myself; and the joyful thing is, that Julian is too young. He drills constantly with a company of lads, and means to enlist as soon as he reaches the minimum age; but I trust we shall either be victorious or vanquished before that time. Meantime (though I approve the war as much as any man) I don't quite understand what we are fighting for, or what definite result can be expected. If we pummel the South ever so hard, they will love us none the better for it; and even if we subjugate them, our next step should be to cut them adrift. If we are fighting for the annihilation of slavery, to be sure, it may be a wise object, and offers a tangible result, and the only one which is consistent with a future Union between North and South. A continuance of the war would soon make this plain to us; and we should see the expediency of preparing our black brethren for future citizenship by allowing them to fight for their own liberties, and educating them through heroic influences.

What ever happens next, I must say that I rejoice that the old Union is smashed. We never were one people, and never really had a country since the Constitution was formed. . . .

## 2. NH to William D. Ticknor,[8] Concord, May 26, 1861

. . . I wish they would push on the war a little more briskly. The excitement had an invigorating effect on me for a time, but it begins to lose its influence. But it is rather unreasonable to wish my countrymen to kill one another for the sake of refreshing my pallid spirits: so I shall pray for peace.

## 3. NH to Francis Bennoch,[9] Concord [July 1861]

. . . The truth is that, at present, I have little heart for anything. We are, as you know, at the beginning of a great war—a war, the issue of which no man can predicate; and I, for one, have no inclination to attempt prophecy. It is not long since the acute ruler of France—the epigrammatic speech-maker—announced to a startled Europe and a delighted country that he had gone to war for an idea—a very NICE, if not absoluteley true idea.[10] But we Yankees have cast him entirely into the shade. We, also, have gone to war, and we seem to have little, or, at least, a very misty idea of what we are fighting for. It depends upon the speaker, and that, again, depends upon the section of the country in which his sympathies are enlisted. The Southern man will say, we fight for states rights, liberty, and independence. The middle and Western states-man will avow that he fights for the Union; whilst our Northern and Eastern man will swear that, from the beginning, his only idea was liberty to the Blacks, and the annihilation of slavery. All are thoroughly in earnest, and all pray for the blessing of Heaven to rest upon the enterprise. The appeals are so numerous, fervent, and yet so contradictory, that the Great Arbiter to whom they so piously and solemnly appeal, must be sorely puzzled how to decide. One thing is indisputable; the spirit of our young men is thoroughly aroused. Their enthusiasm is boundless; and the smiles of our fragile and delicate women cheer them on. When I hear their drums beating, and see their banners flying, and witness their steady marching, I declare, were it not for certain silvery monitors hanging by my temples, suggesting prudence, I feel as if I could catch the infection, shoulder a musket, and be off to the war myself!

Meditating on these matters, I begin to think our custom as to war a mistake. Why draw from our young men, in the bloom and hey-day of their youth, the soldiers who are to fight our battles? Had I my way, no man should go to war under fifty years of age, such men having already had their natural share of worldly pleasures and life's enjoyments. And I don't see how they could make a more creditable or more honourable exit from the world's stage than by becoming food for powder, and gloriously dying in defense of their home and country. Then, I would add a premium in favour of recruits of three score years and upwards; as, virtually, with one foot in the grave, they would not be likely to run away. I apprehend that no people ever built up the skeleton of a warlike history so rapidly as we are doing. What a fine theme for a poet! If you were not a born Britisher, from whose country we expect no help and little sympathy, I would ask you for a martial strain—a song to be sung by our camp fires, to sooth the feelings, and rouse the energies of our troops; inspiring them to meet like men the great conflict that awaits them, resolved to conquer or to die—if dying, still to conquer. Ten thousand poetasters have tried and tried in vain to give us a rousing "Scots wha hae wi' Wallace bled."[11] If we fight no better than we sing, may the Lord have mercy upon us and upon the nation! . . .

### 4. NH to Rose Hawthorne, Beverly Farms, August 5, 1861

. . . Tell Mamma that I see no newspapers, and do not know at this moment, whether the Rebels have taken Washington, or what other misfortune may have happened. Almost every hour, however, I hear the noise of drums, over the water, from Marblehead to Salem, and very often the thunder of cannon, which sometimes continues for an hour together; so that I begin to think the war has overspread the whole country except just this little precinct in the neighborhood of West Beach. On the whole, I enjoy this respite from the daily repetition and contradiction of telegraphs about skirmishes, victories, and defeats, and could almost be content to remain in the same ignorance till the war is over. . . .

### 5. NH to Horatio Bridge, Concord, October 12, 1861

. . . I don't hope (nor, indeed, wish) to see the Union restored as it was; amputation seems to me much the better plan, and all we ought to fight for is, the liberty of selecting the point where our diseased members shall be lopt off. I would fight to the death for the Northern slave-states, and let the rest go.... I have not found it possible to occupy my mind with its usual trash and nonsense, during these anxious times; but as the autumn advances, I find myself sitting down to my desk, and blotting successive sheets of paper, as of yore....

### 6. NH to Henry A. Bright, Concord, November 14, 1861

... By the by, you talk (in common with all other Englishmen) most wretched rubbish about this war. You are so wrong, that you and I have no common ground together, on which I can attempt to set you right. Can you see nothing in this view of the case?—for instance; if we had not fought, the North would unquestionably have lost its Capital, and its identity as a nation, and would have had to make an entirely new position for itself, and probably three or four separate positions. If we stop fighting at this juncture, we give up Maryland, Virginia, Kentucky, Missouri, all of which are fully capable of being made free-soil, and will be so in a few years, if we possess them, but not in a hundred years, if we lose them. We give up our Capital too, and retire under a load of disgrace, which, to my mind, would make national extinction the lesser evil of the two. Cannot an Englishman's common sense help you to see that this is so? Cannot your English pride of country win any sympathy from you for a people who have all their moral inheritance at stake? Who cares what the war costs, in blood or treasure? People must die, whether a bullet kills them or no; and money must be spent, if not for gunpowder, then for worse luxuries. My countrymen choose to spend themselves and their prosperity in war; and they find, at this very moment, an enjoyment in it worth all their sacrifices. I never imagined what a happy state of mind a civil war produces, and how it invigorates every man's whole being. You will live to see the Americans another people than they have hitherto been; and I truly regret that my youth was not cast in these days, instead of in a quiet time.

When we have established our boundary lines to our satisfaction, and demonstrated that we are strong enough to subjugate the whole South, I trust we shall cast off the extreme southern states, and giving them a parting kick, let them go to perdition in their own way. I want no more of their territory than we can digest into free soil; but now that we have actually come to swords' points, it would be a sin and shame to take less.

To drop this subject, (in which, of course, I do not expect you to agree with me, for I know Englishmen too well, and know that every man of you wishes to see us both maimed and disgraced, and looks upon this whole trouble as a god-send—if only there were cotton enough at Liverpool and Manchester,) to drop the subject, however—I have spent personally a very quiet summer, seldom leaving home, except for a visit to the seashore, or an occasional dinner in

Boston. The war at first drew my thoughts wholly to itself, but latterly, I am meditating a Romance, and hope to have it finished by the time the public shall be ready for any other literature than the daily bulletin, or treatises on warlike strategy. . . .

Lowell had a nephew (whom he dearly loved) killed, and another wounded, in one battle; and a son of Holmes received two wounds in the same. The shots strike all round us, but even the mothers bear it with wonderful fortitude.

Emerson is breathing slaughter, like the rest of us; and it is really wonderful how all sorts of theoretical nonsense, to which we New Englanders are addicted in peaceful times, vanish in the strong atmosphere which we now inhale. The grim endurance of the merchants, and even of the shopkeepers, surprises me. The whole world, on this side of the Atlantic, appears to have grown more natural and sensible, and walks more erect and cares less about childish things. If the war only lasts long enough (and not too long) it will have done us infinite good. . . .

### 7. NH to Horatio Bridge, Concord, February 13, 1862

. . . Frank Pierce[12] came here and spent a night, a week or two since; and we drank a bottle of arrack together, and mingled our tears and condolements for the state of the country. Pierce is truly patriotic, and thinks there is nothing left for us but to fight it out; but I should be sorry to take his opinion implicitly as regards our chances in the future. He is bigoted to the Union, and sees nothing but ruin without it; whereas, I (if we can only put the boundary far enough south) should not much regret an ultimate separation. A few weeks will decide how this is to be; for, unless a powerful Union feeling shall be developed by the military successes that seem to be setting in, we ought to turn our attention to the best mode of resolving ourselves into two nations. It would be too great an absurdity, to spend all our Northern strength, for the next generation, in holding on to a people who insist upon being let loose. If we do hold them, I should think Sumner's territorial plan the best way. . . .

P.S. I ought to thank you for a shaded map of Negrodom, which you sent me a little while ago. What a terrible amount of trouble and expense, in washing the sheet white!—and, after all, I am afraid we shall only variegate it with blood and dirt.

### 8. A Peaceable Man [Nathaniel Hawthorne], "Chiefly About War-Matters," *Atlantic Monthly*, 10 (July 1862): 43–61

There is no remoteness of life and thought, no hermetically sealed seclusion, except, possibly, that of the grave, into which the disturbing influences of this

war do not penetrate. Of course, the general heart-quake of the country long
ago knocked at my cottage-door, and compelled me, reluctantly, to suspend the
contemplation of certain fantasies, to which, according to my harmless custom,
I was endeavoring to give a sufficiently life-like aspect to admit of their figuring
in a romance. As I make no pretensions to statecraft or soldiership, and could
promote the common weal neither by valor nor counsel, it seemed, at first, a
pity that I should be debarred from such unsubstantial business as I had con-
trived for myself, since nothing more genuine was to be substituted for it. But
I magnanimously considered that there is a kind of treason in insulating one's
self from the universal fear and sorrow, and thinking one's idle thoughts in the
dread time of civil war; and could a man be so cold and hard-hearted, he would
better deserve to be sent to Fort Warren than many who have found their way
thither on the score of violent, but misdirected sympathies. I remembered the
touching rebuke administered by King Charles to that rural squire the echo of
whose hunting-horn came to the poor monarch's ear on the morning before a
battle, where the sovereignty and constitution of England was to be set at stake.
So I gave myself up to reading newspapers and listening to the click of the telegraph, like other people; until, after a great many months of such pastime, it
grew so abominably irksome that I determined to look a little more closely at
matters with my own eyes. . . .

On our way, we heard many rumors of the war, but few signs of it. The
people were staid and decorous, according to their ordinary fashion; and business seemed about as brisk as usual—though, I suppose, it was considerably
diverted from its customary channels into warlike ones. In the cities, especially
in New York, there was a rather prominent display of military goods at the
shop-windows,—such as swords with gilded scabbards and trappings, epaulets,
carabines, revolvers, and sometimes a great iron cannon at the edge of the pavement, as if Mars had dropped one of his pocket-pistols there, while hurrying
to the field. As railway-companions, we had now and then a volunteer in his
French-gray great-coat, returning from furlough, or a new-made officer trav-
elling to join his regiment, in his new-made uniform, which was perhaps all of
the military character that he had about him,—but proud of his eagle-buttons,
and likely enough to do them honor before the gilt should be wholly dimmed.
The country, in short, so far as bustle and movement went, was more quiet than
in ordinary times, because so large a proportion of its restless elements had
been drawn towards the seat of conflict. But the air was full of a vague disturbance. To me, at least, it seemed so, emerging from such a solitude as has been
hinted at, and the more impressible by rumors and indefinable presentiments,
since I had not lived, like other men, in an atmosphere of continual talk about
the war. A battle was momentarily expected on the Potomac; for, though our
army was still on the hither side of the river, all of us were looking toward the

mysterious and terrible Manassas, with the idea that somewhere in its neighborhood lay a ghastly battlefield, yet to be fought, but foredoomed of old to be bloodier than the one where we had reaped such shame. Of all haunted places, methinks such a destined field should be thickest thronged with ugly phantoms, ominous of mischief through ages beforehand. . . .

Will the time ever come again, in America, when we may live half a score of years without once seeing the likeness of a soldier, except it be in the festal march of a company on its summer tour? Not in this generation, I fear, nor in the next, nor till the Millennium; and even that blessed epoch, as the prophecies seem to intimate, will advance to the sound of the trumpet.

One terrible idea occurs, in reference to this matter. Even supposing the war should end to-morrow, and the army melt into the mass of the population within the year, what an incalculable preponderance will there be of military titles and pretensions for at least half a century to come! Every country-neighborhood will have its general or two, its three or four colonels, half a dozen majors, and captains without end,—besides non-commissioned officers and privates, more than the recruiting-offices ever knew of,—all with their campaign stories, which will become the staple of fireside-talk forevermore. Military merit, or rather, since that is not so readily estimated, military notoriety, will be the measure of all claims to civil distinction. One bullet-headed general will succeed another in the Presidential chair; and veterans will hold the offices at home and abroad, and sit in Congress and the State legislatures, and fill all the avenues of public life. And yet I do not speak of this deprecatingly, since, very likely, it may substitute something more real and genuine, instead of the many shams on which men have heretofore founded their claims to public regard; but it behooves civilians to consider their wretched prospects on the future, and assume the military button before it is too late.

We were not in time to see Washington as a camp. On the very day of our arrival sixty thousand men had crossed the Potomac on their march towards Manassas; and almost with their first step into the Virginia mud, the phantasmagory of a countless host and impregnable ramparts, before which they had so long remained quiescent, dissolved quite away. It was as if General McClellan had thrust his sword into a gigantic enemy, and, beholding him suddenly collapse, had discovered to himself and the world that he had merely punctured an enormously swollen bladder. There are instances of a similar character in old romances, where great armies are long kept at bay by the arts of necromancers, who build airy towers and battlements, and muster warriors of terrible aspect, and thus feign a defence of seeming impregnability, until some bolder champion of the besiegers dashes forward to try an encounter with the foremost foeman, and finds him melt away in the death-grapple. With such heroic adventures let the march upon Manassas be hereafter reckoned. The whole business, though connected with the destinies of a nation, takes inevitably a tinge of the ludicrous. The vast preparation of men and warlike material,—the majestic patience and docility with which the people waited through those weary and dreary months,—the martial skill, courage, and caution, with which our movement was ultimately made,—and, at last, the tremendous shock with which we were brought suddenly up against nothing at all! The Southerners show little sense of humor nowadays, but I think they must have meant to provoke a laugh at our expense, when they planted those Quaker guns. At all events, no other Rebel artillery has played upon us with such overwhelming effect. . . .

We found one man . . . at the Capitol, who was satisfactorily adequate to the business which brought him thither. . . . It was an absolute comfort, indeed, to find Leutze[13] so quietly busy at this great national work, which is deemed to glow for centuries on the walls of the Capitol, if that edifice shall stand, or must share its fate, if treason shall succeed in subverting it with the Union which it represents. It was delightful to see him so calmly elaborating his design, while other men doubted and feared, or hoped treacherously, and whispered to one another that the nation would exist only a little longer, or that, if a remnant still held together, its centre and seat of government would be far northward and westward of Washington. But the artist keeps right on, firm of heart and hand, drawing his outlines with an unwavering pencil, beautifying and idealizing our rude, material life, and thus manifesting that we have an indefeasible claim to a more enduring national existence. In honest truth, what with the hope-inspiring influence of the design, and what with Leutze's undisturbed evolvement of it, I was exceedingly encouraged, and allowed these cheerful auguries to weigh against a sinister omen that was pointed out to me in another part of the Capitol. The freestone walls of the central edifice are pervaded with great cracks, and threaten to come thundering down, under the immense weight of the iron dome,—an appropriate catastrophe enough, if it should occur on the day when we drop the Southern stars out of our flag. . . .

[At the White House] we formed a very miscellaneous collection of people, mostly unknown to each other, and without any common sponsor, but all with an equal right to look our head-servant in the face. By-and-by there was a little stir on the staircase and in the passage-way, etc., etc.*

---

*We are compelled to omit two or three pages, in which the author describes the interview, and gives his idea of the personal appearance and deportment of the President. The sketch appears to have been written in a benign spirit, and perhaps conveys a not inaccurate impression of its august subject; but it lacks *reverence*, and it pains us to see a gentleman of ripe age, and who has spent years under the corrective influence of foreign institutions, falling into the characteristic and most ominous fault of Young America.

[The omitted text, published in April 1871, read as follows: By and by there was a little stir on the staircase and in the passage-way, and in lounged a tall, loose-jointed figure, of an exaggerated Yankee port and demeanor, whom (as being about the homeliest man I ever saw, yet by no means repulsive or disagreeable) it was impossible not to recognize as Uncle Abe.

Unquestionably, Western man though he be, and Kentuckian by birth, President Lincoln is the essential representative of all Yankees, and the veritable specimen, physically, of what the world seems determined to regard as our characteristic qualities. It is the strangest and yet the fittest thing in the jumble of human vicissitudes, that he, out of so many millions, unlooked-for, unselected by any intelligible process that could be based upon his genuine qualities, unknown to those who chose him, and unsuspected of what endowment may adapt him for his tremendous responsibility, should have found the way open for him to fling his lank personality into the chair of state,—where, I presume, it was his first impulse to throw his legs on the council-table, and tell the Cabinet Ministers a story. There is no describing his lengthy awkwardness, nor the uncouthness of his movement; and yet it seemed as if I had been in the habit of seeing him daily, and had shaken hands with him a thousand times in some village street; so true was he to the aspect of the pattern American, though with a certain extravagance which, possibly, I exaggerated still further by the delightful eagerness with which I took it in. If put to guess his calling and livelihood, I should have taken him for a country schoolmaster as soon as anything else. He was dressed in a rusty black frock-coat and pantaloons, unbrushed, and worn so faithfully that the suit had adapted itself to the curves and angularities of his figure, and had grown to be an outer skin of the man. He had shabby slippers on his feet. His hair was black, still unmixed with gray, stiff, somewhat bushy, and had apparently been acquainted with neither brush nor comb that morning, after the disarrangement of the pillow; and as to a nightcap, Uncle Abe probably knows nothing of such effeminancies. His complexion is dark and sallow, betokening, I fear, an insalubrious atmosphere around the White House; he has thick black eyebrows and an impending brow: his nose is large, and the lines about his mouth are very strongly defined.

The whole physiognomy is as coarse a one as you would meet anywhere in the length and breadth of the States; but, withal, it is redeemed, illuminated, softened, and brightened, by a kindly though serious look out of his eyes, and an expression of homely sagacity, that seems weighted with rich results of village experience. A great deal of native sense; no bookish cultivation, no refinement; honest at heart, and thoroughly so, and yet, in some sort, sly,—at least, endowed with a sort of tact and wisdom that are akin to craft, and would impel him, I think, to take an antagonist in flank, rather to make a bull-run at him right in front. But, on the whole, I liked this sallow, queer, sagacious visage, with the homely human sympathies that warmed it; and, for my small share in the matter, would as lief have Uncle Abe for a ruler as any man whom it would have been practicable to put in his place. . . .]

. . . I tried to imagine how very disagreeable the presence of a Southern army would be in a sober town of Massachusetts; and the thought considerably lessened my wonder at the cold and shy regards that are cast upon our troops, the gloom, the sullen demeanor, the declared or scarcely hidden sympathy with rebellion, which are so frequent here. It is a strange thing in human life, that the greatest errors of both men and women often spring from their sweetest and most generous qualities; and so, undoubtedly, thousands of warm-hearted, sympathetic, and impulsive persons have joined the Rebels, not from any zeal for the cause, but because, between two conflicting loyalties, they chose that which necessarily lay nearest the heart. There never existed any other Government against which treason was so easy, and could defend itself by such plausible arguments as against that of the United States. The anomaly of two allegiances (of which that of the State comes nearest home to a man's feelings, and includes the altar and the hearth, while the General Government claims his devotion only to an airy mode of law, and has no symbol but a flag) is exceedingly mischievous in this point of view; for it has converted crowds of honest people into traitors, who seem to themselves not merely innocent, but patriotic, and who die for a bad cause with as quiet a conscience as if it were the best. In the vast extent of our country,—too vast by far to be taken into one small human heart,—we inevitably limit to our own State, or, at farthest, to our own section, that sentiment of physical love for the soil, which renders an Englishman, for example, so intensely sensitive to the dignity and well-being of his little island, that one hostile foot, treading anywhere upon it, would make a bruise on each individual breast. If a man loves his own State, therefore, and is content to be ruined with her, let us shoot him, if we can, but allow him an honorable burial in the soil he fights for.*

*We do not thoroughly comprehend the author's drift in the foregoing paragraph, but are inclined to think its tone reprehensible, and its tendency impolitic in the present stage of our national difficulties.

. . . The fortifications, so numerous in all this region, and now so unsightly with their bare, precipitous sides, will remain as historic monuments, grass-grown and picturesque memorials of an epoch of terror and suffering: they will serve to make our country dearer and more interesting to us, and afford fit soil for poetry to root itself in: for this is a plant which thrives best in spots where blood has been spilt long ago, and grows in abundant clusters in old ditches, such as the moat around Fort Ellsworth will be a century hence. It may seem to be paying dear for what many will reckon but a worthless weed; but the more historical associations we can link with our localities, the richer will be the daily life that feeds upon the past, and the more valuable the things that have been long established: so that our children will be less prodigal than their fathers in sacrificing good institutions to passionate impulses and impracticable theories. This herb of grace, let us hope, may be found in the old footprints of the war. . . .

One very pregnant token of a social system thoroughly disturbed was presented by a party of contrabands, escaping out of the mysterious depths of Secessia; and its strangeness consisted in the leisurely delay with which they trudged forward, as dreading no pursuer, and encountering nobody to turn them back. They were unlike the specimens of their race whom we are accustomed to see at the North, and, in my judgment, were far more agreeable. So rudely were they attired,—as if their garb had grown upon them spontaneously,—so picturesquely natural in manners, and wearing such a crust of primeval simplicity, (which is quite polished away from the Northern black man), that they seemed a kind of creature by themselves, not altogether human, but perhaps quite as good, and akin to the fauns and rustic deities of olden times. I wonder whether I shall excite anyone's wrath by saying this. It is no great matter. At all events, I felt most kindly towards these poor fugitives, but knew not what precisely to wish in their behalf, nor in the least how to help them. For the sake of the manhood which is latent in them, I would not have turned them back; but I should have felt almost as reluctant, on their own account, to hasten them forward to the stranger's land; and I think that my prevalent idea was, that, whoever may be benefited by the results of this war, it will not be the present generation of negroes, the childhood of whose race is now gone forever, and who must henceforth fight a hard battle with the world, on very unequal terms. On behalf of my own race, I am glad, and can only hope that an inscrutable Providence means good to both parties.

There is an historical circumstance, known to few, that connects the children of the Puritans with these Africans of Virginia, in a very singular way. They are our brethren, as being lineal descendants from the Mayflower, the fated womb of which, in her first voyage, sent forth a brood of Pilgrims upon Plymouth Rock, and, in a subsequent one, spawned slaves upon the Southern soil,—a monstrous birth, but with which we have an instinctive sense of kindred, and so are stirred by an irresistible impulse to attempt their rescue, even at the cost of blood and ruin. The character of our sacred ship, I fear, may suffer a little by this revelation; but we must let her white progeny offset her dark one,—and two such portents never sprang from an identical source before. . . .

His face [a young officer's] had a healthy hue of exposure and an expression of careless hardihood; and, as I looked at him, it seemed to me that the war had brought good fortune to the youth of this epoch, if to none beside; since they now make it their daily business to ride a horse and handle a sword, instead of lounging listlessly through the duties, occupations, pleasures—all tedious alike—to which the artificial state of society limits a peaceful generation. The atmosphere of the camp and the smoke of the battle-field are morally invigorating; the hardy virtues flourish in them, the nonsense dies like a wilted weed. The enervating effects of centuries of civilization vanish at once, and leave these young men to enjoy a life of hardship, and the exhilarating sense of danger,—to kill men blamelessly, or to be killed gloriously,—and to be happy in following out their native instincts of destruction, precisely in the spirit of Homer's heroes, only with some considerable change of mode. One touch of Nature makes not only the whole world, but all time, akin. Set men face to face, with weapons in their hands, and they are as ready to slaughter one another now, after playing at peace and good-will for so many years, as in the rudest ages, that never heard of peace-societies, and thought no wine so delicious as what they quaffed from an enemy's skull. Indeed, if the report of a Congressional committee may be trusted, that old-fashioned kind of goblet has again come into use, at the expense of our Northern head-pieces,—a costly drinking cup to him that furnishes it! Heaven forgive me for seeming to jest on such a subject!—only, it is so odd, when we measure our advances from barbarism, and find ourselves just here!*

*We hardly expected this outbreak in favor of war from the Peaceable Man; but the justice of our cause makes us all soldiers at heart, however quiet in our outward life. We have heard of twenty Quakers in a single company of a Pennsylvania regiment.

... I shall not pretend to be an admirer of old John Brown, any farther than sympathy with Whittier's excellent ballad about him may go; nor did I expect ever to shrink so unutterably from any apothegm of a sage, whose happy lips have uttered a hundred golden sentences, as from that saying, (perhaps falsely attribute to so honorable a source), that the death of this blood-stained fanatic has "made the Gallows as venerable as the Cross!"[14] Nobody was ever more justly hanged. He won his martyrdom fairly, and took it firmly. He himself, I am persuaded, (such was his natural integrity), would have acknowledged that Virginia had a right to take the life which he had staked and lost; although it would have been better for her, in the hour that is fast coming, if she could generously have forgotten the criminality of his attempt in its enormous folly. On the other hand, any common-sensible man, looking at the matter unsentimentally, must have felt a certain intellectual satisfaction in seeing him hanged, if it were only in requital of his preposterous miscalculation of possibilities.*

*Can it be a son of old Massachusetts who utters this abominable sentiment? For shame!

But, cooly as I seem to say these things, my Yankee heart stirred triumphantly when I saw the use to which John Brown's fortress and prison-house has now been put. What right have I to complain of any other man's foolish impulses, when I cannot possibly control my own? The engine-house is now a place of confinement for Rebel prisoners. . . . Looking round at these poor prisoners, therefore, it struck me as an immense absurdity that they should fancy us their enemies; since, whether we intend it so or no, they have a far greater stake on our success than we can possibly have. For ourselves, the balance of advantages between defeat and triumph may admit of question. For them, all truly valuable things are dependent on our complete success; for thence would come the regeneration of a people,—the removal of a foul scurf that has overgrown their life, and keeps them in a state of disease and decrepitude, one of the chief symptoms of which is, that, the more they suffer and are debased, the more they imagine themselves strong and beautiful. No human effort, on a grand scale, has ever yet resulted according to the purpose of its projectors. Man's accidents are God's purposes. We miss the good we sought, and do the good we little cared for.*

*The author seems to imagine that he has compressed a great deal of meaning into these little, hard, dry pellets of aphoristic wisdom. We disagree with him. The counsels of wise and good men are often coincident with the purposes of Providence; and the present war promises to illustrate our remark.

. . . It is a pity old men grow unfit for war, not only by their incapacity for new ideas, but by the peaceful and unadventurous tendencies that gradually possess themselves of the once turbulent disposition, which used to snuff the battle-smoke as its congenial atmosphere. It is a pity; because it would be such an economy of human existence, if time-stricken people (whose value I have the better right to estimate, as reckoning myself one of them) could snatch from their juniors the exclusive privilege of carrying on the war. In case of death upon the battle-field, how unequal would be the comparative silence! On one part, a few unenjoyable years, the little remnant of a life grown torpid; on the other, the many fervent summers of manhood in its spring and prime, with all that they include of possible benefit to mankind. Then, too, a bullet offers such a brief and easy way, such a pretty little orifice, through which the weary spirit might seize the opportunity to be exhaled! If I had the ordering of these matters, fifty should be the tenderest age at which a recruit might be accepted for training; at fifty-five or sixty, I would consider him eligible for most kinds of military duty and exposure, excluding that of a forlorn hope, which no soldier should be permitted to volunteer upon, short of the ripe age of seventy. As a general rule, these venerable combatants should have the preference for all dangerous and honorable service in the order of their seniority, with a distinction in favor of those whose infirmities might render their lives less worth the keeping. Methinks there would be no more Bull Runs; a warrior with gout in his toe, or rheumatism in his joints, or with one foot in the grave, would make a sorry fugitive!

On this admirable system, the productive part of the population would be undisturbed even by the bloodiest war; and, best of all, those thousands upon thousands of our Northern girls, whose proper mates will perish in camp-hospitals or on Southern battle-fields, would avoid their doom of forlorn old-maidenhood. But, no doubt, the plan will be pooh-poohed by the War Department; though it could scarcely be more disastrous than the one on which we began the war, when a young army was struck with paralysis through the age of its commander. . . .

There will be other battles, but no more such tests of seamanship and manhood as the battles of the past; and, moreover, the Millennium is certainly approaching, because human strife is to be transferred from the heart and personality of man into cunning contrivances of machinery, which by-and-by will fight out our wars with only the clank and smash of iron, strewing the field with broken engines, but damaging nobody's little finger, except by accident. Such is obviously the tendency of modern improvement. But, in the mean while, so long as manhood retains any part of its pristine value, no country can afford to let gallantry like that of Morris and his crew, any more than that of the brave Worden, pass unhonored and unrewarded. If the Government do nothing, let the people take the matter into their hands, and cities give him swords, gold boxes, festivals of triumph, and, if he needs it, heaps of gold. Let poets brood upon the theme, and make themselves sensible how much of the past and future is contained within its compass, till its spirit shall flash forth in the lightning of a song! . . .

Since the matter has gone so far, there seems to be no way but to go on winning victories, and establishing peace and a truer union in another generation, at the expense, probably of greater trouble, in the present one, than any other people ever voluntarily suffered. We woo the South "as the Lion wooes his bride"; it is a rough courtship, but perhaps love and a quiet household may come a bit at last. Or, if we stop short of that blessed consummation, heaven was heaven still, as Milton sings, after Lucifer and a third part of the angels had seceded from its golden palaces,—and perhaps all the more heavenly, because so many gloomy brows, and soured, vindictive hearts, had gone to plot ineffectual schemes of mischief elsewhere.*

*We regret the innuendo in the concluding sentence. The war can never be allowed to terminate, except in the complete triumph of Northern principles. We hold the event in our hands, and may choose whether to terminate it by the methods already so successfully used, or by other means equally within our control, and calculated to be still more speedily efficacious. In truth, the work is already done.


### 9. NH to Francis Bennoch, Concord, October 12, 1862

. . . I wish you could come and see us; for I don't expect ever to see England again. I did think that I might come over with a new Romance, the English copyright of which would pay Mrs. Hawthorne's and my own expences for a year; but it is impossible to possess one's mind in the midst of a civil war to such a degree as to make thoughts assume life. I hear the cannon and smell the gunpowder through everything. Besides, I feel as if the great convulson were going to make an epoch in our literature as in everything else (if it does not annihilate all,) and that when we emerge from the war-cloud, there will be another and better (at least, a more national and seasonable) class of writers than the one I belong to. So be it. I do not reckon literary reputation as a heavy item on the debtor side of my account with Providence;—indeed, I never realized that I had any at all, and am in doubt about it now. . . .

### 10. NH to Henry A. Bright, Concord, March 8, 1863

I ought to be heartily ashamed of my long silence, but in these revolutionary times, it is impossible to be ashamed of anything. When society is about to be overturned from its foundations, the courtesies of life must needs be a little damaged in advance of the general ruin; nor is it easy to write gossiping epistles when an earthquake is shaking one's writing table. So pardon me; and I will be as merciful to you when England is in a similar predicament.

You must not suppose, however, that I make myself very miserable about the war. The play (be it tragedy or comedy) is too long drawn out, and my chief feeling about it now is a sense of infinite weariness. I want the end to come, and the curtain to drop, and then go to sleep. I never did really approve of the war, though you may have supposed so from the violence and animosity with which I controverted your notions about it, when I wrote last. But you are an Englishman, you know, and of course cannot have any correct ideas about our country, and even if you had, a true American is bound not to admit them. The war-party here do not look upon me as a reliably loyal man, and, in fact, I have been publicly accused of treasonable sympathies;—whereas. I sympathize with nobody and approve of nothing: and if I have any wishes on the subject, it is that New England might be a nation by itself. But, so far as I can judge of the temper of the people, they mean to have a re-union; and if they really mean it, it will be accomplished. The North has never yet put out half its means, and there is a great deal of fight left in us yet. . . .

I went to the Club, last Saturday, and met all the usual set, besides some generals and colonels, fresh from the battle-field, war-worn and wounded.[15] The tone of feeling was very patriotic, the mildest men and most abstract philosophers being, as it seemed to me, the most truculent. Emerson is as merciless as a steel bayonet; and I would not give much for a rebel's life if he came within a sword's length of your friend Charles Norton. For Heaven's sake don't tell him what I say, or he will turn his weapon against me.—But, seriously, this Club may fairly be considered as representing the most enlightened public opinion of New England, at least, if not of the whole North; and it is unreservedly and enthusiastically in favor of continuing the war, and stedfastly confident of the result. We had a consultation about establishing a weekly Journal, of a military character, chiefly for the purpose of operating on the minds of the soldiers and sailors; but I doubt whether these poets and philosophers know how to bring their abilities to bear on that class of men. At any rate, I expressed my distrust, and declined having anything to do with it. . . .

11.  NH to Elizabeth P. Peabody,[16] Concord, July 20, 1863

I do not think that the Dedication to Genl Pierce can have the momentous political consequences which you apprehend. I determined upon it long since, as a proper memorial of our life-long intimacy, and as especially suitable in the case of this book, which could not have been in existence without him. I expressly say that I dedicate the book to the friend, and decline any present colloquy with the statesman, to whom I address merely a few lines expressing my confidance in his loyalty and unalterable devotion to the Union—which I am glad to have the opportunity of saying, at this moment, when all the administration and abolition papers are calling him a traitor. A traitor? Why, he is the only loyal man in the country, North or South! Every body else has outgrown the old faith in the Union, or got outside of it in one way or another; but Pierce retains it in all the simplicity with which he inherited it from his father. . . .

The Dedication can hurt nobody but my book and myself. I know that it will do that, but am content to take the consequences, rather than go back from what I deliberately judge it right to do. As for Posterity, it will have formed a truer opinion of Genl Pierce than you can do; and yet I should suppose that you have breadth and insight enough (however disturbed by the potent elixir of political opinions) to appreciate the sterling merits of this kind of man.

You do not in the least shake me by telling me that I shall be supposed to disapprove of the war; for I always thought that it should have been avoided, although, since it has broken out, I have longed for military success as much as any man or woman of the North. . . . [T]he war will only effect by a horrible convulsion the self-same end that might and would have been brought about by a gradual and peaceful change. Nor am I at all certain that it will effect that end. Even these recent successes have not an indubitable tendency in that direction. They will suggest to the rebels that their best hope lies in the succor of the Peace Democrats of the North, whom they have heretofore scorned, and by amalgamation with whom I really think that the old Union might be restored, and slavery prolonged for another hundred years, with new bulwarks; while the people of the North would fancy that they had got the victory, and never know that they had shed their blood in vain, and so would become Peace Democrats to a man. In that case, woe to the Abolitionists! . . .

The best thing possible, as far as I can see, would be to effect a separation of the Union, giving us the West Bank of the Mississippi, and a boundary line affording as much Southern soil as we can hope to digest into freedom in another century. Such a settlement looks impossible, to be sure, and so does every other imaginable settlement, except through the medium of the Peace Democrats, who (as I have just said) would speedily comprise the whole population, in view of such a result. You cannot possibly conceive (looking through spectacles of the tint which yours have acquired) how little the North really cares for the negro-question, and how eagerly it would grasp at peace if recommended by a delusive show of victory. Free soil was never in so great danger as now. If the Southern statesmen manage their matters sagaciously, there may come a revulsion of feeling that would give them more than they ever asked. Do you suppose that the pendulum is not to swing back again? . . .

I do not write (if you will please to observe) for my letter to be read to others; for this is the first time that I have written down ideas which exist in a gaseous state in my mind, and perhaps they might define themselves rather differently on another attempt to condense them. My views about Dis-Union, for example, though long crudely entertained, are not such as I should choose to put forth at present; and I am very often sensible of an affectionate regard for the dead old Union, which leads me to say a kind thing or two about it, though I had as lief see my grandfather's ghost as have it revive. . . .

The older I grow, the more I hate to write notes, and I trust I have written nothing now that may make it necessary for me to write another.

Thomas Wentworth Higginson, 1862

# Thomas Wentworth Higginson
## (1823–1911)

The Civil War made Higginson a writer. It gave him scenes and characters as well as a field of action that featured himself and hundreds of
former slaves. With increasing radicalism he had become devoted to the
elimination of slavery, and war came just in time to make violent means
acceptable and save Higginson from treason. In 1854 he had tried unsuccessfully to rescue the fugitive slave Anthony Burns from a Boston jail
and in the process probably became an accessory to murder, though he
was never charged. In 1859, he served as one of the Secret Six who
funded John Brown's raid on the arsenal at Harper's Ferry. On the eve of
war, he began an historical investigation into slave insurrections, and he
published pieces on Denmark Vesey and Nat Turner, pieces that sought
to transform Southern demons into Northern heroes. Now, in 1862, he
served in the Sea-Islands as the Colonel of the First South Carolina Volunteers, an all-black regiment, and while drilling his troops and awaiting
combat he wrote.

It is not that he never before worked with words. By 1861, Higginson
was a well-known minister and abolitionist. A student at Harvard Divinity School, he thought the Unitarian ministry must engage in the
reforms of the day or grow even more irrelevant—"corpse-cold" in the
words of the Transcendentalists. And so he participated in antislavery,
women's rights, temperance, and the abolition of capital punishment. He
published sermons, essays, and newspaper columns on these and other
issues. He also wrote poetry, short stories, and reviews of books (he later
claimed that Lydia Maria Child's work made him an abolitionist). But he
pictured himself still an activist, not an author. Only toward the end of
the war, when illness forced him to leave his troops behind and head
home, did Higginson inform his intellectual idol and friend, Ralph Waldo

Emerson, that he hoped to be "an artist" having been "lured by the joy of expression itself."[1]

"The joy of expression" found its way into Higginson's earliest Civil War writings. In "Ordeal by Battle," the literary references mount (Dickens, Richardson, Fielding, and Shakespeare) as Higginson denounces the South and proclaims that the war must be fought to eliminate slavery. In "Regular and Volunteer Officers," he draws on his own experience to puncture the romantic ideal of heroic combat. While stationed near Beaufort, South Carolina, Higginson continued the journal he began in his youth. His entries became the basis for "Leaves from an Officer's Journal" and several other essays published in the *Atlantic Monthly* during and after the war; without revision, Higginson incorporated these pieces into *Army Life in a Black Regiment*, first published in 1869.

The Colonel sought to document the transition from slavery to *armed* freedom. There was much debate over whether blacks should or even could help fight for the Union cause, and Higginson had an acute sense of the historical importance of his position at the head of the first legally authorized black regiment. Although the published journal entries moderate Higginson's unpublished doubts about black capabilities, they still capture the tensions between condescension and admiration that characterized his thinking. He never extricated himself from the paternalism that typified nineteenth-century liberals: his troops were his children, and he often viewed the black soldiers as "simple, docile, and affectionate." Only when he stepped outside the role of leader, and became instead an observer, did he notice the vitality of black spiritualism and record the grace and sophistication of black story-telling. Beneath the ancient South Carolina trees, Higginson felt the presence and experienced the reinvention of the past. He tried after the war to write a novel about a time before the war, but *Malbone: An Oldport Romance* (1869) was a failure. It was through non-fiction that Higginson turned experience into art and, in so doing, created a literary triumph.

At the end of the century, Higginson came back to *Army Life in a Black Regiment* and made some minor changes. By then, he was a leading critic and editor. His *Young Folks' History of the United States* (1875) sold tens of thousands of copies. He wrote studies of Longfellow and Whittier and had the good sense to praise Hawthorne, Crane, and Howells, but the bad sense to dismiss Whitman, in part because the poet's scrutiny of the human body embarrassed him and in part because the old Colonel dismissed those who did not carry a gun during during the Civil War.

We remember Higginson now, if at all, for his relationship to Emily Dickinson and for editing her poetry for publication. But he would have preferred to be remembered for his actions and writings during the war. At his funeral, the tattered flag of the First South Carolina Volunteers draped his coffin.

### 1. TWH to Louisa Higginson, Worcester, May 30, 1861[2]

I have just sent an article to the next *Atlantic*, called the Ordeal by Battle, about the war and its probable results. I have never written any political article there before, because there never has been a time when I could write fully without being too radical, so I thought I would use the present opportunity. The main ground taken is that *however* the present war may end it must put the slavery question in a wholly new aspect. If our success is swift and easy, the South proving weak, then although the formal position of slavery may be untouched after the peace, its prestige of power will be gone, it will have done its worst and yet proved feeble, and thenceforward will be treated with far less respect. If on the other hand, the war is protracted by slavery's proving strong, then the ultimate military emancipation of slaves to a considerable extent, is inevitable. So that in either case the logic of events must leave slavery much weakened, even should we end the war with a compromise. In either case the action of the South is suicidal. As to which will be the case, it has already been my impression that the strength of the South has been overrated and that they will accomplish nothing great by way of fighting. Still this is a point about which persons equally well informed differ so entirely that one must be cautious. Montgomery Blair[3] told my friend G. L. Stearns that he thought there would be no fighting after all—that before winter the South would yield without it, and the general tendency of impression seems now to go in the direction of less respect for Southern army operations. On the other hand, many persons of good opportunities for judging still hold out differently. . . .

### 2. [Thomas Wentworth Higginson] "The Ordeal by Battle," *Atlantic Monthly*, 8 (July 1861): 88–95

Virginia, which began by volunteering as peacemaker in our civil troubles, seems likely to end by being their battleground; as Mr. Pickwick, interfering between the belligerent rival editors, only brought upon his own head the united concussion of their carpet-bags. And as Dickens declares that the warriors engaged far more eagerly in that mimic strife, on discovering that all blows were to be received by deputy, so there is evidently an increased willingness to deal hard knocks on both sides, in the present case, so long as it is clear that only Virginia will take them. Maryland, under protection of our army, adroitly contrives to shift the scene of action farther South. The Gulf States, with profuse courtesies for the Old Dominion, consent to shift it farther

North. The Southern Confederacy has talked about paying Richmond the "compliment" of selecting it for the seat of government;—as if a bully, about to be lynched in his own house by the crowd, should compliment his next-door neighbor by climbing in at his window. It is very pleasant to have a hospitable friend; but it is counting on his hospitality rather too strongly, when you make choice of his apartments to be tarred and feathered in.

Thus fades the fancy of an "independent neutrality" for the Old Dominion. It ought to fade;—for neutrality is a crime, where one's mother's life is at stake; and the Border theory of independence only reminds one of Pitt's definition of an independent statesmen, "a statesman not to be depended on." How sad has been the decline of Virginia! . . .

It is rare that any great contest begins by a blow so unequivocal as the bombardment of Fort Sumter; and rare in recent days for any set of belligerents to risk the ignominy of privateering. But, after all, it is the startling social theories announced by the new "government" which form the chief strength of its enemies. Either slavery is essential to a community, or it must be fatal to it,—there is no middle ground; and the Secessionists have taken one horn of the dilemma with so delightful a frankness as to leave us no possible escape from taking the other. Never, in modern days, has there been a conflict in which the contending principles were so clearly antagonistic. The most bigoted royal house in Europe never dreamed of throwing down the gauntlet for the actual ownership of man by man. Even Russia never fought for serfdom, and Austria has only enslaved nations, not individuals. In civil wars, especially, all historic divergences have been trivial compared to ours, so far as concerned the avowed principles of strife. In the French wars of the Fronde, the only available motto for anybody was the *Tout arrive en France*, "Anything may happen in France," which gayly recognized the absurd chaos of the conflict. In the English civil wars, the contending factions first disagreed upon a shade more or less of royal prerogative, and it took years to stereotype the hostility into the solid forms with which we now associate it. Even at the end of that contest, no one had ventured to claim such a freedom as our Declaration of Independence asserts, on the one side,—nor to recognize the possibility of such a barbarism as Jefferson Davis glorifies, on the other. The more strongly the Secessionists state their cause, the more glaringly it is seen to differ from any cause for which any sane person has taken up arms since the Roman servile wars. Their leaders may be exhibiting very sublime qualities; all we can say is, as Richardson said of Fielding's heroes, that their virtues are the vices of a decent man. . . .

The Secessionists have suggested to us a fatal argument. "The superior race must control the inferior." Very well; if they insist on invoking the ordeal by battle to decide which is the superior, let it be so. It will be found that they have made the common mistake of confounding barbarism with strength. Because the Southern masses are as ignorant of letters and of arts as the Scottish Highlanders, they infer themselves to be as warlike. But even the brave and hardy Highlanders proved powerless against the imperfect military resources of England, a century ago, and it is not easy to see why those who now parody them should fare better. The absence of the alphabet does not necessarily prove the presence of strength, nor is the ignorance of all useful arts the best preparation for the elaborate warfare of modern times. . . .

Insurrection is one of the risks voluntarily assumed by Slavery,—and the greatest of them. The slaves know it, and so do the masters. When they seriously assert that they feel safe on this point, there is really no answer to be made but that by which Traddles in "David Copperfield" puts down Uriah Heep's wild hypothesis of believing himself an innocent man. "But you don't, you know," quoth the straightforward Traddles; "therefore, if you please, we won't suppose any such thing." They cannot deceive us, for they do not deceive themselves. Every traveller who has seen the faces of a household suddenly grow pale, in a Southern city, when some street tumult struck to their hearts the fear of insurrection,—every one who has seen the heavy negro face brighten unguardedly at the name of John Brown, though a thousand miles away from Harper's Ferry,—has penetrated the final secret of the military weakness which saved Washington for us and lost the war for them. . . .

Should the war cease tomorrow, it has inaugurated a new era in our nation's history. The folly of the Gulf States, in throwing away a political condition where the conservative sentiment stood by them only too well, must inevitably recoil on their own heads, whether the strife last a day or a generation. No man can estimate the new measures and combinations to which it is destined to give rise. There stands the Constitution, with all its severe conditions,—severe or weak, however, according to its interpretations;—which interpretations, again, will always prove plastic before the popular will. The popular will is plainly destined to a change; and who dare predict the results of its changing? The scrupulous may still hold by the letter of the bond; but since the South has confessedly prized all legal guaranties only for the sake of Slavery, the North, once free to act, will long to construe them, up to the very verge of faith, in the interest of Liberty. Was the original compromise a Shylock bond?—the war has been our Portia. Slavery long ruled the nation politically. The nation rose and conquered it with votes. With desperate disloyalty, Slavery struck down all political safeguards, and appealed to arms. The nation has risen again, ready to meet it with any weapons, sure to conquer with any. Twice conquered, what further claim will this defeated desperado have? If it was a disturbing element before, and so put under restriction, shall it be spared when it has openly proclaimed itself a destroying element also? Is this to be the last of American civil wars, or only the first one? These are the questions which will haunt men's minds, when the cannon are all hushed, and the bells are pealing peace, and the sons of our hearthstones come home. The watchword "Irrepressible Conflict" only gave the key, but War has flung the door wide open, and four million slaves stand ready to file through. It is merely a question of time, circumstance, and method. There is not a statesman so wise but this war has given him new light, nor an Abolitionist so self-confident but must own its promise better than his foresight. Henceforth, the first duty of an American legislator must be, by the use of all legitimate means, to weaken Slavery. *Delenda est Servitudo.* What the peace which the South has broken was not doing, the war which she has instituted must secure.

### 3. [Thomas Wentworth Higginson] "Regular and Volunteer Officers," *Atlantic Monthly*, 14 (September 1864): 348–357

. . . The relation between officer and soldier is something so different in kind from anything which civil life has to offer, that it is has proved almost impossible to transfer methods or maxims from the one to the other. If a regiment is merely a caucus, and the colonel the chairman,—or merely a fire-company, and the colonel the foreman,—or merely a prayer-meeting, and the colonel the moderator,—or merely a bar-room, and the colonel the landlord,—then the failure of the whole thing is a foregone conclusion. War is not the highest of human pursuits, certainly; but an army comes very near to being the completest of human organizations, and he alone succeeds in it who readily accepts its inevitable laws, and applies them. An army is an aristocracy, on a three-years' lease, supposing that the period of enlistment. No mortal skill can make military power effective on democratic principles. A democratic people can perhaps carry on a war longer and better than any other; because no other can so well comprehend the object, raise the means, or bear the sacrifices. But these sacrifices include the surrender, for the time being, of the essential principle of the government. Personal independence in the soldier, like personal liberty in the civilian, must be waived for the preservation of the nation. With shipwreck staring men in the face, the choice lies between despotism and anarchy, trusting to the common sense of those concerned, when the danger is over, to revert to the old safeguards. It is precisely because democracy is an advanced stage in human society, that war, which belongs to a less advanced stage, is peculiarly inconsistent with its habits. Thus the undemocratic character, so often lamented in West Point and Annapolis, is in reality their strong point. Granted that they are no more appropriate to our stage of society than are revolvers and bowie-knives, that is precisely what makes them all serviceable in time of war. War being exceptional, the institutions which train its officers must be exceptional likewise. . . .

It is hard to appreciate, without the actual experience, how much of military life is a matter of mere detail. The maiden at home fancies her lover charging at the head of his company, when in reality he is at that precise moment endeavoring to convince his company-cooks that salt-junk needs five hours' boiling, or is anxiously deciding which pair of worn-out trousers shall be ejected from a drummer-boy's knapsack. Courage is, no doubt, a good quality in a soldier, and luckily not often wanting; but, in the long run, courage depends largely on the haversack. Men are naturally brave, and when the crisis comes, almost all men will fight well, if well commanded. As Sir Philip Sidney said, an army of stags led by a lion is more formidable than an army of lions led by a stag.[4] Courage is cheap; the main duty of an officer is to take good care of his men, so that every one of them shall be ready, at a moment's notice, for any reasonable demand. A soldier's life usually implies weeks and months of waiting, and then one glorious hour; and if the interval of leisure has been wasted, there is nothing but a wasted heroism at the end, and perhaps not even that. The penalty for misused weeks, the reward for laborious months, may be determined within ten minutes. Without discipline an army is a mob, and the larger the worse; without rations the men are empty uniforms; without ammunition they might as well have no guns; without shoes they might almost as well have no legs. And it is in this practical appreciation of all these matters that the superiority of the regular officer is to be shown. . . .

What is called military glory is a fitful and uncertain thing. Time and the newspapers play strange tricks with reputations, and of a hundred officers whose names appear with honor in the morning's dispatches ninety may never be mentioned again till it is time to write their epitaphs. Who, for instance, can recite the names of the successive cavalry-commanders who have ridden on their bold forays through Virginia, since the war began? All must give place to the latest Kautz or Sheridan, who has eclipsed without excelling them all.[5] Yet each is as brave and as faithful to-day, no doubt, as when he too glittered for his hour before all men's gaze, and the obscurer duty may be the more substantial honor. So when I lift my eyes to look on yonder level ocean-floor, the fitful sunshine now glimmers white on one far-off sail, now on another; and yet I know that all canvas looks snowy while those casual rays are on it, and that the best vessel is that which, sunlit or shaded, best accomplishes its destined course. The officer is almost as powerless as the soldier to choose his opportunity or his place. Military glory may depend on a thousand things,—the accident of a local position, the jealousy of a rival, the whim of a superior. But the merit of having done one's whole duty to the men whose lives are in one's keeping, and to the nation whose life is staked with theirs,—of having held one's command in such a state, that, if at any given moment it was not performing the most brilliant achievement, it might have been,—this is the substantial triumph which every faithful officer has always within reach. . . .

When some future Bancroft or Motley[6] writes with philosophic brain and poet's hand the story of the Great Civil War, he will find the transition to a new era in our nation's history to have been fitly marked by one festal day,—

that of the announcement of the President's Proclamation, upon Port-Royal Island, on the first of January, 1863. That New-Year's time was our second contribution to the great series of historic days, beads upon the rosary of the human race, permanent festivals of freedom. Its celebration was one beside whose simple pageant the superb festivals of other lands might seem but glittering counterfeits. Beneath a majestic grove of the great live-oaks which glorify the South Carolina soil a liberated people met to celebrate their own peaceful emancipation. They came thronging, by land and water, from plantations which their own self-imposed and exemplary industry was beginning already to redeem. The military escort which surrounded them had been organized out of their own numbers, and had furnished to the nation the first proof of the capacity of their race to bear arms. The key-note of the meeting was given by spontaneous voices, whose unexpected anthem took the day from the management of well-meaning patrons, and swept all away into the great currents of simple feeling. It was a scene never to be forgotten: the moss-hung trees, with their hundred-feet diameter of shade; the eager faces of women and children in the foreground; the many-colored headdresses; the upraised hands; the neat uniforms of the soldiers; the outer row of mounted officers and ladies; and beyond all the blue river, with its swift, free tide. . . .

4. [Thomas Wentworth Higginson] "Leaves from an Officer's Journal," *Atlantic Monthly*, 14 and 15 (November 1864, December 1864, and January 1865): 521–529; 740–748; 65–73

I wish to record, as truthfully as I may, the beginnings of a momentous experiment, which, by proving the aptitude of the freed slaves for military drill and discipline, their ardent loyalty, their courage under fire, and their self-control in success, contributed somewhat towards solving the problem of the war, and towards remoulding the destinies of two races on this continent. . . . It is possible, therefore, that some extracts from a diary kept during that period may still have an interest; for there is nothing in human history so momentous as the transit of a race from chattel-slavery to armed freedom; nor can this change be photographed save by the actual contemporaneous words of those who saw it in the process. Perhaps there may also appear an element of dramatic interest in the record, when one considers that here, in the delightful regions of Port Royal, the descendants of the Puritan and the Huguenot, after two centuries, came face to face,—and that son of Massachusetts, reversing the boastful threat which has become historic, here called the roll, upon South Carolina soil, of her slaves, now freemen in arms. . . .

November 27, 1862. . . . The chilly sunshine and the pale blue river seem like New England, but those alone. The air is full of noisy drumming and of gun-shots; for the prize-shooting is our great celebration of the day, and the drumming is chronic. My young barbarians are all at play. I look out from the broken windows of this forlorn plantation-house, through avenues of great live-oaks, with their hard, shining leaves, and their branches hung with a universal drapery of soft, long moss, like fringe-trees struck with grayness. Below, the sandy soil, scantly covered with coarse grass, bristles with sharp palmettoes and aloes; all the vegetation is stiff, shining, semi-tropical with nothing soft or delicate in its texture. Numerous plantation-buildings totter around, all slovenly and unattractive, while the interspaces are filled with all manner of wreck and refuse, pigs, fowls, dogs, and omnipresent Ethiopian infancy. All this is the universal Southern panorama; but five minutes' walk beyond the hovels and the live-oaks bring one to something so un-Southern that the whole Southern coast at this moment trembles at the suggestion of such a thing,—the camp of a regiment of free slaves.

One adapts one's self so readily to new surroundings that already the full zest of the novelty seems passing away from my perception, and I write these lines in an eager effort to retain all I can. Already I am growing used to the experience, at first so novel, of living among five hundred men, and scarce a white face to be seen,—of seeing them go through all their daily processes, eating, frolicking, talking, just as if they were white. Each day at dress-parade I stand with the customary folding of the arms before a regimental line of countenances so black that I can hardly tell whether the men stand steadily or not; black is every hand which moves in ready cadence as I vociferate, "Battalion! Shoulder arms!" nor is it till the line of white officers moves forward, as parade is dismissed, that I am reminded that my own face is not the color of coal. . . .

Strolling in the cool moonlight, I was attracted by a brilliant light beneath the trees, and cautiously approached it. A circle of thirty or forty soldiers sat around a roaring fire, while one old uncle, Cato by name, was narrating an interminable tale, to the insatiable delight of his audience. I came up into the dusky background, perceived only a few, and he still continued. It was a narrative, dramatized to the last degree, of his adventures in escaping from his master to the Union vessels; and even I, who have heard the stories of Harriet Tubman, and such wonderful slave-comedians, never witnessed such a piece of acting. When I came upon the scene, he had just come unexpectedly upon a plantation-house, and, putting a bold face upon it, had walked up to the door.

"Den I go up to de white man, very humble, and say, would you please gib ole man a mouthful for eat?

"He say, he must hab de valeration of half a dollar.

"Den I look berry sorry, and turn for go away.

"Den he say, I might gib him dat hatchet I had.

"Den I say," (this in a tragic vein,) "dat I must habe dat hatchet for defend myself *from de dogs!*"

(Immense applause, and one appreciating auditor says, chuckling, "Dat was your *arms*, ole man," which brings down the house again.)

"Den he say, de Yankee pickets was near by, and I must be very keerful.

"Den I say, 'Good Lord, Mas'r, am day?'"

Words cannot express the complete dissimulation with which these accents of terror were uttered,—this being precisely the piece of information he wished to obtain.

Then he narrated his devices to get into the house at night and obtain some food,—how a dog flew at him,—how the whole household, black and white, rose in pursuit,—how he scrambled under a hedge and over a high fence, etc.,—all in a style of which Gough alone among orators can give the faintest impression, so thoroughly dramatized was every syllable.[7]

Then he described his reaching the river-side at last, and trying to decide whether certain vessels held friends or foes.

"Den I see guns on board, and sure sartin be Union boat, and I pop my head up. Den I been-a-tink Seceshkey had guns too, and my head go down again. Den I hide in de bush till morning. Den I open my bundle, and take ole white shirt and tie him on ole pole and wave him, and ebry time de wind blow, I been-a-tremble, and drap down in de bushes,"—because, being between two fires, he doubted whether friend or foe would see his signal first. And so on, with a succession of tricks beyond Moliere, of acts of caution, foresight, patient cunning, which were listened to with infinite gusto and perfect comprehension by every listener.

And all this to a bivouac of negro soldiers, with the brilliant fire lighting up their red trousers and gleaming from their shining black faces,—eyes and teeth all white with tumultuous glee. Overhead, the mighty limbs of a great live oak, with the weird moss swaying in the smoke, and the high moon gleaming faintly through.

Yet to-morrow strangers will remark on the hopeless, impenetrable stupidity in the daylight faces of many of these very men, the solid mask under which Nature has concealed all this wealth of mother-wit. This very comedian is one to whom one might point, as he hoed lazily in a cotton-field, as a being the light of whose brain had utterly gone out; and this scene seems like coming by night upon some conclave of black beetles, and finding them engaged, with green-room and foot-lights, in enacting "Poor Pillicoddy." This is their university; every young Sambo before me, as he turned over the sweet-potatoes and pea-nuts which were roasting in the ashes, listened with reverence to the wiles of the ancient Ulysses, and meditated the same. It is Nature's compensation; oppression simply crushes the upper faculties of the head, and crowds every-thing into the perceptive organs. Cato, thou reasonest well! When I get into any serious scrape, in an enemy's country, may I be lucky enough to have you at my elbow, to pull me out of it!. . . .

December 3, 1862.—7 P.M.

What a life is this I lead! It is a dark, mild, drizzling evening, and as the foggy air breeds sand-flies, so it calls out melodies and strange antics from this mysterious race of grown-up children with whom my lot is cast. All over the camp the lights glimmer in the tents, and as I sit at my desk in the open doorway, there come mingled sounds of stir and glee. Boys laugh and shout,—a feeble flute stirs somewhere in some tent, not an officer's,—a drum throbs far away in another,—wild kildeer-plover flit and wail above us, like the haunting souls of dead slave-masters,—and from a neighboring cook-fire comes the monotonous sound of that strange festival, half pow-wow, half prayer-meeting, which they know only as a "shout." These fires are usually enclosed in a little booth, made neatly of palm-leaves and covered in at top, a regular native African hut, in short, such is pictured in books, and such as I once got up from dried palmleaves, for a fair, at home. This hut is now crammed with men, singing at the top of their voices, in one of their quaint, monotonous, endless, negro-Methodist chants, with obscure syllables recurring constantly, and slight variations interwoven, all accompanied with a regular drumming of the feet and clapping of the hands, like castanets. Then the excitement spreads: inside and outside the inclosure men begin to quiver and dance, others join, a circle forms, winding monotonously round some one in the centre: some "heel and toe" tumultuously, others merely tremble and stagger on, others stoop and rise, others whirl, others caper sideways, all keep steadily circling like dervishes; spectators applaud special strokes of skill; my approach only enlivens the scene; the circle enlarges, louder grows the singing, rousing shouts of encouragement come in, half bacchanalian, half devout, "Wake 'em brudder!" "Stan' up to 'em, brudder!"—and still the ceaseless drumming and clapping, in perfect cadence, goes steadily on. Suddenly there comes a sort of *snap*, and the spell breaks, amid general sighing and laughter. And this not rarely and occasionally, but night after night,—while in other parts of the camp the soberest prayers and exhortations are proceeding sedately.

A simple and lovable people, whose graces seem to come by nature, and whose vices by training. . . .

December 16 [1862]. . . . I have noticed one man in the regiment who would easily pass for white,—a little sickly drummer, aged fifty at least, with brown eyes and reddish hair, who is said to be the son of one of our commodores. I have seen perhaps a dozen persons as fair or fairer, among fugitive slaves, but they were usually young children. It touched me far more to see this man, who had spent more than half a lifetime in this low estate, and for whom it now seemed too late to be anything but a "nigger." This offensive word, by the way, is almost as common with them as at the North, and far more common than

with well-bred slave-holders. They have meekly accepted it. "Want to go out
to de nigger-houses, Sah," is the universal impulse of sociability, when they
wish to cross the lines. "He hab twenty house-servants and two hundred head
o'nigger," is a still more degrading form of phrase, in which the epithet is limited to the field-hands, and they estimated like so many cattle. This want of self-
respect of course interferes with the authority of the non-commissioned officers, which is always difficult to sustain, even in white regiments. . . .

As one grows more acquainted with the men, their individualities emerge;
and I find first their faces, then their characters, to be as distinct as those of
whites. It is very interesting the desire they show to do their duty and to
improve as soldiers; they evidently think about it, and see the importance of the
thing; they say to me that we white men cannot stay and be their leaders always,
and that they must learn to depend on themselves, or else relapse into their former condition. . . .

December 20. . . . I am perplexed nightly for counter-signs,—their range of
proper names is so distressingly limited, and they make such amazing work of
every new one. At first, to be sure, they did not quite recognize the need of any
variation: one night some officer asked a sentinel whether he had the countersign yet, and was indignantly answered,—"Should tink I hab hab'em, hab'em
for a fortnight"; which seems a long epic for that magic word to hold out. To-
night I thought I would have "Fredericksburg," in honor of Burnside's
reported victory, using the rumor quickly, for fear of a contradiction. Later, in
comes a captain, gets the countersign for his own use, but presently returns,
the sentinel having pronounced it incorrect. On inquiry, it appears that the sergeant of the guard, being weak in geography, thought best to substitute a more
familiar word, "Crockery-ware"; which was, with perfect gravity, confided to
all the sentinels, and accepted without question. O life! what is the fun of fiction
beside thee?. . . .

January 1, 1863 (evening). . . .

The services began at half-past eleven o'clock, with prayer by our chaplain,
Mr. Fowler, who is always, on such occasions, simple, reverential, and impressive. Then the President's Proclamation was read by Dr. W. H. Brisbane, a
thing infinitely appropriate, a South-Carolinian addressing South-Carolinians;
for he was reared among these very islands, and here long since emancipated
his own slaves. Then the colors were presented to us by the Rev. Mr. French,
a chaplain who brought them from the donors in New York. All this was
according to the programme. Then followed an incident so simple, so touching, so utterly unexpected and startling, that I can scarcely believe it on recalling, though it gave the key-note to the whole day. The very moment the
speaker had ceased, and just as I took and waved the flag, which now for the
first time meant anything to these poor people, there suddenly arose, close

beside the platform, a strong male voice, (but rather cracked and elderly), into which two women's voices instantly blended, singing, as if by an impulse that could no more be repressed than the morning note of the song-sparrow,—

"My Country 'tis of thee,
Sweet land of liberty,
Of thee I sing!"

People looked at each other, and then at us on the platform, to see whence came this interruption, not set down in the bills. Firmly and irrepressibly the quavering voices sang on, verse after verse; others of the colored people joined in; some whites on the platform began, but I motioned them to silence. I never saw anything so electric; it made all other words cheap; it seemed the choked voice of a race at last unloosed. Nothing could be more wonderfully unconscious; art could not have dreamed of a tribute to the day of jubilee that should be so affecting; history will not believe it; and when I came to speak of it, after it was ended, tears were everywhere. If you could have heard how quaint and innocent it was! Old Tiff and his children might have sung it; and close before me was a little slave-boy, almost white, who seemed to belong to the party, and even he must join in. Just think of it!—the first day they had ever had a country, the first flag they had ever seen which promised anything to their people, and here, while mere spectators stood in silence, waiting for my stupid words, these simple souls burst out in their lay, as if they were by their own hearths at home! When they stopped, there was nothing to do for it but to speak, and I went on; but the life of the day was in those unknown people's song. . . .

January 12.—Many things glide by without the time to narrate them. On Saturday we had a mail with the President's Second Message of Emancipation, and the next day it was read to the men. The words themselves did not stir them very much, because they have been often told that they were free, especially on New-Year's Day, and, being unversed in politics, they do not understand, as well as we do, the importance of each additional guaranty. But the chaplain spoke to them afterwards very effectively, as usual; and then I proposed to them to hold up their hands and pledge themselves to be faithful to those still in bondage. They entered heartily into this, and the scene was quite impressive, beneath the great oak-branches. I heard afterwards that only one man refused to raise his hand, saying bluntly that his wife was out of slavery with him, and he did not care to fight. The other soldiers of his company were very indignant, and shoved him about among them while marching back to their quarters, calling him "Coward." I was glad of their exhibition of feeling, though it is very possible that the one who had thus the moral courage to stand alone among his comrades might be more reliable, on a pinch, than some who yielded a more ready assent. But the whole response, on their part, was very hearty, and will be a good thing to which to hold them hereafter, at any time of discouragement or demoralization,—which was my chief reason for proposing it. With their simple natures, it is a great thing to tie them to some definite committal; they never forget a marked occurrence, and never seem disposed to evade a pledge. ...

January 13. ... I often notice how their griefs may be dispelled, like those of children, merely by permission to utter them: if they can tell their sorrows, they go away happy, even without asking to have anything done about them. I observe also a peculiar dislike of all *intermediate* control: they always wish to pass by the company officer, and deal with me personally for everything. General Saxton notices the same thing with the people on the plantations as regards himself.[8] I suppose this proceeds partly from the old habits of appealing to the master against the overseer. Kind words would cost the master nothing, and he could easily put off any non-fulfillment upon the overseer. Moreover, the negroes have acquired such constitutional distrust of white people, that it is perhaps as much as they can do to trust more than one person at a time. Meanwhile this constant personal intercourse is out of the question in a well-ordered regiment; and the remedy for it is to introduce by degrees more and more of a system, so that their immediate officers will become all-sufficient for the daily routine. ...

Another childlike attribute in these men, which is less agreeable, is a sort of blunt insensibility to giving physical pain. If they are cruel to animals, for instance, it always reminds me of children pulling off flies' legs, in a sort of pitiless, untaught, experimental way. Yet I should not fear any wanton outrage from them. After all their wrongs, they are not really revengeful; and I would far rather enter a captured city with them than with white troops, for they would be more subordinate. But for mere physical suffering they would have no fine sympathies. The cruel things they have seen and undergone have helped to blunt them; and if I ordered them to put to death a dozen prisoners, I think they would do it without remonstrance.

Yet their religious spirit grows more beautiful to me in living longer with them: it is certainly far more so than at first, when it seemed rather a matter of phrase and habit. It influences them both on the negative and the positive side. That is, it cultivates the feminine virtues first,—makes them patient, meek, resigned. This is very evident in the hospital; there is nothing of the restless, defiant habit of white invalids. Perhaps, if they had more of this, they would resist disease better. Imbued from childhood with the habit of submission, drinking in through every pore the other-world trust which is the one spirit of their songs, they can endure everything. This I expected; but I am relieved to find that their religion strengthens them on the positive side also,—gives zeal, energy, daring. They could easily be made fanatics, if I chose; but I do not choose. Their whole mood is essentially Mohammedian, perhaps, in its strength and its weakness; and I feel the same degree of sympathy that I should, if I had a Turkish command,—that is, a sort of sympathetic admiration, not tending towards agreement, but towards cooperation. Their philosophizing is often the highest form of mysticism; and our dear surgeon declares that they are all natural transcendentalists. The white camps seem rough and secular, after this; and I hear our men talk about "a religious army," "a Gospel army," in their prayer-meetings. They are certainly evangelizing the chaplain, who was rather a heretic at the beginning; at least, this is his own admission. We have recruits on their way from St. Augustine, where the negroes are chiefly Roman Catholics; and it will be interesting to see how their type of character combines with that elder creed. . . .

January 14. . . . Sergeant Prince Rivers, our color-sergeant, who is provost-sergeant also, and has entire charge of the prisoners and the daily policing of the camp . . . is a man of distinguished appearance, and in old times was the crack coachman of Beaufort, in which capacity he once drove Beauregard from this plantation to Charleston, I believe. They tell me he was once allowed to present a petition to the Governor of South Carolina in behalf of slaves, for the redress of certain grievances; and that a placard, offering two thousand dollars for his recapture, is still to be seen by the wayside between here and Charleston. . . . There is not a white man officer in this regiment who has more administrative ability, or more absolute authority over the men; they do not love him, but his mere presence has controlling power over them. He writes well enough to prepare for me a daily report of his duties in the camp: if his education reached a higher point, I see no reason why he should not command the Army of the Potomac. He is jet-black, or rather, I should say, *wine-black;* his complexion, like that of others of my darkest men, having a sort of rich, clear depth, without a trace of sootiness, and to my eye very handsome. His features are tolerably regular, and full of command, and his figure superior to that of any of our white officers,—being six feet high, perfectly proportioned, and of apparently inexhaustible strength and activity. His gait is like a panther's; I never saw such a tread. No anti-slavery novel has described a man of such marked ability. He makes Toussaint perfectly intelligible; and if there should ever be a black monarchy in South Carolina, he will be its king. . . .

January 21 . . . "What care I how black I be?/ Forty pounds will marry me," quoth Mother Goose. Forty *rounds* will marry us to the American Army, past divorcing, if we can only use them well. Our success or failure may make or mar the prospects of colored troops. But it is well to remember in advance that military success is really less satisfactory than any other, because it may depend on a moment's turn of events, and that may be determined by some trivial thing, neither to be anticipated nor controlled. Napoleon ought to have won at Waterloo by all reasonable calculations; but who cares? All that one can expect is, to do one's best, and to take with equanimity the fortune of war.

Herman Melville, 1861 *(Courtesy of the Berkshire Athenaeum)*

# Herman Melville
## (1819–1891)

The Civil War shook Melville out of his writing doldrums. In just over a decade, he had published nine books and a collection of stories. The first three of these, *Typee* (1846), *Omoo* (1847), and *Mardi* (1849), brought him some early success and acclaim. *Redburn* (1849) and *White-Jacket* (1850) poured out of him, done as jobs, for the money, Melville claimed. Then came *Moby-Dick* (1851), a book Hawthorne loved but the critics failed to understand. Melville persevered. *Pierre* (1852), *Israel Potter* (1855), *The Piazza Tales* (1856), and *The Confidence-Man* (1857) followed. Then silence. He traveled, he read, he lectured—but he did not publish. Even with the outbreak of the Civil War, Melville was hardly heard from. At one point, he visited a cousin at the front, but there is little record of his attitude toward the war. And then, near the end of the conflict, with the fall of Richmond in 1865, Melville found his subject and voice.

Published in 1866, *Battle-Pieces and Aspects of the War* consists of seventy-one poems and a prose supplement. A complex work, the poems of *Battle-Pieces* attempted to tell in chronological order the stories of the Civil War. It is a work filled with multiple perspectives, a work with poems about North and South, white and black, hope and despair. The tensions multiply. As one leading critic has observed, the poems include "variations on the theme of Order and Anarchy, illumination through pain and terror, the triumph of mechanic power and its psychic and social costs, Nature's indifference to humanity's travail, manhood and heroism, pessimistic meditations on the future of democracy after fratricidal war." In sum, the volume is a "sustained debate between belief and disbelief, which abounds in paradoxes, ironies, and conflicts, and which keeps denying what it affirms."[1]

In form and content, the prose "Supplement" to *Battle-Pieces* counter-
balances the complexities of the poetry. Here, Melville the artist recedes
in order to let Melville the citizen speak. Like his friend Hawthorne,
Melville never blindly embraced the Civil War. It was a "terrible historic
tragedy," he proclaims at the end of the "Supplement," and his only hope
is that something was learned. That something should be moderation,
compassion, and understanding toward the defeated South. In the "Supplement," he asks his readers to consider the plausibility of the Southern
position on the eve of war; he asks them to realize that superior force, not
superior virtue, won the war for the Union; he asks them to respect the
Southern dead and their mourners. Melville acknowledges here the
"atheistical iniquity" of slavery, but the freedmen are not his primary
concern. He anticipates conflict in the transition period from slavery to
freedom but asks that no one quarter be blamed. It is not that Melville,
one of the most acute commentators on slavery and race prior to the Civil
War, desired to abandon blacks. But he believed that the bitterness
between sections had to be eliminated if there was ever to be cooperation
between races. Without sectional reconciliation, he imagined another
holocaust of war somewhere down the line.

Given the complexity of the volume, it is little wonder that *Battle-
Pieces* was a critical and commercial failure. "Nature did not make him a
poet," averred the reviewer for the *Nation;* the work shows that "the
poetic nature and the technical faculty of poetry writing are not identical," commented another reviewer, Richard Henry Stoddard. The "Supplement" received greater praise from some: a "good and patriotic
action," proclaimed the *New York Herald.* Stoddard thought the whole
book would have succeeded had Melville transformed the poetry into
prose, shrewdly observing that "the habit of his mind is not lyric, but historical." William Dean Howells was more searching in his evaluation. He
couldn't find the real war in Melville's poetry and wondered about Melville's "inner consciousness" which had been perturbed not by "words
and blood, but words alone." As for the theme of the "Supplement,"
Howells doubted that "all the Rebels were as pleasingly impalpable as
those the poet portrays."[2]

Published in an edition of 1200 copies, only 486 copies of *Battle-Pieces*
were sold. Again, Melville withdrew into silence.

### 1. *Battle-Pieces and Aspects of the War* (New York, 1866)

[With few exceptions, the Pieces in this volume originated in an impulse
imparted by the fall of Richmond. They were composed without reference to

collective arrangement, but, being brought together in review, naturally fall into the order assumed.

The events and incidents of the conflict—making up a whole, in varied amplitude, corresponding with the geographical area covered by the war—from these but a few themes have been taken, such as for any cause chanced to imprint themselves upon the mind.

The aspects which the strife as a memory assumes are as manifold as are the moods of involuntary meditation—moods variable, and at times widely at variance. Yielding instinctively, one after another, to feelings not inspired from any one source exclusively, and unmindful, without purposing to be, of consistency, I seem, in most of these verses, to have but placed a harp in a window, and noted the contrasted airs which wayward winds have played upon the strings.]

. . .

### THE PORTENT
### (1859)

*Hanging from the beam,*
*Slowly swaying (such the law),*
*Gaunt the shadow on your green,*
*Shenandoah!*
*The cut is on the crown*
*(Lo, John Brown).*
*And the stabs shall heal no more.*

*Hidden in the cap*
*Is the anguish none can draw;*
*So your future veils its face,*
*Shenandoah!*
*But the streaming beard is shown*
*(Weird John Brown),*
*The meteor of the war.*

. . .

### APATHY AND ENTHUSIASM
### (1860–61)

### I

O the clammy cold November,
  And the winter white and dead,
And the terror dumb with stupor,
  And the sky a sheet of lead;

And events that came resounding
  With the cry that *All was lost,*
Like the thunder-cracks of massy ice
  In intensity of frost—
Bursting one upon another
  Through the horror of the calm.
  The paralysis of arm
In the anguish of the heart;
And the hollowness and dearth.
  The appealings of the mother
  To brother and to brother
Not in hatred so to part—
And the fissure in the hearth
  Growing momently more wide.
Then the glances 'tween the Fates,
  And the doubt on every side,
And the patience under gloom
In the stoniness that waits
The finality of doom.


## II

So the winter died despairing,
  And the weary weeks of Lent;
And the ice-bound rivers melted,
  And the tomb of Faith was rent.
O, the rising of the People
  Came with springing of the grass,
They rebounded from dejection
  After Easter came to pass.
And the young were all elation
  Hearing Sumter's cannon roar,
And they thought how tame the Nation
  In the age that went before.
And Michael seemed gigantical,
  The Arch-fiend but a dwarf;
And at the towers of Erebus
  Our striplings flung the scoff.
But the elders with foreboding
  Mourned the days forever o'er,
And recalled the forest proverb,
  The Iroquois' old saw:

> *Grief to every graybeard*
> *When young Indians lead the war.*

. . .

### SHILOH

#### A REQUIEM

#### (APRIL 1862)

Skimming lightly, wheeling still,
  The swallows fly low
Over the field in clouded days,
  The forest-field of Shiloh—
Over the field where April rain
Solaced the parched one stretched in pain
Through the pause of night
That followed the Sunday fight
  Around the church of Shiloh—
The church so lone, the log-built one,
That echoed to many a parting groan
    And natural prayer
Of dying foemen mingled there—
Foemen at morn, but friends at eve—
  Fame or country least their care:
(What like a bullet can undeceive!)
  But now they lie low,
While over them the swallows skim
And all is hushed at Shiloh.

. . .

### THE COLLEGE COLONEL

He rides at their head;
  A crutch by his saddle just slants in view,
One slung arm is in splints, you see,
  Yet he guides his strong steed—how coldly too.

He brings his regiment home—
  Not as they fled two years before,
But a remnant half-tattered, and battered, and
    worn,
Like castaway sailors, who—stunned
    By the surf's loud roar,
  Their mates dragged back and seen no more—

Again and again breast the surge,
　　And at last crawl, spent, to shore.

A still rigidity and pale—
　　An Indian aloofness lones his brow;
He has lived a thousand years
Compressed in battle's pains and prayers,
　　Marches and watches slow.

There are welcoming shouts, and flags;
　　Old men off hat to the Boy,
Wreaths from gay balconies fall at his feet,
　　But to *him*—there comes alloy.

It is not that a leg is lost,
　　It is not that an arm is maimed,
It is not that the fever has racked—
　　Self he has long disclaimed.

But all through the Seven Days' Fight,
　　And deep in the Wilderness grim,
And in the field-hospital tent,
　　And Petersburg crater, and dim
Lean brooding in Libby, there came—
　　Ah heaven!—what *truth* to him.

. . .

THE MARTYR
INDICATIVE OF THE PASSION OF THE PEOPLE ON THE
15TH OF APRIL 1865

Good Friday was the day
　　Of the prodigy and crime,
When they killed him in his pity,
　　When they killed him in his prime
Of clemency and calm—
　　　When with yearning he was filled
　　　To redeem the evil-willed,
And, though conqueror, be kind;
　　But they killed him in his kindness,
　　In their madness and their blindness,
And they killed him from behind.

　　　There is sobbing of the strong,

And a pall upon the land;
But the People in their weeping
Bare the iron hand:
Beware the People weeping
When they bare the iron hand.

He lieth in his blood—
The father in his face;
They have killed him, the Forgiver—
The Avenger takes his place,
The Avenger wisely stern,
Who in righteousness shall do
What the heavens call him to,
And the parricides remand;
For they killed him in his kindness
In their madness and their blindness,
And his blood is on their hand.

There is sobbing of the strong,
And a pall upon the land;
But the People in their weeping
Bare the iron hand:
Beware the people weeping
When they bare the iron hand.

. . .

"FORMERLY A SLAVE"
AN IDEALISED PORTRAIT BY E. VEDDER, IN THE SPRING
EXHIBITION OF THE NATIONAL ACADEMY, 1865

The sufferance of her race is shown,
And retrospect of life,
Which now too late deliverance dawns upon;
Yet she is not at strife.

Her children's children they shall know
The good withheld from her;
And so her reverie takes prophetic cheer—
In spirit she sees the stir

Far down the depth of thousand years,
And marks the revel and shine;
Her dusky face is lit with sober light,
Sibylline, yet benign.

• • •

### ON THE SLAIN COLLEGIANS

YOUTH is the time when hearts are large,
    And stirring wars
Appeal to the spirit which appeals in turn
    To the blade it draws.
If woman incite, and duty show
    (Though made the mask of Cain),
Or whether it be Truth's sacred cause,
    Who can aloof remain
That shares youth's ardor, uncooled by the snow
    Of wisdom or sordid gain?

The liberal arts and nurture sweet
Which give his gentleness to man—
    Train him to honour, lend him grace
Through bright examples meet—
That culture which makes never wan
With underminings deep, but holds
    The surface still, its fitting place,
    And so gives sunniness to the face
And bravery to the heart; what troops
    Of generous boys in happiness thus bred—
    Saturnians through life's Tempe led,
Went from the North and came from the South,
With golden mottoes in the mouth,
    To lie down midway on a bloody bed.

Woe for the homes of the North,
And woe for the seats of the South:
All who felt life's spring in prime,
And were swept by the wind of their place and time—
    All lavish hearts, on whichever side,
Of birth urbane or courage high,
Armed them for the stirring wars—
Armed them—some to die.
        Apollo-like in pride,
Each would slay his Python—caught
The maxims in his temple taught—
    Aflame with sympathies whose blaze
Perforce enwrapped him—social laws,

Friendship and kin, and by-gone days—
Vows, kisses—every heart unmoors,
And launches into the seas of wars.
What could they else—North or South?
Each went forth with blessings given
By priests and mothers in the name of Heaven;
  And honour in both was chief.
Warred one for Right, and one for Wrong?
So be it; but they both were young—
Each grape to his cluster clung,
All their elegies are sung.

The anguish of maternal hearts
  Must search for balm divine;
But well the striplings bore their fated parts
  (The heavens all parts assign)—
Never felt life's care or cloy.
Each bloomed and died an unabated Boy;
Nor dreamed what death was—thought it mere
Sliding into some vernal sphere.
They knew the joy, but leaped the grief,
Like plants that flower ere comes the leaf—
Which storms lay low in kindly doom,
And kill them in their flush of bloom.

. . .

### SUPPLEMENT

Were I fastidiously anxious for the symmetry of this book, it would close with the notes. But the times are such that patriotism—not free from solicitude—urges a claim overriding all literary scruples.

It is more than a year since the memorable surrender, but events have not yet rounded themselves into completion. Not justly can we complain of this. There has been an upheaval affecting the basis of things; to altered circumstances complicated adaptations are to be made; there are difficulties great and novel. But is Reason still waiting for Passion to spend itself? We have sung of the soldiers and sailors, but who shall hymn the politicians?

In view of the infinite desirableness of Re-establishment, and considering that, so far as feeling is concerned, it depends not mainly on the temper in which the South regards the North, but rather conversely; one who never was a blind adherent feels constrained to submit some thoughts, counting on the indulgence of his countrymen.

And, first, it may be said that, if among the feelings and opinions growing immediately out of a great civil convulsion, there are any which time shall modify or do away, they are presumably those of a less temperate and charitable cast.

There seems no reason why patriotism and narrowness should go together, or why intellectual impartiality should be confounded with political trimming, or why serviceable truth should keep cloistered because not partisan. Yet the work of Reconstruction, if admitted to be feasible at all, demands little but common sense and Christian charity. Little but these? These are much.

Some of us are concerned because as yet the South shows no penitence. But what exactly do we mean by this? Since down to the close of the war she never confessed any for braving it, the only penitence now left her is that which springs solely from the sense of discomfiture; and since this evidently would be a contrition hypocritical, it would be unworthy in us to demand it. Certain it is that penitence, in the sense of voluntary humiliation, will never be displayed. Nor does this afford just ground for unreserved condemnation. It is enough, for all practical purposes, if the South have been taught by the terrors of civil war to feel that Secession, like Slavery, is against Destiny; that both now lie buried in one grave; that her fate is linked with ours; and that together we comprise a Nation.

The clouds of heroes who battled for the Union it is needless to eulogise here. But how of the soldiers on the other side? And when of a free community we name the soldiers, we thereby name the people. It was in subserviency to the slave-interest that Secession was plotted; but it was under the plea, plausibly urged, that certain inestimable rights guaranteed by the Constitution were directly menaced that the people of the South were cajoled into revolution. Through the arts of the conspirators and the perversity of fortune, the most sensitive love of liberty was entrapped into the support of a war whose implied end was the erecting in our advanced century of an Anglo-American empire based upon the systematic degradation of man.

Spite this clinging reproach, however, signal military virtues and achievements have conferred upon the Confederate arms historic fame, and upon certain of the commanders a renown extending beyond the sea—a renown which we of the North could not suppress, even if we would. In personal character, also, not a few of the military leaders of the South enforce forbearance; the memory of others the North refrains from disparaging; and some, with more or less of reluctance, she can respect. Posterity, sympathising with our convictions, but removed from our passions, may perhaps go farther here. If George IV. could, out of the graceful instinct of a gentleman, raise an honourable monument in the great fane of Christendom over the remains of the enemy of his dynasty, Charles Edward, the invader of England and victor in the rout at Prestonpans—upon whose head the king's ancestor but one reign removed had set a price—is it probable that the grandchildren of General Grant will pursue with rancour, or slur by sour neglect, the memory of Stonewall Jackson?

But the South herself is not wanting in recent histories and biographies which record the deeds of her chieftains—writings freely published at the North by loyal houses, widely read here, and with a deep though saddened interest. By students of the war such works are hailed as welcome accessories, and tending to the completeness of the record.

Supposing a happy issue of present perplexities, then, in the generation next to come, Southerners there will be yielding allegiance to the Union, feeling all their interests bound up in it, and yet cherishing unrebuked that kind of feeling for the memory of the soldiers of the fallen Confederacy that Burns, Scott, and the Ettrick Shepherd felt for the memory of the gallant clansman ruined through their fidelity to the Stuarts—a feeling whose passion was tempered by the poetry imbuing it, and which in no wise affected their loyalty to the Georges, and which, it may be added, indirectly contributed excellent things in literature. But, setting this view aside, dishonourable would it be in the South were she willing to abandon to shame the memory of brave men who with signal personal disinterestedness warred in her behalf, though from motives, as we believe, so deplorably astray.

Patriotism is not baseness, neither is it inhumanity. The mourners who this summer bear flowers to the mounds of the Virginian and Georgian dead are, in their domestic bereavement and proud affection, as sacred in the eye of Heaven as are those who go with similar offerings of tender grief and love into the cemeteries of our Northern martyrs. And yet, in one aspect, how needless to point the contrast.

Cherishing such sentiments, it will hardly occasion surprise that, in looking over the battle-pieces in the foregoing collection, I have been tempted to withdraw or modify some of them, fearful lest in presenting, though but dramatically and by way of a poetic record, the passions and epithets of civil war, I might be contributing to a bitterness which every sensible American must wish at an end. So, too, with the emotion of victory as reproduced on some pages, and particularly toward the close. It should not be construed into an exultation misapplied—an exultation as ungenerous as unwise, and made to minister, however indirectly, to that kind of censoriousness too apt to be produced in certain natures by success after trying reverses. Zeal is not of necessity religion, neither is it always of the same essence with poetry or patriotism.

There were excesses which marked the conflict, most of which are perhaps inseparable from the civil strife so intense and prolonged, and involving warfare in some border countries new and imperfectly civilised. Barbarities also there were, for which the Southern people collectively can hardly be held responsible, though perpetrated by ruffians in their name. But surely other qualities—exalted ones—courage and fortitude matchless, were likewise displayed, and largely; and justly may these be held the characteristic traits, and not the former.

In this view, what Northern writer, however patriotic, but must revolt from acting on paper a part anyway akin to that of the live dog to the dead lion; and yet it is right to rejoice for our triumph, so far as it may justly imply an advance for our whole country and for humanity.

Let it be held no reproach to any one that he pleads for reasonable consideration for our late enemies, now stricken down and unavoidably debarred, for the time, from speaking through authorised agencies for themselves. Nothing has been urged here in the foolish hope of conciliating those men—few in number, we trust—who have resolved never to be reconciled to the Union. On such hearts everything is thrown away except it be religious commiseration, and the sincerest. Yet let them call to mind that unhappy Secessionist, not a military man, who with impious alacrity fired the first shot of the Civil War at Sumter, and a little more than four years afterward fired the last one into his own heart at Richmond.

Noble was the gesture into which patriotic passion surprised the people in a utilitarian time and country; yet the glory of the war falls short of its pathos—a pathos which now at last ought to disarm all animosity.

How many and earnest thoughts still rise, and how hard to repress them. We feel what past years have been, and years, unretarded years, shall come. May we all have moderation; may we all show candour. Though, perhaps, nothing could ultimately have averted the strife, and though to treat of human actions is to deal wholly with second causes, nevertheless, let us not cover up or try to extenuate what, humanly speaking, is the truth—namely, that those unfraternal denunciations, continued through years, and which at last inflamed to deeds that ended in bloodshed, were reciprocal; and that, had the preponderating strength and the prospect of its unlimited increase lain on the other side, on ours might have lain those actions which now in our late opponents we stigmatise under the name of Rebellion. As frankly let us own—what it would be unbecoming to parade were foreigners concerned—that our triumph was won not more by skill and bravery than by superior resources and crushing numbers; that it was a triumph, too, over a people for years politically misled by designing men, and also by some honestly-erring men, who from their position could not have been otherwise than broadly influential; a people who, though, indeed, they sought to perpetuate the curse of slavery, and even extend it, but (less fortunate, not less righteous than we) were the fated inheritors; a people who, having a like origin with ourselves, share essentially in whatever worthy qualities we may possess. No one can add to the lasting reproach which hopeless defeat has now cast upon Secession by withholding the recognition of these verities.

Surely we ought to take it to heart that that kind of pacification, based upon principles operating equally all over the land, which lovers of their country yearn for, and which our arms, though signally triumphant, did not bring about, and which law-making, however anxious, or energetic, or repressive, never by itself can achieve, may yet be largely aided by generosity of sentiment public and private. Some revisionary legislation and adaptive is indispensible; but with this should harmoniously work another kind of prudence, not unallied with entire magnanimity. Benevolence and policy—Christianity and Machiavelli—dissuade from penal severities toward the subdued. Abstinence here is as obligatory as considerate care for our unfortunate fellow-men late in bonds, and, if observed, would equally prove to be wise forecast. The great qualities of the South, those attested in the War, we can perilously alienate, or we may make them nationally available at need.

The blacks, in their infant pupilage to freedom, appeal to the sympathies of every humane mind. The paternal guardianship which for the interval Government exercises over them was prompted equally by duty and benevolence. Yet such kindliness should not be allowed to exclude kindliness to communities who stand nearer to us in nature. For the future of the freed slaves we may well be concerned; but the future of the whole country, involving the future of the blacks, urges a paramount claim upon our anxiety. Effective benignity, like the Nile, is not narrow in its bounty, and true policy is always broad. To be sure, it is vain to seek to glide, with moulded words, over the difficulties of the situation. And for them who are neither partisans nor enthusiasts, nor theorists, nor cynics, there are some doubts not readily to be solved. And there are fears. Why is not the cessation of war now at length attended with the settled calm of peace? Wherefore in a clear sky do we still turn our eyes toward the South, as the Neapolitan, months after the eruption, turns his toward Vesuvius? Do we dread lest the repose be deceptive? In the recent convulsion has the crater but shifted? Let us revere that sacred uncertainty which forever impends over men and nations. Those of us who always abhorred slavery as an atheistical iniquity, gladly we join in the exulting chorus of humanity over its downfall. But we should remember that emancipation was accomplished not by deliberate legislation; only through agonised violence could so mighty a result be effected. In our natural solicitude to confirm the benefit of liberty to the blacks, let us forbear from measures of dubious constitutional rightfulness toward our white countrymen—measures of a nature to provoke, among other of the last evils, exterminating hatred of race toward race. In imagination let us place ourselves in the unprecedented position of the Southerners—their position as regards the millions of ignorant manumitted slaves in their midst, for whom some of us now claim the suffrage. Let us be Christians toward our fellow-whites, as well as philanthropists toward the blacks, our fellow-men. In all things, and toward all, we are enjoined to do as we would be done by. Nor should we forget that benevolent desires, after passing a certain point, cannot undertake their own fulfillment without incurring the risk of evils beyond those sought to be remedied. Something may well be left to the graduated care of future legislation, and to heaven. In one point of view the co-existence of the two races in the South—whether the negro be bond or free—seems (even as it did to Abraham Lincoln) a grave evil. Emancipation has ridded the country of the reproach, but not wholly of the calamity. Especially in the present transition period for both races in the South, more or less of trouble may not unreasonably be anticipated; but let us not hereafter be too swift to charge the blame exclusively in any one quarter. With certain evils men must be more or less patient. Our institutions have a potent digestion, and may in time convert and assimilate to good all elements thrown in, however originally alien.

But, so far as immediate measures looking toward permanent Re-establishment are concerned, no consideration should tempt us to pervert the national victory into oppression for the vanquished. Should plausible promise of eventual good, or a deceptive or spurious sense of duty, lead us to essay this, count we must on serious consequences, not the least of which would be divisions among the Northern adherents of the Union. Assuredly, if any honest Catos there be who thus far have gone with us, no longer will they do so, but oppose us, and as resolutely as hitherto they have supported. But this path of thought leads toward those waters of bitterness from which one can only turn aside and be silent.

But supposing Re-establishment so far advanced that the Southern seats in Congress are occupied, and by men qualified in accordance with those cardinal principles of representative government which hitherto have prevailed in the land—what then? Why, the Congressmen elected by the people of the South will—represent the people of the South. This may seem a flat conclusion; but, in view of the last five years, may there not be latent significance in it? What will be the temper of those Southern members? and, confronted by them, what will be the mood of our own representatives? In private life true reconciliation seldom follows a violent quarrel; but, if subsequent intercourse be unavoidable, nice observances and mutual are indispensable to the prevention of a new rupture. Amity itself can only be maintained by reciprocal respect, and true friends are punctilious equals. On the floor of Congress North and South are to come together after a passionate duel, in which the South, though proving her valour, has been made to bite the dust. Upon differences in debate shall acrimonious recriminations be exchanged? shall censorious superiority assumed by one section provoke defiant self-assertion on the other? shall Manassas and Chickamauga be retorted for Chattanooga and Richmond? Under the supposition that the full Congress will be composed of gentlemen, all this is impossible. Yet, if otherwise, it needs no prophet of Israel to foretell the end. The maintenance of Congressional decency in the future will rest mainly with the North. Rightly will more forbearance be required from the North than the South, for the North is victor.

But some there are who may deem these latter thoughts inapplicable, and for this reason: Since the test-oath operatively excludes from Congress all who in any way participated in Secession, therefore none but Southerners wholly in harmony with the North are eligible to seats. This is true for the time being. But the oath is alterable; and in the wonted fluctuations of parties not improbably it will undergo alteration, assuming such a form, perhaps, as not to bar the admission into the National Legislature of men who represent the population lately in revolt. Such a result would involve no violation of the principles of democratic government. Not readily can one perceive how the political existence of the millions of late Secessionists can permanently be ignored by this Republic. The years of the war tried our devotion to the Union; the time of peace may test the sincerity of our faith in democracy.

In no spirit of opposition, not by way of challenge, is anything here thrown out. These thoughts are sincere ones; they seem natural—inevitable. Here and there they must have suggested themselves to many thoughtful patriots. And, if they be just thoughts, ere long they must have that weight with the public which already they have with individuals.

For that heroic band—those children of the furnace who, in regions like Texas and Tennessee, maintained their fidelity through terrible trials—we of the North felt for them, and profoundly we honour them. Yet passionate sympathy, with resentments so close as to be almost domestic in their bitterness, would hardly in the present juncture tend to discreet legislation. Were the Unionists and Secessionists but as Guelphs and Ghibellines? If not, then far be it from a great nation now to act in the spirit that animated a triumphant town-faction in the Middle Ages. But crowding thoughts must at last be checked; and, in times like the present, one who desires to be impartially just in the expression of his views, moves as among sword-points presented on every side.

Let us pray that the terrible historic tragedy of our time may not have been enacted without instructing our whole beloved country through terror and pity; and may fulfillment verify in the end those expectations which kindle the bards of Progress and Humanity.

William Gilmore Simms, circa 1859 *(Courtesy of the South Caroliniana Library)*

# William Gilmore Simms
## (1806–1870)

"Most of our young writers," Simms commented in 1862, "have exchanged the pen for the Sword." Simms wished he was young enough to do so as well. Instead, he offered military advice to Confederate officers, monitored the actions of his son who joined the army, and tried every way possible short of enlisting to boost the Southern cause. He continued writing, and managed some critical essays for *De Bow's Review*, poetry for the *Charleston Mercury* and the *Southern Literary Messenger*, and poetry and drama for the *Magnolia Weekly*. His only extended work was *Paddy McGann* (1863), a short novel about the humorous tales and adventures of an Irish immigrant to the South, serialized in the *Southern Illustrated News*. But he could not stay focused. "I am literally doing nothing in letters," he confided to his Northern friend and literary agent James Lawson. "I am so much excited in the present condition of things that the labour of the desk is irksome—I go to it with reluctance, and leave it on the slightest pretext." Eighteen months later it was much the same: "It will need a year of peace to bring me back to that calm mood which Literature demands."[1]

For the most prolific and best-known Southern writer of the day, this was an astonishing admission. Since 1825, when he published his first work, a poem on the death of Charles Pinckney, Simms had produced a huge and diverse body of work. He was a critic, historian, biographer, poet, dramatist, and novelist. He made his reputation, as well as a sizable income, from his historical romances of colonial and revolutionary America. These included, in one brief period, *Guy Rivers* (1834), *The Yemasee* (1835), *The Partisan* (1835), and *Mellichampe* (1836), and in another, *Katherine Walton* (1851), *Woodcraft* (1852), and *The Forayers* (1855).

Admired nationally, Simms regularly traveled north to lecture and renew literary friendships.

The war forced Simms away from his desk because it forced him away from history and romance. He had to think about money—secession meant the temporary loss—and possible confiscation—of his Northern copyrights, worth some $20,000. He had to think about money and loss—Woodlands, his home, burned down once in 1862 and again in 1865. He had to think about loss and death—buried was his daughter in 1862, his wife in 1863, his dearest friend in 1864, and the sons of others throughout the war. He suffered physically and wished that he could take up his old work: "I am far from well myself. I feel jaded & fagged, yet have been doing nothing at the desk. If I could get back into the old traces, my brains & bowels would both be better."[2] But with the start of the war, the old work had become extinct.

Less than a year into the Rebellion he proclaimed he was "sick of hearing & talking of the war, though the terrible anxiety forces all speech in this one direction."[3] All writing was forced in that direction as well. The paradox with Simms, as with so many other writers during the Civil War, is that he characterized himself as a spent and beaten author, but he did so through writings, particularly correspondence, that we must consider, even if he could not, a significant part of the literary output of his day. His letters contemplate and, in themselves, capture the creative and tragic dimensions of the war. His pamphlet, *Sack and Destruction of the City of Columbia* (1865), reveals a man overwhelmed by the horror that now enveloped his world.

Following the war, Simms tried to revive his literary life, but after five years of writing about war and death, hope and disappointment, his new romances lacked urgency. Few Southerners and even fewer Northerners cared. He was more successful as a booster of Southern letters, compiling and editing a volume of *War Poetry of the South* (1866). Even Southern reviewers, however, criticized the volume for including too many "ambiguous and inelegant" poems which "might very well have remained unpublished."[4] He edited several newspapers, but like so many former slaveholders and planters he had great difficulty understanding the new order being born around him. He had convinced himself that his slaves were loyal and loving, but after the war, when only three of the remaining fifty freedmen agreed to be hired by their former master's son, Simms lashed out at Southern blacks and Northern whites and the new economic arrangements that would require a flexibility of which Simms was incapable. He considered writing an autobiography, but he knew now that it could never be the story that he would have wanted, the story of the successful "self-development" of a man's character and career. Perhaps that is why he never began it. The outline of his life, he thought in 1866, looked something like this: "I have personally known a large number of the chief men of the South, for the last forty years; have been ruined, as a Union Man, by Nullification, and more lately by Secession; & have to commence life *de novo*, but with youth gone."[5]

There is a passage in *Paddy McGann* where one of the characters proclaims, "It is not all over—our happy life, my friend! . . . It cannot be that God will deliver us into the hands of these atrocious heathens. As between us and the Deity, there is no doubt a sad reckoning to make; but as between us and these accursed Yankees, no reproach lies at our doors, unless that single one of having too long slept within the coil of the serpent. I have faith in God, my friend.—He may punish us, and we must suffer, for this is the meed of our desert; but he will not let us sink. . . . After this tribulation, our peace shall return once more—our prosperity—our friends."[6] Maybe for others, but the happy life for Simms never returned.

### 1. WGS to Margaret Maxwell Martin[7] [*c.* April 15, 1861]

I have just returned from an eight days' absence in Charleston, where I witnessed the bombardment of Fort Sumter. I congratulate you on the expulsion of the enemy from the sacred soil of Carolina, now *doubly* sacred to you since your first-born was one of the first sacrifices in its redemption.[8] May his memory blossom anew in your hearts with love, to mature hereafter to a glorious ripeness, while it remains enshrined in the tender regrets of his countrymen! God is surely with us, my dear friend, thus far, in our progress to independence. May we never, by any vain exultation leading to presumptuous confidence, forfeit the powerful favor of the mighty King of all nations who hath thus far been our shield and strength in the day of our trial. But in times like these words fail us, and, as you say, prayer itself sometimes becomes impossible. Certainly, all such prayer as seeks utterance in mere words must be feeble as idle. But silent thought is perhaps the most valuable form of prayer—that thought which blends with feeling and wings its way to God through tears and truthful emotions, through an imagination which soars above the earth, and seeks only to spread its wings of rejoicing directly under the living sunlight, and in the generous smile of heaven. We do not the less pray, my friend—the heart being right, and the purpose just and true—though we speak never a word, and though we breathe with a difficult delight. Rapture, when at the highest, grows dumb, and all our finer pleasures are inarticulate things. Let us only feel how great are God's mercies to us, and so act as not to forfeit them, and the ordinary thought of our waking hours is prayer sublimed for heaven.

### 2. WGS to William Porcher Miles,[9] Woodlands, S.C. May 11, [1861]

I know not, my friend, if I am capable of giving it, but the position of the country, & of our State, keeps me dreadfully anxious, & though my own family is a subject of anxiety, that which I feel, touching our affairs, will not suffer me to be silent. I have been reasoning, or trying to reason, out the project & plans of the U.S. Govt. It is difficult to reason in the case of a desperate party, which knows that if once the excitement sleeps, the thought of the people awakes. The Black Republicans can only save themselves by keeping up the excitement. How are they to do it. The plea of Washington menaced has been more potent than any thing besides. The vanity of the North has been sorely hurt by the fall of Sumter. In the first rages of the people the mob is in the ascendant. But, meanwhile, they get 25,000 at Washington. What to do with them? As the summer approaches, active operations in the South are almost impossible on the part of Northern men. But their policy will be to quarter their troops in the South, at healthy situations. I have no doubt that Scott has arranged to hurl 10,000 men upon Beaufort, establishing a camp, occupying the country, & giving him a base of operations at once against S.C. and Georgia. A detachment will occupy Bluff-town. In November, they will be prepared with 15,000 more, to act upon Charleston & Savannah, and to ascend to Augusta & Columbia. For the details, you must use your conjectures. . . .

### 3. WGS to William Porcher Miles, Woodlands, June 8, 1861

. . . My heart and head are so full that I cannot help but write, though perhaps I shall say nothing of value. Even now, I have a sick family, & your little God Daughter is down with fever. But not, I trust, seriously. I write at midnight. All are sleeping. I cannot sleep. I have just closed up two large batches of editorials for the *Mercury*, which, I am sorry to see, is beginning that sort of fire upon the Confederate Govt. in the management of the army, which it kept up, on our own, before the taking of Sumter. This sort of writing, is the cause of great indignation among many here. It is wild, mischievous & idle. I have faith in our officers & soldiers & fear not. Still, my friend, as you know me to [be of] a restless mind, anxious to be doing—not permitted to do—striving to teach some things which may help our poor country, you will understand why I write. I have some suggestions to make, which, if you please, you may empty into the ears of Gen. Beauregard.[10] I would have him pick ten men for each company in every regiment, have them well officered, painted and disguised as Indians. They will inspire terror. They should be habited in the yellow Hunting Shirt of Cotton—they should be turbanned,—armed with rifle, bowie knife & hatchet, and each company, thus formed, should be attached to its own regiment as an auxiliary force. Once produce disorder in the enemy's line or column, & let these fellows put in for close action. But the officer should be a rare fellow, & should know his business. These should be your Seminole Zouaves. It should be made as public as possible that every regiment has its band of Indians. The tumeric will dye the garments—the blood root,—*poccoon*, or *sanguinaria canadensis*, the face, hands, arms & neck. If there be any thing which will inspire terror in the souls of the citizens soldiery of the North, it will be the idea that scalps are to be taken by the redmen. Encourage this idea. You will have in your masses thousands, I trust, who will be familiar with the Indian mode of warfare. Beauregard himself, will know all about it. Your Texans should be freely employed in this fashion, and for your officers you should have live, daring, reckless fellows—the boys chosen should be at once bold & expert. . . .

If you can destroy [Scott's] columns, then you must take Washington, destroy it, expel the conqueror, rouse up Maryland, & penetrate Pennsylvania with fire & sword. A merely defensive war, dealing with the most presumptuous & aggressive people in the world, is simply child's play. You must *dictate* a peace, & this you will only be enabled to do, when you have obtained two or three decisive victories, & when the European powers shall be implicated in the war. In less than six weeks, I expect to see Great Britain in the field. There will be an *ex tempore sea fight*, in which *she will not be worsted*. Then comes the rest, & the rest will be conclusive. . . . I need not say to you that I feel like a bear chained to the stake. I can neither ride nor march. I can only pass sleepless nights, fuming to my friends, of what I think may be done. May the Great & Good God shelter you, dear friend, & render you to us in safety.

4. WGS to James Henry Hammond,[11] Woodlands, June 14, 1861

My House for the last two months has been something of a Hospital. I have had three children down, seriously, with Bilious remittent, in one case running into typhoid. The are now better, but my anxiety & suffering have been great, & I now tremblingly watch against relapse. Half a dozen little negroes sick also, one of whom will probably die tonight. The rest doing well. I, too, have been suffering from (I suppose) both mind & body; with nothing to console & every thing to distract me. No more books to make—no money—some debt,—and plain living. Othello's occupation is gone for the present, and my copyrights, worth $20,000—the whole of my life earnings—not only temporarily value-less to me but liable to confiscation! The North takes away from me, and the South has never given! . . .

### 5.  WGS to James Lawson,[12] Woodlands, July 4, 1861

. . . [L]iterature, poetry especially, is effectually overwhelmed by the drums, & the cavalry, and the shouting. War is here the only idea. Every body is drilling and arming. Even I practise with the Colt. I am a dead shot with rifle & double barrel, & can now kill rabbit or squirrel with the pistol. Our women practise, & they will fight, too, like she wolves. Your Yankees are converting our whole people to Unionism. If you ask me about myself, I have only to say that I am sad & sick & suffering. Gilmore is feverish to buckle on armour & go to Vir-ginia. We have lost our youngest son, the boy Sydney Hammond, 2 years old, teething,—and, I think, with a spinal affection. . . . Crops are good—mine never better. We shall make abundance of corn, & the Cotton crop will prob-ably exceed that of last year by 300,000 bales. The seasons have been very favorable. We have been eating at Woodlands, for months, strawberries, green peas, green corn, okra, irish potatoes, snap beans, squashes, radishes, blackber-ries, June berries, artichokes, &c. &c. My wife sells $2 of butter weekly. Her pocket money. We have milk, butter milk, curds, clabber, spring chickens & eggs in abundance. But we want peace! We are invaded! Every hour widens & deepens the breach between the two sections; and passion is succeeded by Hate, & Hate by Vindictiveness, and if the war continues, there will be no rem-edy. Your city will be utterly ruined by the Black Republicans who dare not think of peace, and who, if the people once come to their senses, will be torn to pieces. You, perhaps, do not think all this. But you had warning of every syllable a year ago & last summer. The cowardice of your conservatives is the secret of your evil. You have no moral at the North. The mob rules you. If the war is persevered in, it must be a war of extermination. Our people will fight to the last! . . .

### 6.  WGS to James Lawson, Woodlands, August 20, 1861

. . . We should really be glad to see you & Lyde, & all the girls here with us, and, I trust, when this war, at once brutal & ridiculous ceases, we shall have you here again. Oh! how your foolish city has been cutting its own throat. Only think of a people making war on their best customers. What suicide. Your *accounts* are not such as reach us of the events of the war. Our Government is not one to suppress reports of the action; to seize upon telegraphic dispatches; to alter reports for the press & telegraph—in brief to do what it pleases, in violation of Constitution, law & rights of the Citizen. Whether you will hear the truth until the war is ended, is very questionable. But you ought to be shrewd Scotchman enough to guess it for yourself, when, after all the mighty preparations of the North, they still tremble for the safety of Washington, & every step in Virginia has lost them blood & treasure. We do not exult in this. We wish for peace. We desire no war, but are prepared for the worst. We are resolved on Independence. We have been persecuted for 30 years & will stand it no longer—from our brethren. By this time your thinking men see the sort of game that is before them. Let them grow wise before it be too late. Every battle, thus far, has resulted in a Southern Victory.—Sumter, Bethel, Bull Run, Manassas, Harper's Ferry & Missouri,—all tell the same tale. Your Generals are cashiered. Your army demoralized. Your papers are at a loss where to cast the blame. They will be at no loss before long. They will see that their cause is bad. We have now 200,000 men in the field, with 250,000 in preparation for it. We can feed our armies from the fields, without buying any thing but guns & ammunition. We shall make 4,500,000 bales of Cotton. We will look at the piles & if need be, burn them. We do not need to sell a bag. Of all this, you, among others, were well warned long ago. I do not blame *you* for this war. I know that you desired peace. We offered peace. But your people have sacrificed the country for the sake of a party that had no other object in view, than the monopoly of office. Office without revenue! Where are your democrats? Where were they at the passage of the Morrill tariff, for the benefit of Pennsylvania and New England. Between these two, New York is in ruins. We are prepared for a long war—preparing for it. It will fully establish the independence of the South. We are now manufacturing guns, cannon, rifles, powder, shot, oils, machinery, wool & cotton clothing, percussion caps, sewing machines—every thing. Three years of war will be the making of our people; and they are all beginning to perceive it. Not a bale of Cotton will be sent to the seaports. Hardly one off the plantations. Our young men are all profitably employed. Our old men are keeping things straight at home. Our crops are abundant, and we are willing that the vile petty conflict of 30 years, should close, at last, in a final issue of battle. Every day of delay in the conflict strengthens us, & every man feels that our cause is just & that God is with us. Troops for Virginia & our Sea Coast are pouring in daily. New regiments are in constant formation, and such a *personnel* for war is rarely witnessed in any nation. . . .

For my part, I am literally doing nothing in letters. I am so much excited in the present condition of things that the labour of the desk is irksome—I go to it with reluctance, and leave it on the slightest pretext. . . . We shall have bread & meat in plenty, but possibly no money. I am already picking Cotton; and we shall pile it up in pyramids, with piles of light wood beneath it, ready to be fired as soon as your fierce Yankees penetrate the country. We shall admire daily the piles as they grow, and they will make a splendid conflagration, lighting up the country for miles, and showing the bright armour of the enemy on his march. But war is a sad subject for jesting upon & to us, old fellows, it is hateful. You & I might have adjusted the whole issue—i.e. if despotic powers for 24 hours had been given us.

### 7. WGS to William Gilmore Simms, Jr., Woodlands, [November 7, 1861]

. . . Advise me, as soon as you can, of your whereabouts & the mode of reaching you, in the event of our desiring to send you any thing. See that your provision for clothing is warm & sufficient. Leave every thing that you do not need, with your sister; and remember that nobody is more lighthearted than he who has fewest cares, whether of brain or body. Your bowie knife may be very useful. You are to remember that you are to defend your mother country, & your natural mother, from a horde of mercenaries & plunderers, and you will make your teeth meet in the flesh. The less you fear for yourself, the more your security. "He who would save his life, the same shall lose it!" This is a biblical warning against that lack of firmness, that overcaution, always trembling at consequences, & calculating chances, which was the infirmity of Hamlet, and which is fatal to all heroism. And this audacity & courage are not inconsistent with the utmost prudence and circumspection. All generalship, in fact, is so much military prudence, as reconciles valour with judgment & wisdom. Mere inconsiderate rage is not so much valour as blindness, ignorance, presumption & insanity. Obey orders, do your duty faithfully & cheerfully & patiently, and wait your time, & watch your time, and keep your head so, that where your leader may falter, you shall be able to keep him up, counsel him on, & where he falls, take the lead yourself. A strong will, a brave heart & clear head, in the moment of danger, these constitute the essentials of heroism. Let nothing, at any time, divert your mind, from the immediate duty which is before you. This is *first* & therefore *over* all. It will be time enough tomorrow for other matters. But I will not bore you with laws and maxims. Be a man, my son, faithful & firm, and put yourself in God's keeping. All that the love & confidence of parents can do for you will be done. Yourself, with God'said, must do the rest. . . .

### 8. WGS to James Henry Hammond, Woodlands, November 18, 1861

I went to town on Friday last, seeking a Hogshead or a couple of barrels of molasses. Not a gallon was to be had in Charleston, the troops having consumed every thing. And as the troops continue to accumulate, & as we can get nothing except by the slow coach, over the land route, it is almost impossible that things should be more favorable to my wishes a month hence than now. Meanwhile, I wish to feed my negroes, & through sweets, keep them in sweet temper. It is probable that the article may be procurable in Augusta. Will you endeavor to buy me a Hogshead of the cheapest, or a couple of bbls, (which I should prefer) and, as I am not known perhaps, as a man of substance, to the *solid* men of that town, endorse me as good for the nonce. If you can, do so as soon as possible. I hold it to be important, & suggest it to you, that our negroes should, especially just now, be taught to feel that their owners are their best friends. Mine are very docile. I have 70, and most of them are born on the place, and have grown up with my children. I have lost my overseer—gone to the wars. My son, the only one able to do duty—just 18—is in camp & eager for an opportunity. But for my helpless little ones, I should be very much disposed, though I can neither ride nor march, to set off for the seaboard myself, for I can still see to shoot. What have you done for negro clothes and shoes? Or have you been more provident than your friends & laid in a supply of both while it was possible. Will you let me know whether a good thick cotton stuff, of sufficient weight as a substitute for woollen, can be got from your Augusta factories, and at what prices, and whether I can get credit, to the extent of a couple of hundred Dollars, or whether they will take pay in cotton and at what prices? Do see to these matters for me as soon as you conveniently can. I would run up and see about the matter myself, and visit you at the same time, but that I have nobody on the place but myself. . . .

I was fated like Cassandra to speak the truth with nobody to listen. My plans would most effectually have kept the enemy from breaking in at Port Royal. It is not the Yankee race alone that needs purging & scourging. We too need punishment to destroy the packed jury, & old family systems, the logrolling & the corruption every where. . . . Do write me. I am very desolate and disconsolate—able to do little—very much curtailed & cut down. My copyrights, worth $25,000 are, I suppose, all confiscate!

### 9. WGS to James Henry Hammond, Woodlands, December 2 [1861]

. . . I believe that England only waits a *political* necessity, to give her a pretext to elude & escape her philanthropic proclivities. She has been costive, in respect to the Confederate States, simply because she has never regarded the breach as irreparable. We have been mouthing & crying wolf so long—have been so long threatening disruption—that it is now hard to believe it. But, *necessitas non habet legem.* And England is evidently restive. The capture of our

Commissioners is evidently an imbroglio devised for her benefit and digestion.[13] It will give her a pretext. I have come to the conclusion that their capture
was a profound trap laid for the Yankees by Davis. Were it really of importance
to send these Commissioners & send them in safety, then the Confederate
Govt. & the Commissioners themselves played the siliest game in the
world. . . . My hope is that Great Britain will be glad to seize upon the ground
of quarrel which this outrage offers her. She cannot be desirous of the dismemberment of the late Confederacy—cannot be desirous of the perpetuation of a
Union which was in conflict with all her interests—to her shipping, trade,
manufactures & institutions—of which she was jealous—which she at once
feared & despised—cannot be indifferent to Cotton supply, or regardless of the
free trade with 10 millions of people, who do not conflict with her in any way,
but on the contrary, as purely Agricultural, are her natural allies. I should not
be surprised to find her at war with the U.S. in less than 3 weeks. . . .

## 10. WGS to William Porcher Miles, Woodlands, January 15, 1862

Our chief guest, on Christmas Day, was Death. He found his way, without
warning, and tore away our precious little one. The dear baby has arisen. I, who
have so frequently been made to groan and shudder at his coming, am not a whit
better prepared to meet him now, when he thus bears from us, each new bud
of promise. No sooner have new tendrils closed over the old wounds, than they
are rent away, and the scars reopen, & the old hurt bleeds afresh. This child
was very sweet & dear to us. She had served, my friend, as you rightly intimate,
to add new chords to those ties which linked you & ourselves so gratefully
together even over the still unburied corpses of my two noble little boys. And,
in herself, she was so surpassingly lovely. You can have no idea how tall she
had grown, & how beautifully. Her form was perfectly developed; her face very
fine & her forehead & whole head were cast in a mould of peculiar intellectual
strength and beauty! Alas! Alas!—And scarcely had we laid her in the grave
before I was again made to shudder with most awful terrors, when her brother,
Govan, a year older, was taken down with the same loathsome & cruel disease.
But God has been merciful in his case, & the boy has been spared. Yet you can
well coneive my own & the agonies of his poor mother. Ah! my friend, to think
that of 14 children, we have now buried nine! And all of such wonderful promise. Five are yet left us, but for how long—how long? I have no longer any sense
of security. My days & nights teem with apprehension. I wake from fearful
dreams. I walk musing with my fears & terrors. It affects my health, my happiness, my habits, my performances. I no longer read or write with satisfaction,
or success. Briefly, my dear friend, I am under these successive shocks, grow-

ing feebler, rapidly aging, and shudder with a continued sense of winter at my hearth. My occupation utterly gone, in this wretched state of war & confusion, I have no refuge in my wonted employments from the intensive apprehensions engendered by so long & so dreary an experience. Could I go to work, as of old, having a motive, I might escape from much of the domestic thought, and in foreign faring, quiet the oppressive memory. But nobody reads nowadays, and no one prints. My desks are already filled with MS.S. Why add to the number—the mass,—when, I so frequently feel like giving these to the flames? My will is not strong enough, even in obedience to the calls of the mind, to engage in new labours which are so wholly motiveless. I can still continue the work of self-development, though I no longer put pen to paper, or book to print. But I will not press this egotistical matter upon you any further. . . .

### 11. WGS to William Porcher Miles, Woodlands in Ruins, April 10, 1862

. . . Gladly now would I give my dwelling & all that I have saved, for the restoration of my two boys. And since then, a third boy, & a girl, your own protégé, and, I think, one of the most promising & lovely of my children. Truly, I am pursued by a hungry fate! But I will not succumb. It may crush, but shall not subject me, no more than Yankeedom shall subject our country. I am happy to tell you that I have saved all my MS.S. and nearly all my library. I fortunately built, only the last year, a wing to the dwelling, connected by a corridor, 20 ft in length. The wing was saved. But for this removal of my books, they must have been all lost, and only a few days before the fire, I gathered up all my MS.S.—matter enough for 50 vols. and packed it into trunks, not knowing how soon I should have to fly—thinking more of the Yankees, than of midnight fires, & wishing to be ready. Had I lost my library & MS.S. the blow would have been insupportable. As it is, I mean to die with harness on my back. . . .

### 12. WGS to James Henry Hammond, Woodlands in Ruins, April 10, [1862]

. . . . [B]oth of us have had personal experience which inclines us to believe that there are certain persons who seem to be perpetually pursued by some angry Fate, which haunts his steps, & dogs his career, as tenaciously as ever the Furies clung to the heels of Orestes. It seemed to me, a few months ago, when Death became my guest at Christmas,—the day that is usually hallowed to happiness in every porch—when he tore away one of the loveliest & most promising of my little brood—it seemed to me then, that the insatiate archer Fate, had achieved his crowning victory over me, and would be thenceforth satisfied. It seems not. I am still as bitterly pursued as ever, & can now only await patiently and in expectation for other strokes, each perhaps more heavy & more deadly than the last. Now that my homestead is in ruins, it would seem that the next shaft would properly be aimed at the Master. Well, my friend, I who have been required to endure so much, should, by this time, be prepared for any fate. To a certain extent I am; and perhaps the chief regret which I should feel, at being suddenly summoned to the great account, will be at leaving so many helpless ones for whom I have mostly striven, and who have constituted at once my principal cares & joys. That a Fate has pursued me for more than 30 years of loss, trial, trouble, denial, death, destruction, in which youth has passed rapidly to age, & hope into resignation that is only not despondency. It is my chief consolation that I have been able to endure so well; and if the Fate smites, the God strengthens. Even under this severe calamity, which it would have been terrible to me to anticipate, I am patient. I have lost none of my energy & courage, though I may have lost some of my cheerfulness & elasticity. I am bracing myself to bear, and to repair. To restore is impossible. As you say, there are losses in such a calamity as can never be restored. The accumulations of self & family, for 100 years, in a numerous household like ours—several families amalgamated into one, of which mine was the general store house—were wondrous large. As yet we know not the full extent of our losses. . . . The negroes had to be summoned from the negro quarter, a third of a mile off. They worked admirably when they came, with the most eager zeal & the most perfect devotion. *That* fact, my dear H. is to me full of consolation. And when in a moment of personal danger,—for I had to escape from an upper window, while the floor above was falling in—had you heard their passionate cries from below, to save myself, & seen the wonderful efforts which they made to bring a heavy ladder to my relief—you would have been gratified at the tacit proof thus given, that there was no lack of love for their master. . . .

## 13. WGS to Richard Yeadon, Woodlands, June 17, 1862

. . . . [N]ow that I do sit down to write, it is scarcely possible to say anything. All attempts at consolation, from any degree of friendship, must fail in such a case as yours.[14] The ordinary language of sympathy is so completely stereotyped that it sinks usually into the baldest common-place; and in an extreme instance, the last loss, the greatest grief, sorrow and sympathy equally find themselves speechless. Were I with you I should probably do nothing more than silently squeeze your hand. To say anything would seem impertinence. One hoods himself in the house of mourning and takes a silent place beside the desolate hearth, or broods for a moment over the face of the dead, and weeps silently with the living mourner, and so goes drooping to his own habitation, dreading the hour when the case shall become his own. I who have buried so many dear ones, know well how idle are all attempts at consolation, and but too frequently how painful and offensive. In your case it is not only your affections that are stricken. Your pride is crushed also. This lost boy was your nephew, and your *heart* feels the loss of a dear kinsman, the eldest son of the last surviving sister. But he was your adopted son also, chosen to bear your name, to perpetuate it, to maintain your position in society, to gratify your ambitious hopes for the future, and to represent your fortune. In his fate all these calculations are baffled, and these hopes mortified with defeat. . . . For him who has gone you have a two-fold consolation, in the fact that he dies young, ere he had much suffered, and while he was yet pure; and that he perished gallantly striving in battle for the independence of his country. It may not be amiss to refer you now to the uses, to yourself, of this great affliction. Without undertaking to justify the ways of God to man, it is yet only reasonable to assume that he has a purpose in this, as in all other of his providences which we may not readily fathom. This purpose, no doubt, contemplates your ultimate benefit. You, my friend, are at this very moment in as great peril as ever at any moment in your life. You have reached that dangerous state of which the Gods themselves are said to grow jealous.

14. WGS to the Editors of the *Southern Illustrated News,*
September 20, 1862

. . . You have well adverted, in your editorial department, to the difficulty of engaging now in literary composition. To do justice to the public, or to one's self, in letters, implies a perfectly calm mind, much leisure, and freedom from distracting occupation. Your whole mind must be concentrated on your subject. But who can give his whole mind to, or concentrate his thoughts upon abstract topics, when the whole country is heaving with the throes of a mighty revolution—when we are arming our sons for battle—when every dwelling presents daily a scene of parting—and when, from so many thousands, a voice of wailing is sent up from mothers and sisters, weeping for the beloved one, and refusing to be comforted? All our thoughts resolve themselves into the war. We are now *living* the first grand epic of our newly-born Confederacy. We are *making* the materials for the drama, and for future songs and fiction; and, engaged in the actual event, we are in no mood for delineating its details, or framing it to proper laws of art, in any province. This must be left to other generations, which, in the enjoyment of that peace and independence for which we are now doing battle, will be able to command the leisure for those noble and generous arts by which nations best assert their claims to independence, and secure a proud immortality for fame! We shall need to leave this labor to them. . . .

### 15. WGS to Paul Hamilton Hayne,[15] Woodlands, July 29, 1863

. . . Since our last writing, you see that our poor old city has been & is seriously menaced. Our people, so far as I can learn, have shown, if they do not now exhibit, a singular degree of apprehensiveness, not warranted by the circumstances, and not creditable to their manhood & resolve. They are recovering from it, but there is still too much of doubt & despondency among the citizens not to give us great concern. My trust is that as the pressure begins to be seriously felt, and as anxiety & suspense give way to the certainties of conflict, they will rise above the crisis, and prove successful in the encounter with it. It will probably resolve itself into a final trial with the bayonet on James Island. . . . I got a letter yesterday from Thompson, who is now editing a paper in Richmond called "The Record"—an eclectic, which embodies the documentary history of the day & country. It affords him no field, for his nice taste & happy talent, unless in the propriety of his selections; and, as he writes me—probably apprehending that I might seek an organ—he has no literary patronage to bestow. But my heart is too full of anxiety to suffer me to write, and though I have a contract for some $200 worth of prose, I find myself unable to divert my thoughts from the crisis in which the country trembles in suspense. What I write is in a spasm—a single burst of passion—hope, or scorn, or rage or exultation. If, where you are, you can abstract your mind from the present, & throw into the far land of the past, or poesy, do so for your own relief. I cannot! I have sent the last instalments of my dramatic essay on "Arnold" to the "Magnolia," and it will soon be finished. But the business of revision had become a drudgery with me long before it closed, and the horrible corruption & blunders of the press, had disgusted me with every column. I have no news. I have had a child very sick with worm fever, & my wife has been suffering severely with neuralgia in the face. They are now better—but who can be well, while this terrible war lasts, and while so many whom we love are in danger.

### 16. WGS to Paul Hamilton Hayne, Woodlands, September 23 [1863]

. . . I have been ill, my friend, I may say dangerously ill, from the moment when I was struck down by the heaviest bolt of all that ever shattered my roof-tree.[16] I was, I think, insane. I neither slept nor ate for four days and nights. Fever seized me, and I should have gone mad but for the administration of timely opiates. I am once more on my legs, but very weak. Today, is the first that I have given to the desk, and this I could do only in snatches of brief period. I move about the house & try to see things. But every thing seems blank, & waste, & very cheerless. I am alone! Alone! For near 30 years, I had one companion in whose perfect fidelity, I felt sure. To her I could go, and say, "I suffer!"—or "I am glad," always satisfied that she would partake the feeling with me, whatever its character. Your eulogy is not mere varnish & gilding. She was all that you describe,—a dutiful wife, a devoted mother, and the most guileless of women. Ah! God! And I am lone!

We live too much for the world, my dear Paul. It is a poor affair. This ambitious struggle after greatness, is a vanity. Our sole justification must lie in the will & wish to *do*, irrespective of the profit and the loss. What does Milton say in Lycidas—I half forget the passage—

> "But not the *praise*,
> Phoebus replied, & toucht my trembling ears—
> Fame is no plant that grows on mortal soil—" . . .

### 17. WGS to James Henry Hammond, Woodlands, July 28, 1864

. . . . I write (though I trust unnecessarily) to exhort you to a patient submission to the extortion & injustice which we may expect, & which we cannot easily escape.[17] You are such a marked man, and, without any miserable flattery, so far preeminent over all your fellows, that every defiance in your case, of the authorities—every denial of help to the cause, however justifiable as a private right, will be made to show enormously odious. This odiousness you might well brave & despise on your own account. You have little to ask & perhaps quite as little to fear. But the worst is the mischief will not fall upon your shoulders only, but will be entailed through life & for generations to come upon your progeny. Your children will be made to feel the odium in all relations of Life. Your sons will be cut off from all the distinctions—nay, from all the associations of society, and this will not be confined to South Carolina, or the little precinct in which you live. It will pass into history, & be made the topic of debate among all that class of persons who grovel at the base of eminence, seeking its overthrow by sap—men who

> "Distort the truth, accumulate the lie,
> And pile the pyramid of Calumny."

For the sake of your children & grandchildren, you must not incur this danger, or give occasion for this sort of malignity to work. Nor (however little you may value life) must you incur the risk of losing yours, in a miserable brawl. Better lose the money. It is lucky you can afford to lose it, better than anyone I know. Yield gracefully & loftily. No one better knows how to do this than yourself. And believe me, dear H., I speak from my heart to you. I have never, I believe, counseled you in any way inconsistently with your dignity & honour. I think that I do not now. Refer my letter to your wife. Take the woman's counsel with that of your friend. I look upon your wife as a rarely good woman, & a rarely *good* woman is perhaps far wiser in such a case, than a rarely endowed man. Were you as rarely good as you are rarely endowed, you would be one of the most perfect men living. It is your passions, your impetus & too frequently stubborn will, that neutralizes some of your noblest gifts. Forgive me for saying so now, but I have always thought this, & a thousand times said it to yourself. Believe me that this is one of the very cases where I would have you sacrifice your passions along with your interests, to that humbler wisdom which God employs for chastening the one, and keeping the other from getting wholly the better of heart and head. No man knows more thoroughly than myself, the crimes, blunders, indecencies & robberies, of the incompetent, dishonest, and cruelly corrupt character of thousands of the creatures employed in this war, as agents of those in power. But their crimes & blunders must not be suffered to disparage the labour & character of the army, and we must be content to sacrifice interest, even to the spoiler, & to waive a natural & just indignation & resentment, in regard to the safety of paramount interests, which our defiance might endanger. And it is a wise selfishness which makes us fear that unjust odium, entailed upon our children, which we have not deserved ourselves, but from which, in a struggle with the blind passions & prejudices of the multitude, we may not be able to relieve ourselves. Pray, my dear H. take all these things to heart. Let your friend, as I may fearlessly claim to be, prevail with you. Let your wife decide, for once, in a matter, which, while it is business, becomes a question of selfish policy in which she is deeply interested for her children & grandchildren. . . .

### 18. WGS to Paul Hamilton Hayne, Woodlands, September 19, 1864

. . . I am tired down, worn out & sickish. . . . At this moment, Wilmington is menaced by a concurrent attack by land & sea. Beauregard is there in command. All can be saved, if the exempts, detailed men & skulks can be brought promptly into the field, & subjected to timely discipline. Otherwise, we shall die by inches like the tail of a snake. Imbecility in office, civil & military, is tolling on the young life of our country, our youth, to unproductive peril & sure destruction. We are made daily to sup on horrors. The war will probably be of continued duration till both parties are exhausted,—unless God shall more emphatically interpose—how he may, or will do so—we may conjecture, but none can predict. . . .

### 19. WGS to William Gilmore Simms, Jr., Woodlands, November 14, 1864

. . . My purpose in writing to you, in lessons of economy, were to prevent you from wasting money, or your pay, when you happen to have it. Neither you nor I can afford to be guilty of waste or luxury, having all these children to provide for, and having to provide against the contingencies of an obscure & very uncertain future. In the diseased unrest of your mind, your desultory & purposeless mode of life, it is easy to expend money in the attainment of the means of temporary excitement. It will need that you exert all your will & moral force, to subject your mind to patience, so that you may reach a wholesome condition of the blood,—calming yourself to methodical & regular movements, & so toning down your moods, as to get rid of that feverish impatience of the staid & prosaic, which your present and recent mode of life has naturally engendered. It is a great misfortune to find yourself forever in a hurry—forever seeking change—and feeling as irksome, the restraints of place or duty. Think how monotonous will be any mode of life to you, after the war is over—unless you can now gradually subdue yourself to some method in your daily walks, & to a patient dogged determination, to do the work before you, and this done, fold your hands quietly for such meditations as should naturally occur to one in your situation, having a future purpose of self-development, and cogitating upon its plans. It was painful to me to witness in you, the irritable & feverish restlessness which marked all your movements while here—the impatience of the uniform—the fidgetting & nervous desire for change of scene, place & action—all of which, if indulged, must lead to a frivolous future—unsettled, unmethodical, without aim or purpose, beyond the mercurial impulse of the moment. Of course this habit has been engendered by the life you have been leading; but you must not let yourself be mastered by such a life, or your whole future will be lost. . . .

### 20. WGS to Edward Spann Hammond, Woodlands, November 20, 1864

Language fails me in any effort to embody my feelings in words.[18] I will not speak of my loss in comparison with that of your mother—you—all of you. Yet your father was my most cherished friend for near twenty five years. Never were thoughts more intimate than his & mine. We had few or no secrets from each other—we took few steps in life without mutual consultation. We had,—

I am sure I had—perfect confidence in him. I believe he had in me. I felt that there was something kindred in our intellectual nature. Certainly, there was much, very much, in common between us. Never did man more thoroughly appreciate his genius—its grasp—its subtlety—its superiority of aim. And most deeply did I sympathize with him, under that denial of his aim, and the exercise of his powers,—which, permitted, I verily believe he would have lived to a mature old age—lived for far higher triumphs even than those which he achieved. But the will of God be done. . . . This day, I feel doubly alone. I have seen committed to the grave, year after year, children, wife & friends. The fiery circle of Fate is drawing rapidly around me. We shall meet before many days, and, I trust in God, that we shall meet not only for the renewal of old ties, but for the exercise of those faculties, in which I felt proudly that we were kindred. Preserve all his papers. I hope someday to render a proper tribute to his memory. We have no chance for this now. There is no organ. There are no means. Do not suffer his *revised* publications to be mislaid. Have them carefully preserved, compactly put up & sealed against mischance. With God's blessing, I hope to put on record my appreciation of his claims and to illustrate them by his works. . . . I write with painful effort. I have been too much staggered by recent events fully to command the resources of my mind. I cannot *will* myself to thought. I can only fold hands, & wonder, and perhaps pray. What awaits us in the future, is perhaps foreshown to us by the Past, of trial and loss and suffering. Or it may be that God designs that we should surrender in sacrifice our choicest professions, that we may become worthy of the great boon of future Independence. Yet while I write, and hope, and pray, the day grows more clouded. I trembled & had sore misgivings when Johnson was removed from the army, & Hood put in his place. I predicted evil then to your father & to others. He concurred with me. And when Hood removed from Sherman's front, I then declared my opinion that if Sherman had the requisite audacity— it did not need Genius,—he would achieve the greatest of his successes, by turning his back on the enemy in his rear, & march boldly forward towards the Atlantic coast. I fear that such is his purpose. If so,—what have we to oppose him? I dare not look upon the prospect before us. It may become necessary for you, for me, & all to prepare as we can, for the overrunning of Carolina! All's very dark. . . .

### 21. WGS to Theophilus Hunter Hill,[19] Woodlands, November 22, 1864

. . . In regard to the poem which you send me now, I would not advise its publication in its present state. As a specimen of very *felicitous versification*, it is highly creditable; but as a creation, a conception bold & original duly worked out,—you have done nothing with the subject. It is still, as you found it, a naked statement of fact—viz: that Narcissus, a beautiful youth, became so enamored of his own beauty as to pine away to death in consequence. In your effort at musical effects, you have been content with giving this history in a happy collection of rhymes, but the only moral which you work from it, is to be found in that very portion which your friend urges you to omit. I, myself, do not see the necessity of making a poem to illustrate a moral; but every poem must embody *thought*, conception, & a poem of this class should show design. The earlier efforts of all young writers in Poetry, are designed to acquire mastery in utterance. They naturally strive to make language deliver itself in rhythm. Until this faculty be acquired, thought cannot become malleable in language. Now, it is not infrequently the case that, after a while, the young writer continues his practise, *seeking musical* effects only. He forgets that these musical *effects* are only means to an end, and that rhyme & rhythm are only agents for utterance in Poetry. Poetry is *winged thought*, and flies like an arrow to its mark. Having, as you have done, acquired a sufficient mastery of rhythmical utterance, your aim must be now embody your *thoughts* in this mode of speech. You are not merely to rhyme, however musical the rhyming may be—you are to design, conceive, think, seek, find & deliver. You are to *extort* from every subject its inner secret—for the Poet is a Seer. Whatever of problem there be in the story of Narcissus you are to find out—the moral of himself and story, which is its vital principle. Narcissus was passionless. He had no earnest passions. He loved himself only. He could not love women. He had no blood for it. He was probably an onanist, and his story, probably founded on a fact, was a satire. . . . That Poetry which is simply graceful & harmonious verse, has no vitality. Nothing lives long in literature of any sort but that which is informed by vigorous original thought; & it must be thought beyond the time.

## 22. [WGS] *Sack and Destruction of the City of Columbia, South Carolina* (Columbia, 1865)

The march of the Federals into our State was characterized by such scenes of license, plunder and general conflagration, as very soon showed that the threats of the Northern press, and of their soldiery, were not to be regarded as mere *brutum fulmen*. Day by day brought to the people of Columbia tidings of atrocities committed, and more extended progress. Daily did long trains of fugitives line the roads, with wives and children, and horses and stock and cattle, seeking refuge from the pursuers. Long lines of wagons covered the highways. Half-naked people cowered from the winter under bush tents in the thickets, under the eaves of houses, under the railroad sheds, and in old cars left them along the route. All these repeated the same story of suffering, violence, poverty and nakedness. Habitation after habitation, village after village—one sending up its signal flames to the other, presaging for it the same fate—lighted the winter and midnight sky with crimson horrors.

No language can describe nor can any catalogue furnish an adequate detail of the wide-spread destruction of homes and property. Granaries were emptied, and where the grain was not carried off, it was strewn to waste under the feet of the cavalry or consigned to the fire which consumed the dwelling. The negroes were robbed equally with the whites of food and clothing. The roads were covered with butchered cattle, hogs, mules and the costliest furniture. Valuable cabinets, rich pianos, were not only hewn to pieces, but bottles of ink, turpentine oil, whatever could efface or destroy, was employed to defile and ruin. Horses were ridden into the houses. People were forced from their beds, to permit the search after hidden treasures.

The beautiful homesteads of the parish country, with their wonderful tropical gardens, were ruined, ancient dwellings of black cypress, one hundred years old, which had been reared by the fathers of the republic—men whose names were famous in Revolutionary history—were given to the torch as recklessly as were the rude hovels; choice pictures and works of art, from Europe, select and numerous libraries, objects of peace wholly, were all destroyed. The inhabitants, black no less than white, were left to starve, compelled to feed only upon the garbage to be found in the abandoned camps of soldiers. The corn scraped up from the spots where the horses fed, has been the only means of life left to thousands but lately in affluence. . . .

All the precious things of a family, such as the heart loves to pore on in quiet hours when alone with memory—the dear miniature, the photograph, the portrait—these were dashed to pieces, crushed under foot, and the more the trembler pleaded for the object so precious, the more violent the rage which destroyed it. Nothing was sacred in their eyes, save the gold and silver which they bore away. Nor were these acts those of common soldiers. Commissioned officers, of rank so high as that of colonel, were frequently among the most active in spoliation, and not always the most tender or considerate in the manner and acting of their crimes. And, after glutting themselves with spoil, would often utter the foulest speeches, coupled with oaths as condiment, dealing in what they assumed, besides, to be bitter sarcasm upon the cause and country. . . .

The shocking details should not now be made, but that we need, for the sake of truth and humanity, to put on record the horrid deeds. And yet, we should grossly err if, while showing the forbearance of the soldiers in respect to our *white* women, we should convey to any innocent reader the notion that they exhibited a like forbearance in the case of the *black*. The poor negroes were terribly victimized by their assailants, many of them, besides the instance mentioned, being left in a condition little short of death. Regiments, in successive *relays*, subjected scores of these poor women to the torture of their embraces, and—but we dare not further pursue the subject. There are some horrors which the historian dare not pursue—which the painter dare not delineate. They both drop the curtain over crimes which humanity bleeds to contemplate.

Harriet Beecher Stowe, circa 1860

# Harriet Beecher Stowe
## (1811–1896)

"The agitations and mental excitements of the war have, in the case of the writer, as in the case of many others, used up the time and strength which would have been devoted to authorship. Who could write on stories that had a son to send to battle, with Washington beleaguered and the whole country shaken as with an earthquake? Who could write fiction when fact was so imperious and terrible, in the days of Bull Run and Big Bethel?" With this explanation, Harriet Beecher Stowe, the best-selling author in America, ceased after two installments a story she was writing for the New York *Independent*. Six months later, when she resumed the tale, she informed her readers that "no great romance is coming,—only a story pale and colorless as real life, and sad as truth."[1]

Stowe's own "real life" was anything but "pale and colorless." The daughter of Lyman Beecher, America's fiery evangelical preacher, she lost her mother at age four and spent her childhood contemplating the most profound questions of religious faith. At age twenty-one, she moved with her family from Hartford to Cincinnati, where her father headed Lane Theological Seminary and where she met her husband, Calvin Ellis Stowe, a professor of Biblical literature. It was here that she became interested in the public questions of the day, especially abolition. And it was here that she began writing, publishing sketches in the *Western Monthly Magazine*.

In 1850 the Stowes returned to the East. Harriet was now physically closer to the brother with whom she had strong emotional links. Henry Ward Beecher had inherited his father's pyrotechnics and applied them to the question of slavery. Harriet told her brother of her plans to write a book that would awaken the nation to the sin of slavery. Sometime that year, settled in Brunswick, Maine, she wrote about the death of a slave named Uncle Tom. From there, she derived the rest of the story and it appeared in installments between June 1851 and April 1852 in the *National Era,* an anti-slavery newspaper centered in Washington. Published in 1852, *Uncle Tom's Cabin; or, Life Among the Lowly* became, next to the Bible, the best-selling book of the century.

A decade later, Abraham Lincoln met Mrs. Stowe at the White House. "So this is the little lady who made the big War," he is reported to have said. Lincoln was simply being his droll self, but the comment is revealing. The Civil War was very much made by and of words, and every writer knew it. For Stowe, this knowledge carried a particular burden. Looked to for leadership, she had trouble deciding what to say. She could not write romance, but what could she write? The letters on behalf of her son Frederick came easily; afflicted by uncertain physical ailments, the withdrawal into family was comforting. But Stowe was a professional writer and a devoted opponent of slavery. She had to find a way during the Civil War to speak out. When she did, the result helped shape the outcome of the war as much as her work had initiated it.

In November 1862, over the course of two days, Stowe wrote a letter that was nearly ten years overdue. In 1853, she had received a document from the women of Great Britain and Ireland, some half-million of them, imploring their sisters in America to devote themselves to the destruction of slavery. The address remained unanswered until now, until the British themselves had disgusted Stowe and other Unionists with their tacit support of the Confederacy, until Lincoln had given assurances that the Emancipation Proclamation would indeed be issued on the first of January.

Stowe's reply effectively rebuked the British for their inconsistencies and celebrated what she saw as the inexorable progress toward emancipation. It served as a vehicle for Stowe to re-emerge on the national scene as a spokesperson not only for the Union cause but for female moral authority. Published in January 1863, her reply also reinforced what was now widely known: Lincoln had indeed issued the Emancipation Proclamation. On the day of its signing, Stowe was present at the Boston Music Hall for the Emancipation Jubilee. When word finally arrived, her name was called out by the audience. She stood at the balcony and received cheers; it was the moment toward which she had been writing.

Stowe continued after that day. She knew all the abstractions of the war and she learned all the realities of it. Her son, wounded at Gettysburg, was never the same, living out his life in a confusion of pain and alcohol. Stowe herself suffered from headaches and facial paralysis. She increasingly invested her energies in the building of a new home and took to writing about home beautification for the *Atlantic*. Home was not merely a subject for essays, it was the emotional and symbolic fulcrum of her life. The war had balanced the "home nest." It was time now to rebuild: "Home is the thing we must strike for now, for it is here that we must strengthen the things that remain."[2]

Home would form a basis for the new Christian benevolence that must envelop the nation after the war. In the *Chimney Sweep*, published near the end of the war, Stowe fused her religious pieties with poetic visions of a regenerated landscape. As with many other writers and photographers at the time, Stowe imagined that nature would renew the lives wrenched and scarred by the sacrifices of war. She awaited the growth of "flowers of healing." The lilac, in which she placed her hopes of rebirth, would within months be employed by Whitman as the flower of mourning.[3]

After the war, Stowe bought a home in Florida and spent many of her last years there. The ironies here run deep, for she partially abandoned her native state, Connecticut, for a Southern state where she even invested in schemes to raise cotton. In her writing, Stowe returned to the themes of her youth. The power behind her claim that Lord Byron had an incestuous relationship with his sister must have been connected at some level to her own complex family relations. Accusations put her at the center of a public controversy that damaged her reputation. *Uncle Tom's Cabin* was still a presence in the country; its author less so. She spent her last years drifting, not so much in space as in mind: "now I rest me, like a moored boat, rising and falling on the water, with loosened cordage and flapping sail."[4] Before slipping out of view on the horizon, she had forever shifted the currents of history.

## 1. Harriet Beecher Stowe to Hattie,[5] May 2, 1861[6]

I am writing with a pencil *in bed* because I am too much worn out today to get up—Ever since war was declared which is now about two weeks—a little over—I have been like a person struggling in a night mare dream—Fred[7] immediately wanted to go—& I was willing he should, if he could only get a situation where he could do any good—But as a mere soldier I felt he was not strong enough & might therefore only get sick & do no good—He applied to go as a surgeon's aid—but as he was only in his first year of study & so many graduated medical men applied he could not get any situation of that kind. At last Mrs. Field's[8] brother Dr. Adams (a splendid fellow who is surgeon of the first regiment) said that if Fred would enlist with him as a private he would immediately choose him for Hospital Steward when the army got in action—

I can't describe the confusion in the house when Fred came rushing up Saturday before last with the news that he was going. I was lying in bed quite worn out having done a great deal about the house that day—Immediately I got up late as it was & we hurried & threw his & my things together. . . . [B]y Friday all was ready & I took him to Boston. . . . He may start off any time or minute. . . .

Fred & I had a long talk Saturday night & he said he was willing to lay down his life cause & that if he died he felt he should go to the pure & good he always longed for & he & I kneeled down hand in hand and prayed for each other. . . . This is no holiday frolic or child's play but it is taking the plunge of life in real earnest. . . . This has come like a whirlwind this war so that really I have yet got things adjusted yet.

2. HBS to Calvin Stowe,[9] Brooklyn, June 11, 1861

Yesterday noon Henry came in, saying that the Commonwealth, with the First Regiment on board, had just sailed by. Immediately I was of course eager to get to Jersey City to see Fred. Sister Eunice[10] said she would go with me, and in a few minutes she and I were in a carriage, driving towards the Fulton Ferry. Upon reaching Jersey City we found that the boys were dining in the depot, an immense building with many tracks and platforms. It has a great cast-iron gallery just under the roof, apparently placed there with prophetic instinct of these times. There was a crowd of people pressing against the grated doors, which were locked, but through which we could see the soldiers. It was with great difficulty that we were at last permitted to go inside, and that object seemed to be greatly aided by a bit of printed satin that some man gave Mr. Scoville.[11]

When we were in, a vast area of gray caps and blue overcoats were presented. The boys were eating, drinking, smoking, talking, singing, and laughing. Company A was reported to be here, there, and everywhere. At last S. spied Fred in the distance, and went leaping across the tracks towards him. Immediately afterwards a blue-overcoated figure bristling with knapsack and haversack, and looking like an assortment of packages, came rushing towards us.

Fred was overjoyed, you may be sure, and my first impulse was to wipe his face with my handkerchief before I kissed him. He was in high spirits, in spite of the weight of the blue overcoat, knapsack, etc., etc., that he would formerly have declared intolerable for half an hour. I gave him my handkerchief and Eunice gave him hers, with a sheer motherly instinct that is so strong within her, and then we filled his haversack with oranges.

We stayed with Fred about two hours, during which time the gallery was filled with people, cheering and waving their handkerchiefs. Every now and then the band played inspiriting airs, in which the soldiers joined with hearty voices. While some of the companies sang, others were drilled, and all seemed to be having a general jollification. The meal that had been provided was plentiful, and consisted of coffee, lemonade, sandwiches, etc.

On our way out, we were introduced to the Rev. Mr. Cudworth, chaplain of the regiment. He is a fine-looking man, with black eyes and hair, set off by a white havelock. He wore a sword, and Fred, touching it, asked, "Is this for use or ornament, sir?"

"Let me see you in danger," answered the chaplain, "and you'll find out."

I said to him I supposed he had had many a one confided to his kind offices, but I could not forbear adding one more to the number. He answered, "You may rest assured, Mrs. Stowe, I will do all in my power."

We parted from Fred at the door. He said he felt lonesome enough Saturday evening on the Common in Boston, where everybody was taking leave of somebody, and he seemed to be the only one without a friend, but that this interview made up for it all.

I also saw young Henry. Like Fred he is mysteriously changed, and wears an expression of gravity and care. So our boys come to manhood in a day. . . .

### 3. Harriet Beecher Stowe, "A Reply," *Atlantic Monthly*, 11 (January 1863): 120–33

The time has come . . . when such an astonishing page has been turned in the anti-slavery history of America, that the women of our country, feeling that the great anti-slavery work to which their English sisters exhorted them is almost done, may properly and naturally feel moved to reply to their appeal, and lay before them the history of what has occurred since the receipt of their affectionate and Christian address.

Your address reached us just as a great moral conflict was coming to its intensest point.

The agitation kept up by the anti-slavery portion of America, by England, and by the general sentiment of humanity in Europe, had made the situation of the slaveholding aristocracy intolerable. As one of them at the time expressed it, they felt themselves under the ban of the civilized world. Two courses only were open to them: to abandon slave institutions, the sources of their wealth and political power, or to assert them with such an overwhelming national force as to compel the respect and assent of mankind. They chose the latter.

To this end they determined to seize on and control all the resources of the Federal Government, and to spread their institutions through new States and Territories until the balance of power should fall into their hands and they should be able to force slavery into all the Free States.

A leading Southern senator boasted that he would yet call the roll of his slaves on Bunker Hill; and, for a while, the political successes of the Slave Power were such as to suggest to New England that this was no impossible event.

They repealed the Missouri Compromise, which had hitherto stood, like the Chinese wall, between our Northwestern Territories and the irruptions of slaveholding barbarians.

Then came the struggle between Freedom and Slavery in the new Territory,—the battle for Kansas, and Nebraska, fought with fire and sword and blood, where a race of men, of whom John Brown was the immortal type, acted over again the courage, the perseverence, and the military religious ardor of the old Covenanters of Scotland, and, like them, redeemed the Ark of Liberty at the price of their own blood and blood dearer than their own.

The time of the Presidential canvass which elected Mr. Lincoln was the crisis of this great battle. The conflict had become narrowed down to the one point of the extension of slave-territory. If the slaveholders could get States enough, they could control and rule; if they were outnumbered by Free States, their institutions, by the very law of their nature, would die of suffocation. Therefore, Fugitive-Slave Law, District of Columbia, Inter-State Slave-Trade, and what not, were all thrown out of sight for a grand rally on this vital point. A President was elected pledged to opposition to this one thing alone,—a man known to be in favor of the Fugitive-Slave Law and other so-called compromises of the Constitution, but honest and faithful in his determination on this one subject. That this was indeed the vital point was shown by the result. The moment Lincoln's election was ascertained, the slaveholders resolved to destroy the Union they could no longer control.

They met and organized a Confederacy which they openly declared to be the first republic founded on the right and determination of the white man to enslave the black man, and, spreading their banners, declared themselves to the Christian world of the nineteenth century as a nation organized with the full purpose and intent of perpetuating slavery.

But in the course of the struggle that followed, it became important for the new Confederation to secure the assistance of foreign powers, and infinite pains were then taken to blind and bewilder the mind of England as to the real issues of the conflict in America.

It has been often and earnestly asserted that slavery had nothing to do with this conflict; that it was a mere struggle for power; that the only object was to restore the Union as it was, with all its abuses. It is to be admitted that expressions have proceeded from the National Administration which naturally gave rise to misapprehension, and therefore we beg to speak to you on this subject more fully.

And, first, the declaration of the Confederate States themselves is proof enough, that, whatever may be declared on the other side, the maintenance of slavery is regarded by them as the vital object of their movement. . . . On the other hand, the declarations of the President and the Republican party, as to their intention to restore "the Union as it was," require an explanation. It is the doctrine of the Republican party, that Freedom is national and Slavery sectional; that the Constitution of the United States was designed for the promotion of liberty, and not of slavery; that its framers contemplated the gradual abolition of slavery; and that in the hands of an anti-slavery majority it could be so wielded as peaceably to extinguish this great evil.

They reasoned thus. Slavery ruins land, and requires fresh territory for profitable working. Slavery increases a dangerous population, and requires an expansion of this population for safety. Slavery, then, being hemmed in by impassable limits, emancipation in each State becomes a necessity.

*By restoring the Union as it was* the Republican party meant the Union in the sense contemplated by the original framers of it, who, as has been admitted by [Alexander] Stephens, . . . were from principle opposed to slavery. It was, then, restoring a *status* in which, by the inevitable operation of natural laws, peaceful emancipation would become a certainty.

In the mean while, during the past year, the Republican Administration, with all the unwonted care of organizing an army and navy, and conducting military operations on an immense scale, have proceeded to demonstrate the feasability of overthrowing slavery by purely Constitutional measures. To this end they have instituted a series of movements which have made this year more fruitful in anti-slavery triumphs than any other since the emancipation of the British West Indies.

The District of Columbia, as belonging strictly to the National Government, and to no separate State, has furnished a fruitful subject of remonstrance from British Christians with America. We have abolished slavery there, and thus wiped out the only blot of territorial responsibility on our escutcheon.

By another act, equally grand in principle, and far more important in its results, slavery is forever excluded from the Territories of the United States.

By another act, America has consummated the long-delayed treaty with Great Britain for the suppression of the slave-trade. In ports where slave-vessels formerly sailed with the connivance of the port-officers the Administration has placed men who stand up to their duty, and for the first time in our history the slave-trader is convicted and hung as a pirate. This abominable secret traffic has been wholly demolished by the energy of the Federal Government.

Lastly, and more significant still, the United States Government has in its highest official capacity taken distinct anti-slavery ground, and presented to the country a plan of peaceable emancipation with suitable compensation. This noble-spirited and generous offer has been urged on the Slaveholding States by the Chief Executive with an earnestness and sincerity of which history in after-times will make honorable account in recording the events of Mr. Lincoln's administration.

Now, when a President and Administration who have done all these things declare their intention of restoring *"the Union as it was,"* ought not the world fairly to interpret their words by their actions and their avowed principles? Is it not *necessary* to infer that they mean by it the Union as it was in the intent of its anti-slavery framers, under which, by the exercise of normal Constitutional powers, slavery should be peaceably abolished?

We are aware that this theory of the Constitution has been disputed by certain Abolitionists; but it is conceded, as you have seen, by the Secessionists. Whether it be a just theory or not is, however, nothing to our purpose at present. We only assert that such is the professed belief of the present Administration of the United States, and such are the acts by which they have illustrated their belief.

But this is but half the story of the anti-slavery triumphs of this year. We have shown you what has been done for freedom by the simple use of the ordinary Constitutional forces of the Union. We are now to show you what has been done to the same end by the Constitutional war-power of the nation.

By this power it has been this year decreed that every slave of a Rebel who reaches the lines of our army becomes a free man; that all slaves found deserted by masters become free men; that every slave employed in any service for the United States thereby obtains his liberty; and that every slave employed against the United States in any capacity obtains his liberty; and lest the army should contain officers disposed to remand slaves to their masters, the power of judging and delivering up slaves is denied to army-officers, and all such acts are made penal.

By this act, the Fugitive-Slave Law is for all present purposes practically repealed. With this understanding and provision, wherever our armies march, they carry liberty with them. For be it remembered that our army is almost entirely a volunteer one, and that the most zealous and ardent volunteers are those who have been for years fighting with tongue and pen the Abolition battle. So marked is the character of our soldiers in this respect, that they are now familiarly designated in the official military dispatches of the Confederate States as "The Abolitionists." Conceive the results, when an army, so empowered by national law, marches through a slave-territory. One regiment alone has to our certain knowledge liberated two thousand slaves during the past year, and this regiment is but one out of hundreds. . . .

It is conceded on all sides, that, wherever our armies have had occupancy, there slavery has been practically abolished. The fact was recognized by Pres-

ident Lincoln in his last appeal to the loyal Slave States to consummate emancipation.

Another noticeable act of our Government in behalf of Liberty is the official
provision it makes for the wants of the thousands of helpless human beings thus
thrown upon our care. Taxed with the burden of an immense war, with the care
of thousands of sick and wounded, the United States Government has cheerfully voted rations for helpless slaves, no less than wages to the helpful ones.
The United States Government pays teachers to instruct them, and overseers
to guide their industrial efforts. A free-labor experiment is already in successful
operation among the beautiful sea-islands in the neighborhood of Beaufort,
which, even under most disadvantageous circumstances, is fast demonstrating
how much more efficiently men will work from hope and liberty than from fear
and constraint. Thus, even amid the roar of cannon and the confusion of war,
cotton-planting, as a free-labor institution, is beginning its instant life, to grow
hereafter to a glorious manhood.

Lastly, the great, decisive measure of the war has approached,—*The President's Proclamation of Emancipation.*

This also has been much misunderstood and misrepresented in England. It
has been said to mean virtually this:—Be loyal, and you shall keep your slaves;
rebel, and they shall be free.

But let us remember what we have just seen of the purpose and meaning of
the Union to which the rebellious States are invited back. It is to a Union which
has abolished slavery in the District of Columbia, and interdicted slavery in the
Territories,—which vigorously represses the slave-trade, and hangs the convicted slaver as a pirate,—which necessitates emancipation by denying expansion to slavery, and facilitates it by the offer of compensation. Any Slaveholding
States which should return to such a Union might fairly be supposed to return
with the purpose of peaceable emancipation. The President's Proclamation
simply means this:—Come in, and emancipate peaceably with compensation;
stay out, and I emancipate, nor will I protect you from the consequences. . . .

And now, Sisters of England, in this solemn, expectant hour, let us speak to
you of one thing which fills our hearts with pain and solicitude.

It is an unaccountable fact, and one which we entreat you seriously to pon-
der, that the party which has brought the cause of Freedom thus far on its way,
during the past eventful year, has found little or no support in England. Sadder
than this, the party which makes Slavery the chief corner-stone of its edifice
finds in England its strongest defenders.

The voices that have spoken for us who contend for Liberty have been few
and scattering. God forbid that we should forget those few noble voices, so
sadly exceptional in the general outcry against us! They are, alas, too few to be

easily forgotten. False statements have blinded the minds of your community, and turned the most generous sentiments of the British heart against us. The North are fighting for supremacy and the South for independence, has been the voice. Independence? for what? to do what? To prove the doctrine that all men are *not* equal. To establish the doctrine that the white may enslave the negro.

It is natural to sympathize with people who are fighting for their rights; but if these prove to be the right of selling children by the pound and trading in husbands and wives as merchantable articles, should not Englishmen think twice before giving their sympathy? A pirate-ship on the high seas is fighting for *independence!* Let us be consistent.

It has been said that we have been over-sensitive, thin-skinned. It is one inconvenient attendant of love and respect, that they do induce sensitiveness. A brother or father turning against one in the hour of trouble, a friend sleeping in the Gethsemane of our mortal anguish, does not always find us armed with divine patience.[12] We loved England; we respected, revered her; we were bound to her by ties of blood and race. Alas! must all these declarations be written in the past tense? . . .

This very day the writer of this has been present at a solemn religious festival in the national capital, given at the home of a portion of those fugitive slaves who have fled to our lines for protection,—who, under the shadow of our flag, find sympathy and succor. The national day of thanksgiving was there kept by over a thousand redeemed slaves, and for whom Christian charity had spread an ample repast. Our Sisters, we wish *you* could have witnessed the scene. We wish you could have heard the prayer of a blind old negro, called among his fellows John the Baptist, when in touching broken English he poured forth his thanksgivings. We wish you could have heard the sound of that strange rhythmical chant which is now forbidden to be sung on Southern plantations,—the psalm of this modern exodus,—which combines the barbaric fire of the Marseillaise with the religious fervor of the old Hebrew prophet.

> Oh, go down Moses,
> 'Way down into Egypt's land
> Tell King Pharoah
> To let my people go!. . . .

As we were leaving, an aged woman came and lifted up her hands in blessing. "Bressed be de Lord dat brought me to see dis first happy day of my life! Bressed be de Lord!" In all England is there no Amen?

We have been shocked and saddened by the question asked in an association of Congregational ministers in England, the very blood-relations of the liberty-loving Puritans,—"Why does not the North let the South go?"

What! give up the point of emancipation for these four million slaves? Turn our backs on them, and leave them to their fate? What! leave our white brothers to run a career of oppression and robbery, that, as sure as there is a God that ruleth in the armies of heaven, will bring down a day of wrath and doom?

Is it any advantage to people to be educated in man-stealing as a principle, to be taught systematically to rob the laborer of his wages, and to tread on the necks of weaker races? Who among you would wish your sons to become slave-planters, slave-merchants, slave-dealers? And shall we leave our brethren to this fate? Better a generation should die on the battle-field, that their children may grow up in liberty and justice. Yes, our sons must die, their sons must die. We give ours freely; they die to redeem the very brothers that slay them; they give their blood in expiation of this great sin, begun by you in England, perpetuated by us in America, and for which God in this great day of judgment is making inquisition in blood.

In a recent battle fell a Secession colonel, the last remaining son of his mother, and she a widow. That mother had sold eleven children of an old slave-mother, her servant. That servant went to her and said,—"Missis, we even now. You sold all my children. God took all yours. Not one to bury either of us. *Now,* I forgive you."

In another battle fell the only son of another widow. Young, beautiful, heroic, brought up by his mother in the sacred doctrines of human liberty, he gave his life an offering as to a holy cause. He died. No slave-woman came to tell *his* mother of God's justice, for many slaves have reason to call her blessed.

Now we ask you, Would you change places with that Southern mother? Would you not think it a great misfortune for a son or daughter to be brought into such a system?—a worse one to become so perverted as to defend it? Remember, then, that wishing success to this slavery-establishing effort is only wishing to the sons and daughters of the South all the curses that God has written against oppression. *Mark our words!* If we succeed, the children of these very men who are now fighting us will rise up to call us blessed. Just as surely as there is a God who governs in the world, so surely all the laws of national prosperity follow in the train of equity; and if we succeed, we shall have delivered the children's children of our misguided brethren from the wages of sin, which is always and everywhere death. . . .

## 4. HBS to Frederick Stowe, July 11, 1863

You may imagine the anxiety with which we waited for news from you after the battle. The first we heard was on Monday morning from the paper, that you were wounded in the head. On hearing this your Father set off immediately to go to you & took the twelve o'clock train to Boston & the five o'clock New York cars to go right on to Baltimore.

Before he left Andover we got a telegraph from Robert saying that you were wounded, but not dangerously and would be sent home in a few days.

At Springfield that night a gang of pick pockets hustled your father among them as he was getting out of the cars & took from him his pocket book containing 1 30 dollars & all the letters which your sisters & I wrote to you—He went on to Baltimore & when he arrived there was so sick as to have to send for a doctor who told him that he was going to be very sick & must go back immediately where he could be taken care of.

He however saw a Mr. Clark (uncle of our student Clark) who was going on to Gettysburg to attend to the wounded, & Gen. H. Wilson who both promised to look for you.

Several other friends also volunteered & Papa returned to Brooklyn where Jack Howard nursed him & this morning Saturday the 11th he is home & in bed—quite unwell but not so but what good news from you would revive him—Do get some one to write for you & tell us how to visit [?], & what we shall do for you.—Do let us know when we may expect you—We have been looking for you every night, all your sisters waiting at the cars—We *must* see you & return thanks [one illegible word] that your life is saved. God bless you. At last you have helped win a glorious victory. The cause is triumphant! God be thanked!—Your loving mother.

### 5. [HBS] "The Chimney-Corner," *Atlantic Monthly*, 15 (January 1865): 109–15

Here comes the First of January, Eighteen Hundred and Sixty-Five, and we are all settled comfortably into our winter places, with our winter surroundings and belongings; all cracks and openings are calked and listed, the double windows are in, the furnace dragon in the cellar is ruddy and in good liking, sending up his warming respirations through every pipe and register in the house; and yet, though an artificial summer reigns everywhere, like bees, we have our swarming-place,—in my library. There is my chimney-corner, and my table permanently established on one side of the hearth; and each of the female genus has, so to speak, pitched her own winter-tent within sight of the blaze of my camp-fire. . . .

Peaceable, ah, how peaceable, home and quiet and warmth in winter! And how, when we hear the wind whistle, we think of you, O our brave brothers, our saviours and defenders, who for our sake have no home but the muddy camp, the hard pillow of the barrack, the weary march, the uncertain fare,—you, the rank and file, the thousand unnoticed ones, who have left warm fires, dear wives, loving little children, without even the hope of glory or fame,—without even the hope of doing anything remarkable or perceptible for the cause you love,—resigned only to fill the ditch or bridge the chasm over which your country shall walk to peace and joy! Good men and true, brave unknown hearts, we salute you, and feel that we, in our soft peace and security, are not worthy of you! When we think of you, our simple comforts seem luxuries all too good for us, who give so little when you give all!

But there are others to whom from our bright homes, our cheerful firesides, we would fain say a word, if we dared.

Think of a mother receiving a letter with such a passage as this in it! It is extracted from one we have just seen, written by a private in the army of Sheridan, describing the death of a private. "He fell instantly, gave a peculiar smile and look, and then closed his eyes. We laid him down gently at the foot of a large tree. I crossed his hands over his breast, closed his eyelids down, but the smile was still on his face. I wrapped him in his tent, spread my pocket-handkerchief over his face, wrote his name on a piece of paper, and pinned it on his breast, and there we left him: we could not find pick or shovel to dig a grave." There it is!—a history that is multiplying itself by hundreds daily, the substance of what has come to so many homes, and must come to so many more before the great price of our ransom is paid!

What can we say to you, in those many, many homes where the light has gone out forever?—you, O fathers, mothers, wives, sisters, haunted by a name that has ceased to be spoken on earth,—you, for whom there is no more news from the camp, no more reading of lists, no more tracing of maps, no more letters, but only a blank, dead silence! The battle-cry goes on, but for you it is passed by! the victory comes, but, oh, never more to bring him back to you! your offering to this great cause has been made, and been taken; you have thrown into it *all* your living, even all that you had, and from henceforth your house is left unto you desolate! O ye watchers of the cross, ye waiters by the sepulchre, what can be said to you? We could almost extinguish our own home-fires, that seem too bright when we think of your darkness; the laugh dies on our lip, the lamp burns dim through our tears, and we seem scarcely worthy to speak words of comfort, lest we seem as those who mock a grief they cannot know.

But is there no consolation? Is it nothing to have had such a treasure to give, and to have given it freely for the noblest cause for which ever battle was set,— for the salvation of your country, for the freedom of all mankind? Had he died a fruitless death, in the track of common life, blasted by fever, smitten or rent by crushing accident, then might his most precious life seem to be as water spilled upon the ground; but now it has been given for a cause and a purpose worthy even the anguish of your loss and sacrifice. He has been counted worthy to be numbered with those who stood with precious incense between the living and the dead, that the plague which was consuming us might be stayed. The blood of these young martyrs shall be the seed of the future church of liberty, and from every drop shall spring up flowers of healing. O widow! O mother! blessed among bereaved women! there remains to you a treasure that belongs not to those who have lost in any other wise,—the power to say, "He dies for his country." In all the good that comes of this anguish you shall have a right and share by virtue of this sacrifice. The joy of freedmen bursting from chains, the glory of a nation new-born, the assurances of a triumphant future for your country and the world,—all these become yours by the purchase-money of that precious blood.

Besides this, there are other treasures that come through sorrow, and sorrow alone. There are celestial plants of root so long and so deep that the land must be torn and furrowed, ploughed up from the very foundation, before they can strike and flourish; and when we see how God's plough is driving backward and forward and across this nation, rending, tearing up tender shoots, and burying soft wild-flowers, we ask ourselves, What is He going to plant?

Not the first year, nor the second, after the ground has been broken up, does the purpose of the husbandman appear. At first we see only what is uprooted and ploughed in,—the daisy drabbled, and the violet crushed,—and the first trees planted amid the unsightly furrows stand dumb and disconsolate, irresolute in leaf, and without flower or fruit. Their work is under the ground. In darkness and silence they are putting forth long fibres, searching hither and thither under the black soil for the strength that years hence shall burst into bloom and bearing.

What is true of nations is true of individuals. It may seem now winter and desolation with you. Your hearts have been ploughed and harrowed and are now frozen up. There is not a flower left, nor a blade of grass, not a bird to sing,—and it is hard to believe that any brighter flowers, any greener herbage, shall spring up, than those which have been torn away: and yet there will. Nature herself teaches you to-day. Out-doors nothing but bare branches and shrouding snow; and yet you know that there is not a tree that is not patiently holding out at the end of its boughs next year's buds, frozen indeed, but unkilled. The rhododendron and the lilac have their blossoms all ready, wrapped in cere-cloth, waiting in patient faith. Under the frozen ground the crocus and hyacinth and the tulip hide in their hearts the perfect forms of future flowers. And it is even so with you: your leaf-buds of the future are frozen, but not killed; the soil of your heart has many flowers under it cold and still now, but they will yet come up and bloom.

The dear old book of comfort tells of no present healing for sorrow. *No* chastening for the present seemeth joyous, but grievous, but *afterwards* it yieldeth peaceable fruits of righteousness. We, as individuals, as a nation, need to have faith in that AFTERWARDS. It is sure to come,—sure as spring and summer to follow winter.

There is a certain amount of suffering which must follow the rending of the great chords of life, suffering which is natural and inevitable; it cannot be argued down; it cannot be stilled; it can no more be soothed by any effort of faith and reason than the pain of a fractured limb, or the agony of fire on the living flesh. All that we can do is to brace ourselves to bear it, calling on God, as the martyrs did in the fire, and resigning ourselves to let it burn on. We must be willing to suffer, since God so wills. There are just so many waves to go over us, just so many arrows of stinging thought to be shot into our soul, just so many faintings and sinkings and revivings only to suffer again, belonging to and inherent in our portion of sorrow; and there is a work of healing that God has placed in the hands of Time alone.

Time heals all things at last; yet it depends much on us in our suffering, whether time shall send us forth healed, indeed, but maimed and crippled and callous, or whether, looking to the great Physician of sorrows, and coworking with him, we come forth stronger and fairer even for our wounds. . . .

The report of every battle strikes into some home; and heads fall low, and hearts are shattered, and only God sees the joy that is set before them, and that shall come out of their sorrow. He sees our morning at the same moment that He sees our night,—sees us comforted, healed, risen to a higher life, at the same moment that He sees us crushed and broken in the dust; and so, though tenderer than we, He bears our great sorrows for the joy that is set before us. . . .

The apathy of melancholy must be broken by an effort of religion and duty. The stagnant blood must be made to flow by active work, and the cold hand warmed by clasping the hands outstretched towards it in sympathy or supplication. One orphan child taken in, to be fed, clothed, and nurtured, may save a heart from freezing to death; and God knows this war is making but too many orphans.

It is easy to subscribe to an orphan asylum, and go on in one's despair and loneliness. Such ministries may do good to the children who are thereby saved from the street, but they impart little warmth and comfort to the giver. One destitute child housed, taught, cared for, and tended personally, will bring more solace to a suffering heart than a dozen maintained in an asylum. Not that the child will probably prove an angel, or even an uncommonly interesting mortal. It is a prosaic work, this bringing up of children, and there can be little rose-water in it. The child may not appreciate what is done for him, may not be particularly grateful, may have disagreeable faults, and continue to have them after much pains on your part to eradicate them,—and yet it is a fact, that to redeem one human being from destitution and ruin, even in some homely every-day course of ministrations, is one of the best possible tonics and alternatives to a sick and wounded spirit.

But this is not the only avenue to beneficence which the war opens. We need but name the service of hospitals, the care and education of the freedmen,—for these are charities that have long been before the eyes of the community, and have employed thousands of busy hands: thousands of sick and dying beds to tend, a race to be educated, civilized, and Christianized, surely were work enough for one age; and yet this is not all. War shatters everything, and it is hard to say what in society will not need rebuilding and binding up and strengthening anew. Not the least of the evils of war are the vices which a great army engenders wherever it moves,—vices peculiar to military life, as others are peculiar to peace. The poor soldier perils for us not merely his body, but his soul. He leads a life of harassing and exhausting toil and privation, of violent strain on the nervous energies, alternating with sudden collapse, creating a craving for stimulants, and endangering the formation of fatal habits. What furies and harpies are those that follow the army, and that seek out the soldier in his tent, far from home, mother, wife, and sister, tired, disheartened, and tempt him to forget his troubles in a momentary exhilaration, that burns only to chill and to destroy! Evil angels are always active and indefatigable, and there must be good angels enlisted to face them; and here is employment for the slack hand of grief. Ah, we have known mothers bereft of sons in this war, who have seemed at once to open wide their hearts, and to become mothers to every brave soldier in the field. They have lived only to work,—and in place of one lost, their sons have been counted by thousands.

And not least of all the fields for exertion and Christian charity opened by this war is that presented by womanhood. The war is abstracting from the community its protecting and sheltering elements, and leaving the helpless and dependent in vast disproportion. For years to come, the average of lone women will be largely increased; and the demand, always great, for some means by which they may provide for themselves, in the rude jostle of the world, will become more urgent and imperative.

Will any one sit pining away in inert grief, when two streets off are the midnight dance-houses, where girls of twelve, thirteen, and fourteen are being lured into the way of swift destruction? How many of these are daughters of soldiers who have given their hearts' blood for us and our liberties!

Two noble women of the Society of Friends have lately been taking the gauge of suffering and misery in our land, visiting the hospitals at every accessible point, pausing in our great cities, and going in their purity to those midnight orgies where mere children are being trained for a life of vice and infamy. They have talked with these poor bewildered souls, entangled in toils as terrible and inexorable as those of the slave-market, and many of whom are frightened and distressed at the life they are beginning to lead, and earnestly looking for the means of escape. In the judgment of these holy women, at least one third of those with whom they have talked are children so recently entrapped, and so capable of reformation, that there would be the greatest hope in efforts for their salvation. While such things are to be done in our land, is there any reason why any one should die of grief? One soul redeemed will do more to lift the burden of sorrow than all the blandishments and diversions of art, all the alleviations of luxury, all the sympathy of friends. . . .

In such associations and others of kindred nature, how many of the stricken and bereaved women of our country might find at once a home and an object in life! Motherless hearts might be made glad in a better and higher motherhood; and the stock of earthly life that seemed cut off at the root, and dead past recovery, may be grafted upon with a shoot from the tree of life which is in the Paradise of God.

So the beginning of this eventful 1865, which finds us still treading the winepress of our great conflict, should bring with it a serene and solemn hope, a joy such as those had with whom in the midst of the fiery furnace there walked one like unto the Son of God.

The great affliction that has come upon our country is so evidently the purifying chastening of a Father, rather than the avenging anger of a Destroyer, that all hearts may submit themselves in a solemn and holy calm still to bear the burning that shall make us clean from dross and bring us forth to a higher national life. Never, in the whole course of our history, have such teachings of the pure abstract Right been so commended and forced upon us by Providence. Never have public men been so constrained to humble themselves before God, and to acknowledge that there is a Judge that ruleth in the earth. Verily His inquisition for blood has been strict and awful; and for every stricken household of the poor and lowly, hundreds of households of the oppressor have been scattered. The land where the family of the slave was first annihilated, and the negro, with all the loves and hopes of a man, was proclaimed to be a beast to be bred and sold in market with the horse and the swine,—that land, with its fair name, Virginia, has been made a desolation so signal, so wonderful, that the blindest passer-by cannot but ask for what sin so awful a doom has been meted out. The prophetic vision of Nat Turner, who saw the leaves drop blood and the land darkened, have been fulfilled. The work of justice which he predicted is being executed to the uttermost.

But when this strange work of judgment and justice is consummated, when our country, through a thousand battles and ten thousands of precious deaths, shall have come forth from this long agony, redeemed and regenerated, then God Himself shall return and dwell with us, and the Lord God shall wipe away all tears from all faces, and the rebuke of His people shall He utterly take away.

Walt Whitman, photographed by Mathew Brady, 1862 *(Courtesy of the National Archives)*

# Walt Whitman
## (1819–1892)

The war, he claimed, could not, should not, be written, yet he never stopped writing. Notebooks, letters, editorials, poems, during the war; *Memoranda During the War* (1875–76) afterwards; *Specimen Days* (1882–83) after that. In 1888, a friend of Whitman's asked: "Do you go back to those days?" "I do not need to," the poet responded: "I have never left them."[1]

Of all American writers at the time, no one was touched more deeply by the war than Whitman. He often recalled where he had been when news of the attack on Fort Sumter first spread. Returning from the opera around midnight, he was walking down Broadway on his way home to Brooklyn when he heard the shrieks of newsboys. He bought one of the Extras and crossed to Niblo's, where a crowd had gathered. He stood in stunned silence and then trudged home. Forty-one at the time, Whitman may have been expected to enlist; years later critics such as Thomas Wentworth Higginson would condemn him for not fighting. But Whitman found another way to serve. He devoted himself to the sick and wounded and dying soldiers.

"I am he bringing help for the sick as they pant on their backs," the poet proclaimed in "Song of Myself" (1855). And so it was to be. Before the war, Whitman was often seen at New York Hospital, attending to injured stage drivers and others. In March and April 1862 he regularly visited the Hospital and wrote about it in a series of articles for the *New York Leader*. Each ward, he thought, contained a "volume of meaning," a "tragic poem." He was especially drawn to the soldiers and could not help desiring to "cheer and change a little the monotony of their sickness and confinement." He took special notice of one woman who visited regularly and brought small but useful items such as papers and books, candies and gowns. Numerous benevolent women came to the hospital, observed Whitman. "And men, too," he added.[2]

When his brother George was listed as wounded at the battle of Fredericksburg in December 1862, Whitman rushed to Washington in search of him. He found him in good health and almost immediately started visiting wounded soldiers in the hospitals and convalescent camps. There were over fifty to choose from, including the Patent Office Hospital, Campbell Hospital, and Armory Square Hospital, where Whitman devoted most of his time because it contained "the worst cases, most repulsive wounds." "I have been almost daily calling as a missionary," he wrote in the New York Times, "distributing now & then little sums of money—and regularly letter-paper and envelopes, oranges, tobacco, jellies, &c. &c."[3]

He gave more than sundries; he gave his love, and he gave himself. Whitman was comrade, brother, and father to these wounded and dying young men. He hovered over open sores and festering wounds, witnessed amputations, stood by vomit and diarrhea. When necessary, he held and kissed his "poor, poor boys." He treated each one individually, each one as a "specimen," both of himself and something larger. The wounded soldiers were "America brought to Hospital in her fair youth." Through them, Whitman felt he gained special insight into the nation and access to a "new world."

He described himself at this time as a "great wild buffalo," near 200 pounds with flowing hair and bearded scarlet face. In time, however, his own health began to suffer. By June 1863 he complained of "sore throat & distress in my head." Though his health soon improved, he returned to Brooklyn in November, mainly to vote but also to check on family affairs. He wrote to soldiers in Armory Square Hospital and complained that he had "had enough of going around New York." By early December, he was back in Washington.[4]

Whitman's health held out for several months; at one point, he even described his condition as "first rate." But by June 1864 the physicians were warning him to refrain from visiting the hospitals. In addition to a sore throat, Whitman complained of "spells of faintness" and a "bad feeling" in his head. Admitting to being homesick, he returned to Brooklyn to recuperate. Within two months, though, he had resumed his regimen of visiting hospitalized soldiers. The Brooklyn City Hospital on Raymond Street was but a quarter of a mile from his home and he walked there throughout August and September. "So you see I am still in business," he wrote a friend.[5]

And so he continued this way to the end of the war. He estimated that he had made over 600 visits and been among 80,000 to 100,000 of the wounded and sick. He knew that his presence had saved many lives, that the "magnetic flood of sympathy and friendship" he provided was more beneficial than "all the medicine in the world." He loved the rank and file; their individual stories were the stories that mattered most, the stories that captured the essence of the war. Though he knew words could never convey his experience in the hospitals, could never convey the multiple meanings in a wounded soldier's smile, he never stopped trying to express the beauty and terror of it all. The voices, faces, touches of thousands of soldiers lived inside him; their wounds and agonies were his. He carried them with him wherever he went, carried them to his grave and beyond.[6]

He had great hopes of writing a book worthy of the time, a book "considerably beyond mere hospital sketches," he snorted in dismissing Louisa Alcott's effort. *Drum-Taps* (1865) and *Sequel to Drum-Taps* (1865–66) was that work. Whitman thought the work superior to *Leaves of Grass* because he was able finally to capture in poetry what he could not convey in prose. The poems in that work continue to resonate, continue to move us with their juxtapositions of grief and hope, agony and love, death and rebirth. Whitman indeed never left those days. We too, across the "action of this *Time & Land we swim in*," cannot leave those days behind.[7]

## 1. WW to Louisa Van Velsor Whitman,[8] Washington, December 29, 1862

Friday the 19th inst. I succeeded in reaching the camp of the 51st New York, and found George alive and well[9]. . . . Mother, how much you must have suffered, all that week, till George's letter came—and all the rest must too. As to me, I know I put in about three days of the greatest suffering I ever experienced in my life. I wrote to Jeff[10] how I had my pocket picked in a jam and hurry, changing cars, at Philadelphia, so that I landed here without a dime. The next two days I spent hunting through the hospitals, walking all day and night, unable to ride, trying to get information, trying to get access to big people, &c—I could not get the least clue to anything—Odell[11] would not see me at all—But Thursday afternoon, I lit on a way to get down on the government boat that runs to Aquia creek, and so by railroad to the neighborhood of Falmouth, opposite Fredericksburg—So by degrees I worked my way to Ferrero's[12] brigade, which I found Friday afternoon without much trouble after I got in camp. When I found dear brother George, and found that he was alive and well, O you may imagine how trifling all my little cares and difficulties seemed—they vanished into nothing. And now that I have lived for eight or nine days amid such scenes as the camps furnish, and had a practical part in it all, and realize the way that hundreds of thousands of good men are now living, and have had to live for a year or more, not only without any of the comforts, but with death and sickness and hard marching and hard fighting, (and no success at that,) for their continual experience—really nothing we call trouble seems worth talking about. One of the first things that met my eyes in camp was a heap of feet, arms, legs, &c. under a tree in front a hospital, the Lacy house. . . .

### 2. WW to Martha Whitman,[13] Washington, January 3, 1863

. . . Yesterday I went out to the Campbell Hospital to see a couple of Brooklyn boys, of the 51st. They knew I was in Washington, and sent me a note, to come and see them. O my dear sister, how your heart would ache to go through the rows of wounded young men, as I did—and stopt to speak a comforting word to them. There were about 100 in one long room, just a long shed neatly whitewashed inside. One young man was very much prostrated, and groaning with pain. I stopt and tried to comfort him. He was very sick. I found he had not had any medical attention since he was brought here—among so many he had been overlooked. So I sent for the doctor, and he made an examination of him—the doctor behaved very well—seemed to be anxious to do right—said that the young man would recover—he had been brought pretty low with diarrhoea, and now had bronchitis, but not so serious as to be dangerous. I talked to him some time—he seemed to have entirely give up, and lost heart—he had not a cent of money—not a friend or acquaintance—I wrote a letter for him to his sister—his name is John A. Holmes, Campbello, Plymouth county, Mass. I gave him a little change I had—he said he would like to buy a drink of milk, when the woman came through with milk. Trifling as this was, he was overcome and began to cry. Then there were many, many others. I mention the one as a specimen. My Brooklyn boys were John Lowery, shot at Fredericksburgh, and lost his left forearm, and Amos H. Vliet—Jeff knows the latter—he has his feet frozen, and is doing well. The 100 are in a ward, (6.)—and there are, I should think, eight or ten or twelve such wards in the Campbell Hospital—indeed a real village. Then there are some 38 more Hospitals here in Washington, some of them much larger.

### 3. WW to Ralph Waldo Emerson, Washington, January 17, 1863

. . . I go a great deal into the Hospitals. Washington is full of them—both in town and out around the outskirts. Some of the larger ones are towns in themselves. In small and large, all forty to fifty thousand inmates are ministered to, as I hear. Being sent for by a particular soldier, three weeks since, in the Campbell Hospital, I soon fell to going there and elsewhere to like places daily. The first shudder has long passed over, and I must say I find deep things, unreckoned by current print or speech. The Hospital, I do not find it, the repulsive place of sores and fevers, nor the place of querulousness, nor the bad results of morbid years which one avoids like bad s[mells]—at least [not] so it is under the circumstances here—other hospitals may be, but not here.

I desire and intend to write a little book out of this phase of America, her masculine young manhood, its conduct under most trying of and highest of all exigency, which she, as by lifting a corner in a curtain, has vouchsafed me to see America, already brought to Hospital in her fair youth—brought and deposited here in this great, whited sepulchre of Washington itself—(this union Capital without the first bit of cohesion—this collect of proofs how low and swift a good stock can deteriorate—) Capital to which these deputies most strange arrive from every quarter, concentrating here, well-drest, rotten, meagre, nimble and impotent, full of gab, full always of their thrice-accursed *party*—arrive and skip into the seats of mightiest legislation, and take the seats of judges and high executive seats—while by quaint Providence come also sailed and wagoned hither this other freight of helpless worn and wounded youth, genuine of the soil, of darlings and true heirs to me the first unquestioned and convincing western crop, prophetic of the future, proofs undeniable to all men's ken of perfect beauty, tenderness and pluck that never race yet rivalled.

But more, a new world here I find as I would show—a world full of its separate action, play, suggestiveness—surely a medium world, advanced between our well-known practised one of body and of mind, and one there may-be somewhere on beyond, we dream of, of the soul.

Not to fly off to these clouds, however, I must abruptly say to my friends, where interested, that I find the best expression of American character I have ever seen or conceived—practically here in these ranks of sick and dying young men—nearly all I have seen, (five-sixths I think of those I have seen,) farmers' sons from the West, northwest—and from Pennsylvania, New York, and from largely among the rest your Massachusetts, &c—now after great and terrible experiences, here in their barracks they lie—in those boarded Washington hospital barracks, whitewashed outside and in, one story, high enough, airy and clean enough—one of the Wards, for sample, a long stretch, a hundred and sixty feet long, with aisle down the middle, with cots, fifty or more on each side—and Death there up and down the aisle, tapping lightly by night or day here and there some poor young man, with relieving touch—that is one Ward, a cluster of ten or twelve make a current Washington Hospital—wherein this moment lie languishing, burning with fever or down with diarrhea, the imperial blood and rarest marrow of the North—here, at any rate, as I go for a couple of hours daily, and get to be welcome and useful, I find the masses fully justified by closest contact, never vulgar, ever calm, without greediness, no flummery, no frivolity—responding electric and without fail to affection, yet no whining—not the first unmanly whimper have I yet seen or heard. . . .

The Army (I noticed it first in camp, and the same here among the wounded) is *very young*—and far more American than we supposed—ages range mainly from 20 to 30—a slight sprinkling of men older—and a bigger sprinkling of young lads of 17 and 18—

As I took temporary memoranda of names, items, &c of one thing and another, commissioned to get or do for the men—what they wished and what their cases requried from outside, &c—these memoranda grow bulky, and suggest something to me—so I now make fuller notes, or a sort of journal, (not a mere dry journal though, I hope)—This thing I will record—it belongs to the time, and to all the States—(and perhaps it belongs to me)—

### 4. "The Great Army of the Sick," *New York Times*, February 26, 1863

The military hospitals, convalescent camps, &c. in Washington and its neighborhood sometimes contain over fifty thousand sick and wounded men. Every form of wound, (the mere sight of some of them having been known to make a tolerably hardy visitor faint away,) every kind of malady, like a long procession, with typhoid fever and diarrhoea at the head as leaders, are here in steady motion. The soldier's hospital! how many sleepless nights, how many woman's tears, how many long and aching hours and days of suspense, from every one of the Middle, Eastern and Western States, have concentrated here! Our own New-York, in the form of hundreds and thousands of her young men, may consider herself here—Pennsylvania, Ohio, Indiana and all the West and Northwest the same—and all the New-England States the same.

Upon a few of these hospitals I have been almost daily calling as a missionary, on my own account, for the sustenance and consolation of some of the most needy cases of sick and dying men, for the last two months. One has much to learn in order to do good in these places. Great tact is required. These are not like other hospitals. By far the greatest proportion (I should say five-sixths) of the patients are American young men, intelligent, of independent spirit, tender feelings, used to a hardy and healthy life; largely the farmers are represented by their sons—largely the mechanics and workingmen of the cities. Then they are *soldiers*. All these points must be borne in mind.

People through our Northern cities have little or no idea of the great and prominent feature which these military hospitals and convalescent camps make in and around Washington. There are not merely two or three or a dozen, but some fifty of them, of different degrees of capacity. Some have a thousand or more patients. The newspapers here find it necessary to print every day a directory of the hospitals; a long list, something like what a directory of the churches would be in New-York, Philadelphia or Boston. . . .

A few weeks ago the vast area of the second story of that noblest of Washington buildings, the Patent Office, was crowded close with rows of the sick, badly wounded, and dying soldiers. They were placed in three very large apartments. I went there several times. It was a strange, solemn, and, with all its features of suffering and death, a sort of fascinating sight. I went sometimes at night, to sooth and relieve particular cases; some, I found, needed a little cheering up and friendly consolation at that time, for they went to sleep better afterward. Two of the immense apartments are filled with high and ponderous glass cases, crowded with models in miniature of every kind of utensil, machine, or invention, it ever entered into the mind of man to conceive, and with curiosities and foreign presents. Between these cases were lateral openings, perhaps eight feet wide and quite deep, and in these were placed many of the sick; besides a great long double row of them up and down through the middle of the hall. Many of them were very bad cases, wounds and amputations. Then there was a gallery running above the hall, in which there were beds also. It was, indeed, a curious scene at night, when lit up. The glass cases, the beds, the sick, the gallery above, and the marble pavement under foot—the suffering, and the fortitude to bear it in the various degrees—occasionally, from some, the groan that could not be repressed—sometimes a poor fellow dying, with emaciated face and glassy eye, the nurse by his side, the doctor also there, but no friend, no relative—such were the sights but lately in the Patent Office. The wounded have since been removed from there, and it is now vacant again.

Of course, there are among these thousands of prostrated soldiers in hospitals here, all sorts of individual cases. On recurring to my note-book, I am puzzled which cases to select to illustrate the average of these young men and their experiences. I may here say, too, in general terms, that I could not wish for more candor and manliness, among all their sufferings, than I find among them.

Take this case in Ward 6, Campbell Hospital—a young man from Plymouth Country, Massachusetts, a farmer's son, aged about 20 or 21, a soldierly American young fellow, but with sensitive and tender feelings. Most of December and January last, he lay very low, and for quite a while I never expected he would recover. He had become prostrated with an obstinate diarrhoea; his stomach would hardly keep the least thing down, he was vomiting half the time. But that was hardly the worst of it. Let me tell his story—it is but one of thousands.

He had been some time sick with his regiment in the field, in front, but did his duty as long as he could—was in the battle of Fredericksburgh—soon after was put in the regimental hospital. He kept getting worse—could not eat anything they had there—the doctor told him nothing could be done for him there—the poor fellow had fever also—received (perhaps it could not be helped) little or no attention—lay on the ground getting worse. Toward the latter part of December, very much enfeebled, he was sent up from the front, from Falmouth Station, in an open platform car; (such as hogs are transported upon north,) and dumped with a crowd of others on the boat at Aquia Creek, falling down like a rag where they deposited him, too weak and sick to sit up or help himself at all. No one spoke to him, or assisted him—he had nothing to eat or drink—was used (amid the great crowds of sick) either with perfect indifference, or, as in two or three instances, with heartless brutality.

On the boat, when night came and when air grew chilly, he tried a long time to undo the blankets he had in his knapsack, but was too feeble. He asked one of the employees, who was moving around deck, for a moment's assistance, to get the blankets. The man asked him back if he could not get them himself. He answered no, he had been trying for more than half an hour, and found himself too weak. The man rejoined, he might then go without them, and walked off. So H. lay, chilled and damp, on deck all night, without anything under or over him, while two good blankets were within reach. It caused him a great injury—nearly cost him his life.

Arrived at Washington, he was brought ashore and again left on the wharf, or above it, amid the great crowds, as before, without any nourishment—not a drink for his parched mouth—no kind hand had offered to cover his face from the forenoon sun. Conveyed at last some two miles by the ambulance to the hospital and assigned a bed, (bed 47, ward 6, Campbell Hospital, January and February, 1863,) he fell down exhausted upon the bed; but the Ward-master (he has since been changed) came to him with a growling order to get up—the rules, he said, permitted no man to lie down in that way with his old clothes on—he must sit up—must first go the the bath-room, be washed, and have his clothes completely changed. (A very good rule, properly applied.) He was taken to the bath-room and scrubbed well with cold water. The attendants, callous for a while, were soon alarmed, for suddenly the half-frozen and lifeless body fell limpsy in their hands, and they hurred it back to the cot, plainly insensible, perhaps dying.

Poor boy! the long train of exhaustion, deprivation, rudeness, no food, no friendly word or deed, but all kinds of upstart airs and impudent, unfeeling speeches and deeds from all kinds of small officials (and some big ones,) cutting like razors into that sensitive heart, had at last done the job. He now lay, at times out of his head but quite silent, asking nothing of anyone, for some days, with death getting a closer and a surer grip upon him—he cared not, or rather, he welcomed death. His heart was broken. He felt the struggle to keep up any longer to be useless. God, the world, humanity—all had abandoned him. It would feel so good to shut eyes forever on the cruel things around him and toward him.

As luck would have it, at this time, I found him. I was passing down Ward No. 6 one day, about dusk (4th of January, I think,) and noticed his glassy eyes, with a look of despair and hopelessness, sunk low in his thin, pallid-brown young face. One learns to divine quickly in the hospital, and as I stopped by him and spoke some commonplace remark (to which he made no reply,) I saw as I looked that it was a case for ministering to the affections first and other nourishment and medicines afterward. I sat down by him without any fuss—talked a little—soon saw that it did him good—led him to talk a little himself—got him somewhat interested—wrote a letter for him to his folks in Massachusetts, (to L. H. Campbell, Plymouth County,)—soothed him down as I saw he was getting a little too much agitated, and tears in his eyes—gave him some small gifts, and told him I should come again soon. (He has told me since that this little visit, at that hour, just saved him—a day more, and it would have been perhaps too late.)

Of course I did not forget him, for he was a young fellow to interest any one. He remained very sick—vomiting much every day, frequent diarrhoea, and also something like bronchitis, the doctor said. For a while I visited him almost every day—cheered him up—took him some little gifts, and gave him small sums of money, (he relished a drink of new milk, when it was brought through the ward for sale). For a couple of weeks his condition was uncertain—sometimes I thought there was no chance for him at all. But of late he is doing better—is up and dressed, and goes around more and more (Feb. 21) every day. He will not die, but will recover.

The other evening, passing through the ward, he called me—he wanted to say a few words, particular. I sat down by his side on the cot, in the dimness of the long ward, with the wounded soldiers there in their beds, ranging up and down. He told me I had saved his life. He was in the deepest earnest about it. It was one of those things that repay a soldiers' hospital missionary a thousand-fold—one of the hours he never forgets.

A benevolent person with the right qualities and tact, cannot perhaps make a better investment of himself, at present, anywhere upon the varied surface of the whole of this big world, than in these same military hospitals, among such thousands of most interesting young men. The army is very young—and so much more American than I supposed. Reader, how can I describe to you the mute appealing look that rolls and moves from many a manly eye, from many a sick cot, following you as you walk slowly down one of these wards? To see these, and to be incapable of responding to them, except in a few cases, (so very few compared to the whole of the suffering men,) is enough to make one's heart crack. I go through in some cases cheering up the men, distributing now and then little sums of money—and regularly letter-paper and envelopes, oranges, tobacco, jellies, &c., &c.

Many things invite comment, and some of them sharp criticism, in these hospitals. The Government, as I said, is anxious and liberal in its practice toward its sick; but the work has to be left, in its personal application to the men, to hundreds of officials of one grade or another about the hospitals, who are sometimes entirely lacking in the right qualities. There are tyrants and shysters in all positions, and especially those dressed in subordinate authority. Some of the ward doctors are careless, rude, capricious, needlessly strict. One I found who prohibited the men from all enlivening amusements. I found him sending men to the guard-house for the most trifling offence. In general, perhaps, the officials—especially the new ones, with their straps or badges—put on too many airs. Of all places in the world, the hospitals of American young men and soldiers wounded in the volunteer service of their country, ought to be exempt from mere conventional military airs and etiquette of shoulder-straps. But they are not exempt.

### 5. WW to Louisa Van Velsor Whitman, Washington, March 8, 1863

. . . The poor Frenchman d'Almeida[14] I told you about in my last, got out of the Old Capitol prison this morning—has been in a week—it was a most ridiculous thing putting him in—he was as square a man as I am—while he was in, the chief officer of the prison laughed sarcastically one day at his broken English, and d'Almeida said, "Sir you ought not to laugh—you ought much more to weep, to see a poor traveler like me in such a misfortune"—and Mr. Chief Officer immediately called the guard and sent d'Almeida to the guard-house for that *awful offence* of making such an answer. The guard-house is a nasty, lousy dungeon without light—in it was a nigger with his wrists in manacles, and four white deserters—there is among the Old Capitol prisoners a little boy of seven years old—he and his father were taken as secesh guerillas in Virginia, and the government is holding on to the child, to exchange him for some Union prisoner south, in an exchange. Mother, my heart bleeds all sorts of such damnable things of one kind or another I meet with every day—it is not the fault of the President—he would not harm any human being—nor of Seward or Stanton—but the heartless mean-souled brutes that get in positions subordinate but where they can show themselves, and their damned airs and pomposity—they think nothing of treating a man like the worst slaveowner is supposed to treat his niggers—

Meanwhile the great officers of the Government have every minute occupied with pressing business, and these wretches have full swing. It seems impossible that there could be in the Free States such tyrants, as many you see hereabout. . . .

### 6. WW to Nathaniel Bloom and John Gray,[15] Washington, March 19, 1863

Since I left New York, I was down in the Army of the Potomac in front with my brother a good part of the winter, commencing time of the battle of Fredericksburgh—have seen *war-life*, the real article—folded myself in a blanket, lying down in the mud with composure—relished salt pork & hard tack—have been on the battle-field among the wounded, the faint and the bleeding, to give them nourishment—have gone over with a flag of truce the next day to help direct the burial of the dead—have struck up a tremendous friendship with a young Mississippi captain (about 19) that we took prisoner badly wounded at Fredericksburgh—(he has followed me here, is in Emory hospital here, minus a leg—he wears his confederate uniform, proud as the devil—I met him first at Falmouth, in the Lacy house, middle of December last, his leg just cut off, and cheered him up—poor boy, he has suffered a great deal, and still suffers— has eyes bright as a hawk, but face pale—our affection is quite an affair, quite romantic—sometimes when I lean over to say I am going, he puts his arm round my neck, draws my face down, &c. quite a scene for the New Bowery.)

I spent the Christmas holidays on the Rappahannock—during January came up hither, took a lodging room here—did the 37th Congress, especially the night sessions the last three weeks, explored the Capitol then, meandering the gorgeous painted interminable senate corridors, getting lost in them, (a new sensation, rich & strong, that endless painted interior at night)—got very much interested in some particular cases in Hospitals here—go now steadily to more or less of said Hospitals by day or night—find always the sick and dying soldiers forthwith begin to cling to me in a way that makes a fellow feel funny enough. These Hospitals, so different from all others—these thousands, and tens and twenties of thousands of American young men, badly wounded, all sorts of wounds, operated on, pallid with diarrhea, languishing, dying with fever, pneumonia, &c. open a new world somehow to me, giving closer insights, new things, exploring deeper mines than any yet, showing our humanity, (I sometimes put myself in fancy in the cot, with typhoid, or under the knife,) tried by terrible, fearfulest tests, probed deepest, the living soul's, the body's tragedies, bursting the petty bounds of art. To these, what are your dramas and poems, even the oldest and the tearfulest? Not old Greek mighty ones, where man contends with fate, (and always yields)—not Virgil showing Dante on and on among the agonized & damned, approach what here I see and take a part in. For here I see, not at intervals, but quite always, how certain, man, our American man—how he holds himself cool and unquestioned master above all pains and bloody mutilations. It is immense, the best thing of all, nourishes me

of all men. This then, what frightened us all so long! Why it is put to flight with
ignominy, a mere stuffed scarecrow of the fields. O death where is thy sting?
O grave where is thy victory? &c. In the Patent Office, as I stood there one
night, just off the cot-side of a dying soldier, in a large Ward that had received
the worst cases of 2d Bull Run, Antietam and Fredericksburgh, the surgeon,
Dr. Stone, (Horatio Stone, the sculptor,)[16] told me, of all who had died in that
crowded ward the past six months, he had still to find the *first man* or *boy* who
had met the approach of death with a single tremor, or unmanly fear. But let
me change the subject—I have given you screed enough about death and Hospitals—and too much, since I got started. Only I have some curious yarns I
promise you, my darlings and gossips, by word of mouth, whene'er we meet.

Washington and its points I find bear a second and third perusal, and doubtless indeed many. My first impressions, architectural, &c. were not favorable;
but upon the whole, the city, the spaces, buildings, &c make no unfit emblem
of our country, so far, so broadly planned, every thing in plenty, money &
materials staggering with plenty, but the fruit of the plans, the knit, the combination yet wanting—Determined to express ourselves greatly in a capital but
no fit capital yet here—(time, associations, wanting, I suppose)—many a hiatus
yet—many a thing to be taken down and done over again yet—perhaps an
entire change of base—may-be a succession of changes. Congress does not
seize very hard upon me—I studied it and its members with curiosity, and
long—much gab, great fear of public opinion, plenty of low business talent, but
no masterful man in Congress, (probably best so.) I think well of the President.
He has a face like a hoosier Michael Angelo, so awful ugly it becomes beautiful
with its strange mouth, its deep cut, criss-cross lines, and its doughnut complexion. My notion is, too, that underneath his outside smutched mannerism,
and stories from third-class county bar-rooms, (it is his humor,) Mr. Lincoln
keeps a fountain of first-class practical telling wisdom. I do not dwell on the
supposed failures of his government; he has shown, I sometimes think, an
almost supernatural tact in keeping the ship afloat at all, with head steady, not
only not going down, and now certain not to, but with proud and resolute spirit,
and flag flying in sight of the world, menacing and high as ever. I say never yet
captain, never ruler, had such a perplexing, dangerous task as his, the past two
years. I more and more rely upon his idiomatic western genius, careless of court
dress or court decorums. . . .

I miss you all, my darlings & gossips, Fred Gray, and Bloom and Russell and
every body. I wish you would all come here in a body—that would be divine.
(We would drink ale, which is here of the best.) My health, strength, personal
beauty &c. are, I am happy to inform you, without diminution, but on the contrary quite the reverse. I weigh full 220 pounds avoirdupois, yet still retain my
usual perfect shape—a regular model. My beard, neck, &c. are woolier, fleec-

ier, whiteyer than ever. I wear army boots, with magnificent black morocco tops, the trousers put in, wherein shod and legged confront I Virginia's deepest mud with supercilious eyes. The scenery around Washington is really fine, the Potomac a lordly river, the hills, woods, &c all attractive. I poke about quite a good deal. Much of the weather here is from heaven—of late, though a stretch decidedly from the other point. To-night (for it is night, about 10) I sit alone writing this epistle, (which will doubtless devour you all with envy and admiration,) in the room adjoining my own particular. A gentleman and his wife, who occupy the two other apartments on this floor, have gone to see Heron in Medea[17]—have put their little child to bed, and left me in charge. The little one is sleeping soundly there in the back room, and I, (plagued with a cold in the head,) sit here in the front, by a good fire, writing as aforesaid to my gossips & darlings. The evening is lonesome & still. I am entirely alone. "O solitude where are the charms," &c &c. . . .

### 7. WW to Louisa Van Velsor Whitman, Washington, April 15, 1863

. . . I fancy the reason I am able to do some good in the hospitals, among the poor languishing & wounded boys, is that I am so large and well—indeed like a great wild buffalo, with much hair—many of the soldiers are from the west, and far north—and they take to a man that has not the bleached shiny & shaved cut of the cities of the east. I spent three to four hours yesterday in Armory Hospital—One of my particular boys there was dying, pneumonia—he wanted me to stop with him awhile—he could not articulate—but the look of his eyes, and the holding on of his hand, was deeply affecting. His case is a relapse— eight days ago, he had recovered, was up, was perhaps a little careless—at any rate took cold, was taken down again and has sunk rapidly. He has no friends or relatives here—Yesterday he labored & panted so for breath, it was terrible—he is young man from New England, from the country—I expect to see his cot vacated this afternoon or evening, as I shall go down then. Mother, if you or Mat was here a couple of days, you would cry your eyes out. I find I have to restrain myself and keep my composure—I succeed pretty well.

### 8. WW to Thomas P. Sawyer, Washington, April 21, 1863

. . . Well, Tom, the war news is not lovely, is it? We feel disappointed here about Charleston—I felt as blue about it as anybody.[18] I was so in hopes they would take the conceit out of that grassy city. It seems to me always as if Charleston has done the biggest business of blowing & mischief, on a small capital of industry or manliness, of any city the world ever knew. But for all our bad success at Charleston, and even if we fail for a while elsewhere, I believe this Union will conquer in the end, as sure as there's a God in heaven. This country can't be broken up by Jeff Davis, & all his damned crew. Tom, I sometimes feel as if I didn't want to live—life would have no charm for me, if this country should fail after all, and be reduced to take a third rate position, to be domineered over by England & France & the haughty nations of Europe &c and we unable to help ourselves. But I have no thought that will ever be, this country I hope would spend her last drop of blood, and last dollar, rather than submit to such humiliation.

O I hope Hooker[19] will have good success in his plans, whatever they may be. We have been foiled so often in our plans, it seems as though it was too much. And our noble Army of the Potomac, so brave, so capable, so full of good men, I really believe they are this day the best in the world. God grant Hooker may have success, and his brave boys may at last achieve the victory they deserve. O how much I think about them though. I suppose that does no good. Tom, you tell the boys of your company there is an old pirate up in Washington, with the white wool growing all down his neck—an old comrade who thinks about you & them every day, for all he don't know them, and will probably never see them, but thinks about them as comrades & younger brothers of his, just the same.

These lines may never reach you, as it is talked here that the Army of the Potomac is in for a real fighting march, at last, may be something desperate, it may continue some time when it once begins. Tom, I thought I would write you a few words, hoping they might reach you. Dear comrade, you must not forget me, for I never shall you. My love you have in life or death forever. I don't know how you feel about it, but it is the wish of my heart to have your friendship, and also that is you should come safe out of this war, we should come together again in some place where we could make our living, and be true comrades and never be separated while life lasts—and take Lew Brown[20] too, and never separate from him. Or if things are not so to be—if you get these lines, my dear, darling comrade, and any thing should go wrong, so that we do not meet again, here on earth, it seems to me, (the way I feel now,) that my soul could never be entirely happy, even in the world to come, without you, dear comrade. . . .

### 9. WW to Louisa Van Velsor Whitman, Washington, May 13, 1863

I am late with my letter this week—my poor, poor boys occupy my time very much—I go every day, & sometimes nights—I believe I mentioned a young man in Ward F, Armory Square, with a bad wound in the leg, very agonizing, had to have it propt up, & an attendant all the while dripping water on night &

day—I was in hopes at one time he would get through with it, but a few days ago he took a sudden bad turn, & died about 3 o'clock the same afternoon—it was horrible—he was of good family (handsome, intelligent man, about 26, married) his name was John Elliott of Cumberland Valley, Bedford Co., Penn., belonged to 2d Pennsylvania Cavalry. I felt very bad about it—I have wrote to his father—have not rec'd any answer yet—no friend nor any of his folks were here & have not been here nor sent, probably didn't know of it at all. The surgeons put off amputating the leg, he was so exhausted, but at last it was imperatively necessary to amputate—mother, I am shocked to tell you, that he never came alive off the amputating table—he died under the operation—it was what I had dreaded & anticipated—poor young man, he suffered much, very *very* much, for many days & bore it so patiently—so it was a release to him— Mother, such things are awful—not a soul here he knew or cared about, except me—yet the surgeons & nurses were good to him—I think all was done for him that could be—there was no help but to take off the leg—he was under chloroform—they tried their best to bring him to—three long hours were spent, a strong smelling bottle held under his nostrils, with other means, three hours. Mother, how contemptible all the usual little wordly prides & vanities & striving after appearances, seems in the midst of such scenes as these—such tragedies of soul & body. To see such things & not be able to help them is awful—I feel almost ashamed of being so well & whole. . . .

### 10. WW to Louisa Van Velsor Whitman, Washington, June 30, 1863

. . . Mother, I have had quite an attack of sore throat & distress in my head for some days past, up to last night, but to-day I feel nearly all right again. I have been about the city same as usual, nearly—to the Hospitals, &c, I mean—I am told that I hover too much over the beds of the hospitals, with fever & putrid wounds, &c. One soldier, brought here about fifteen days ago, very low with typhoid fever, Livingston Brooks, Co B 17th Penn Cavalry, I have particularly stuck to, as I found him in what appeared to be a dying condition, from negligence, & a horrible journey of about forty miles, bad roads & fast driving—& then after he got here, as he is a simple country boy, very shy & silent, & made no complaint, they neglected him—I found him something like I found John Holmes last winter—I called the doctor's attention to him, shook up the nurses, had him bathed in spirits, gave him lumps of ice, & ice to his head, he had a painful bursting pain in his head, & his body was like fire—he was very quiet, a very sensible boy, old fashioned—he did not want to die, & I had to lie to him without stint, for he thought I knew everything, & I always put in of course that what I told him was exactly the truth, & that if he got really dangerous I would tell him & not conceal it.

The rule is to remove bad fever patients out from the main wards to a tent by themselves, & the doctor told me he would have to be removed. I broke it gently to him, but the poor boy got it immediately in his head that he was marked with death, & was to be removed on that account—it had a great effect upon him, & although I told the truth this time it did not have as good a result as my former fibs—I persuaded the doctor to let him remain—for three days he lay just about an even chance, go or stay, with a little leaning toward the first—But, mother, to make a long story short, he is now out of any immediate danger—he has been perfectly rational throughout—begins to taste a little food, (for a week he eat nothing, I had to compel him to take a quarter of an orange, now & then)—& I will say, whether any one calls it pride or not, that if he *does* get up & around again, it's me that saved his life. Mother, as I have said in former letters, you can have no idea how these sick & dying youngsters cling to a fellow, & how fascinating it is, with all its hospital surroundings of sadness & scenes of repulsion & death.

In this same hospital, Armory Square, where this cavalry boy is, I have about fifteen or twenty particular cases I see much too, some of them as much as him—there are two from East Brooklyn, George Monk, Co A 78th N Y, & Stephen Redgate, (his mother is a widow in E[ast] B[rooklyn], I have written her,) both are pretty badly wounded—both are youngsters under 19—O mother, there seems to me as I go through these rows of cots, as if it was too bad to accept these *children*, to subject them to such premature experiences— I devote myself much to Armory Square Hospital because it contains by far the worst cases, most repulsive wounds, has the most suffering & most need of consolation—I go every day without fail, & often at night—sometimes stay very late—no one interferes with me, guards, doctors, nurses, nor any one—I am let to take my own course. . . .

Mr. Lincoln passes here (14th st) every evening on his way out—I noticed him last evening about ½ past 6, he was in his barouche, two horses, guarded by about thirty cavalry. The barouche comes first under a slow trot, driven by one man in the box, no servant or footman beside—the cavalry all follow closely after with a lieutenant at their head—I had a good view of the President last evening—he looks more careworn even than usual—his face with deep cut lines, seams, & his *complexion gray*, through very dark skin, a curious looking man, very sad—I said to a lady who was looking with me, "Who can see that man without losing all wish to be sharp upon him personally? Who can say he has not a good soul?" The lady assented, although she is almost vindictive on the course of the administration, (thinks it wants nerve &c., the usual complaint). The equipage is rather shabby, horses indeed almost what my friends the Broadway drivers would call *old plugs*. The President dresses in plain black clothes, cylinder hat—he was alone yesterday—As he came up, he first drove over to the house of the Sec of War, on K st about 300 feet from here, sat in his carriage while Stanton came out & had a 15 minutes interview with him (I can see from my window)—& then wheeled around, & slowly trotted around the corner & up Fourteenth st., the cavalry after him—I really think it would be safer for him just now to stop at the White House, but I expect he is too proud to abandon the former custom—Then about an hour after, we had a large cavalry regiment pass, with blankets, arms, &c, on the war march over the same track—the reg't was very full, over a thousand, indeed thirteen or fourteen hundred—it was an old reg't, veterans, *old fighters,* young as they were—they were preceded by a fine mounted band of sixteen, (about ten bugles, the rest cymbals & drums)—I tell you, mother it made every thing ring—made my heart leap, they played with a will—then the *accompaniment*—the sabres rattled on a thousand men's sides—they had pistols, their heels spurred—handsome American young men (I make no acc't of any other)—rude uniforms, well worn, but good cattle prancing—all good riders, full of the devil, nobody shaved, all very sunburnt. The regimental officers (splendidly mounted, but just as roughly drest as the men) came immediately after the band, then company after company, with each its officers at its head—the tramping of so many horses (there is a good hard turnpike)—then a long train of men with led horses, mounted negroes, & a long long string of baggage wagons, each with four horses—& then a strong rear guard—I tell you it had the look of *real war*—noble looking fellows—a man looks & feels so proud on a good horse, & armed—They are off toward the region of Lee's (supposed) rendezvous, toward the Susquehannah, for the great anticipated battle—Alas, how many of these healthy handsome rollicking young men will lie cold in death, before the apples ripe in the orchards. . . .

11. WW to Louisa Van Velsor Whitman, Washington, July 7, 1863

Mother, it seems to be certain that Meade[21] has gained the day, & that the battles there in Pennsylvania have been about as terrible as any in the war—O what a sight must have been presented by the field of action—I think the killed & wounded there on both sides were as many as eighteen or twenty thousand—in one place, four or five acres, there were a thousand dead, at daybreak on Saturday morning—Mother, one's heart grows sick of war, after all, when you see what it really is—every once in a while I feel so horrified & disgusted—it seems to me like a great slaughter-house & the men mutually butchering each other—then I feel how impossible it appears, again, to retire from this contest, until we have carried our points—(it is cruel to be so tossed from pillar to post in one's judgment). . . .

[T]here are camps here of every thing—I went once or twice to the Contraband Camps, to the Hospital, &c. but I could not bring myself to go again—

when I meet black men or boys among my own hospitals, I use them kindly, give them something, &c.—I believe I told you that I do the same to the wounded rebels, too—but as there is a limit to one's sinews & endurance & sympathies, &c. I have got in the way after going lightly as it were all through the wards of a hospital, & trying to give a word of cheer, if nothing else, to every one, then confining my special attentions to the few where the investment seems to tell best, & who want it most—Mother, I have real pride in telling you that I have the consciousness of saving quite a little number of lives by saving them from giving up & being a good deal with them—the men say it is so, & the doctors say it is so—& I will candidly confess I can see it is true, though I say it of myself. . . .

### 12. WW to Louisa Van Velsor Whitman, Washington, July 15, 1863

So the mob has risen at last in New York[22]—I have been expecting it, but as the day for the draft had arrived & every thing was so quiet, I supposed all might go on smoothly—but it seems the passions of the people were only sleeping, & have burst forth with terrible fury, & they have destroyed life & property, the enrolment buildings &c as we hear—the accounts we get are a good deal in a muddle, but it seems bad enough—the feeling here is savage & hot as fire against New York, (the mob—"*copperhead mob*" the papers here call it,) & I hear nothing in all directions but threats of ordering up the gunboats, cannonading the city, shooting down the mob, hanging them in a body, &c &c—meantime I remain silent, partly amused, partly scornful, or occasionally put a dry remark, which only adds fuel to the flame—I do not feel it in my heart to abuse the poor people, or call for rope or bullets for them, but that is all the talk here, even in the hospitals—

The acc'ts from N Y this morning are that the gov't has ordered the draft to be suspended there—I hope it is true, for I find that the deeper they go in with the draft, the more trouble it is likely to make—I have changed my opinions & feelings on the subject—we are in the midst of strange & terrible times—one is pulled a dozen different ways in his mind, & hardly knows what to think or do. . . .

My hospital life still continues the same. . . . I see so much of butcher sights, so much sickness & suffering I must get away a while I believe for self-preservation. . . .

### 13. To Lewis K. Brown, Washington, August 1, 1863

. . . Lew, I must tell you what a curious thing happened in the chaplain's house night before last—there has been a man in ward I, named Lane, with two fingers amputated, very bad with gangrene, so they removed him to a tent by himself—last Thursday his wife came to see him, she seemed a nice woman but very poor, she stopt at the chaplain's—about 3 o'clock in the morning she got up & went to the sink, & there she gave birth to a child, which fell down the sink into the sewer runs beneath, fortunately the water was not turned on— the chaplain got up, carried Mrs. Lane out, & then roused up a lot of men from the hospital, with spades &c. dug a trench outside, & got into the sink, & took out the poor little child, it lay there on its back, in about two inches of water— well, strange as it may seem, the child was alive, (it fell about five feet through the sink)—& is now living & likely to live, is quite bright, has a head of thick black hair—the chaplain took me in yesterday, showed me the child, & Mrs. Jackson, his wife, told me the whole story, with a good deal I havn't told you— & then she treated me to a good plate of ice cream. . . .

Well, Lew, they had the great battle of Gettysburgh, but it does not seem to have settled any thing, except to have killed & wounded a great many thousand men—It seems as though the two armies were falling back again to near their old positions on the Rappahannock—it is hard to tell what will be the next move—yet, Lewy, I think we shall conquer yet—I don't believe it is destined that this glorious Union is to be broken up by all the secesh south, or copheads north either—. . . .

### 14. WW to Mr. and Mrs. S. B. Haskell, Washington, August 10, 1863

Dear friends, I thought it would be soothing to you to have a few lines about the last days of your son Erastus Haskell of Company K, 141st New York Volunteers. I write in haste, & nothing of importance—only I thought any thing about Erastus would be welcome. From the time he came to Armory Square Hospital till he died, there was hardly a day but I was with him a portion of the time—if not during the day, then at night. I had no opportunity to do much, or any thing for him, as nothing was needed, only to wait the progress of his malady. I am only a friend, visiting the wounded & sick soldiers, (not connected with any society—or State.) From the first I felt that Erastus was in danger, or at least was much worse than they in the hospital supposed. As he made no complaint, they perhaps [thought him] not very bad—I told the [doctor of the ward] to look him over again—he was a much [sicker boy] than he supposed, but he took it lightly, said, I know more about these fever cases than you do— the young man looks very sick, but I shall certainly bring him out of it all right. I have no doubt the doctor meant well & did his best—at any rate, about a week or so before Erastus died he got really alarmed & after that he & all the doctors tried to help him, but without avail—Maybe it would not have made any difference any how—I think Erastus was broken down, poor boy, before he came to the hospital here—I believe he came here about July 11th—Somehow I took to him, he was a quiet young man, behaved always correct & decent, said little—I used to sit on the side of his bed—I said once, You don't talk any, Erastus, you leave me to do all the talking—he only answered quietly, I was never much of a talker. The doctor wished every one to cheer him up very lively—Only once I tried to tell him some amusing narratives, but after a few moments I stopt, I saw that the effect was not good, & after that I never tried it again—I used to sit by the side of his bed, pretty silent, as that seemed most agreeable to him, & I felt it so too—he was generally opprest for breath, & with the heat, & I would fan him—occasionally he would want a drink—some days he dozed a good deal—sometimes when I would come in, he woke up, & I would lean down and kiss him, he would reach out his hand & pat my hair & beard a little, very friendly, as I sat on the bed & leaned over him. . . .

While he lay sick here he had his fife laying on the little stand by his side—he once told me that if he got well he would play me a tune on it—but, he says, I am not much of a player yet.

I was very anxious he should be saved, & so were they all—he was well used by the attendants—poor boy, I can see him as I write—he was tanned & had a fine head of hair, & looked good in the face when he first came, & was in pretty good flesh too—(had his hair cut close about ten or twelve days before he died)—He never complained—but it looked pitiful to see him lying there, with such a look out of his eyes. He had large clear eyes, they seemed to talk better than words—I assure you I was attracted to him much—Many nights I sat in the hospital by his bedside till far in the night—The lights would be put out—yet I would sit there silently, hours, late, perhaps fanning him—he always liked to have me sit there, but never cared to talk—I shall never forget those nights, it was a curious & solemn scene, the sick & wounded lying around in their cots, just visible in the darkness, & this dear young man close at hand lying on what proved to be his death bed—I do not know his past life, but what I do know, & what I saw of him, he was a noble boy—I felt he was one I should get very much attached to. I think you have reason to be proud of such a son, & all his relatives have cause to treasure his memory.

I write to you this letter, because I would do something at least in his memory—his fate was a hard one, to die so—He is one of the thousands of our unknown American young men in the ranks about whom there is no record or fame, no fuss made about their dying so unknown, but I find in them the real precious & royal ones of this land, giving themselves up, aye even their young & precious lives, in their country's cause—Poor dear son, though you were not my son, I felt to love you as a son, what short time I saw you sick & dying here—it is well as it is, perhaps better—for who knows whether he is not better off, the patient & sweet young soul, to go, than we are to stay? So farewell, dear boy—it was my opportunity to be with you in your last rapid days of death—no chance as I have said to do any thing particular, for nothing [could be done—only you did not lay] here & die among strangers without having one at hand who loved you dearly, & to whom you gave your dying kiss—. . . .

### 15. WW to Nathaniel Bloom, Washington, September 5, 1863

. . . What a difference it is with me here—I tell you, Nat, my evenings are frequently spent in scenes that make a terrible difference—for I am still a hospital visitor, there has not passed a day for months (or at least not more than two) that I have not been among the sick & wounded, either in hospitals or down in camp—occasionally here I spend the evenings in hospital—the experience is a profound one, beyond all else, & touches me personally, egotistically, in unprecedented ways—I mean the way often the amputated, sick, sometimes dying soldiers cling & cleave to me as it were as a man overboard to a plank, & the perfect content they have if I will remain with them, sit on the side of the cot awhile, some youngsters often, & caress them &c.—It is delicious to be the object of so much love & reliance, & to do them such good, sooth & pacify torments of wounds &c—You will doubtless see in what I have said the reason I continue so long in this kind of life—as I am entirely on my own hook too.

Life goes however quite well with me here—I work a few hours a day at copying &c, occasionally write a newspaper letter, & make enough money to pay my expenses—I have a little room, & live a sort of German or Parisian student life—always get my breakfast in my room, (have a little spirit lamp) & rub on free & happy enough, untrammeled by business, for I make what little employment I have suit my moods—walk quite a good deal, & in this weather the rich & splendid environs of Washington are an unfailing fountain to me—go down the river, or off into Virginia once in a while—All around us here are forts, by the score—great ambulance & teamsters' camps &c—these I go to—some have little hospitals, I visit, &c &c—. . . .

### 16. WW to Margaret Curtis,[23] Washington, October 4, 1863

. . . I try to distribute something, even if but the merest trifle, all round, without missing any, when I visit a ward, going round rather rapidly—& then devoting myself, more at leisure, to the cases that need special attention. One who is experienced may find in almost any ward at any time one or two patients or more, who are at that time trembling in the balance, the crises of the wound, recovery uncertain, yet death also uncertain. I will confess to you, madam, that I think I have an instinct & faculty for these cases. Poor young men, how many have I seen, & known—how pitiful it is to see them—one must be calm &

cheerful, & not let on how their case really is, must stop much with them, find
out their idiosyncracies—do any thing for them—nourish them, judiciously
give the right things to drink—bring in the affections, soothe them, brace them
up, kiss them, discard all ceremony, & fight for them, as it were, with all weapons. I need not tell your womanly soul that such work blesses him that works
as much as the object of it. I have never been happier than in some of these
hospital ministering hours. . . .

### 17. WW to James Redpath,[24] Washington, October 21, 1863

My idea is a book of the time, worthy the time—something considerably
beyond mere hospital sketches—a book for sale perhaps in a larger American
market—the premises or skeleton memoranda of incidents, persons, places,
sights, the past year (mostly jotted down either on the spot or in the spirit of
seeing or hearing what is narrated)—(I left New York early last December, &
have been around the front or here ever since)—full of interest I think—in
some respects somewhat a combination in handling of the Old French
Memoires, & my own personality (things seen through my eyes, & what my
vision brings)—a book full enough of mosaic, but all fused to one comprehensive thing—one of the drifts is to push forward the very big & needed truth,
that our national military system needs shifting, revolutionizing & made to tally
with democracy, the people—The officers should almost invariably rise from
the ranks—there is an absolute want of democratic spirit in the present system
& officers—it is the feudal spirit exclusively—nearly the entire capacity, keen-
ness & courage of our army are in the ranks—(what has been done has been
unavoidable so far, but the time has arrived to discuss the change)—

I have much to say of the hospitals, the immense national hospitals—in them
too most radical changes of premises are demanded—(the air, the spirit of a
thing is every thing, the details follow & adjust themselves). I have many hospital incidents, [that] will take with the general reader—I ventilate my general
democracy with details very largely & with reference to the future—bringing
in persons, the President, Seward, Congress, the Capitol, Washington City,
many of the actors of the drama—have something to say of the great trunk
America, the West &c &c—do not hesitate to diffuse *myself*—the book is very
rapid—is a book that can be read by the five or ten minutes at (being full of
small parts, pieces, paragraphs with their dates, incidents &c)—I should think
two or three thousand sale ought to be certainly depended on here in hospitals
in Washington, among departments &c—. . . .

I have been & am in the midst of these things, I feel myself full of them, & I
know the people generally now are too (far more than they know,) & would
readily absorb & understand my mem[oranda]. Wherefore let us make & publish
the book, & out with it so as to have it for sale by middle or 20th of November.

### 18. WW to Louisa Van Velsor Whitman, Washington, October 27, 1863

... Well, dear Mother, how the time passes away—to think it will soon be a year I have been away—it has passed away very swiftly somehow to me—O what things I have witnessed during that time—I shall never forget them—& the war is not settled yet, but I have finally got for good I think into the feeling that our triumph is assured, whether it be sooner or whether it be later, or whatever roundabout way we are led there, & I find I dont change that conviction from any reverses we meet, or any delays or government blunders—there are blunders enough, heaven knows, but I am thankful things have gone on as well for us as they have—thankful the ship rides safe & sound at all—then I have finally made up my mind that Mr. Lincoln has done as good as a human man could do—I still think him a pretty big President—I realize here in Washington that it has been a big thing to have just kept the United States from being thrown down & having its throat cut—& now I have no doubt it will throw down secession & cut its throat—& I have not had any doubt since Gettysburgh—....

### 19. WW to Louisa Van Velsor Whitman, Washington, April 10, 1864

... Mother, we expect a commencement of the fighting below very soon, there is every indication of it—we have had about as severe rain storms here lately as I ever see—it is middling pleasant now—there are exciting times in Congress—the Copperheads are getting furious, & want to recognize the Southern Confederacy—this is a pretty time to talk of recognizing such villains after what they have done, and after what has transpired the last three years—After first Fredericksburgh I felt discouraged myself, & doubted whether our rulers could carry on the war—but that has past away, the war *must* be carried on—& I would willingly go myself in the ranks if I thought it would profit more than at present, & I don't know sometimes but I shall as it is—

Mother, you dont know what a feeling a man gets after being in the active sights & influences of the camp, the Army, the wounded &c.—he gets to have a deep feeling he never experienced before—the flag, the tune of Yankee Doodle, & similar things, produce an effect on a fellow never such before—I have seen some bring tears on the men's cheeks, & others turn pale, under such circumstances—I have a little flag (it belonged to one of our cavalry reg'ts) presented to me by one of the wounded—it was taken by the secesh in a cavalry fight, & rescued by our men in a bloody little skirmish, it cost three men's lives, just to get one little flag, four by three—our men rescued it, & tore it from the breast of a dead rebel—all that just for the name of getting their little banner back again—this man that got it was very badly wounded, & they let him keep it—I was with him a good deal, he wanted to give me something he said, he didn't expect to live, so he gave me the little banner as a keepsake—I mention this, Mother, to show you a specimen of the feeling—there isn't a reg't, cavalry or infantry, that wouldn't do the same, on occasion—. . . .

### 20. "Visits Among Army Hospitals," *New York Times,* December 11, 1864

. . . The work of the Army Hospital Visitor is indeed a trade, an art, requiring both experience and natural gifts, and the greatest judgment. A large number of the visitors to the hospitals do no good at all, while many do harm. The surgeons have great trouble from them. Some visitors go from curiosity—as to a show of animals. Others give the men improper things. Then there are always some poor fellows in the crises of sickness or wounds, that imperatively need perfect quiet—not to be talked to by strangers. Few realize that it is not the mere giving of gifts that does good: it is the proper adaptation. Nothing is of any avail among the soldiers except conscientious personal investigation of cases, each one for itself; with sharp, critical faculties, but in the fullest spirit of human sympathy and boundless love. The men feel such love, always, more than anything else. I have met very few persons who realize the importance of humoring the yearnings for love and friendship of these American young men, prostrated by sickness and wounds. . . .

I shall have to omit any detailed account of the wounded of May and June, 1864, from the battles of the Wilderness, Spottsylvania, etc. That would be a long history in itself. The arrivals, the numbers, and the severity of the wounds, outvied anything that we had seen before. For days and weeks the melancholy tide set in upon us. The weather was very hot; the wounded had been delayed in coming, and much neglected. Very many of the wounds had worms in them. An unusual portion mortified. It was among these that, for the first time in my life, I began to be prostrated with real sickness, and was, before the close of the Summer, imperatively ordered North by the physicians, to recuperate and have an entire change of air. . . .

The reader has doubtless inferred the fact that my visits among the wounded and sick have been as an Independent Missionary, in my own style, and not as agent of any commission. Several noble women and men of Brooklyn, Boston, Salem and Providence have voluntarily supplied funds at times. I only wish they could see a tithe of the actual work performed by their generous and benevolent assistance, among these suffering men.

He who goes among the soldiers with gifts, &c., must beware how he proceeds. It is much more of an art than one would imagine. They are not charity-patients, but American young men, of pride and independence. The spirit in which you treat them, and bestow your donations, is just as important as the gifts themselves; sometimes more so. Then there is continual discrimination necessary. Each case requires some peculiar adaptation to itself. It is very important to slight nobody—not a single case. Some hospital visitors, especially the women, pick out the handsomest looking soldiers, or have a few for their pets. Of course some will attract you more than others, and some will need more attention than others; but be careful not to ignore any patient. A word, a friendly turn of the eye, or touch of the hand in passing, if nothing more. . . .

To many of the wounded and the sick, especially the youngsters, there is something in personal love, caresses and the magnetic flood of sympathy and friendship that does, in its way, more good than all the medicine in the world. I have spoken of my regular gifts of delicacies, money, tobacco, special articles of food, nick-nacks, &c., &c. But I steadily found more and more that I could help and turn the balance in favor of cure, by the means here alluded to, in a curiously large proportion of cases. The American soldier is full of affection, and the yearning for affection. And it comes wonderfully grateful to him to have this yearning gratified when he is laid up with painful wounds or illness, far away from home, among strangers. Many will think this merely sentimentalism, but I know it is the most solid of facts. I believe that even the moving around among the men, or through the ward, of a hearty, healthy, clean, strong, generous-souled person, man or woman, full of humanity and love, sensing out invisible, constant currents thereof, does immense good to the sick and wounded.

To those who might be interested in knowing it, I must add, in conclusion, that I have tried to do justice to all the suffering that fell in my way. While I have been with wounded and sick in thousands of cases from the New-England States, and from New-York, New-Jersey and Pennsylvania, and from Michigan, Wisconsin, Indiana, Illinois and the Western States, I have been with more or less from all the States North and South, without exception. I have been with many from the border States, especially from Maryland and Virginia, and found far more Union Southerners than is supposed. I have been with many rebel officers and men among our wounded, and given them always what I had, and tried to cheer them the same as any. I have been among the army teamsters considerably, and indeed always find myself drawn to them. Among the black soldiers, wounded or sick, and in the contraband camps, I also took my way whenever in their neighborhood, and did what I could for them.

### 21. WW to William D. O'Connor,[25] Brooklyn, January 6, 1865

It may be Drum-Taps may come out this winter, yet, (in the way I have mentioned in times past.) It is in a state to put right through, a perfect copy being ready for the printers—I feel at last, & for the first time without any demur, that I am satisfied with it—content to have it go to the world verbatim & punctuation. It is in my opinion superior to Leaves of Grass—certainly more perfect as a work of art, being adjusted in all its proportions, & its passion having the indispensable merit that though to the ordinary reader let loose with wildest abandon, the true artist can see it is yet under control. But I am perhaps mainly satisfied with Drum-Taps because it delivers my ambition of the task that has haunted me, namely, to express in a poem (& in the way I like, which is not at all by directly stating it) the pending action of this *Time & Land we swim in,* with all their large conflicting fluctuations of despair & hope, the shiftings, masses, & the whirl & deafening din, (yet over all, as by invisible hand, a definite purport & idea)—with the unprecedented anguish of wounded & suffering, the beautiful young men, in wholesale death & agony, everything sometimes as if in blood color, & dripping blood. The book is therefore unprecedently sad, (as these days are, are they not?)—but it also has the blast of the trumpet, & the drum pounds & whirrs in it, & then an undertone of sweetest comradship & human love, threading its steady thread inside the chaos, & heard at every lull & interstice thereof—clearly also it has clear notes of faith & triumph. . . .

## 22. *Drum-Taps* (1865)

### THE WOUND-DRESSER

1

An old man bending I come among new faces,
Years looking backward resuming in answer to children,
Come tell us old man, as from young men and maidens that love me,
(Arous'd and angry, I'd thought to beat the alarum, and urge relentless war,
But soon my fingers fail'd me, my face droop'd and I resign'd myself,
To sit by the wounded and soothe them, or silently watch the dead;)
Years hence of these scenes, of these furious passions, these chances,
Of unsurpass'd heroes, (was one side so brave? the other was equally brave;)
Now be witness again, paint the mightiest armies of earth,
Of those armies so rapid so wondrous what saw you to tell us?
What stays with you latest and deepest? of curious panics,
Of hard-fought engagements of sieges tremendous what deepest remains?

2

O maidens and young men I love and that love me,
What you ask of my days those the strangest and sudden your talking recalls,
Soldier alert I arrive after a long march cover'd with sweat and dust,
In the nick of time I come, plunge in the fight, loudly shout in the rush of
    successful charge,

Enter the captur'd works—yet lo, like a swift-running river they fade,
Pass and are gone they fade—I dwell not on soldiers' perils or soldiers' joys,
(Both I remember well—many the hardships, few the joys, yet I was
  content.)

But in silence, in dreams' projections,
While the world of gain and appearance and mirth goes on,
So soon what is over forgotten, and waves wash the imprints off the sand,
With hinged knees returning I enter the doors, (while for you up there,
Whoever you are, follow without noise and be of strong heart.)

Bearing the bandages, water and sponge,
Straight and swift to my wounded I go,
Where they lie on the ground after the battle brought in,
Where their priceless blood reddens the grass the ground,
Or to the rows of the hospital tent, or under the roof'd hospital,
To the long rows of cots up and down each side I return,
To each and all one after another I draw near, not one do I miss,
An attendant follows holding a tray, he carries a refuse pail,
Soon to be fill'd with clotted rags and blood, emptied, and fill'd again.

I onward go, I stop,
With hinged knees and steady hand to dress wounds,
I am firm with each, the pangs are sharp yet unavoidable,
One turns to me his appealing eyes—poor boy! I never knew you,
Yet I think I could not refuse this moment to die for you, if that would save
  you.

3
On, on I go, (open doors of time! open hospital doors!)
The crush'd head I dress, (poor crazed hand tear not the bandage away,)
The neck of the cavalry-man with the bullet through and through I examine,
Hard the breathing rattles, quite glazed already the eye, yet life struggles hard,
(Come sweet death! be persuaded O beautiful death!
In mercy come quickly.)

From the stump of the arm, the amputated hand,
I undo the clotted lint, remove the slough, wash off the matter and blood,
Back on his pillow the soldier bends with curv'd neck and side-falling head,
His eyes are closed, his face is pale, he dares not look on the bloody stump,
And has not yet look'd on it.

I dress a wound in the side, deep, deep,
But a day or two more, for see the frame all wasted and sinking,
And the yellow-blue countenance see.

I dress the perforated shoulder, the foot with the bullet-wound,
Cleanse the one with a gnawing and putrid gangrene, so sickening, so
   offensive,
While the attendant stands behind aside me holding the tray and pail.

I am faithful, I do not give out,
The fractur'd thigh, the knee, the wound in the abdomen,
These and more I dress with impassive hand, (yet deep in my breast a fire, a
   burning flame.)

4

Thus in silence in dreams' projections,
Returning, resuming, I thread my way through the hospitals,
The hurt and wounded I pacify with soothing hand,
I sit by the restless all the dark night, some are so young,
Some suffer so much, I recall the experience sweet and sad,
(Many a soldier's loving arms about this neck have cross'd and rested
Many a soldier's kiss dwells on these bearded lips.)

## 23. *Memoranda During the War* (1875–76)

During the Union War I commenced at the close of 1862, and continued steadily through '63, '64 and '65, to visit the sick and wounded of the Army, both
on the field and in the Hospitals in and around Washington city. From the first
I kept little note-books for impromptu jottings in pencil to refresh my memory
of names and circumstances, and what was specially wanted, &c. In these I
brief'd cases, persons, sights, occurrences in camp, by the bedside, and not seldom by the corpses of the dead. Of the present Volume most of its pages are
*verbatim* renderings from such pencillings on the spot. Some were scratched
down from narratives I heard and itemized while watching, or waiting, or tending somebody amid those scenes. I have perhaps forty such little note-books
left, forming a special history of those years, for myself alone, full of associations never to be possible said or sung. I wish I could convey to the reader the
associations that attach to these soil'd and creas'd little livraisons, each composed of a sheet or two of paper, folded small to carry in the pocket, and fas-
ten'd with a pin. I leave them just as I threw them by during the War, blotch'd
here and there with more than one blood-stain, hurriedly written, sometimes
at the clinique, not seldom amid the excitement of uncertainty, or defeat, or of
action, or getting ready for it, or a march. Even these days, at the lapse of many
years, I can never turn their tiny leaves, or even take one in my hand, without
the actual army sights and hot emotions of the time rushing like a river in full
tide through me. Each line, each scrawl, each memorandum has its history.

Some pang of anguish—some tragedy, profounder than ever poet wrote. Out of them arise active and breathing forms. They summon up, even in this silent and vacant room as I write, not only the sinewy regiments and brigades, marching or in camp, but the countless phantoms of those who fell and were hastily buried by wholesale in the battle-pits, or whose dust and bones have been since removed to the National Cemeteries of the land. . . .

## 24. *Specimen Days* (1882–83)

And so good-bye to the war. I know not how it may have been, or may be, to others—to me the main interest I found, (and still, on recollection, find,) in the rank and file of the armies, both sides, and in those specimens amid the hospitals, and even the dead on the field. To me the points illustrating the latent personal character and eligibilities of these States, in the two or three millions of American young and middle-aged men, North and South, embodied in those armies—and especially the one-third or one-fourth of their number, stricken by wounds or disease at some time in the course of the contest—were of more significance even than the political interests involved. (As so much of a race depends on how it faces death, and how it stands personal anguish and sickness. As, in the glints of emotions under emergencies, and the indirect traits and asides in Plutarch, we get far profounder clues to the antique world than all its more formal history.)

Future years will never know the seething hell and the black infernal background of countless minor scenes and interiors, (not the official surface-courteousness of the Generals, not the few great battles) of the Secession War; and it is best they should not—the real war will never get in the books. In the mushy influences of current times, too, the fervid atmosphere and typical events of those years are in danger of being totally forgotten. I have at night watch'd by the side of a sick man in the hospital, one who could not live many hours. I have seen his eyes flash and burn as he raised himself and recurr'd to the cruelties on his surrender'd brother, and mutilations of the corpse afterward. . . .

Such was the war. It was not a quadrille in a ball-room. Its interior history will not only never be written—its practicality, minutiae of deeds and passions, will never even be suggested. The actual soldier of 1862–'65, North and South, with all his ways, his incredible dauntlessness, habits, practices, tastes, language, his fierce friendship, his appetite, rankness, his superb strength and animality, lawless gait, and a hundred unnamed lights and shades of camp, I say, will never be written—perhaps must not and should not be.

# Notes

## Preface

1. Walter Lowenfels, editor, *Walt Whitman's Civil War* (New York, 1961), p. 13. Also see Charles I. Glicksberg, editor, *Walt Whitman and the Civil War* (Philadelphia, 1933).

2. John Weiss, "War and Literature," *Atlantic Monthly* 9 (June 1862): 676; William Dean Howells, "Reviews and Literary Notices," *Atlantic Monthly* 20 (July 1867): 121.

3. Edmund Wilson, *Patriotic Gore: Studies in the Literature of the American Civil War* (New York, 1962), p. xiii; Daniel Aaron, *The Unwritten War: American Writers and the Civil War* (New York, 1973), pp. xvii–xix. Also see Robert A. Lively, *Fiction Fights the Civil War* (Chapel Hill, 1957) and David Madden and Peggy Bach (eds.), *Classics of Civil War Fiction* (Jackson, Miss., 1991). Scholars are beginning to re-examine the literature generated during the War. For example, Kathleen Diffly, "Where My Heart Is Turning Ever: Civil War Stories and National Stability from Fort Sumter to the Centennial," *American Literary History* 2 (Fall 1990): 627–58.

4. The question of canon formation has received a great deal of attention in recent years. For a scholarly treatment of the issue see Robert von Hallberg (ed.), *Canons* (Chicago, 1984) and Paul Lauter, *Canons and Contexts* (New York, 1991).

5. The issue of Southern intellectual life is discussed in Michael O'Brien, *Rethinking the South: Essays in Intellectual History* (Baltimore, 1988), pp. 19–37; and Eugene Genovese, "Foreword," in Richard J. Calhoun (ed.), *Witness to Sorrow: The Antebellum Autobiography of William J. Grayson* (Columbia, S.C., 1990).

6. Herman Melville to Nathaniel Hawthorne, August 13, 1852, in Jay Leyda, editor, *The Portable Melville* (New York, 1952), p. 464.

## Adams

1. HA to CFA, Jr., Dec. 9, 1860, in J. C. Levenson et al. (eds.), *The Letters of Henry Adams, Volume 1: 1858–1868* (Cambridge, Mass., 1982), p. 204 (hereafter cited as *Letters*).

2. *The Education of Henry Adams* (Boston, 1918; Houghton Mifflin Sentry Edition, 1961), p. 4.

3. HA to CFA, Jr., Dec. 18, 1863, *Letters*, p. 415.

4. Daniel Aaron, editor, "'Strongly-Flavored Imitation Cynicism': Henry Adams' *Education* Reviewed by John Jay Chapman," *New England Quarterly* 63 (June 1990): 291.

5. *Education*, p. 111; p. 153; HA to CFA, Jr., July 17, 1863, *Letters*, p. 371.

6. Henry Adams's papers are located at the Massachusetts Historical Society. For complete texts of Adams's letters during the Civil War, see J. C. Levenson et al. (eds.), *The Letters of Henry Adams, Volume 1: 1858–1868.*

7. The "Chief" was Charles Francis Adams (1807–86), HA's father and United States Minister to the Court of St. James's.

8. War correspondent for the London *Times*, William Howard Russell (1821–1907) had just reported on the Union loss at Bull Run.

9. James M. Mason (1798–1871) was Confederate diplomatic commissioner to England.

10. William Henry Seward (1801–72) was Secretary of State under Lincoln. Charles Sumner (1811–74), Zachariah Chandler (1813–79), and Lyman Trumbull (1813–96) served as Republican Senators from Massachusetts, Wisconsin, and Illinois respectively.

11. Both Stephen George Perkins (1835–62) and James Hamilton Kuhn (1838–62) were killed in action.

12. Adams is referring to the Battle of Gettysburg.

13. The battles at Marathon (490 B.C.) and Naseby (1645 A.D.) resulted in minor victories.

14. HA is referring to the nomination of George McClellan as the Democratic Presidential candidate.

## Alcott

1. LMA to Alfred Whitman, May 19, 1861, in *The Selected Letters of Louisa May Alcott.* Edited by Joel Myerson and Daniel Shealy (Boston, 1987), p. 65.

2. *The Journals of Louisa May Alcott.* Edited by Joel Myerson and Daniel Shealy (Boston, 1989), p. 118.

3. See Madeleine Stern, "Louisa M. Alcott: Civil War Nurse," *Americana* 37 (April 1943): 322–23.

4. LMA to Mary Elizabeth Waterman, Nov. 6, 1863, in *Letters*, p. 95.

5. LMA to James Redpath, Dec. 2, 1863, in *Letters*, p. 97.

6. Alcott's journals are located at Houghton Library, Harvard University, and have been published in Joel Myerson and Daniel Shealy, editors, *The Journals of Louisa May Alcott* (Boston, 1989).

7. A reference to the unsuccessful attack by Ambrose E. Burnside (1824–81) against well-entrenched Confederate forces at Fredericksburg in December 1863.

8. By force of arms.

9. A reference to Baron Munchausen, the hero of a tale of fantastic adventures written by Rudolf Raspe in 1785.

10. *Romeo and Juliet*, Act III, Scene I.

## Child

1. LMC to Elizabeth Cady Stanton, May 24, 1863, in Milton Meltzer and Patricia Holland (eds.), *Lydia Maria Child: Selected Letters, 1817–1880* (Amherst, Mass., 1982), p. 431 (hereafter cited as *Letters*).

2. Jean Fagan Yellin (ed.), *Incidents in the Life of a Slave Girl* (Cambridge, Mass., 1987), p. 4.

3. *Letters*, p. 441.

4. L. Maria Child, *The Freedmen's Book* (Boston, 1865), p. iii.

5. *Letters*, p. 356.

6. John Greenleaf Whittier (1807–92), American poet and abolitionist.

7. Child's papers are scattered but are available in microform in *The Collected Correspondence of Lydia Maria Child, 1817–1880* (Millwood, 1980). Milton Meltzer and Patricia Holland published a selection of the correspondence they gathered for the microform edition in *Lydia Maria Child: Selected Letters, 1817–1880*.

8. The daughter of a Unitarian minister in Medford, Lucy Osgood (1791–1873) was Child's friend and a frequent correspondent.

9. In Greek mythology, the three-headed dog who guarded the entrance to Hades.

10. Benjamin Butler (1818–93), brigadier-general of the Massachusetts militia, is acknowledged as having been the first to refer to escaped slaves as "contraband."

11. Lucy Searle (1794–?) was a schoolteacher in Newburyport, Mass.

12. Sarah Shaw (1815–1902) was Child's dearest friend; her son, Robert Gould Shaw, led a regiment of black troops and was killed at Fort Wagner on July 18, 1863.

13. Nathaniel Willis (1806–67) was the Washington correspondent for New York's *Home Journal*.

14. In Greek myth, King Tantalus was condemned to stand in a chin-high pool of water in Hades beneath fruit-laden boughs only to have the fruit or water recede whenever he tried to eat or drink.

15. Republican Congressman from Indiana, George Julian (1817–99) early on urged Lincoln to emancipate the slaves.

16. William Cutler (1812–89) was a Congressman from Ohio.

17. Henry Wilson (1812–75), the son of a day laborer, was Senator from Massachusetts.

18. Former governor of Massachusetts, Nathaniel Banks (1816–94) was commissioned a major-general during the War. He was the son of a mill superintendent.

19. Fredrika Bremer (1801–65) was a Swedish writer whose works Child read in translation and greatly enjoyed.

## Cooke

1. Richard Barksdale Harwell, "John Esten Cooke, Civil War Correspondent," *Journal of Southern History* 19 (1953): 504.

2. Mary Jo Bratton, "John Esten Cooke and His 'Confederate Lies'," *Southern Literary Journal* 13 (Spring 1991): 76; also see Ritchie D. Watson, Jr., "John Esten Cooke," in Robert Bain and Joseph Flora (eds.), *Fifty Southern Writers Before 1900* (New York, 1987).

3. Jay B. Hubbell, "The War Diary of John Esten Cooke," *Journal of Southern History* 7 (1941): 526.

4. *The Southern Illustrated News*, Sept. 6, 1862.

5. Hubbell, "The War Diary of John Esten Cooke," p. 536.

6. Bratton, "John Esten Cooke . . . ," p. 72.

7. First printed anonymously, "Stonewall Jackson's Way" was written by John Williamson Palmer, Southern correspondent for the *New York Times*.


## De Forest

1. James F. Light, *John William De Forest* (New York, 1965), p. 65; William Dean Howells, "Reviews and Literary Notices," *Atlantic Monthly* 20 (July 1867): 120–22.

2. *Atlantic Monthly* 4 (July 1859): 131–32; reprinted in James W. Gargano (ed.), *Critical Essays on John William De Forest* (Boston 1981), p. 48.

3. "Charleston Under Arms," *Atlantic Monthly* 7 (April 1861): 488–505.

4. William Dean Howells, "Reviews and Literary Notices," p. 121; Henry James, "Miss Ravenel's Conversion," *Nation* 4 (June 20, 1867): 491–492.

5. Edwin Oviatt, "J. W. De Forest in New Haven," *New York Times*, Dec. 17, 1898; reprinted in Gargano, *Critical Essays*, p. 38.

6. De Forest to Brander Mathews, Jan. 24, 1902; quoted in Frank Bergmann, *The Worthy Gentleman of Democracy: John William De Forest and the American Dream* (Heidelberg, 1971), p. 102.

7. DeForest's papers are located at Yale University.

8. The mortar fleet of David Dixon Porter (1813–91) helped in the capture of New Orleans in March 1862.

9. Benjamin Butler served as military governor of New Orleans in 1862 and later became a leading Republican Congressman.

10. Orator and politician, Edward Everett (1794–1865) was the featured speaker at the consecration of Gettysburg Cemetery.

11. John Wolcott Phelps (1813–85) was the abolitionist commander of the Ship Island Expedition.

12. Meriwether Jefferson Thompson (1826–76) was best known for his leadership of the Missouri State Guard, members of which came to be known as "Swamp Rats."

13. Confederate General John Cabell Breckinridge (1821–75) ran against Lincoln in the Election of 1860. He would be appointed Secretary of War in February 1865.

14. Chief engineer and brigadier general, Godfrey Weitzel (1835–84) would command the all-black 25th Corps of the Army of the James.

15. David Glasgow Farragut (1801–70) commanded the naval expedition in the capture of New Orleans.

16. Wounded at Shiloh, Alfred Mouton (1829–64) commanded a Louisiana brigade.

## Douglass

1. *Christian Recorder* quoted in William S. McFeely, *Frederick Douglass* (New York, 1991), p. 213.

2. John W. Blassingame (ed.), *The Frederick Douglass Papers. Series One: Speeches, Debates, and Interviews. Volume 3: 1855–1863* (New Haven, 1985), p. 429; p. 435.

3. *Life and Times of Frederick Douglass* (1892; New York, 1967), p. 373.

4. McFeely, *Frederick Douglass*, p. 363.

5. *Life and Times of Frederick Douglass*, p. 364.

6. Douglass's papers, located at Yale University, are currently being published in a series of volumes edited by John W. Blassingame. The complete texts of Douglass's Civil War addresses can be found in *The Frederick Douglass Papers. Series One: Speeches, Debates, and Interviews. Volume 3: 1855–63* and *Volume 4: 1864–80* (New Haven, 1991). I have omitted the parenthetic audience exclamations included in some of the speeches.

7. Unitarian minister and activist Samuel J. May (1797–1871) often allowed his house to serve as a stopping place along the Underground Railroad.

8. *Hamlet*, Act III, Scene 1.

9. *Julius Caesar*, Act IV, Scene 2.

10. James Kent (1763–1847) was a prominent New York jurist and author of *Commentaries on American Law* (1830).

11. English historian Edward Gibbon (1737–94) was best known for his *Decline and Fall of the Roman Empire* (1776).

12. *As You Like It*, Act II, Scene 7.

13. In an attempt to save the Union, Kentucky Senator John J. Crittenden (1787–1863) proposed to restore the terms of the Missouri Compromise and protect slavery in the District of Columbia.

## Emerson

1. *The Journals and Miscellaneous Notebooks of Ralph Waldo Emerson*, 16 vols., William Gilman et al. (eds.) (1960–82), 15: 163 (hereafter referred to as *JMN*).

2. "Nature," in *Selections from Ralph Waldo Emerson*. Edited by Stephen E. Whicher (Boston, 1957), p. 24.

3. *JMN*, 5: 298.

4. *JMN*, 15: 77–78.

5. Emerson maintained multiple journals simultaneously and referred to each one by different letters and names. The original journals are located in Houghton Library, Harvard University. They have been published in a definitive modern edition by Harvard

University Press: *The Journals and Miscellaneous Notebooks of Ralph Waldo Emerson*, 16 vols., William Gilman et al. (eds.) For Emerson's correspondence during the Civil War see Volume 5 of Ralph Rusk, editor, *The Letters of Ralph Waldo Emerson* (New York, 1939).

6. This is most likely the draft for a speech RWE delivered at a meeting to raise funds for Robert Gould Shaw's black regiment.

7. Thomas Carlyle (1795–1881), distinguished essayist and historian, whose work was introduced to an American audience by Emerson.

8. Hideous cause.

### Forten

1. Quoted in Brenda Stevenson (ed.), *The Journals of Charlotte Forten Grimké* (New York, 1988), p. 433; p. 403 (hereafter cited as *Journals*).

2. *Journals*, p. 33; p. 50.

3. Forten's journals are located at Howard University. For a superb introduction to Forten's life and definitive text of the journals, see Brenda Stevenson, *The Journals of Charlotte Forten Grimké*.

4. Physician at a Worcester clinic, Seth Rogers would journey to South Carolina as a surgeon for the First South Carolina Volunteers, the black regiment under Thomas Wentworth Higginson's command. Forten became emotionally involved with the married Rogers.

5. Earlier in the day, Forten had heard Wendell Phillips speak at the Music Hall.

6. François-Dominique Toussaint Louverture (1750?–1803) led the successful slave revolt in Haiti in 1791.

7. Garrison published two letters from Forten. See *Liberator*, Dec. 12 and 19, 1862.

8. Compare Forten's account of the day with Higginson's in "Leaves from an Officer's Journal," *Atlantic Monthly* 14 (Dec. 1864): 747–48.

9. Harriet Tubman (1821–1913) was a runaway slave who led scores of slaves to freedom and labored for black civil rights.

10. Robert Shaw (1837–63) commanded the 54th Massachusetts, a black regiment whose actions at Fort Wagner on July 18, 1863, helped win support for black military involvement.

### Hawthorne

1. NH to Horatio Bridge, Feb. 13, 1862, in *The Centenary Edition of the Works of Nathaniel Hawthorne. Vol. 18: The Letters, 1857–1864*. Edited by Thomas Woodson et al. (Columbus, 1987) (Hereafter cited as *Letters*).

2. NH to Sidney Webster, March 14, 1864, in *Letters*, p. 648.

3. NH to James Fields, May 23, 1862, in *Letters*, p. 461.

4. NH to James Fields, July 18, 1863, in *Letters*, p. 586.

5. *The Centenary Edition of the Works of Nathaniel Hawthorne. Volume 5: Our Old Home: A Series of English Sketches* (Columbus, 1970), pp. 3–5.

6. Horatio Bridge (1806–93) graduated from Bowdoin College with Hawthorne in 1825. He was chief of the Bureau of Provisions and Clothing in Washington, and Hawthorne's "best friend."

7. Hawthorne's letters are scattered but the extraordinary Centenary edition of his works, published by Ohio State University Press, has made his complete correspondence available for the first time. Complete texts of the letters included below can be found in *The Centenary Edition of the Works of Nathaniel Hawthorne. Volume 18: The Letters, 1857–1864.* Edited by Thomas Woodson et al. (Columbus, 1987).

8. Publisher of leading American and English literary figures, William Ticknor (1810–64) was especially close to Hawthorne. On a trip in March 1864 planned to revitalize Hawthorne, Ticknor took ill in Philadelphia. Hawthorne "blistered, and powdered, and pilled him" and observed "medical science and the sad and comic aspects of human misery." On April 10, Ticknor died and Hawthorne returned to Concord in a state of "pallid exhaustion." See *Letters,* pp. 651–53.

9. Francis Bennoch (1812–90), English merchant and aspiring poet, introduced Hawthorne to London literary society.

10. Hawthorne is referring to Napoleon III who, in 1860, dispatched troops to Beirut in defense of Christian lives.

11. A reference to Robert Burn's *Scots, What Hae* (1793).

12. The fourteenth President of the United States, Franklin Pierce (1804–69) was Hawthorne's classmate at Bowdoin.

13. Emmanuel Gottlieb Leutze (1816–68), German immigrant to Philadelphia and world-renowned artist with studios in Düsseldorf, had been commissioned by the House to paint "Westward the Course of Empire." Hawthorne had his portrait painted by Leutze, a pleasant experience, he told his publisher, because for each sitting Leutze "gives me a first-rate cigar, and when he sees me getting tired, he brings out a bottle of splendid champagne."

14. Prior to the execution of John Brown (1800–1859) for his attack on the arsenal at Harper's Ferry, Virginia, Emerson was reported to have predicted that the hanging would "make the gallows as glorious as the cross."

15. Founded in 1856, the Saturday Club met for dinner and conversation at the Parker House in Boston on the last Saturday of every month. As of 1861, the members included Hawthorne, Emerson, Longfellow, Lowell, and Whittier.

16. Hawthorne's sister-in-law, Elizabeth Peabody (1804–94), was a prominent abolitionist, educator and member of the Transcendentalist Circle in and around Concord.

## Higginson

1. TWH to RWE, July 6, 1864, quoted in Tilden G. Edelstein, *Strange Enthusiasm: A Life of Thomas Wentworth Higginson* (New Haven, 1968), p. 297.

2. Most of Higginson's papers are located at Houghton Library, Harvard University.

3. Postmaster-General in Lincoln's cabinet, Montgomery Blair (1813–83) had defended Dred Scott and helped arrange counsel for John Brown.

4. Philip Sidney (1554–86), statesman, poet, and soldier, was mortally wounded in combat against the Spanish.

5. August Kautz (1828–95) was chief of cavalry in the Department of Virginia; and Philip Sheridan (1831–1888) commanded all cavalry in the Army of the Potomac.

6. George Bancroft (1800–1891) and John Lothrop Motley (1814–77) were two of the most distinguished living historians. Bancroft was a Northern Democrat; Motley served during the war as minister to Austria.

7. John Gough (1817–86) was a renowned temperance orator on the lecture circuit.

8. Rufus Saxton (1824–1908) was Commander of Union forces at Beaufort.


## Melville

1. Daniel Aaron, *The Unwritten War: American Writers and the Civil War* (New York, 1973), pp. 79, 88.

2. For the reviews of *Battle-Pieces,* see Watson G. Branch (ed.), *Melville: The Critical Heritage* (London, 1974), pp. 388–98.


## Simms

1. WGS to George William Bagby, March 24, 1862, in Mary Simms Oliphant (ed.), *The Letters of William Gilmore Simms* (Columbia, S.C., 1982), Vol. 6, Supplement, p. 228 (hereafter cited as *Letters*); WGS to James Lawson, Aug. 20, 1861, in *Letters,* Vol. 4, p. 374; WGS to John Reuben Thompson, Jan. 10, 1863, in *Letters,* Vol. 4, p. 421.

2. WGS to James Henry Hammond, Oct. 28, 1862, in *Letters,* Vol. 4, p. 414.

3. WGS to John Reuben Thompson, Jan. 16, 1862, in *Letters,* Vol. 6, p. 223.

4. *Crescent Monthly* (New Orleans) quoted in *Letters,* Vol. 4, p. 622n.

5. WGS to Evert Augustus Duyckinck, July 7, 1866, in *Letters,* Vol. 4, p. 577.

6. *The Writings of William Gilmore Simms: Centennial Edition. Volume 3: Paddy McGann* (Columbia, S.C., 1972), p. 221.

7. Wife of a Methodist minister, Margaret Martin (b. 1807) was a Scottish native who occasionally wrote religious verse.

8. William Maxwell Martin (1837–61) was a member of the Columbia Artillery. He died at Fort Moultrie on Feb. 21 from typhoid fever.

9. William Porcher Miles (1822–99) was a prominent United States and Confederate Congressman from South Carolina.

10. Brigadier General of the Confederate Army, Pierre Gustave Toutant Beauregard (1818–93) would play a key role in the Confederate victory at Bull Run.

11. Elected Senator from South Carolina in 1857, James Henry Hammond (1807–64) is best known for proclaiming "Cotton is King." With Lincoln's election, he resigned from the Senate.

12. A dear friend of Simms's, James Lawson (1799–1880) was a New York author, editor, and expert on marine insurance.

13. On Nov. 8, Captain Charles Wilkes (1798–1877) seized the Confederate States

diplomatic commissioners to England and France, James Murray Mason (1798–1871) and John Slidell (1793–1871).

14. Yeadon's adopted son, his nephew Richard, had been killed in battle in Virginia.

15. Paul Hamilton Hayne (1830–86), poet, editor, and critic from South Carolina, was referred to as the "poet laureate of the South" in the decades following the war.

16. Simms refers here to the death of his wife, Chevillette, on Sept. 10.

17. An 1863 act of the Confederate States Congress authorized the impressment of goods; Hammond threatened to resist the impressment of his corn.

18. James Henry Hammond died on Nov. 13.

19. Teacher, journalist, and poet, Theophilus Hunter Hill (1836–1901) did not take the advice offered here by Simms.

## Stowe

1. Annie Fields, *Life and Letters of Harriet Beecher Stowe* (Boston, 1898), p. 286.

2. Stowe quoted in Forrest Wilson, *Crusader in Crinoline: The Life of Harriet Beecher Stowe* (Philadelphia, 1941), p. 502.

3. On the pastoral and the Civil War, see Timothy Sweet, *Traces of War: Poetry, Photography, and the Crisis of the Union* (Baltimore, 1990).

4. Stowe quoted in Wilson, *Crusader in Crinoline*, p. 636.

5. Harriet Beecher Stowe and Eliza Tyler Stowe, twin daughters born in 1836, devoted themselves to their mother's life and career.

6. Most of Stowe's correspondence is located at the Stowe-Day Foundation in Hartford, Connecticut.

7. Frederick William Stowe was born in 1840. Disabled at the Battle of Gettysburg, his alcoholism caused the family great distress. He disappeared in 1870 after sailing for San Francisco.

8. Annie Fields (1834–1915) was the wife of publisher James T. Fields and the close friend of a number of writers including Stowe, Hawthorne, Child, Whittier, and Lowell.

9. Calvin Stowe (1802–86), educator and theologian, held positions at Dartmouth, Lane Theological Seminary, Bowdoin, and Andover Theological Seminary.

10. Eunice was Henry Ward Beecher's wife.

11. Samuel Scoville was a friend of Fred's. In 1859 the two traveled together in Europe.

12. Gethsemane, a garden outside of Jerusalem, was the scene of Christ's suffering the night before he died.

## Whitman

1. Edwin Haviland Miller (ed.), *The Correspondence of Walt Whitman, Volume I: 1842–1867* (New York, 1961), p. 127n. (hereafter cited as *Correspondence*).

2. Charles I. Glicksberg, editor, *Walt Whitman and the Civil War* (New York, 1933), p. 29; p. 42; p. 43.

3. "The Great Army of the Sick," *New York Times*, Feb. 26, 1863.

4. *Correspondence*, p. 89; p. 111; p. 187.

5. *Correspondence*, p. 240.

6. "Visits Among Army Hospitals," *New York Times*, Dec. 11, 1864.

7. *Correspondence*, p. 246.

8. Walt Whitman's mother Louisa (1795–1873) lived in Brooklyn during the war.

9. George Washington Whitman (1829–1901) remained in combat throughout the war. See Jerome M. Loving (ed.), *Civil War Letters of George Washington Whitman* (Durham, 1975).

10. Thomas Jefferson Whitman (1833–90) was not drafted having paid a commutation fee so as not to serve.

11. Moses Fowler Odell (1818–66) was a House member from New York.

12. Edward Ferrero (1831–99) commanded George's regiment of the Fifty-first New York Volunteers.

13. Martha Whitman (d. 1873) was Jeff's wife and the mother of Manahatta and Jessie Louisa Whitman.

14. French professor Joseph-Charles d'Almeida (1822–80) was confined as a refugee to the Old Capitol Prison.

15. Nathaniel Bloom was a New York grocer and importer; John Frederick Schiller Gray served in the Twentieth New York Infantry and had fought at Antietam.

16. Horatio Stone (1808–75) was Patent Office Hospital surgeon.

17. Matilda Agnes Heron (1830–77) was a well-known actress of the day.

18. A reference to naval defeat of Union Admiral Samuel F. du Pont on April 7.

19. Joseph Hooker (1814–79) commanded the Army of the Potomac between Jan. 26 and June 28, 1863.

20. Like Thomas Sawyer, about whom little is known, Brown (1843–1926) was one of many soldiers to whom Whitman felt a close attachment.

21. George Gordon Meade (1815–72) assumed command of the Army of the Potomac just days before the battle of Gettysburg.

22. Between July 13 and July 17, draft riots erupted in New York City that left over a hundred persons dead and destroyed extensive amounts of property. They were put down by Union regiments recalled from Gettysburg.

23. Wife of Boston lawyer Charles Curtis, Margaret (d. 1888) was one of a number of supporters who sent Whitman funds to help him in his hospital work.

24. Redpath (1833–91) had a varied career as author, correspondent, editor, and publisher. He tried to raise funds for Whitman among the Boston reform community but did not succeed. He earlier wrote Whitman that "there is a prejudice agst you here among the 'fine' ladies & gentlemen of the transcendental School. It is believed that you are not ashamed of your reproductive organs, and, somehow, it wd seem to be the result of their logic—that eunuchs only are fit for nurses." Quoted in Miller, *Correspondence*, p. 123n.

25. For part of his time in Washington, Whitman lived with William O'Connor (1832–89) and his wife Ellen. O'Connor had published an abolitionist novel, *Harrington*, in 1860.

# Index